D0405591

WITHDRAWN
UTSA LIBRARIES

Nikita Khrushchev

Nikita Khrushchev

EDITED BY

William Taubman, Sergei Khrushchev, and Abbott Gleason

Translated by David Gehrenbeck, Eileen Kane, and Alla Bashenko

Yale University Press   New Haven & London

To Artemis Joukowsky: Colleague, Benefactor, Friend

Copyright © 2000 by Yale University.
All rights reserved.
This book may not be reproduced, in whole or in part, including illustrations,
in any form (beyond that copying permitted by Sections 107 and 108 of the U.S.
Copyright Law and except by reviewers for the public press), without written
permission from the publishers.

Designed by James J. Johnson and set in E+F Scala type
by The Composing Room of Michigan, Inc.
Printed in the United States of America by Sheridan Books, Chelsea, Michigan.

Library of Congress Cataloging-in-Publication Data

Nikita Khrushchev / edited by William Taubman, Sergei Khrushchev, and Abbott Gleason;
translated by David Gehrenbeck, Eileen Kane, and Alla Bashenko.

    p.   cm.

Includes bibliographical references and index.

ISBN 0-300-07635-5 (alk. paper)

1. Khrushchev, Nikita Sergeevich, 1894–1971.   2. Heads of state—Soviet Union—
Biography.   3. Soviet Union—Politics and government—1953–1985.   I. Taubman,
William.   II. Khrushchev, Sergei.   III. Gleason, Abbott.

DK275 .K5 N485 2000
947.085′2′092—dc21
[B]   99-051323

A catalogue record for this book is available from the British Library.
The paper in this book meets the guidelines for permanence and durability
of the Committee on Production Guidelines for Book Longevity of the
Council on Library Resources.

10 9 8 7 6 5 4 3 2 1

Library
University of Texas
at San Antonio

Contents

Contributors

IURII AKSIUTIN, historian, Russian Humanities University, Moscow

NIKOLAI BARSUKOV, historian, formerly of the Institute on Marxism-Leninism in Moscow

NANCY CONDEE, professor of Slavic languages and literatures, University of Pittsburgh

ABBOTT GLEASON, professor of history, Brown University

SERGEI KHRUSHCHEV, senior fellow, Watson Institute, Brown University

VLADIMIR NAUMOV, executive secretary, Presidential Commission on Rehabilitation of Victims of Repression, Moscow

PETER REDDAWAY, professor of political science, George Washington University

GEORGII SHAKHNAZAROV, former official of the Central Committee of the Soviet Communist party; advisor to Mikhail Gorbachev

IURII SHAPOVAL, historian, Institute on Nationality Relations and Political Science, Ukrainian Academy of Sciences

ANATOLII STRELIANYI, Russian journalist currently working for Radio Free Europe

WILLIAM TAUBMAN, professor of political science, Amherst College

WILLIAM J. TOMPSON, Nestle Lecturer in Politics, Birkbeck College, University of London

OLEG TROYANOVSKY, former foreign policy assistant to Nikita Khrushchev, later Soviet ambassador to the United Nations, to China and to Japan

ELENA ZUBKOVA, researcher, Institute of Russian History, Russian Academy of Sciences

VLADISLAV ZUBOK, senior fellow, National Security Archive, Washington, D.C.

Introduction

WILLIAM TAUBMAN, SERGEI KHRUSHCHEV, AND ABBOTT GLEASON

Alone among Soviet rulers, Nikita Khrushchev left the Soviet Union better off than when he became its leader. (Arguably, Mikhail
Gorbachev did likewise, except that the Soviet Union no longer existed
when he left office). Yet until Khrushchev became first secretary of the
Soviet Communist party in 1953, not much was generally known about
him in the West or even in the Soviet Union outside of high party circles. He had worked in the mines in Ukraine, served in the Ukrainian
party apparatus, and then risen to become Moscow party leader, Stalin's
viceroy in Ukraine, a high-ranking wartime political commissar, and,
after World War II, one of Stalin's closest Kremlin associates. Even
Khrushchev's real date of birth in the village of Kalinovka near Kursk
was not known. Khrushchev himself listed his birth date as April 17,
1894, but Iurii Shapoval, digging in local records, has unearthed the
true date, April 15.

Once Stalin died and Khrushchev took over as party leader, the
world learned a lot more about him, perhaps more than it wanted to
know. In contrast to the laconic Stalin, Khrushchev was endlessly lo-
quacious. His speeches on agriculture alone fill eight volumes; his interviews appeared in many languages; he almost never stuck to a prepared text; he may never have told an anecdote the same way twice; he
could be stunningly indiscreet. Given his importance as Soviet leader,
not to mention the colorfulness of some of his utterances, it is not surprising that the outside world snapped to attention. During the 1950s
and 1960s three Khrushchev biographies appeared in the West, as did
studies of Khrushchev-era Kremlin politics, cultural politics, civil-mil-
itary relations, foreign and security policy, agricultural policy, Khrushchev's fall from power, and the Khrushchev regime as a whole.[1]

The day after his October 1964 ouster from power, however, Khrushchev became a "non-person" in the Soviet Union, forced to live under virtual house arrest, isolated from almost all contact with foreigners, and cut off from most of his compatriots. Yet he also became the first Soviet leader (and the last until Mikhail Gorbachev) to write his memoirs, and he even managed to get many of them to the West, where they were published as *Khrushchev Remembers*, in two volumes, just before and after his death in September 1971.[2] Khrushchev's memoirs offered a rich lode of reminiscence, but they were mostly dictated alone, long after the events in question, without any access to documents or archives, and with one eye on the internal security police, the KGB. Although Khrushchev had a remarkable memory and a burning desire to set his record straight, his recollections could not help but contain numerous omissions and errors.

Between Khrushchev's death and the arrival of glasnost in the late 1980s, the official Soviet silence about him deepened. Still, two dissidents, Roy and Zhores Medvedev, produced a short, incisive study of Khrushchev's years in power, and Roy Medvedev added another Khrushchev biography.[3] Other Western books appeared, evaluating Khrushchev's domestic and foreign policy and comparing Khrushchev's leadership with Leonid Brezhnev's.[4]

When Gorbachev finally lifted the taboo on Khrushchev's name in the late 1980s, the spotlight fell on him again—all the more so since, at a time of reformation, he could be cited as the originator of reform. Sergei Khrushchev's book about his father appeared at this time, as did books by Khrushchev's son-in-law, Aleksei Adzhubei, and a former Central Committee official, Fedor Burlatskii.[5] Some Khrushchev memoir material not transmitted to the West during his lifetime was now published as a third volume of *Khrushchev Remembers*. A nearly full Russian text of Khrushchev's memoirs, edited by Sergei Khrushchev, appeared in the Moscow scholarly journal *Voprosy istorii*, between 1990 and 1995, and new Western books on Khrushchev-era diplomacy were published as well.[6] Yet even under Gorbachev, vast lacunae remained, pending the opening of Soviet archives.

With the fall of the Soviet Union in 1991, the documentary floodgates finally opened—erratically, and not necessarily permanently, but at least for a while. Although the Presidential Archive, which contains the most sensitive material on Soviet leaders, was not opened, and KGB and military archives remained closed to all but a favored few, party and government depositories became available to Russian and foreign researchers, not only in Moscow but throughout the former Soviet Union.[7] Meanwhile, the stream of memoirs by and about former Communist officials grew from a trickle into a flood—even as the attention of ordinary Russians shifted from their glorious/inglorious past to the hard-pressed present and uncertain future.[8]

This sort of new information is the basis for the articles in this book. Most of them were originally written for an international conference on the centennial of Khrushchev's birth and have been revised since then.[9] Three chapters (by Naumov, Tompson, and Reddaway) were specially commissioned for this volume. Most of the authors are Russians, but American and British scholars have also contributed. Several Russian authors (Shapoval, Barsukov, Zubkova, Aksiutin, and Zubok) are professional historians; those who are not include the executive secretary of a post-Soviet commission investigating Soviet-era repressions and rehabilitations (Naumov), a top Gorbachev aide (Shakhnazarov), a gifted journalist (Strelianyi), Khrushchev's former foreign policy assistant (Troyanovsky), and the Soviet leader's son, Sergei Khrushchev. Having had little or no access to Western literature on Khrushchev until very recently, the Russian contributors quote from it infrequently. But several of them cite their own personal experience during the Khrushchev era to telling effect. The editors have done their best to make sure that sources used in all articles are carefully referenced, but given the erratic state of post-Soviet archives, as well as difficulties in communicating with distant authors, that has not always been possible. In addition, one of the authors, Nikolai Barsukov, has alas died.

The amount of information about Khrushchev has changed over time, and so have the questions asked about him. When he was in power those questions were mostly policy-oriented and Kremlinological: What was he trying to do? How was he trying to do it? Who was for and against him? During the late 1980s, the main issue became why Khrushchev had failed and been deposed, and whether Gorbachev could avoid the same fate. Since the collapse of the Soviet Union the focus has shifted—or rather, should shift—once again, to the question of what Khrushchev's career (which stretched from before the revolution to the beginning of the end of the Soviet system) can tell us about the Soviet period as whole. What attracted him to revolution and communism in the first place? How, in the light of his complicity in Stalin's terrible bloodletting, could he make an attempt to break with Stalin and Stalinism? Why, in the end, did he falter and fail? Khrushchev's failure, like Gorbachev's twenty-five years later, raises the crucial question of whether communism was reformable at all. What was the nature of Khrushchev's failure, and what does it suggest about the final collapse of communism?

The articles in this volume touch on all these issues, and more. Iurii Shapoval, drawing on research he has done in Kiev, Donetsk, and other cities, chronicles Khrushchev's career in Ukraine, providing new information about his early years—including a 1923 Trotskyite "deviation" that haunted Khrushchev as long as Stalin lived; his initial ties with his mentor, Lazar Kaganovich; and early evidence of both Khrushchev's Stalinism and his budding anti-Stalinism. Most significantly, Shapoval shows how Khrushchev's Ukrainian experience influenced his later behavior as Soviet leader.

Nikolai Barsukov concentrates on turning points after 1953: Beria's fall; Khrushchev's defeat of Malenkov and Molotov; the origins and consequences of his 1956 speech unmasking Stalin, and of the coup attempted against him in 1957; the paradox of the 1961 party program, which promised abundance even as economic conditions worsened; and Khrushchev's decline and fall.

Elena Zubkova focuses on Khrushchev's relationship with Georgii Malenkov—not just because the two were rivals for power but also because if they had joined together, the reforms that both men supported might have been more sustainable. In Zubkova's rendition, the story of why they did not cooperate, of why Khrushchev broke with Malenkov, reveals a great deal about why Khrushchev's career eventually ran aground.

Khrushchev's role in both the repression and the rehabilitation of Stalin's victims, and in the further repression of those who wanted a wholesale transformation of the Soviet system, is the subject of Vladimir Naumov's account. Although incriminating documentation from the 1930s is still hard to come by, even for someone with Naumov's extraordinary access to archives, enough is available to substantiate Khrushchev's complicity in both Moscow and Ukraine. His role in releasing and rehabilitating prisoners in the 1950s is far clearer, of course, but so is the number of arrests he authorized when his 1956 attack on Stalin produced more unrest than he bargained for.

Anatolii Strelianyi's ostensible subject is agriculture: he traces Khrushchev's far-reaching reforms of September 1953, his Virgin Lands and corn-growing campaigns, his early success in boosting the

Soviet harvest, and the agricultural disasters that befell him in the early 1960s. But beyond that, Strelianyi's essay dissects Khrushchev's true belief in communism, plus his ironical reliance on the hidebound party bureaucracy (the *apparat*) to implement his utopian dream. Unlike others, who blame the apparat for undermining Khrushchev, Strelianyi's Khrushchev confounds the apparat, which would have liked to carry out his orders; its inability to do so ruined Soviet agriculture and Khrushchev's career.

William Tompson, the author of a biography of Khrushchev published in 1995,[10] examines Khrushchev's economic reforms—or rather, the lack of them—in the light of post-Communist experience. The fact that Khrushchev was no economic reformer used to be held against him. Nowadays, Tompson points out, when we know that Gorbachev's half-measures only made things worse, Khrushchev's non-measures don't seem so bad.

Nancy Condee brings the perspective of modern (and postmodern) cultural studies to an examination of the Khrushchev Thaw. Her subject is not so much literature and film, although she discusses both, or even the politics of culture narrowly defined, but rather the politics of culture in the largest sense and the culture of Khrushchev-era politics itself.

Iurii Aksiutin mines long-secret party and police reports, as well as unpublished letters to Soviet newspaper editors, to gauge public opinion about key issues between 1953 and 1964. Stalin's death, Khrushchev's secret speech, the Polish and Hungarian upheavals of 1956, the "anti-party group's" attempted coup of 1957, and the economic troubles of Khrushchev's last years—opinions differed on all these episodes and issues, but according to Aksiutin, the Soviet people were less supportive of Khrushchev than one might have supposed. It was not just die-hard Stalinists, entrenched bureaucratic interests, and Chinese adversaries who resisted Khrushchev, Aksiutin concludes. A substantial portion (precisely how substantial is impossible to say on the basis of the evidence) of the Soviet population was instinctively hostile to his efforts.

With Oleg Troyanovsky's well-informed memoir, which deals with Khrushchev's decade at the helm of Soviet foreign policy, the focus shifts to diplomacy. Troyanovsky's recollections help to resolve the much-debated question of why Khrushchev declared a Berlin ultimatum in November 1958, thus transforming his hitherto measured efforts to ease East-West tensions into the Berlin crisis, which lasted until 1961 and beyond. The answer, which sounds simple but is quite nuanced in Troyanovsky's fine-grained account, is that after the West snubbed Soviet peace overtures for five years, Khrushchev resolved to force the Western powers to accept them.

Nuclear bluster and bluff were among the means that Khrushchev used to pressure the West. As Sergei Khrushchev describes in his essay, both tactics were employed in the service of his father's strategic thinking. The problem Khrushchev faced was how to deter any Western attack and advance his strategic objectives, while at the same time easing the defense burden on the Soviet economy. Khrushchev's answer was to cut back on conventional weapons and rely on nuclear rockets, even before Soviet intercontinental missiles were deployed in substantial numbers. The horrors he encountered firsthand during World War II convinced Khrushchev that nuclear conflict must be avoided at all costs, even as he manipulated the threat of it to intimidate the West.

Khrushchev's handling of Germany and Berlin—perhaps the central problem of Soviet foreign policy—reflected both his diplomatic and military thinking. After trying to make Communism work in East Germany, if possible with West German cooperation, Khrushchev resorted first to threats and ultimatums and then to the Berlin Wall. As described by Vladislav Zubok, Khrushchev's German policies were thwarted by international forces beyond his control (including not just Western resistance but East German recalcitrance too), just as similar forces at home undermined his domestic programs.

The final two chapters compare Khrushchev and Gorbachev. They differ about whether Gorbachev really believed in communism (as Reddaway thinks) or was seeking to transcend it (Shakhnazarov's view). But beyond that, both essays compare and contrast the two leaders and their personalities; the degree to which the times facilitated or hindered their work; the role of the nomenklatura elite, in particular, in opposing reform; and other reasons that both leaders were defeated in the end. The biggest question both Shakhnazarov and Reddaway raise, one that haunted Khrushchev and Gorbachev and continues to haunt Russians today, is not whether communism was reformable but whether Russia itself is.

We would like to acknowledge bountiful help from Brown University, where the Khrushchev centennial conference was held, and particularly assistance from Brown's Watson Institute for International Studies. Mark Garrison, former director of the Watson Institute's Center for Foreign Policy Development, made the conference possible in the first place; his successor, P. Terrence Hopmann, helped bring it to fruition; and Deana Arsenian, also of the institute, directed preparations for the conference. The Watson Institute director Thomas Biersteker provided financial and logistical aid of all sorts for both the conference and this book. Without the munificent support of Artemis Joukowsky neither the conference nor the book would have been possible. We are grateful to Nikita Khrushchev's daughter, Rada Adzhubei; his grandchildren, Yuliia Khrushcheva, Iurii Khrushchev, Nikita Khrushchev, Jr., and Alyosha Adzhubei; and his great-granddaughter, Nina Khrushcheva, all of whom took part in the centennial conference. Sergei Khrushchev's wife, Valentina Golenko, also assisted us, as did Nikita Khrushchev, Jr., who helped keep us in contact with Moscow-based authors of chapters in this book. We would also like to thank the Cold War International History Project at the Woodrow Wilson International Center for Scholars for supporting the centennial conference, Amherst College for sustaining editorial work on the book, and Christina Cathey Schutz and Margaret Wessling for help in preparing the final manuscript.

1

The Ukrainian Years, 1894–1949

IURII SHAPOVAL

The Ukrainian pages of Nikita Khrushchev's biography remain among the least studied, even though a considerable part of his life was associated with Ukraine. He began his political career there, and his appointment in early 1938 as leader of the Ukrainian party organization turned out to be a peculiar sort of salvation for him. The English journalist and diplomat Edward Crankshaw correctly noted that it was in Ukraine that Khrushchev became as much his own boss as was possible under Stalin, developed his abilities and talents, and saw with his own eyes the horrible suffering through which people were forced to live, as well as how the same people rose up and fought against the Germans. He himself was changed as a result.[1]

I have here attempted to give a short survey of Khrushchev's life and career from his birth until his second departure from Ukraine for Moscow in 1949, and to consider the formative influence of Khrushchev's Ukrainian experience on his criticism of Stalin's crimes, his agricultural policies, his way of choosing and handling the party cadres who worked for him, and other aspects of his political life.[2]

The more involved one becomes in the study of Khrushchev's life and work, the more surprising the many facets of his character turn out to be. He was born in the village of Kalinovka, in the Dmitrievsk district of Kursk province, in 1894. Although his birthday is generally thought to be April 17, the village of Kalinovka's registration book shows that his parents, Sergei Nikanorovich and Aksinia Ivanovna, baptized their child on his birthday, April 15 (April 3, old style). He was the eleventh newborn registered on that day.[3]

During winters Sergei Nikanorovich left his family, newly enlarged by Nikita's sister, Irina, and worked in the Donbass as a cabinetmaker and then as a miner at the Uspenskii mine. With the Khrushchev household struggling to make ends meet, Nikita started working himself, looking after the landowner Shaufusova's cows.

In 1908 Sergei Nikanorovich moved his family to the Donbass for good, living at the Uspenskii mine, five kilometers south of Iuzovka. Not far away were the Rutchenkov mine and the German Bosse ironworks factory. Until he was fifteen, Nikita worked as a farm laborer for the landowner Kirsh, and on days off he and other boys his age cleaned boilers at local mines. Soon he was accepted as a metalworker's apprentice at the Bosse factory. His first teachers were the old worker F. P. Golovach and the master craftsman T. S. Pukhno. Contemporaries recall that Nikita once astonished his teachers and friends by putting together a motorcycle from spare parts and riding it into the workers' quarters.

Roy Medvedev has noted that Khrushchev's closest friend was the miner and book lover Pantelei Makhinia.[4] Panko, as the locals called him, a native of Cherkashchina, a quick-witted young man and a self-taught poet, had a fairly significant influence on Khrushchev. Makhinia died during the civil war, and as if trying to preserve the memory of his friend, Khrushchev would recite the amateurish but sincere lines of Makhinia's poetry at meetings of the creative intelligentsia in the late 1950s.

There is virtually no serious evidence of Nikita Khrushchev's revolutionary proclivities. We do know that he first participated in oppositional politics in the aftermath of the shooting of workers at the Lena gold fields on April 4, 1912; he helped gather provisions for the families of the executed workers. A May 28, 1912, dispatch from the head of the Ekaterinaslav provincial gendarme division mentions the name of a young metalworker from the Bosse factory, Nikita Khrushchev.[5]

The young worker's behavior did not pass unnoticed; he soon had to leave the factory, eventually finding work again at Rutchenkov shaft 31, where he worked as a machinist. He distributed the Bolshevik newspaper, *Pravda,* and organized collective readings.

The Rutchenkov mine belonged to the French capitalists Lebern, Ferier, and Company. With the intensification of labor unrest in Russia, the French soon sold the mine and the mechanical workshops. But working conditions were difficult under the new owners too, leading to workers' protests. In the fall of 1913, a new wave of political strikes swept the area. The old worker I. A. Pisarev's apartment became a meeting place for the discussion of burning social issues and stories about mines and miners in the press.

At the end of 1914, Khrushchev began working at the mechanical workshops, which served approximately ten shafts. He spent time in all of them and was thus able to extend his circle of acquaintances and contacts. In the same year, he married Pisarev's oldest daughter, Efrosinia Ivanovna. As Anna Ivanovna, her sister, remembers, Efrosinia and Khrushchev met in 1911.[6] Not long after they married, two children were born: a son, Leonid, and a daughter, Iuliia.

In 1915, there were 113 strikes in Ukraine, in which approximately forty-eight thousand workers participated. The Rutchenkov mine was also shaken by disturbances in March 1915, and Khrushchev was one of the organizers. The police apparently wanted to arrest him, but the workers are said to have stepped forward in his defense and ejected the gendarmes from the workshops.[7]

At the end of April and the beginning of May 1916, there were again strikes in the Donbass region, particularly in the coal-mining regions of Gorlovsko-Shcherbinovskii and in Iuzovka, where Khrushchev was one of the leaders. The former second secretary of the Ukrainian Communist party Central Committee, R. Ia. Terekhov, recalls how "Nikita Sergeevich came by our place more than once to discuss this or that question. It once happened that he spent the night at my house, and we sat up practically the entire night, talking about issues at the mine."[8]

Following the February revolution of 1917, Khrushchev became even more involved in political activity. He was chosen first as a member of the Temporary Executive Committee and then, on May 29, 1917, as a representative of the Rutchenkov Union of Workers' Deputies.[9] It was in this period that he met Lazar M. Kaganovich (whose pseudonym in Iuzovka was Boris Kosherovich) at a demonstration in Iuzovka. As Khrushchev later noted in his memoirs, "I did not know that he was Kaganovich; I knew him as Kosherovich. Not only did I trust and respect Kaganovich, but, as they say, I stood behind him completely."[10] In his turn Kaganovich supported Khrushchev in every possible way.

The Iuzovka soviets were under the influence of the Mensheviks and the SRs. There is some evidence that Khrushchev sympathized with the Bolshevik faction, although he was not a formal member of the party. Khrushchev always gave 1918 as the year he entered the party. In his own words, "I became a Bolshevik and a member of the Communist Party after the revolution, and shortly thereafter joined the Red Army."[11] During the Civil War, he was a Red Army soldier, chairman of a party cell, army political instructor, commissar of a battalion, and party instructor with the 9th Kuban Army.

In the book *The Story of an Honored Miner,* published in 1961, Khrushchev is described as "one of those under whose leadership the Red Army disrupted the sinister plans of the American, English, and French imperialists, who planned to save Denikin's army from complete ruin with the help of the Entente's fleet."[12] The authors of the book further characterized Khrushchev as "one of the active creators of the Red Army and one of the organizers of the victories of the young Republic of Soviets over foreign interventionists and internal counterrevolution."[13] Khrushchev's activity during the Civil War demands further careful study, but there are currently no grounds for such a lofty appraisal of his activity in 1918–20.

After the Civil War, Khrushchev returned to the Rutchenkov mine, which was managed by a leadership team consisting of a chairman and two deputies, one for technical and one for political work. As this second deputy, Khrushchev fulfilled his responsibilities so successfully that he was offered the post of manager of the Pastukhov mine. Instead, he decided to enter the *rabfak,* or worker's training school, at the Iuzovka Mining Institute. Several times he requested approval for the change from A. P. Zaveniagin, secretary of the mine, and finally received it.[14] In filling out his application to Zaveniagin, Khrushchev described his reasons for pursuing his studies as follows: "To obtain technical knowledge for more productive work in the industry of the RSFSR."[15] Even in the rabfak, however, he did not cease his involvement with politics. At the 9th Iuzovka district party conference on December 23, 1923, he was elected to the district party committee.[16]

In February 1924 Khrushchev was elected a member of the Iuzovka district party committee bureau.[17] This meant that the thirty-year-old Khrushchev's energetic work had been noticed. An important event in his personal life occurred that same year: he married for the second time. (His first wife had died of typhus during the Civil War.) His wife, Nina Petrovna Kukharchuk, recalled, "In the fall of 1922, I was sent to Iuzovka (now Donetsk) to the district party school as a teacher of political economy. There I met Nikita Sergeevich Khrushchev, who was studying in the rabfak in Iuzovka . . . we married in 1924 and from then on worked together at the Petrov mine of the Iuzovka district."[18] Khrushchev and Nina Petrovna had three children: Rada, Sergei, and Elena.

A little-known but very interesting event in Khrushchev's biography occurred around that time. Khrushchev relates the circumstances in his memoirs: "In 1923, while studying at the rabfak, I slipped into vacillations of a Trotskyist character . . . . I was fascinated at that time by Kharechko, a rather well-known Trotskyite. . . . I knew that he was a revolutionary, but I didn't know that he was a Social Democrat. At the time I knew absolutely nothing about the basic ideas of the Social Democratic Party, although I knew that this was a person who had fought for the people before the revolution. . . . When he arrived in Iuzovka, I naturally sympathized with Kharechko and supported him."[19]

During the tragic year of 1937, Khrushchev told Kaganovich about this incident and asked him whether to inform Stalin. Kaganovich advised against doing so, but Khrushchev told Stalin everything and asked if he should inform delegates to a Moscow province party conference, who were electing province party leaders. Stalin at first suggested keeping quiet, but later advised telling the whole story, which Khrushchev did.[20]

History arranged things in such a way, however, that nineteen years later, in June 1957, Khrushchev had to recall once again his youthful political "sin" during the famous Central Committee plenum that crushed the "anti-party" group of Kaganovich, Georgii Malenkov, and Viacheslav Molotov. Kaganovich accused Khrushchev of Trotskyism. Khrushchev explained his vacillations of 1923 as a response to violations of internal party democracy:

> For those violations, the secretary of the district committee was eventually dismissed. Because I understood the urgency of struggling against those who distorted and violated internal party democracy, I actively and rather harshly denounced the secretary of the district party committee, Moiseenko, and other leading workers. But it turned out that my speeches came at the beginning of the discussion raised by the Trotskyites. . . . And so it turned out that my speeches . . . objectively were in support of the Trotskyites. I soon understood that I had made a mistake . . . . When a plenum of the party Central Committee adopted a decision on internal party conditions in October 1923, I immediately took the correct positions.[21]

Kaganovich publicly apologized to Khrushchev in June 1957 "for incorrect and uncomradely behavior, when I used Comrade Khrushchev's short-lived mistake of thirty years ago in our struggle."[22] Much later, however, in conversation with the writer Feliks Chuev, he again called Khrushchev a Trotskyite and admitted that he told Stalin about Khrushchev's Trotskyism in 1937[23].

Khrushchev was not a Trotskyite, of course. His "vacillations" display T. I. Kharechko's influence,[24] but they also reflect the fact that the Trotskyite opposition quite properly criticized bureaucratism in the party, the restriction of minority rights, and the degeneration of many party workers. In opposing these abuses, Khrushchev was not so much supporting the opposition as denouncing real shortcommings.

After his stint at the rabfak, Khrushchev worked as party secretary of the Petrov-Mariinsk district committee between July 1925 and December 1926. He was then transferred to Stalino (Iuzovka's new name) to head the party's organizational department there. In that capacity he in effect served as deputy to K. V. Moiseenko, the Stalino party committee secretary.

By that time Khrushchev had accumulated sufficient political experience to put an end to his admittedly slight but still dangerous "vacillations of a Trotskyist character." Now he consistently followed the Stalinist line. His experience as a delegate to the 14th and 15th party congresses of 1925 and 1927 played a key role in establishing this conformity. On January 11, 1926, in his report to a plenum of the Petrov-Mariinsk district committee on the work of the 14th Party Congress, he emphasized that Petrov-Mariinsk "will not follow in the footsteps of the *Zinovievshchina*, but will be strong in relation to the Central Committee."[25]

At a plenum of the Stalino party committee in the fall of 1925, Khrushchev had said, "I remember Kamenev's speech at the all-union congress: I had the impression that he considered the dismissal of Comrade Stalin from the post of general secretary imperative." In criticizing the opposition for striving to demonstrate the difference between Leninist and Stalinist policies, Khrushchev offered the following "counter-argument": "We know that Stalin became the general secretary not after Lenin's death, but when he was still alive. It cannot be that Lenin would have promoted someone with an unclear political line as general secretary; that is why it is easy for us to beat back the attacks of the opposition."[26] Thirty years later, Khrushchev would tell astonished delegates at a secret session of the 20th Party Congress the story of Lenin's final, deathbed conflict with Stalin over "those negative characteristics of Stalin that appeared only in embryonic form during Lenin's life but developed later into terrible abuses of power on Stalin's part."[27]

In the 1920s, however, Khrushchev did everything possible to prevent the Petrov-Mariinsk party committee, the Stalino and Kiev committees, and later the Industrial Academy in Moscow from becoming bastions of what Stalin characterized as "anti-party elements." Speaking to the First All-Ukrainian Party Conference in October 1926, Khrushchev said:

> Comrades, I would like to say a few words about the declaration of the opposition. . . . Their statements are only a strategic maneuver—they want to show now that they are against a schism. . . . But, in admitting their mistakes, they at the same time are trying to create opportunities for conducting schismatic policy in the future. . . . They must tell us frankly their positions on the main questions we now have to decide, and they must show true remorse. Only if this is demonstrated by actions, not by words, will the party forgive them for the mistakes they have made. Otherwise, we will have to demand that our highest party organs, without taking into account any merits of individual oppositionists, unconditionally apply the most repressive measures against the incorrigible ones.[28]

In November 1926 Khrushchev was confirmed as a full member of the Stalino party committee bureau.[29] But he did not remain in Stalino for long. In 1928 Kaganovich, who had headed the Ukrainian party since 1925, summoned Khrushchev to Kharkov (the capital of Ukraine at the time) and offered him the position of deputy chief of the Central Committee's organizational assignment department. Kaganovich made his offer because there were few blue-collar workers in the apparat of the Central Committee,[30] and because Khrushchev and Kaganovich had known each other since 1917. The top Ukrainian leadership had already come to know Khrushchev after the scandalous affair of K. V. Moiseenko, who was removed as Stalino party leader for "petty bourgeois tendencies."

Khrushchev himself characterized Moiseenko in his memoirs as "a student who had not finished the medical institute, a wonderful orator and a good organizer. He and I went our different ways later on. He was distinguished by petty bourgeois tendencies; his connections and close associates were virtually NEP-men. Therefore we later dismissed him from the post of secretary. This scandalous affair reached the Ukrainian Central Committee, and a commission was sent to check us out. They analyzed the disagreements, recognized our arguments as sound, and he was relieved of his position as secretary."[31] Khrushchev defended his position before a commission of the Ukrainian Central Committee and before the Politburo of the Ukrainian Central Committee in September 1927.[32]

Alas, no one has been able to determine just what constituted Moiseenko's NEP-man-like behavior. At the June 1957 plenum of the Central Committee, Khrushchev explained it this way: "We routed the violent and corrupt bosses in the Donbass. This group was headed by Ukrainian Politburo member Radchenko and supported by the secretary of the Stalino committee, Moiseenko, and the secretary of the Artemov district committee, Mikhnenko. During this period, I went to the Ukrainian Central Committee in Kharkov several times. At that time, Kaganovich relied on us and I supported him, because he followed the line of the Central Committee."[33]

When Kaganovich invited him to move to Kharkov, Khrushchev did not at first agree, probably because he wanted to succeed Moiseenko as Stalino party secretary. On September 26, 1927, however, a plenum of the Stalino committee elected V. A. Stroganov secretary.[34] In Khrushchev's opinion, Stroganov did not meet the requirements for the secretary of a party organization as large as Stalino's. He was a mediocrity and soon began engaging in intrigues. Party activists quickly understood the situation, preferring to take important issues up with Khrushchev rather than Stroganov.[35] Naturally, this created difficult and sometimes impossible situations for Khrushchev, and Kaganovich's proposal gave him a way out.

Khrushchev left for Kharkov in the spring of 1928 but did not remain there long. "I did not like Kharkov as much as I expected," he recalled. "The trouble with working in an office is that you can't see real life for all the paper-pushing. That is a certain kind of work, but I am a man of the earth, of concrete action, of coal, metal, chemicals, and to a certain extent agriculture."[36] On April 28, 1928, the Ukrainian Central Committee secretariat chose him to direct the organizational department of the Kiev district party committee, headed by N. N. Demchenko.[37]

That is how Khrushchev ended up in Kiev. But even though relations between him and his new boss were constructive this time, Khrushchev soon asked to leave Kiev. His request surprised many, including

S. V. Kosior, who had headed the Ukrainian Central Committee since July 1928. Suspicions arose that Khrushchev was at odds with Demchenko. In fact, Khrushchev simply understood that without further study or improved qualifications, there would be no higher official post for him. After speaking with Kosior, he received permission to attend the Industrial Academy in Moscow. But actually enrolling turned out to be difficult, since Khrushchev had not served the required length of time in a significant economic post. So he turned to Kaganovich, then already a secretary of the Central Committee in Moscow, who made sure the issue was settled immediately.

Khrushchev's time at the Industrial Academy gave yet another boost to his career when he launched a fight against "right deviationists" who were allegedly "clogging" the student body. Khrushchev's experience at struggling with oppositionists in Ukraine came in handy when he was asked to attach his name to an article in *Pravda* denouncing "rightists." On May 28, 1930, he was elected secretary of the academy's party cell, apparently at the direct order of Kaganovich, who then headed the Moscow party committee. It was Kaganovich who categorically told the secretary of the Bauman district party committee, A. P. Shirin, "Make [Khrushchev] the secretary of the cell."[38]

In 1931 Khrushchev moved on to Moscow party work. Between 1931 and 1938 he occupied the following positions: secretary of two district committees in Moscow, and then of the city party committee; second secretary of the Moscow provincial committee; first secretary of the city party committee; and, shortly thereafter, first secretary of both the provincial and the city party organizations of Moscow. Naturally, he was appointed to these positions with the knowledge and approval of Stalin.[39] Khrushchev replaced Kaganovich as head of the Moscow party organization, and as Nikita Sergeevich himself said to "Iron Lazar" at a Central Committee plenum in 1957, "The question arises: how could a 'Trotskyite' be tolerated in such positions?"[40] While working in Moscow during this period, Khrushchev earned Stalin's trust. In 1934 he was elected a member of the Central Committee, and in January 1938 he was made a candidate member of the Politburo.

That same January, Stalin proposed sending Khrushchev back to Ukraine. The "Great Terror," which began in Ukraine much earlier than is usually understood (essentially in 1933), had destroyed experienced party workers, who had been declared "nationalists" or "enemies of the people." New persons had to be found for party and government organs. In contrast to Kaganovich, who had become infamous in Ukraine in the 1920s, Khrushchev was the perfect candidate to become Ukrainian party leader.

It is worth noting, however, that Khrushchev himself claims not to have wanted to return. He says he considered himself less qualified than Kosior. In addition, he had grave doubts about his ability to orient himself in nationality politics and find a common language with the Ukrainian intelligentsia. But Stalin was not responsive. According to Khrushchev, Stalin said "that I must work in Ukraine."[41]

Khrushchev asked Malenkov to recommend Ukrainians who were working at that time in the Central Committee apparat and in other managerial organs in Moscow for his "team." People chosen included M. A. Burmistenko, Z. T. Serdiuk, and D. S. Korotchenko.

Once he arrived in Kiev, Khrushchev brought to a virtual halt the process of "Ukrainianization" or "indigenization" *(korenizatsiia)*, which had been dominant since the beginning of the 1920s. An April 10, 1938, resolution of the Ukrainian Central Committee, "On the reorganization of schools in Ukraine," branded schools in which instruction took place in the languages of national minorities as hotbeds of "bourgeois-nationalist influence on children," whose operation was considered "inadvisable and harmful." Such educational institutions were liquidated and the students transferred to schools with instruction in both Ukrainian and Russian.[42]

Khrushchev spoke in detail about these measures in his report at the 14th Ukrainian Party Congress in June 1938, insisting that "it is necessary to purge the teachers of hostile elements. And we must look carefully at the workers of the schools, for there are Petliurists [members of a Ukrainian nationalist group] and [White Army] officers there."[43] Khrushchev also recalled the former Ukrainian people's commissar for education, V. P. Zatonskii, who had been arrested at the end of 1937: "Enemy of the people Zatonskii tells in his testimony how they altered the study plans, how they caused harm by corrupting the teachers. . . . Zatonskii says that the re-evaluation of teachers, which has been ordered by the government, is being conducted so as to compromise and kick out honest teachers and retain Petliurist, Trotskyist-Bukharinist, and bourgeois-nationalist spy gangs."[44]

The resolution adopted by the congress emphasized the need to "liquidate the consequences of sabotage in the teaching of Russian language in schools ending at the middle school level, as well as in institutions of higher learning."[45] It is not surprising that at the subsequent 15th Party Congress in 1940, neither Khrushchev's report nor presentations by the delegates mentioned the terms "indigenization" or "Ukrainianization."

What influence did Khrushchev's Ukrainian experience have on the formation of his conviction that Stalin's crimes must be criticized? Khrushchev's own involvement in repressive actions in Ukraine is indisputable, although many documents that show his involvement have not been preserved. We can hardly consider this dearth of documents an accident; Khrushchev himself must have played a role in the matter. Beginning in 1935, when he worked in Moscow, his own personal archive included transcripts of speeches, presentations, and conferences in which he took part, as well as copies of letters to Stalin and other materials. This archive was maintained in a secretariat; some 205 folders of documents were accumulated just during Khrushchev's first Moscow period (until 1938). He brought them along to Ukraine and significantly expanded the archive there.

In 1949, after Khrushchev's departure for Moscow, these documents were removed from the secret section of the Ukrainian Central Committee on his orders and sent to his secretariat in Moscow. The list of headings of these documents alone runs to fifty-two pages. Included among the documents removed to Moscow were seventy transcripts of his speeches, nine copies of his letters to Stalin between 1938 and 1941, and more than 260 transcripts from the period 1944–1949. The list also mentions the so-called Front Archive of N. S. Khrushchev,—copies of wartime letters and notes to Stalin, correspondence with partisan units, a file of documents connected with his activities at the Stalingrad front, and six folders with topographic maps and diagrams, all in addition to the 205 files mentioned above.[46]

On January 10, 1967, the Ukrainian party leader P. E. Shelest officially raised the question of the documents that had been removed in 1949 in a letter to the Central Committee in Moscow. "After Comrade Khrushchev's departure," he wrote, "all transcripts of his reports and speeches between 1938 and 1949 and other materials were removed on his orders from the archive of the Ukrainian Central Committee and sent first to the Moscow province party committee and then to the apparat of the Central Committee. At the present time they are being held in the Central Committee. . . . We ask you to consider returning to the Ukrainian Central Committee those archival materials sent to Comrade Khrushchev in Moscow in 1949 by the secretariat."[47]

There was no reaction at all to this request; the documents wound up in the Politburo's archive in Moscow. Since August 1991 they have been located at the Archive of the President of Russia, where they are unavailable to researchers. Other materials, which are available in Ukraine, show that many repressive actions were carried out with Khrushchev's knowledge and sanction, and that he personally signed the arrest warrants of prominent political figures. For example, after Kosior's departure to Moscow, a "conspiracy" within the Ukrainian Komsomol was discovered. According to NKVD "playwrights," this conspiracy was headed by the Ukrainian Komsomol first secretary, S. I. Usenko. A Ukrainian NKVD report asserted that Usenko "is the leading participant in a counterrevolutionary right-Trotskyist organization." Handwritten across the first page of this document is the following: "Arrest! N. S. Khrushchev. November 18, 1938."[48]

It was after Khrushchev's arrival in Kiev that Kosior and his brother Kazimir were accused of involvement in and leadership of the "Polish Organization of Troops." A number of leaders, including N. N. Popov, a former secretary of the Ukrainian Communist party, and V. A. Balitsky, the former people's commissar of internal affairs, were accused of founding and leading the "right-Trotskyist center" in Ukraine, which supposedly had "provincial branches." Also "exposed" were a "military-nationalist organization," a "sacred union of partisans," an organization of the "young generation of Ukrainian nationalists," which was charged with planning an assassination attempt on Khrushchev, and many other "organizations."[49]

Arriving in Ukraine in the last year of the "Great Terror," Khrushchev was involved in many of its monstrous acts. In the Usenko affair, he acted on the basis of a detailed account of the "plot," including "admitted testimonies" of those involved. But we should recall that organs of state security had significant autonomy at that time, and that regional leaders like Khrushchev were often forced to take NKVD accusations on faith.

The main director of the policy of destroying "enemies of the people" in Ukraine was the people's commissar of internal affairs, A. I. Uspenskii. His activity increased significantly after the Soviet security police chief N. I. Ezhov's visit to Ukraine in February 1938. For Khrushchev himself, this visit was a reminder that Moscow was watching his struggle with "enemies of the people" and "nationalists." It was no accident that Khrushchev reported to the 14th Ukrainian Party Congress, "This was a unique year for the Soviet nation. By destroying enemies of the people and purging the party, government apparat, and Red Army, we have achieved an even greater strengthening of our government, an even greater strengthening of the ranks of the Communist party. . . . By destroying enemies of the people, we have dealt a blow to the Polish, German, Japanese, and other intelligence agencies that is equal to a victory in a great war. . . . After Nikolai Ivanovich Ezhov's trip to Ukraine . . . the real destruction of hidden enemies began. And I think that with the help of all toilers, we will purge Ukrainian soil of all traitors and betrayers."[50]

Khrushchev cited what in his words were "interesting statistics on promotion to leadership work in provincial committees of the Ukrainian Communist party": from May 1937 to February 1938, thirteen first secretaries were promoted, nine were repressed as enemies of the people, three were transferred, and one remained. Further on, Khrushchev noted, "Starting from February 1938, of the 31 first and second secretaries of province committees, 18 had to be arrested. The picture is similar for people's commissariats and province executive political committees. The enemies of the people have been putting their cadres in position."[51]

According to NKVD documents, "a fundamental change in the routing of enemy units and the Trotskyist underground" occurred after Khrushchev's arrival in Kiev; the pattern of punishment was changed so that henceforth almost all those arrested were shot. This was done, one of the documents points out, "on the basis of direct orders of the people's commissar of internal affairs of the USSR, Ezhov, regarding the liquidation of the anti-Soviet underground, [orders] given by him during his trip to Ukraine, which is under the leadership of the secretary of the Ukrainian Central Committee, N. S. Khrushchev."[52]

Actually, the peak of mass repressions in Ukraine preceded Khrushchev's arrival. In fact, a January 1938 plenum of the Ukrainian Central Committee began to "correct mistakes that took place in expelling Communists from the party." In his report at the 14th Ukrainian Party Congress, Khrushchev referred to unfounded repressions. Between April 1937 and May 1938 alone, 15,611 individuals, or 5.8 percent of the entire party membership of the republic, were expelled from the party.[53]

Khrushchev noted at the same congress that from January to May 1938, 3,135 persons were restored to party ranks.[54] It would obviously be naive to suggest that with his arrival justice prevailed. It would also be unhistorical, however, to ignore the fact that it was in Ukraine that Khrushchev first gained experience in rehabilitating people, restoring them to the party, and freeing them from jails and concentration camps. Even during the Terror, Khrushchev defended the Ukrainian poet Maksim Rylskii and several other figures against the morbidly suspicious people's commissar Uspenskii.

Incidentally, the fate of Uspenskii served to convince Khrushchev of the correctness of his own actions. Stalin called Khrushchev at one point, indicated that Uspenskii was seriously "compromised," and ordered that he be arrested.[55] After Uspenskii's "exposure," the head of the Ukrainian NKVD was for a short time A. Z. Kobulov, the younger brother of B. Z. Kobulov, Beria's deputy in the federal NKVD. After that, I. A. Serov, whom Khrushchev was to put in charge of the KGB after Stalin's death, took over the NKVD in Kiev, where he and Khrushchev developed a very close and even "trusting relationship."[56] This did not, however, occur immediately

At the end of 1938, the terror in Ukraine began to abate. In the meantime, Khrushchev was officially named Ukrainian party leader, having served as acting first secretary until the 14th Congress in June. In 1939 he became a full member of the Politburo in Moscow. As Ukrainian party chief, Khrushchev devoted much time to redividing several provinces and setting up new party organizations. In addition, he focused his attention on agriculture. Upon sending Khrushchev to Ukraine, Stalin said to him, "I know your weakness for cities and industry. I must warn you not to get too engrossed in the Donbass, since you are from there, but to pay more attention to agriculture, since Ukrainian agriculture has enormous significance for the Soviet Union."[57]

On the whole, Khrushchev carried out Stalin's instructions. He traveled a lot and spent time on collective farms, meeting not only with officials but also with agronomists and village laborers. But he still believed that agricultural difficulties were largely brought about by "hostile" forces, and he had a Stalinist understanding of the place and role of the peasantry in the country's economy.

Khrushchev first met T. D. Lysenko, the charismatic quack agricultural scientist who already enjoyed Stalin's support, before the war. On

July 15, 1939, in a speech at a conference of workers in animal husbandry, Khrushchev said, "Comrades, our breeders are literally working miracles. Take our Academician Trofim Denisovich Lysenko, a
wonderful person; he has an entire school of wonderful people."[58] Such
an utterly false evaluation contributed to Lysenko's frenetic pseudo-sci-
entific activity and to his intrigues, which so adversely affected the fates
of many scientists.[59]

On the other hand, Khrushchev actively supported many truly outstanding scholars. Even before the war, he met Academician E. O. Paton, who told Khrushchev about his discovery of a unique method of
welding steel. Khrushchev recalled, "The conversation with Paton produced a very strong impression on me. I immediately dictated a note to
Stalin, in which I related everything the academician had told me, and
what I had seen myself when I traveled to his institute and became acquainted with his work. In the note, I praised Paton a good deal, wrote
how I was enchanted with his work and how important such work will
be for welding in the future, and stressed that we should speed up Paton's projects so we could introduce them sooner in the work of our factories."[60]

Stalin approved Khrushchev's initiative. Paton was sent to the tank
factory in Kharkov, where his welding technique was used on the assembly line. It is characteristic of Khrushchev that he found time during the war to support this scientist. In a March 25, 1943, letter from the
Voronezh front to authorities in Sverdlovsk, Khrushchev wrote, "The
Hero of Socialist Labor, Academician Paton, is doing work of great importance to the government. Special equipment is necessary in order
to incorporate automatic electrical welding in defense factory production on a broad scale. This equipment is made by workshops of the Institute of the Ukrainian Academy of Sciences, headed by Academician
Paton. Please assist the institute so that its workshops can produce
more equipment for our defense factories. N. Khrushchev."[61]

In January 1944, Khrushchev personally recommended Paton for
admission into the party. This seemingly insignificant event was actually a serious step. Although those who came from what was regarded
as a bourgeois or intelligentsia background ordinarily had to undergo
a trial period before being accepted as party members, Paton was admitted immediately upon Khrushchev's recommendation to Stalin.[62]
Nor was Paton the only one. Khrushchev supported the famous Ukrainian poet P. G. Tychina in his application for party membership.

On September 1, 1939, Germany attacked Poland, and on September 17, portions of the Red Army entered the territory of western Ukraine and western Belorussia. Khrushchev participated in this campaign along with the commanding officer of the Kiev military district, S. K. Timoshenko. Until the end of his life, Khrushchev believed in the historical necessity of the Molotov-Ribbentrop pact, which made Germany and the Soviet Union allies at the beginning of the war. The mere fact of an agreement with Nazi Germany, however, was repulsive to Khrushchev. One factor that served as a sort of justification was that "Ukraine has long attempted to join all Ukrainian peoples under one government. These were lands which truly were historically Ukrainian and settled by Ukrainians."[63]

During this "liberation march" into western Ukraine, there occurred an episode that casts the relationship between Khrushchev and I. A. Serov in a somewhat different light and that helps us understand Khrushchev's character at the time. While involved in assessing certain NKVD actions, Serov became frightened, and to give himself some extra insurance, he wrote a secret memorandum to L. P. Beria:

> Khrushchev yelled at me hysterically, began to swear, and stated, 'You are all sitting there in headquarters, you've seen enough of the old enemy Chekist leadership, yet you still continue to use the same methods.' Upset by such conversations, I asked him to think about what he was saying and stated that I had already eliminated old NKVD methods. . . . Then Comrade Khrushchev turned on Comrade Mikheev, the commander of the Special (NKVD) Department of the Front, who had just arrived. . . . I was forced to join in the conversation and express my opinion that Comrade Khrushchev was underestimating operational workers and frequently ignored their work. Khrushchev came up to me with his fists clenched and chewed Comrade Mikheev and me out. . . . Seeing Khrushchev in such a state, I approached him and said that I did not intend to discuss these questions any further. . . . Khrushchev began to back off a little. He began to say that we learn from each other, that we will continue to do so, and so on.

Serov concluded the memorandum with a cogent summation of Khrushchev's character: "I have come to the conclusion that Comrade Khrushchev is arrogant, even though he is not opposed to playing the democrat. He just loves it when his close associates flatter him, and I don't think he is unaware of that. I will do my best to maintain businesslike relations with him at work, but I will not be able to follow the example of some of his close associates."[64]

It is hard to say what caused Khrushchev's irritation. It may well have been the NKVD's crude actions in western Ukraine, where it subjected the local population to repression, under the banner of struggling with the nationalist underground. In general, the new government tried as rapidly as possible to unify Ukraine, to equalize socioeconomic relations in the western lands with those in the rest of the Soviet Union. New institutions were created that did not take local conditions into account. Khrushchev himself was in charge of this process. He also had to carry out the decisions of the USSR Council of People's Commissars on forced deportations from the western provinces. In accordance with a March 2, 1940, resolution, family members of former prisoners of war being held in camps or prisons, private property owners, officials of the state apparatus, members of the Organization of Ukrainian Nationalists, former members of the so-called Sich Division, and refugees from the central regions of Poland were sent off. The archives show that between the fall of 1939 and the fall of 1940, roughly one-tenth of the population of western Ukraine and western Belorussia was deported without a trial, an investigation, or even a written accusation. In November 1940 alone, 318,00 families, or 1,173,170 persons, were deported from these regions.[65] Altogether between 1939 and 1941, some sixty thousand people were arrested in the western Ukrainian lands; more than fifty thousand of them were shot or tortured.[66]

The new government suppressed all former Ukrainian political parties and movements and all social, cultural, scientific, trade, and industrial societies; many representatives of the intelligentsia were arrested (such as Academician K. I. Studinskii, whom Khrushchev mentions in his memoirs); religious and educational institutions were closed; and a series of proceedings against members of the Organization of Ukrainian Nationalists and Ukrainian intellectuals was organized.

In addition, a multitude of documents bearing witness to illegalities and violations of people's rights passed through Khrushchev's hands. He responded to this situation as best he could, trying to use the very system that gave rise to those illegalities. Simultaneous with the prohibition of Ukrainian political institutions, the liquidation of Polish organizations and the arrests of Polish figures, including Communists, began. The Polish Communist party had been dissolved by the Comintern on August 16, 1938, for being "riddled" with spies and provoca-teurs, who had allegedly seized control. After the incorporation of west-ern Ukraine, this repressive policy was continued. Khrushchev recalls: "We were met by many good fellows. . . . These were people who had passed through Polish prisons, these were Communists tested by life itself. . . . And many of them, having been freed by our Red Army, then found themselves in our Soviet prisons. Unfortunately, that's just how it was."[67]

Khrushchev's regrets were not based on hindsight. On November 2, 1940, on his initiative, the Ukrainian Politburo adopted a resolution entitled "On the facts of an incorrect attitude toward former members of the Polish Communist party." This document compelled party or-gans of western provinces to overcome "unfounded political mistrust of former members of the Polish Communist party, to involve them more actively in public work."[68] Khrushchev also decided to address another issue that was sowing seeds of hatred and civil war in the west-ern Ukrainian lands: "dekulakization" and forced collectivization. Once again in 1940, at the level of the Ukrainian Politburo, he con-demned arbitrariness in the carrying out of collectivization in western Ukraine.[69]

But most surprising is the fact that several times before and during the war, Khrushchev risked displaying interest in the fate of "enemies of the people." In the summer of 1939, for example, he made a point of receiving Petr Kovalenko, a former party worker, whom he had known since the 1920s. He spoke for a long time with Kovalenko, who had just been released from prison, asking questions about the camps, about methods of interrogation, beatings, and torture. At the end of the dis-cussion, holding his head in his hands, the disconcerted Khrushchev paced the office, finally saying: "Do you think, Petr, that I understand what is happening in the country? Do you think that I understand why I am sitting in the office of the first secretary of the Ukrainian Central Committee, and not in a cell at the Lubyanka or Lukianovka? Do you think that I am confident in tomorrow, that tomorrow they won't trans-fer me from this office to a prison cell? And yet it is still necessary to work, to do everything possible for the happiness of the people, every-thing within our power."[70]

Since this conversation took place within the walls of the Ukrainian Central Committee, Khrushchev's last remark to Kovalenko was clearly designed for self-protection. But the rest of the conversation is the indisputable result of Khrushchev's observation of the tragic realities of his time and his instinctive protest against the violence.

Moreover, during the war with Nazi Germany he tried to rehabilitate a group of Ukrainian intellectuals—twenty-three writers and literary scholars, ten historians, nine composers, actors, and artists, three linguists, a teacher, and a physicist. On October 31, 1943, a list was sent to V. Savchenko, the people's commissar for Ukrainian state security, with the following postscript from Khrushchev's assistant: "I am sending you this material at the personal order of Comrade Khrushchev . . . [who] will speak with you about this question." On January 6, 1944, Savchenko reported to Khrushchev that forty-one individuals from the list "are on the operational register of the NKVD-NKGB" and provided information on them. According to Iu. V. Aksiutin, "this is probably one of the first documents written during the Great Patriotic War, which had as its goal at least partial rehabilitation. And it was Nikita Khrushchev who, in our opinion, may have comprehended even then the scale of the Stalinist crimes and of what they did to the population."[71]

Even though he was Stalin's protégé, Khrushchev had not lost the capacity for compassion and understanding. And to a considerable extent, his stay in Ukraine contributed to this outcome. The intrigues, lies, and hypocrisy of the Stalinist "court" in Moscow degraded even its most steadfast members. Khrushchev, by contrast, had to come to terms with people's suffering. As a provincial party boss, he also understood more clearly what the Stalinist empire meant for non-Russian nationalities. All of this gradually prepared him to become the father of the Thaw in the 1950s. It is not by accident that his "secret speech" at the 20th Party Congress, and his other speeches against Stalinism, frequently alluded to his Ukrainian experience.

The beginning of the war with Nazi Germany fundamentally changed the character of Khrushchev's activity. As a member of the military council of the Kiev Special Military District, and later of the Southwest Theater, he worked "day in and day out" in the struggle against the Nazis; he directed party mobilization of people, the evacuation of enterprises and of scientific and cultural institutions, and the creation of the underground and partisan formations. Until the end of 1942, he was still signing Ukrainian party resolutions. After that, all his efforts as a member of the military council of the Stalingrad front were directed to the defense of that city. While at Stalingrad he suffered a personal tragedy: in March 1943, his eldest son Leonid was killed.[72] Leonid's wife, Liubov Illarionovna, was soon arrested on trumped-up charges. As he so often did, Stalin was detaining the relative of a close associate (he sometimes executed them as well). Fortunately, Liubov Illarionovna, after serving her time, survived and lives to this day in Kiev.

In 1942 the Nazis completely occupied Ukraine. Since Khrushchev was busy on the Stalingrad front, he did not belong to the "underground" Ukrainian Central Committee that was created on October 2, 1942, and existed until July 1943. From April 1943 on, Khrushchev devoted more attention to partisan operations and, as the territory of Ukraine was liberated, to rebuilding the devastated economy, normalizing daily life, and re-creating provincial party committees. Beginning in July 1943, he resumed leadership of the Politburo, the organizational bureau, and the secretariat of the Ukrainian Central Committee. On November 6, 1943, Lieutenant-General Khrushchev, member of the military council of the First Ukrainian Front, entered Kiev together with the Red Army, and in the fall of 1944 all of Ukraine was liberated from the Nazis. Beginning in February 1944, Khrushchev held the post of first secretary of the Ukrainian Central Committee and simultaneously headed the Ukrainian government, the first time he had combined the leadership of party and state.

With Khrushchev's direct participation, Trans-Carpathian Ukraine was united with the Ukrainian Republic, thus completing the unification of the Ukrainian lands. In mid-1946 complaints reached the Central Committee in Moscow that the Russian population in those regions was being forcibly Ukrainianized. On August 23, 1946, the Central Committee Secretariat responded with a special resolution; and in October 1946, Khrushchev had to report on his progress in carrying out the Secretariat's orders.[73] He does not mention this episode in his memoirs.

Nor does he mention a letter of his to Stalin from June 20, 1944, in which, after reporting that troops of the 1st Ukrainian and 1st Belorussian fronts had reached the state borders of the Soviet Union and in several places had moved even farther west, he suggests expanding the territory of Ukraine: "I consider it necessary, in those regions that have a majority Ukrainian and Russian population, to organize our Soviet administration after liberation, so that later, when it is advantageous, we can announce the entry of those regions into the territory of the Soviet Union, with their annexation to Soviet Ukraine. The following regions should be annexed to Soviet Ukraine: Kholm, Grubeshov, Zamost'e, Tomashov, Iaroslav, and a few other points adjoining the above-mentioned regions. It will be possible to create on the territory of the Ukrainian Republic a Kholm province, with a provincial center in the city Kholm."[74]

Knowing Stalin's paranoia, which might lead him to evaluate this initiative as a manifestation of Ukrainian nationalism, Khrushchev justified his proposal by explaining that the entry of new regions would permit straightening of the border. But Khrushchev's proposals were not accepted in the Kremlin. Stalin decided to resettle "voluntarily" in Ukraine those Ukrainians living on territories that were supposed to be handed over to Poland. Because it would have been dangerous for Khrushchev to insist on his proposals, he did not do so.

Between 1944 and 1946, 482,000 Ukrainians were resettled from Poland to various provinces of Ukraine. A significant number remained on Polish territory, however, and starting on March 29, 1947, the Polish Workers' Party undertook to expel Ukrainian and mixed Ukrainian-Polish families, so as to purge the northeastern part of Poland. As a result, more than 140,000 additional persons were resettled. This action helped the Polish Communists gain the sympathy of Polish chauvinist circles.

Passions run high today on the Crimean question, both in Ukraine and in Russia. Did Khrushchev act legally when he initiated the transfer of the Crimea from Russia to Ukraine in 1954? It turns out that he first tried to do so in 1944. In August of that year, in accordance with the USSR State Defense Committee resolution no. 6372s, "On the resettlement of collective farmers to regions of the Crimea," Ukrainian authorities decided to resettle nine thousand collective farmers from various Ukrainian provinces to the Crimea.[75] On October 3, 1944, 10,017 people arrived there.[76] Having purged the Crimea of Crimean Tatars, Stalin apparently hoped to provide the necessary labor by other means.[77] The Crimea needed laborers to harvest the fruit and to look after animals on former Tatar collective farms.[78] But Khrushchev resisted this resettlement, for fear that Ukraine would give up people and material resources without getting anything in return. Aware of the Crimean peninsula's long-established historical connections with Ukraine, Khrushchev studied several detailed reports on the Crimea and in 1944 took to Moscow his idea of transferring the Crimea to

Ukraine.[79] He described the results of that trip to a party colleague: "There I was in Moscow and I said, 'Ukraine is in ruins, and everybody wants something from her. And what if we give the Crimea to her, no strings attached? Oh, what they didn't call me after that, how they worked me over. They were ready to make mincemeat out of me! But no big deal; as you see, I'm alive!"[80] The author of these reminiscences ascribes the following words to Khrushchev as well: "I'll give up people, but I'll take the Crimea. We'll come out even."[81]

Clearly, despite Khrushchev's genuine internationalism, he strove to promote the interests of Ukraine, which had suffered huge losses and had given so much to the always ravenous "all-union piggy bank." Of course Khrushchev never dreamed that Ukraine could ever secede and become an independent state.

Another episode that helps characterize Khrushchev as a politician occurred in 1944. Despite his support for many representatives of Ukrainian science and culture, his relations with Ukrainian intellectuals in general were largely defined by the political-ideological situation. Consider, for example, the evolution of Khrushchev's evaluation of A. P. Dovzhenko's film, *Ukraine in Flames* (*Ukraina v ogne*). Having praised it to the skies in August 1943, Khrushchev drastically changed his opinion at the end of the same year, because the film seemed "nationalistic" to Kremlin leaders and to Stalin personally. On December 31, 1943, Khrushchev refused to meet with Dovzhenko. On January 3, 1944, Dovzhenko noted in his diary, "Today I was with N. S. Kh[rushchev]. A difficult meeting, and now two hours have already gone by and I have still not gotten through an oppressive desire to die, so as not to feel this human harshness. It seemed as if he wasn't N. S. and I wasn't myself. . . . There was a cold, merciless atheist and judge, and a guilty, amoral criminal and enemy of the people, i.e. me. And I understood that no arguments, even those pronounced with the anguish of a heavy heart and reflecting the most honest self-analysis, had changed his mind in anything, nor would they. . . . I left N.S. with the feeling that my life was ruined. 'We'll come back to a consideration of your work,' he said. 'We won't just leave it as it is. No, we'll come back to it yet.' So I have to live and function under the oppressive, unbearable threat of eventual judgment. They will tear me apart before the people, and all my many years of labor will be nullified or even turned into a dishonest trick. Lord, give me strength. Don't let me fall into grief and sorrow, lest my heart dry up and my soul turn bitter. Send me the wisdom to forgive the good N.S., who showed himself to be small in stature, for he is a weak person."[82]

On January 31, 1944, Stalin gave a speech, "On anti-Leninist mistakes and nationalist distortions in Dovzhenko's film *Ukraine in Flames*," at a Politburo session. Not only did he criticize the film, but he declared it to be "anti-Soviet," a clear manifestation of "nationalism."[83] But Dovzhenko's final punishment was left up to the "Ukrainian comrades," headed by Khrushchev. It is his signature that appears under the Ukrainian Central Committee's February 8, 1944, resolution, "On A. P. Dovzhenko," that resulted in Dovzhenko's dismissal from the All-Slavic Committee, the Committee for Stalin Prizes, the editorial board of the journal *Ukraina*, and the Kiev film studio, where he had served as artistic director.[84] Although Dovzhenko thought Khrushchev was sympathetic to him, political exigencies won out. As the "leader of Ukraine," he acted in the way Moscow demanded. This savage criticism of Dovzhenko launched the next stage of the struggle with "nationalistic manifestations" within the Ukrainian creative elite.

Nor was Ukraine spared the consequences of the odious August 1948 session of the Lenin Academy of Agricultural Sciences. In connection with the resolution of the Ukrainian Central Committee of August 1948, "On measures for the reconstruction of the work of scientific establishments, [university] departments, publishers, and magazines and newspapers in the area of biology, and the strengthening of these areas with qualified groups of Michurinists," many Ukrainian scientists who did not support the Lysenko movement lost their jobs, and a devastating criticism of their work was launched. At Kharkov State University the head of the Department of Darwinism and Genetics, Professor I. M. Poliakov, was dismissed, as were S. M. Gershenzon, the head of the Department of Darwinism at Kiev State University, and many others.[85]

In accordance with the laws of the Stalinist system, Khrushchev unwaveringly carried out decisions, even though he could not but understand their unequivocal consequences. On February 21, 1948, the Presidium of the USSR Supreme Soviet adopted a decree "On the expulsion from the Ukrainian SSR of individuals maliciously shirking labor activity in agriculture and leading an antisocial, parasitic way of life." "Public sentences" were soon passed at collective farm meetings on those who were to be expelled from Ukraine. Also discussed were those who, in the opinion of the meeting, did not work diligently enough or failed to complete the minimum number of workdays. Such people usually got off with a warning and had to promise to work better. As Khrushchev noted in a March 27, 1948, speech at the Ukrainian Politburo, it was a "very effective measure" when someone in attendance at a meeting gave his or her word to work well and then strengthened the commitment with a signature.[86] From the time the decree appeared until July 1950, some 11,991 "public sentences" of expulsion were carried out,[87] mostly in 1948. Public sentences were passed on older people, disabled veterans of World War II, and those not belonging to collective farms but nonetheless living in rural areas. Individual collective farm leaders tried to use the decree to settle personal scores with certain collective farmers. Between 1948 and 1950, 2,049 of these "sentences"—17 percent of them—were revoked.[88]

The decree of February 21, 1948, was only one link in a chain of measures inherent in a system that sought to solve economic problems by force. Although Khrushchev resolutely opposed such methods after 1953, he behaved differently in 1948. On April 17 he sent a long letter to Stalin in which he described the implementation of the decree, denounced its errors and excesses, and proposed that similar decrees be adopted in the Russian Republic (RSFSR) and other union republics. "Everywhere," he wrote, "the application of the decree will hasten the strengthening of work discipline, which will guarantee the timely completion of all agricultural work, good harvests, an increase in the productivity of animal husbandry, and a more rapid improvement of the entire collective farm economy."[89]

This decree's "pressure tactics" had an effect, but not the one Khrushchev intended. Indeed, this was the period when Khrushchev, who had always been more interested in industry, realized both the difficult position of the peasants in the feudal Stalinist system and the need to improve peasant life. During the postwar famine (1946–1947) the Ukrainian Central Committee and the Ukrainian government, on Khrushchev's initiative, sought needed aid from the central government. As a result, Ukraine's collective farms received seeds for planting grain in the beginning of 1947, as well as other help, which relieved the shortages somewhat. Agricultural issues were considered sixteen times between 1945 and 1949 at plenums of the Ukrainian Central Committee, at most of which Khrushchev spoke. At his urging, the Ukrainian Central Committee in 1946 resumed the practice of con-

ducting republic-wide conferences of outstanding workers from various branches of agriculture. Between 1946 and 1948, twelve such conferences were held, with approximately eleven thousand individuals
participating. Although there was no small amount of formalism at
these meetings, they nevertheless served as a constant reminder that
agricultural problems did exist and that life in the village was not easy.
This realization led Khrushchev to adopt reformist agricultural policies
in the 1950s.

In the difficult conditions of the postwar period, when the main
burden of reconstruction lay on the peasants but insufficient attention
was paid to them, Khrushchev undertook measures to better their material condition. As early as April 1945, Ukrainian authorities adopted
a resolution "On the construction of housing for collective farmers,
production buildings on collective farms, and cultural-recreational
buildings in the village." It provided for the construction of houses for
collective farmers in an organized fashion, with the help of the collectives themselves. After a short time, groups of builders were formed,
brick-tile factories were started up, and the work of construction enterprises was revived. As a result, between 1945 and 1950, 4,500 villages were planned and built, and 252 model plans for various economic and cultural-recreational structures were drawn up. In the first
postwar Five-Year Plan, 919,000 housing units for collective farmers,
250,000 production buildings on collective farms, and 31,000 cultural-
recreational buildings were either restored or completely rebuilt.

Later, when he was in Moscow, Khrushchev tried to apply his
Ukrainian experience to the Soviet Union at large. In a report given at
a January 1951 party conference and then published in *Pravda* on March
4, he advocated amalgamating smaller collective farms into urban-style
settlements. But after the article provoked a sharply negative reaction
from Stalin, *Pravda*'s editorial board announced on March 5 that it had
failed to note the "tentative" nature of Khrushchev's views. Few knew
that a special secret letter of the Central Committee had sharply criticized the article. But many heads of collective farms halted building
projects, including the construction of housing.

Khrushchev himself, despite his high rank, did penance. One can
only imagine the spiritual torture he suffered in writing the following:
"Dear Comrade Stalin! You absolutely correctly pointed out the mistakes that were committed by me in the report published on March 4 of
this year, 'On the construction of collective farms and equipping them

with services and utilities.' As you instructed me, I have tried to ponder these questions more deeply. Pondering them, I understood that as a whole, the report is fundamentally incorrect. . . . I ask you, Comrade Stalin, to help me to correct the crude mistake that I have made and thus to reduce as much as possible the harm that I have brought upon the party with my incorrect report."[90] Stalin put the letter in the archives. It had no further consequences for Khrushchev, who "corrected" his own "mistake" after the tyrant's death; in 1958 the Central Committee repealed as erroneous the accusations made against his article in 1951.

Stalin condemned one other instance of Khrushchev's consideration for the peasantry. It occurred in the midst of the horrors of the 1946–1947 famine: in May 1947, more than nine hundred thousand people were registered as suffering from potentially fatal dystrophy; parents abandoned their children when there was no possibility of feeding them; between January and June 1947, more than three hundred cases of cannibalism occurred in Ukraine. Altogether, in sixteen eastern provinces and in Izmail and Chernovits provinces in the west, 282,000 people died in 1946, and more than 520,000 died in 1947.[91] These figures reflect only those cases that were officially recognized. Many people died fleeing Ukraine, on the road to Transcaucasia, Central Asia, or the Kuban. Khrushchev requested aid, sending several letters to Moscow. He recalled the reaction he received: "Stalin sent me a most rude and offensive telegram stating that I was a dubious character, saying that I was writing memos in which I proved Ukraine could not fulfill its state orders [for grain] and requesting a huge number of ration cards for feeding people. That telegram crushed me. I understood the tragedy that hung not only over me, but over the Ukrainian people."[92]

When Khrushchev began to provide more detailed information about the developing famine, he provoked Stalin's anger even further: "'Spinelessness! You are being deceived; all this is being brought to your attention just to gain your pity and make you waste reserves.' [Stalin] thought that I was giving in to local Ukrainian influence, that I was being pressured, that I had nearly become an untrustworthy nationalist."[93]

Stalin went on to raise the question of "strengthening" Khrushchev's leadership in Kiev. On March 3, 1947, Politburo member L. M. Kaganovich and Central Committee secretary N. S. Patolichev participated in a Ukrainian Central Committee plenum. Both were elected to the Ukrainian Politburo and Orgburo. The plenum determined that combining the posts of chairman of the Council of Ministers and first secretary of the Ukrainian Central Committee was inadvisable and decided "to confirm Comrade L. M. Kaganovich as first secretary of the Ukrainian Central Committee, so that Comrade Khrushchev can remain chairman of the Ukrainian Council of Ministers."[94]

Thus the political paths of Khrushchev and Kaganovich crossed once again. Their friendly relations in the 1920s and 1930s had continued during the war with Nazi Germany. In 1943 Khrushchev even found time to congratulate Kaganovich on receiving the title of Hero of Socialist Labor.[95] But the situation was different in 1947. Soon after Kaganovich's arrival in Ukraine, many understood that he could potentially play a sinister role. While energetically involving himself in agricultural administration, Kaganovich simultaneously began to create the impression that "all was not in order" in Ukraine, not only in agriculture but in general, and that the reason was nationalism. At one of his meetings with first secretaries of provincial party committees, Kaganovich announced that every failure to fulfill plan assignments in industry and agriculture would be considered a manifestation of Ukrainian bourgeois nationalism. Campaigns of persecution against talented Ukrainian scholars and figures in art and literature gained momentum. Devastating articles about them appeared in the press.

Recollections of Kaganovich's work in Ukraine in the 1920s served as a kind of introduction to these campaigns. On September 2, 1947, the newspaper *Sovetskaia Ukraina* printed an abridged transcript of A. Korneichuk's speech to the leadership of the Soviet Writers' Union. "The struggle with bourgeois nationalism," Korneichuk said, "has a long and instructive history in Ukrainian literature. Under the leadership of the Central Committee and Comrade Stalin personally, Ukraine's Bolsheviks, with Lazar Moiseevich Kaganovich at their head, smashed 'Khvylevism,' that intelligence service of Ukrainian fascism in literature.[96] The bacilli of Khvylevism are still alive in the bodies of some Ukrainian literary figures and continue to harm the successful growth of our literature. The struggle with nationalistic ideology remains even now one of the most important tasks of Ukrainian Soviet literature."[97]

Soon enough the carriers of the "bacilli" of nationalism were named. In particular, the open persecution of Maksim Rylskii began.

In recalling Kaganovich's "unmasking" activities in the postwar period, Khrushchev said:

> I managed with great difficulty to defend such a worthy writer as Maksim Rylskii from destructive criticism for his poem 'Mother,' which is full of profound patriotic feelings. The main reason for the baseless attacks against Rylskii was the fact that in that poem, which praises Soviet Ukraine, Stalin's name was not mentioned. And Comrade Kaganovich, who curried favor and did everything to fan the flames of Stalin's personality cult, began to depict Maksim Rylskii as a Ukrainian bourgeois nationalist. He played on Stalin's weakness, without considering the severe consequences for Ukrainian, and not only Ukrainian, literature. It must be said that this could have led to serious consequences, and not only for literature.[98]

During Kaganovich's stay in Ukraine, the Ukrainian Central Committee adopted a resolution "On the political mistakes and unsatisfactory work of the Ukrainian Academy of Sciences' Institute of History," in which the academy and its fellows were subjected to crude, baseless attacks. The former director of the Institute of the History of Ukraine, Professor M. N. Petrovskii, was subjected to such criticism; his works *The Unification of the Ukrainian People in a Single Ukrainian Soviet State* (1944) and *The Unbending Spirit of the Great Ukrainian People* (1943) were seen as mistakes and distortions of a "bourgeois-nationalistic character."

The *Short Course on the History of Ukraine* (1941; edited by S. Belousov, K. Guslistii, M. Petrovskii, N. Suprunenko, and F. Iastrebov), *Contributions to the History of Ukraine* (Ufa, 1942; edited by K. Guslistii, M. Slavin, and F. Iastrebov), and the first volume of the *History of Ukraine* (1943, edited by M. N. Petrovskii) were characterized as attempts to "revive bourgeois-nationalist views on questions of the history of Ukraine to a greater or lesser extent." Khrushchev felt that all these actions were directed against him as well. When preparation began for a Ukrainian Central Committee plenum with "Struggle against nationalism as the main danger in the Ukrainian Communist Party" on the agenda, it became clear that Khrushchev would not escape unharmed. It was he, after all, who had led the Ukrainian party organization for many years and consequently bore the responsibility for not having removed the "danger." Furthermore, Stalin called Khrushchev at one point and observed that Kaganovich was sending many documents to Moscow without Khrushchev's approval. These facts do not confirm R. A. Medvedev's opinion that in 1947 Kaganovich "tried to smooth things over with Khrushchev."[99]

In my opinion, Khrushchev was almost certainly saved from a direct confrontation with Kaganovich by the extended bout of pneumonia that he mentions in his memoirs.[100] Some Western scholars believe that this "illness," which lasted from June till September 1947, was less a medical than a political ailment. Khrushchev himself, however, contends in his memoirs that it was real, and his son Sergei confirms that fact. Khrushchev's extended isolation allowed him to remain on the sidelines during the hysterical efforts to unmask national dissidents, the undesirable consequences of which soon became clear in Moscow. Shortly after bringing to the capital his list of "bourgeois nationalists," Kaganovich was removed from Ukraine. Stalin apparently realized that Kaganovich's actions could complicate rather than strengthen Moscow's control over the republic. On December 26, 1947, a Ukrainian Central Committee plenum removed Kaganovich as Ukrainian party leader.[101] Khrushchev assumed this position once again, and D. S. Korotchenko took over as head of the Ukrainian Council of Ministers. Thus the history of Khrushchev's demotion came to a close. Stalin's faith was restored. "That," recalled Khrushchev, "improved my morale: I was restored as a full-fledged member of the Politburo, and not in name only."[102]

When Khrushchev is spoken or written about, attention is usually focused on the Thaw, that is, on his attempts to ameliorate the Stalinist administrative-command system. Yet these attempts, as we know, ended in failure, an outcome that can be at least partially explained by his genetic connection with the system he wanted to reform. The administrative-command system was hierarchical; it recognized not only the cult of the "uppermost leader" but also little cults of ministerial and regional leaders. According to the rules of this system, both its successes and its failures had to be personified. It is here, as well as in Khrushchev's human qualities, that we must search for the reasons that he did "not protest" against those who hailed his "personal contribution" or, along with "Comrade Stalin's" accomplishments, recalled the accomplishments of "his very close comrade-in-arms, Comrade Khrushchev."[103] His achievements were extolled more and more often during his last years in Ukraine. The 16th Ukrainian Party Congress in

January 1949 was typical in this regard. Toasts were made in honor of two people: Stalin and Khrushchev.

The composer P. Batiuk and the poet T. Masenko wrote "Song About Khrushchev" even earlier, which included this refrain:

> He went through battles together with our people,
> He is leading our land to happiness.
> May our friend Comrade Khrushchev be praised,
> Sing, o people, of him!

One of the verses of the song went like this:

> Wherever life grows in great renewal,
> We see our friend again and again.
> We meet Khrushchev at Poltava and Lvov,
> At the very heart of resounding successes.[104]

The verse quoted above did in a way correspond to reality: Khrushchev traveled all over Ukraine, attentively following the course of postwar restoration. And successes in this area were obvious. Ukraine's economy suffered significantly during the war and Nazi occupation, but industrial production had attained 71 percent of 1940 levels by the end of 1948, and the overall area under cultivation in all categories of agriculture had reached 93 percent of prewar levels. The Dnepropetrovsk hydroelectric station was resurrected; metallurgical giants like the Zaporozhstal, Azovstal, Makeev, and other factories returned to operation. The Kharkov tractor factory was rebuilt. A new branch of industry—gas—arose in Ukraine with the construction of the Dashava-Kiev gas pipeline.

Parallel with this reconstruction, a little-known and undeclared "war after the war" was waged, one in which Khrushchev was directly involved, to Sovietize the western Ukrainian lands. With his knowledge and sanction, a campaign of oppression was mounted against the Organization of Ukrainian Nationalists (OUN) and the Ukrainian Insurgent Army (UPA). In a letter to Stalin of November 15, 1944, Khrushchev wrote that he had assigned party organizations and NKVD and NKGB organs the task of carefully checking the apparat, especially technical workers recruited from the local population. He also proposed introducing field courts-martial for NKVD troops: "To terrorize the bandits we should not shoot those condemned to execution by the

sentences of the field courts-martial, but hang them. The courts-martial must be conducted openly, with the local population in attendance.
The results of the courts-martial are not to be revealed more widely in
the press."[105]

There was one other proposal in Khrushchev's letter: to "establish
temporarily special troikas at provincial offices of the NKVD in western
Ukrainian provinces, consisting of the provincial party committee secretary, the provincial NKVD office head, and the provincial chief prosecutor. These troikas are to be given the right to consider the cases of
Ukrainian-German nationalists and their helpers and the right to apply the supreme measure of punishment to the guilty—shooting, with
the sentence to be carried out immediately."[106] Khrushchev's proposal
to re-create the infamous troikas, which had been used during the terror of the late 1930s, was not adopted, but executions of those suspected
of participation in the nationalist underground in western Ukraine
were conducted publicly.

Khrushchev understood the seriousness of the confrontation with
the Ukrainian insurgents, who in 1945 were rearranged into small,
well-organized and armed subunits based in local wooded mountain
ranges. The UPA brigades controlled significant territories and strove
to maintain national-state structures, illegal in those conditions, as an
alternative to the organs of Communist power. According to official
data, the Ukrainian underground carried out 14,500 acts of sabotage
and terrorism, which killed no fewer than thirty thousand representatives of the Communist regime, members of the military, and local inhabitants.[107]

After the capitulation of Nazi Germany, the Stalinist leadership was
able to intensify its actions against the OUN and UPA, thus turning
western Ukraine into a virtual war zone. Khrushchev took the lead, occasionally calling conferences with province party leaders and the
heads of provincial NKVD and NKGB offices. Between January and October 1945 he spoke at eight such conferences. He was brusque and demanding in the extreme. On January 10, 1945, in Lvov province, he
warned, "We just won't be respected if we don't take measures; we must
arrest every single one of the participants, whom we must then judge,
perhaps hang, and then exile the rest of them; that way we will take a
hundred for one. . . . They must fear our vengeance."[108]

Under pressure from Khrushchev, the Ukrainian Central Committee assigned provincial leaders the task of liquidating the nationalistic

movement in western Ukraine by March 15, 1945. The OUN and UPA resistance to the Communist regime lasted much longer than that, however. Organized struggle ended after the death of the UPA commander R. Shukhevich ("Taras Chuprinka"), who was killed on March 5, 1950, while scattered armed attacks continued into the mid-1950s. That Khrushchev's original timetable was not achieved seemed to stimulate his aggressiveness; he was convinced, as he said at one of the conferences in 1946, that "banditism now bases itself on terror . . . not on the sympathy of the masses."[109]

Khrushchev was wrong, as he himself began to understand. There was in fact terror, but the sympathies of the population were with the Ukrainian underground. These sympathies were to no small extent engendered by the arbitrary illegalities carried out in western Ukraine by police organs and military units. Between 1944 and 1949, information flooded into Kiev about multiple violations of, as it was then expressed, "socialist legality." In July 1946, for example, the Ukrainian Politburo adopted a special resolution, "On insufficiencies in the work of the MVD and MGB organs, of the courts and the prosecutors in the struggle with violators of Soviet legality in western Ukrainian provinces," which noted "965 violations of socialist legality" during the first five months, of which in 462 cases the "guilty parties were brought to trial."[110]

Khrushchev was well aware of all this. In August 1945 the people's commissar for internal affairs in Ukraine, General-Lieutenant Riasnoi, sent him a report on the "large number of incidents of immoral and criminal conduct on the part of some military personnel" in the western provinces of Ukraine. The document listed rape, murder, robberies and thefts, arbitrariness and outrages, hooligan actions. It also emphasized that "in the conditions of the western provinces of Ukraine, these facts are widely used by anti-Soviet elements for purposes hostile to us."[111] Here is Khrushchev's reaction to one such document: "I strongly request"—in this case the matter involved the command of the Carpathian military district—"that necessary measures be taken to avoid such incidents."[112]

It was impossible for Khrushchev to overcome lawlessness and violence, however, since he himself was involved in the same activities. In particular, he encouraged the creation of so-called special MGB groups, which infiltrated the OUN underground and the UPA. These provocateurs mistreated the local population, luring some people into cooperation to test their loyalty to the Communist regime and then disposing of them, while plundering and destroying others and then ascribing the violence to the OUN or UPA.

In 1949 Khrushchev received a detailed memorandum from the prosecutor, Kosharsky, attached to Ukrainian MVD troops. In it, Kosharskii showed that "the crudely provocative and mindless work of a series of special groups, and the violent acts allowed by their members against the local population, is not only not facilitating the struggle with banditry but, on the contrary, is complicating it, undermining the authority of Soviet legality and undoubtedly bringing harm to the cause of socialist construction in the western provinces of Ukraine."[113]

The actions of these special groups remain little investigated to this day and deserve a separate study, in which one would have to demonstrate Khrushchev's role. Similar attention to his role in the destruction of the Ukrainian Greek Catholic Church (UGKTs) is also necessary. Much evidence suggests that Khrushchev considered the UGKTs to be fully as dangerous as the OUN and UPA, primarily because the church had so much influence on the western Ukrainian population and a solid material base. When an instruction (approved by Stalin) for the destruction of the church appeared in March 1945, Khrushchev, in close contact with security organs, worked out a plan for discrediting the UGKTs hierarchy as "servants of the Vatican," "enemies of the people," and "weapons of Ukrainian bourgeois nationalism." By April 1945 all high-ranking clergy living in the Soviet Union at the time were arrested. Metropolitan Iosif Slepoi (who took over as head of the UGKTs in November 1944 after the death of Metropolitan Andrei Sheptitskii) spent eighteen years in prison.

In May 1945, party and security organs organized an "initiative group" within the church that agitated for breaking the union with Rome and justified aggressive action against the UGKTs. G. Kostelnik was the leader of the group. Between March 8 and 10, 1946, a Lvov assembly of representatives of the UGKTs was held under the control of the NKGB, at which it was decided (216 delegate-priests and 19 civilian representatives voted in favor) to cancel the Brest union of 1596. Kostelnik, who played the chief role in this spectacle, became dangerous to the organizers of the assembly when his conscience began to trouble him. On September 20, 1948, he was killed in mysterious circumstances; moreover, the murderer immediately committed suicide.

Under pressure from the authorities, a decision to end the activities of the UGKTs was also made by the Mukachevskii diocese. Once again, the affair was bloody: the head of the UGKTs in Trans-Carpathia, Bishop Teodor Romzha of Mukachevskii, was eliminated by agents of a special group. On October 27, 1947, he was brought to a hospital (after an organized assassination attempt on him), where, according to a nun serving as a nurse at the time, he was poisoned.[114]

In his memoirs, the former NKVD general P. A. Sudoplatov reports Khrushchev's direct role in organizing this murder. After the unsuccessful attempt on Romzha's life, Khrushchev allegedly convinced Stalin of the need to eliminate the bishop. "Soon," writes Sudoplatov, "we determined that the real threat to Khrushchev came from the nuns who were under Romzha's control, who in turn maintained a close connection with the wife of Ivan Turianitsa, the first secretary of the provincial committee and the chairman of the city administration. Khrushchev knew that Romzha had penetrated both the governmental and the party administration, but he did not quite know how. Fearing the exposure of his own ineffectiveness, Khrushchev ordered Romzha's murder."[115] In time, the story of Bishop Romzha's murder would serve as one concrete explanation of something Khrushchev said in retirement, when he "repented" in a conversation with playwright Mikhail Shatrov: "I'm up to my elbows in blood. I sincerely believed in Stalin at the time and did everything. . . . That's the most terrible thing, what burdens my soul."[116]

All this reminds us once again of the price of those transformations that were carried out in western Ukraine after its annexation by the Soviet Union. In particular, according to incomplete data, 2,196,170 persons, one-fifth of the population, were deported from the region to the eastern part of the Soviet Union between the years 1939 and 1955.[117] And there were others even less fortunate.

Of course the problem of reunification was solved for western Ukraine, far-reaching de-Polonization was conducted, and Sovietization was begun. Khrushchev did his part here as well; he never conceived of western Ukraine as outside Ukraine as a whole, and he never conceived of Ukraine as outside the Soviet Union.

Khrushchev's last year in Ukraine was 1949. The 16th Ukrainian Party Congress, which took place between January 25 and 28, welcomed Khrushchev with a prolonged and thunderous standing ovation, including shouts of "Glory to Comrade Khrushchev!" and "Hurrah!"[118] Many of the leading delegates had been promoted by Khrushchev: L. I.

Brezhnev, A. A. Grechko, A. A. Epishev, A. I. Kirichenko, L. R. Korni-
its, D. S. Korotchenko, L. G. Melnikov, V. E. Semichastnii, Z. T. Serdiuk,
and others were visible in the presidium of the congress, and N. A.
Shchelokov (who was the director of the department of the Ukrainian
Central Committee), V. P. Mzhavanadze (deputy commander of the
Kiev military district for political affairs), and G. T. Shuiskii (assistant
secretary of the Ukrainian Central Committee) were in the Secretariat.
A. P. Kirilenko, R. A. Rudenko, and others were elected to the Ukrainian Central Committee. Almost all these men later became members
of the Khrushchev "administration" when he became Soviet leader.

"In our work with cadres," emphasized Khrushchev, "there are to
this day serious defects. . . . It often happens that a man is judged by the
information on his application and by an impression, but not by his
deeds."[119] Years later, the harsh reality hidden behind this traditional
Communist rhetoric would catch up with Khrushchev himself; many
of those he promoted, who supported him during the period of his rise,
would turn away from him and contribute to his overthrow in October
1964. We are not speaking only of Brezhnev or Kirilenko but, for example, of P. E. Shelest (whom Khrushchev met in 1940) and N. V. Podgornyi (whom Khrushchev also knew well from his work in Ukraine in
the 1940s and whom Khrushchev personally nominated as Ukrainian
first secretary in 1957, then as secretary of the CPSU Central Committee in June 1963). Shelest is apparently the only one of Khrushchev's
"Ukrainian appointees" who eventually, in retirement, expressed a
kind of repentance for his participation in Khrushchev's overthrow. In
1989, in response to the question, "Do you think that Khrushchev's
overthrow and Brezhnev's rise to power were objectively necessary?" he
said, "No, there was no such necessity. That is my firm conviction, although I myself took part in what happened. I see now that I was wrong
and sincerely regret what happened."[120]

Of course, this was repentance with the benefit of hindsight; back
in 1964 virtually all Khrushchev's Ukrainian protégés came out against
him. The only Ukrainian leader who actively supported Khrushchev
in 1964 was the Ukrainian Central Committee secretary O. I. Iva-
shchenko, who unsuccessfully tried to warn Khrushchev of the plot
underway against him.

The year 1949 brought the seventieth birthday of the "leader of peoples," and in time for the celebration Stalin decided to bring Khrushchev back to Moscow. According to Khrushchev, Stalin believed that

another plot was being hatched against him in Moscow and Leningrad: "We want Moscow to be the fulcrum of the party's Central Committee; therefore it is more useful for you to work here."[121] Khrushchev thanked him for his confidence, and soon, at the December 1949 plenum of the Ukrainian Central Committee, he was released from his duties as Ukrainian leader so that he could return to Moscow as CPSU Central Committee secretary and head of the Moscow province party committee. L. G. Melnikov took over the Ukrainian party organization.

In summing up, it is not easy to squeeze Khrushchev into some well-defined framework. Something will always be found in his biography to put that framework in doubt. During his tenure in power, he was depicted as a great friend of Ukraine because his political career began there and he headed the Ukrainian Central Committee for almost twelve years. But that image of him is complicated by the anti-Ukrainian bent of many of his actions.

On the other hand, it is not possible to treat Khrushchev's activities in Ukraine as simply anti-Ukrainian, since more than once Stalin blasted him for falling under the influence of "Ukrainian nationalists." Khrushchev's political biography, including its Ukrainian pages, cannot be understood in fragmentary fashion. His life and work, the varied pieces of his historic-political mosaic, must always be assembled into a complete picture.

2

The Rise to Power

NIKOLAI BARSUKOV

Nikita Khrushchev was elected secretary of the Central Committee of the Communist Party of the Soviet Union at a committee plenum on December 16, 1949.[1] Shortly thereafter he vacated the post of head of the Ukrainian Communist party. The advancement occurred on Stalin's initiative. A few days after his arrival in Moscow, at a celebration of Stalin's seventieth birthday, Khrushchev sat to the leader's immediate left on the stage of the Bolshoi Theater.

Khrushchev also effectively became the first secretary of the party's Moscow province committee, which he had already led between 1935 and 1938. His move reflected Stalin's notion that the "health" of the Moscow party organization needed to be "restored," as that of the Leningrad party organization had recently been. What caused Stalin's concern was an anonymous report of a "plot" against the Central Committee and the government, led by the Moscow party leader G. M. Popov. An experienced, reliable person was needed to deal with this situation, one who knew the rules of the game. Khrushchev fulfilled those requirements perfectly.

Nikita Khrushchev had the courage to be skeptical. He recalled:

> Despite the fact that Stalin disliked it very much when such documents were approached with distrust, I said, "I am completely convinced that this is a document that has nothing in common with reality. I know many people whom it names as conspirators and as part of that group. But these are people of the utmost honesty! In particular, I am completely sure that Popov is not a conspirator. . . ." And apparently my confident tone had an impact on Stalin. He said to me, "So you feel that this does not deserve attention?" I said, "Absolutely not. This is either a provocateur or a madman." He swore. And that was the end of it.[2]

Things might have gone differently, as Khrushchev noted. "To distinguish myself and win Stalin's trust . . . all I had to say was, 'Yes, this is a serious document, we must look into this.' That would have been enough on my part. He would have ordered Popov arrested immediately. The entire group would obviously have confessed. And then you would have had a conspiratorial group in Moscow. Plus a person about whom it is said, so to speak, that he came, he investigated, he uncovered, he destroyed, and so forth. But what a base move that would have been! Yet that's the way it went in Leningrad."[3]

Khrushchev was always close to the rank-and-file party members and to the people; he saw and felt the situation and mood out in the regions better than other leaders did. He understood that a sweeping new repressive action would not result in any good and might even become dangerous, both in the grand scheme of things and for himself personally.

The postwar years were a time of considerable growth of the sociopolitical and spiritual-moral consciousness of the people of the Soviet Union. Victories on the field of battle and then on the working front, as well as the restoration of the economy, instilled a feeling of great national pride and self-respect. And the war had another sort of impact. Millions of Soviet citizens had spent time in foreign countries and had seen a different political system, a higher standard of living, and an alternative culture of daily life. Such experiences inevitably corrected the relentlessly negative representations of the West, first and foremost in the area of material welfare. But these newly found social reference points did not fundamentally alter the belief of the Soviet people in the correctness and eventual triumph of socialism or the impending doom of capitalism. The people, by and large, were convinced that socialism, by virtue of its "superiority over capitalism," would not only provide an equal standard of living but would actually surpass that of capitalism. Hence the nationwide support for the Communist party and its Stalinist leadership.

At the same time, the increase in popular self-consciousness and social activism represented a potential threat to the totalitarian regime. Spontaneous protests against the dictates of the party, political doctrinairism, and ideological dogmatism grew. There appeared occasional instances of free thinking, of a more independent analysis of reality, including history and the results and lessons of military victory. In public life, notes of criticism, calls for change, and resistance to the manipulation of social consciousness from on high sounded more distinctly and loudly. Discussion began about economics, philosophy, language, and literary criticism. The economists A. I. Notkin, A. V. Sanin, V. G. Venzher, and L. D. Iaroshenko dared to disagree with Stalin himself.[4] For Iaroshenko, this opposition led to arrest. Representatives of the "bourgeois sciences" of genetics and cybernetics began to speak out. Valentin Ovechkin exposed the actual state of affairs in rural villages in his work *Raionnye budni* (Regional weekdays).[5] Nonconformist youth circles and groups sprang up.[6] Samizdat—independent, underground publishing—sent out its first shoots.

New preventive actions were therefore undertaken by the Stalinist leadership. A series of repressions was launched in order to paralyze democratic aspirations and to drown out the first expressions of free thought. Political, ideological, social, and administrative persecution once again became an active component in the self-defense of totalitarianism and in the strengthening of the authoritarian party-state system. The number of victims grew daily.

On February 21, 1948, the Presidium of the USSR Supreme Soviet issued a decree, according to which "particularly dangerous state criminals" who had served their sentence would not be set free but would be subject to "settlement in exile."[7] Some political prisoners who had already been released were arrested again. Between 1948 and 1953, 58,218 people were exiled for an indefinite period.[8] As on January 1, 1953, 2,472,247 people remained in corrective labor camps.[9] Of these, more than half a million were "politicals."

As Stalin's health worsened and his inevitable exit approached, tension grew in the highest echelons of power. Prominent party and state figures fell victim to internecine strife: Central Committee Secretary A. A. Kuznetsov, Deputy Chairman of the USSR Council of Ministers N. A. Voznesenskii, and Chairman of the RSFSR Council of Ministers M. I. Rodionov were all shot, as were many others. Secretary of the Central Committee A. A. Zhdanov died. Khrushchev noted in his memoirs, "Zhdanov died because doctors treated him in a certain manner, that is, they 'treated' him in quotation marks, in order not to cure him. And as a result of certain omissions or even intentional actions, Zhdanov died."[10] At the Central Committee plenum after the 19th Party Congress in 1952, Stalin questioned the loyalty of V. M. Molotov and A. I. Mikoyan. He even harbored designs against L. P. Beria. "After the war," said Khrushchev, "when I began to meet frequently with Stalin, I started to feel more and more that Stalin did not trust Beria. More than that, he was afraid of him. What exactly he was afraid of, I did not then understand. Later on, when the whole machinery for the destruction of people, and all of the resources devoted to it were exposed—and it was Beria who used these resources and took the necessary actions on Stalin's orders—I understood that Stalin had apparently reached a conclusion: if Beria was doing this to those singled out by Stalin, then he could do the same thing on his own initiative, if he chose. Stalin was afraid that this choice would fall first of all upon himself."[11] In fact they were all afraid, even Khrushchev. But Stalin either chose not to or could not eliminate Beria, and so he remained outwardly trusting toward him.

Stalin was aware that his time was running out. He grew more and more aloof, and not only on account of his health. He was tired of power and grandeur; he withdrew into himself, and he sharply limited his social interactions. The number of people close to him dropped to four or five, including Khrushchev, Beria, G. M. Malenkov, and N. A. Bulganin. Stalin could not help but ponder the succession of power. I believe that all the "surprises" of the 19th Party Congress and the subsequent Central Committee plenum were the result. Stalin declined to give the keynote address to the 19th Party Congress, leaving it to Malenkov. He himself gave only a short speech and assigned the report on changes in party rules to Khrushchev, thereby passing over such established members of the Politburo as Molotov, Mikoyan, and L. M. Kaganovich.

Stalin, of course, realized his own significance and understood he could not have a successor anything like himself. Hence he strove to prevent anyone from approximating the level of power he had enjoyed and to prepare instead a collective leadership to come after him. At the 19th Party Congress, almost a hundred more people (members and candidates) were elected to the Central Committee than had been at the 18th Congress; its membership was increased by two-thirds. At the Central Committee plenum on October 16, 1952, Stalin proposed replacing the Politburo and the Orgburo with a Presidium unheard of in size: thirty-six people, as compared to the fourteen who had entered the leadership of the party at the 18th Congress. Only nine of Stalin's old comrades remained on the Presidium, making up barely a quarter of its membership.[12]

This rejuvenation of the party leadership brought to power a new generation of people less burdened by the past and, consequently, freer in their political choices. This action provoked confusion and some be-

wilderment among Stalin's comrades, who sensed a threat to their omnipotence. During Stalin's lifetime, however, everything remained unchanged. The leadership remained in the hands of the Presidium's bureau (essentially the former Politburo). The full membership of the
Presidium never met.

When Stalin died on March 5, 1953, the centripetal force of the personality cult, when the will of the leader was supreme in the highest
echelon of power, was lost. In the new atmosphere, those closest to
Stalin were concerned primarily with maintaining their dominant position in the party and the country. Only hours after Stalin's death (the
formal decision is dated March 6), twenty-two members of the Presidium of the Central Committee found themselves ousted from its ranks.
"Stalin's comrades" (Beria, Bulganin, Voroshilov, Kaganovich, Malenkov, Mikoyan, Molotov, Pervukhin, Saburov, and Khrushchev) restored
themselves as sole members of the party leadership. Malenkov became
the chairman of the USSR Council of Ministers. Beria, Molotov, Bulganin, and Kaganovich were named his first deputies. Mikoyan, M. G.
Pervukhin, and M. Z. Saburov received ministerial appointments. K. E.
Voroshilov was elected chairman of the Presidium of the USSR
Supreme Soviet.[13] Thus all members of the party Presidium, except
Khrushchev, entered the government, a situation that reflected Malenkov's obvious effort to transfer the center of the country's leadership to
the state structures. The Council of Ministers' Presidium (its chairman
and his first deputies) essentially became the institutional equivalent
of the Presidium of the Central Committee.

On March 14, 1953, the Central Committee granted Malenkov's request that he be relieved of his responsibilities as Central Committee
secretary so that he could focus completely on leading the Council of
Ministers.[14] He did, however, continue to chair the Central Committee
Presidium. Leadership of the Central Committee itself was assigned to
Khrushchev, who had stepped down as first secretary of the Moscow
party organization. Formally, Khrushchev was one of several secretaries
of the Central Committee, but, as a member of its Presidium, he naturally occupied the dominant position among them. At the same time,
he was the only Presidium member who was not a member of any state
organ, and he was therefore somewhat distanced from strictly state
power. Although Khrushchev had to reconcile himself to this situation,
it naturally did not suit him. He did not yet have enough forces or sup-

port, however, to fight for a position in the government to complement his party leadership post.

One of the primary, although secret, reasons for cutting down the size of the newly enlarged party Presidium was that the question of Stalin's personality cult and dictatorship was bound to arise. Since the majority of the Presidium members elected after the 19th Congress had not been intimate participants in the Terror, a decisive denunciation of Stalin's cult, with all its unlawfulness, did not present the same threat for them as the one hanging over "Stalin's comrades." The restoration of the former narrow party leadership, bound together by a kind of collective guarantee, offered them the opportunity to define their attitude to the personality cult in their corporate interest.

The Central Committee Presidium gathered on the evening of March 10, the day after Stalin's funeral. Malenkov chaired the meeting. He noted that "we have had major abnormalities, much has gone according to the personality cult," and he declared, "We consider it necessary to end the policy of the personality cult."[15] As an experienced and knowledgeable political figure, Malenkov understood that the Stalinist regime of individual power would face a crisis. Moreover, he wanted to deflect the personality cult, so as not to allow it to invade the inner sanctum of the dictatorship, where the controls over the system lay hidden. For the time being, however, the criticism of the personality cult was phrased in terms of "Leninist principles of party life," "collective leadership," and moral-ethical norms. Stalin's name was not mentioned; in fact, it retained its symbolic significance.

In the period following Stalin's death, Khrushchev at first took an extremely passive position regarding the cult of personality; Beria, who was a formidable obstacle on the path to power, occupied him much more. At the July 1953 plenum of the Central Committee, which ratified Beria's ouster and arrest, Khrushchev said not a word about Stalin's dictatorship; the full force of his speech was directed at Beria and the arbitrariness of the Ministries of Internal Affairs (MVD) and State Security (MGB). Khrushchev concluded his speech with an expression of his confidence in the steadfastness of "our Leninist-Stalinist leadership."[16]

By occupying the posts of first deputy chairman of the Council of Ministers and minister of internal affairs (after combining the MVD and MGB), Beria placed himself and the MVD system beyond the control of state and party organs. That gave him a powerful apparatus, both

overt and covert, for seizing power, a fact that his colleagues took fear-
fully into account. The power-loving, despotic adventurer, Beria, posed
the most obvious threat of a new personal dictatorship. As soon as that
threat appeared, the party and government leadership, with the support
of the military command, took decisive preventive measures in which
Khrushchev personally played no small role. Beria was arrested and, in
accordance with Stalinist traditions, shot.

Another circumstance should also be kept in mind. After Stalin's
death, his malicious transgressions of legality and his tyrannical repressions began openly to be discussed. The question inevitably arose
in society as to who was guilty and responsible—not just who had op-
erated the machinery of repression, but who had directed it. Hence an
ulterior motive for eliminating Beria was to blame him and his "assistants" for all the illegalities. The Beria affair served as a lightning rod
for the public mood. Later, Khrushchev noted in his memoirs, "We created one version. To put it bluntly . . . we invented the idea that Beria
was the primary figure in the abuses committed by Stalin. This was the
result of our shock, of the fact that we could in no way free ourselves
from the idea that Stalin was the leader, Stalin was the father, Stalin was
the friend of the people, Stalin was a genius, and so on—that Stalin was
not a murderer, Stalin was not the monster that he turned out to be . . . .
Strictly speaking, we were held prisoner by the very version we ourselves created in the interests of rehabilitating Stalin."[17]

In sum, three leaders—Beria, Malenkov, and Khrushchev—pursued their own political goals to attain power and presented themselves
in various ways after Stalin was gone. In the end, one was destroyed,
the second was eventually forced from the political arena, and the third
took the historical stage as the victor.

The elimination of Beria, and Khrushchev's role in it, drastically
changed Khrushchev's situation and bolstered his authority. The path
to official leadership of the party was now effectively open to him. Other
close associates of Stalin did not aspire to that position, preferring key
positions in the state structure. They trusted Khrushchev, considering
him "their own" and counting on their seniority to guarantee his sub-
ordination and complete controllability. However, as further events
would show, they grossly miscalculated. Khrushchev outplayed them
on all fronts.

I will not attempt to judge when Khrushchev became possessed by the idea of becoming the sole leader, but after the elimination of Beria he proceeded toward this goal firmly and unwaveringly. Stalin's laurels did not entice him; he sincerely and resolutely denounced the repressive regime of the personality cult. His ideal was a truly popular leader for whom there would be no greater goal than the popular good. Khrushchev possessed all the abilities necessary to become such a leader, and he reached his goal. Unfortunately, however, he overstepped it and was inevitably ensnared by a new personality cult that helped destroy his political career.

Khrushchev had great experience in party leadership roles; he possessed highly developed political intuition and outstanding organizational abilities. He was distinguished by his magnetic personal qualities: democratism, accessibility, an ability to laugh and joke, to speak simply and lucidly, and to inspire with his words. All of this helped him to advance to the highest level. In September 1953, a Central Committee plenum established the post of party first secretary and, on Malenkov's recommendation, elected Khrushchev.

Soviet economic and social policy needed to be reoriented toward improving people's living conditions. Foreign policy required correction as well. Malenkov took a series of promising steps in this direction,[18] but Khrushchev gradually gained the initiative. Under his effective leadership, the September plenum conducted a serious and constructive discussion of urgent questions of party politics for the first time in many years. The plenum dramatically increased Khrushchev's authority; it provided him with broad support in the regions, where local party leaders were being replaced at the direction of the Central Committee.

Having strengthened his position, Khrushchev strove actively to counteract Malenkov's reduction of the administrative-command functions of party organs; he sought to assert the leading role of the party fully. All the most important resolutions on the economy began to come jointly from the Central Committee and the Council of Ministers. (Earlier, joint resolutions were rarely adopted, and the titles were in the reverse order: Council of Ministers, then Central Committee.)

After Khrushchev's election as first secretary, Malenkov continued to chair meetings of the Presidium. But such a situation could not last long, and Khrushchev decided to put an end to the duumvirate. In August and September 1954, during his vacation in the Crimea, he met with Mikoyan, Bulganin, the Ukrainian party leader A. I. Kirichenko, the heads of the Moscow, Leningrad, and Crimean party organizations (E. A. Furtseva, F. R. Kozlov, and D. Polianskii), and certain other leading figures, and he received their full support.[19] In November a resolution of the Central Committee Secretariat transferred functions of the office of the Presidium, hitherto under the direction of Malenkov, to the General Department of the Central Committee. Thus the entire apparatus of the Central Committee was now at Khrushchev's disposal.

At the January 1955 Central Committee plenum, Malenkov was harshly criticized for "mistakes" and "insufficiencies" in his leadership of the economy. Nor was his participation in the "Leningrad affair" forgotten.[20] At a February 1955 session of the Council of Ministers, Malenkov was released (officially at his request) from the duties of chairman and was named minister of hydroelectric stations (he remained on the Presidium and became deputy chairman of the Council of Ministers). Bulganin replaced him as prime minister, having been nominated by Khrushchev; they had worked together during the 1930s, when Bulganin headed the Moscow City Soviet. Thus was Khrushchev's second main opponent defeated.

At the same time, new people flooded into the party leadership. A. I. Kirichenko and M. A. Suslov became members of the Presidium, while A. B. Aristov, N. I. Beliaev, and D. T. Shepilov became secretaries of the Central Committee.[21] These reinforcements noticeably strengthened Khrushchev's position and gave him the opportunity to act more resolutely to realize the program he had mapped out in domestic and foreign policy. The center of gravity of the country's leadership moved steadily toward the party Central Committee.

With past experience in mind, Khrushchev gradually established direct Central Committee supervision over the so-called power ministries (defense, internal affairs, and state security), juridical organs, and the office of the public prosecutor; all these had corresponding sections in the Central Committee apparatus. These sections were officially in charge of personnel issues, but their functions were in fact considerably broader. Khrushchev considered it necessary to reorganize once again the Ministry of Internal Affairs, and in March 1954 the Committee for State Security (KGB) was again created under the auspices of the USSR Council of Ministers. I. A. Serov, whom Khrushchev knew well from their work together in Ukraine, became its chairman.

After Stalin's death, Khrushchev immediately adopted a sharply negative position on political repression. In July and August 1953, he conducted the first party rehabilitations through the Committee for Party Control under the Central Committee. At the end of 1954, Khrushchev personally assigned General Prosecutor R. A. Rudenko, Minister of Internal Affairs S. N. Kruglov, and Minister of Justice K. P. Gorshenin the task of preparing a report dealing with those who had been politically repressed. This action was in response to the many signals received by the Central Committee and other party organs about illegal convictions for counterrevolutionary crimes. The report was oriented toward rehabilitation; it was explicitly composed "in accordance with your [Khrushchev's] instruction as to the need to review the cases of individuals who were convicted of counterrevolutionary crimes and who are now being held in camps and prisons." According to the report, 3,777,380 people had been convicted since 1921 of "counter-revolutionary crimes," including 624,980 who were sentenced to the highest level of punishment," that is, death.[22]

It was Khrushchev who initiated this review of the whole practice of Stalinist political repression, the liberation of the unjustly convicted from prisons and camps, and their subsequent rehabilitation. Most of all, thanks to Khrushchev, hundreds of thousands of victims gained their freedom; hundreds of thousands of those deprived of life had their names cleared and were no longer known as "enemies of the people." Between 1954 and 1955, more than 350,000 political convicts were freed from the camps and prisons.[23]

The secretly adopted but clearly expressed decision of the leadership to end the personality cult without looking into its origins was thus carried out with a certain consistency. The old Stalinist circle that remained in power was not prepared to denounce Stalin. Khrushchev himself was not yet prepared to do so either. The myth about the great leader of the peoples, the great continuer of Lenin's work, remained for the time being inviolable. In the style of the cult, the press noted the first anniversary of Stalin's death and his seventy-fifth birthday (December 21, 1954).[24] Study of Stalin's "Economic Problems of Socialism in the USSR" continued in schools and universities. Stalinism as a totalitarian system was only beginning to be undermined. The top party leadership, commanding a vast bureaucratic apparatus, remained in power.

Such a situation was fraught with serious political complications; it eventually had to be resolved. Allusions to the arbitrariness of security organs were supposed to serve as a lightning rod, but the view inevitably spread that the responsibility for repressions and for the flouting of legality was to be found at much higher levels of politics and power. To remain silent and not react to the situation, was no longer possible; it could begin to threaten the leadership of the party and the country. Khrushchev understood this earlier and better than the others. If he had not raised these questions, one of his rivals eventually would have.[25] Khrushchev took this difficult mission upon himself both by virtue of his position and because of his personal beliefs. Despite his convictions, it took no little courage to question the sanctity of the name under whose banner the country had marched for over three decades.

On Khrushchev's initiative, a special commission under the chairmanship of Central Committee secretary P. N. Pospelov was formed in December 1955 to study documents concerning the massive political repression of the 1930s. The summary of its report, delivered on February 9, 1956, the eve of the 20th Party Congress, stated, "In our country, the years 1935–40 were years of mass arrests of Soviet citizens. In all, during those years 1,920,635 individuals were arrested and charged with anti-Soviet activity, of whom 688,503 were shot."[26]

Khrushchev also assigned Pospelov to prepare a speech for possible presentation at the 20th Party Congress, one that would address only prewar repression, primarily that of the majority of delegates to the 17th Party Congress. Pospelov prepared a text, which ended with 1939.[27] This is most likely the text that was considered by the Presidium and at a Central Committee plenum on February 13, when it was decided that the congress should be closed for Khrushchev's speech.[28] Khrushchev apparently understood that otherwise he would be identified with others of "Stalin's comrades," whose responsibility for mass repression must sooner or later arise.

But Khrushchev decided to go even further. He significantly expanded the speech, bringing it up to the death of Stalin. The text of the speech was hurriedly written during the course of the congress itself (Khrushchev plucked D. T. Shepilov right out of its sessions for this work, and others were called in as well).[29] Depicting the consequences of the personality cult broadly, showing the negative sides of Stalin during and after the war, and stripping the "leader of peoples" of his laurels, Khrushchev seemed to extricate himself from the common guilt of Stalin's comrades for arbitrariness and illegality. The speech provided concrete facts about the repressions and Stalin's responsibility for them, but not about the mass political terror of which Khrushchev himself was a part. It is quite characteristic that, in sharing the information about the scale of the arrests and shootings, Khrushchev did not include any precise figures in his speech (except for the repression of the delegates to the 17th Party Congress). They became available only more than thirty years later, in the time of glasnost.[30]

Khrushchev's speech was not published. In the hope of controlling its distribution and avoiding emotional outbursts and confrontations, the party distributed it secretly, primarily by having it read to party members at party meetings. A fuller break with the Stalinist past was an alternative, and the publication of the speech could have served as an effective impetus for this. An open, publicized denunciation of Stalin and of the totalitarian regime he created might well have encouraged a much more profound restructuring of public consciousness, provoked increased critical analysis of the path being followed, and made irreversible the process of democratization of society and its many-sided renewal. The entire course of events could have been different. Instead, this possibility was foreclosed. Stalin's successors were not capable of fundamental political changes. For them, personal power remained all important, and the Stalinist model of socialism remained unshakable.

After the 20th Party Congress, contradictions at the highest level of the leadership intensified. Khrushchev and his new circle gained strength. Molotov, Kaganovich, and Malenkov, on the other hand, did not want to come to terms with the loss of their former power and grandeur. They also understood that Khrushchev's denunciation of Stalin's cult would almost certainly lead to their being held responsible for its consequences. Further tension was provoked by Khrushchev's growing power, by his obvious independence and occasional unpredictability, and by his tendency to ignore other's opinions and his unwillingness to accept criticism. Khrushchev sought to untie his hands by removing the Stalinist old guard from power once and for all. He began his offensive even before the 20th Congress, at the time when Malenkov was removed from his post as chairman of the Council of Ministers. After the congress, in 1956, Molotov lost his position as minister of foreign affairs and Kaganovich was removed as chairman of the State Committee on Labor and Salaries; both were appointed to significantly less important posts.

A situation thus arose that precluded any further peaceful coexistence. Knowing that time was not on their side, the opposition decided on a preemptive strike. In a conversation with M. Z. Saburov, who had been dropped as chairman of Gosplan, Malenkov said, "We must act. If we don't remove them, they'll remove us."[31]

The union of Malenkov, Molotov, and Kaganovich was formed under the pressure of circumstances, by the threat of their banishment from the political arena. To realize their self-seeking plans, they assigned a major role to Bulganin, trying to pit the chairman of the Council of Ministers against the party first secretary. Although Bulganin was mainly beholden to Khrushchev for his lofty post, he undoubtedly sensed the instability of his situation and understood that he would soon have to step down. Bulganin had a propensity for pro-Stalinist moods, and he was no stranger to the love of power. He essentially became the center of the oppositional group; its meetings took place in his office, where tactical questions were discussed.

Voroshilov, who occupied the post of chairman of the USSR Supreme Soviet's Presidium but played virtually no political role, did not have any particular score to settle with Khrushchev. His inner devotion to Stalinism was beyond doubt, however, and his responsibility for repressions, most of all within the military, was equal to that of Stalin's other comrades. So it did not take long to persuade him to oppose Khrushchev. As for Pervukhin and Saburov, they were too connected with the Stalinist period for their own good. Since Khrushchev was already orienting himself toward the new cadres he had promoted, Pervukhin and Saburov hoped to preserve their positions in a bloc with their old comrades.

It is possible that Khrushchev knew about the plot to remove him as party leader. In February 1957 information reached the Central Committee from the Iaroslav, Saratov, and other provincial party committees about rumors that Khrushchev would be demoted to minister of agriculture, Malenkov would be promoted to Central Committee secretary, and other changes in the leadership of the party and state would be made.[32] This information must have reached Khrushchev. Nor could the KGB and its chief, Ivan Serov, have missed it. Perhaps they deliberately did not take preventive measures, which would have been fraught with complications. While keeping an eye on things, they may have simply allowed events to develop in their own way.

The day chosen for the group's action was June 18, when Khrushchev and other party and government leaders were supposed to travel to Leningrad for that city's 250th anniversary celebration. At an urgent meeting of the Council of Ministers' Presidium, which was transformed into a session of the Central Committee Presidium upon Khrushchev's arrival, Bulganin was elected chairman (supported by Molotov, Kaganovich, Bulganin, Voroshilov, and Pervukhin), even though Khrushchev had chaired the party Presidium for several years.

The opposition, which included the head of government (Bulganin) and the titular head of state (Voroshilov), had a majority in the party Presidium. Ultimately, their goal was to recover the key party posts of which they had been deprived. As mere members of the party Presidium, Malenkov, Molotov, and Kaganovich did not have direct access to the party apparat and thus lacked decisive leverage over political life. Hence the opposition's plan: first to remove Khrushchev as first secretary, or to eliminate the post altogether "in the interests of fuller collegiality" (thus returning to the situation that had existed between March and August 1953); next to gain representation themselves in the Central Committee Secretariat; and then to appoint party and government officials beholden to them.

The Presidium sessions were stormy and full of mutual accusations. Malenkov, Kaganovich, and Molotov expressed disagreement with current economic and foreign policy and also aired personal grievances against Khrushchev. Other participants in the session also directed critical remarks at Khrushchev, accusing him of developing his own personality cult and monopolizing the work of the Presidium and the Secretariat. Shepilov, in particular, aggressively addressed these issues, for which he was forever after charged with siding with the opposition.

Khrushchev chose the only plausible tactic: not allowing the Presidium to adopt any decisions and turning all questions over to the Central Committee plenum.[33] At Presidium meetings he could not level the most serious charges against Malenkov, Molotov, or Kaganovich—he could not accuse them directly of participation in mass repressions—because their counteraccusations against him would have been just as strong. The plenum, however, was another story. The overwhelming majority of its members (the membership had been renewed by almost two-thirds since the 19th Congress) had not been directly involved in the repressions and condemned them. Hence they could boldly raise the question of the personal guilt of Malenkov, Molotov, Kaganovich, and Voroshilov.

The special plenum convened on June 22, 1957, at two o'clock in the afternoon. (Even before the Presidium officially called the meeting, more than two-thirds of the Central Committee members were already in Moscow.) Since it was clear from the start that the removal of Khrushchev was a dead issue, the plenum could have adjourned the same day. Yet it continued for seven days. Its task was the full political compromising of Malenkov, Molotov and Kaganovich in order to label them the "anti-party group" and thus banish them from the political arena. The pretext—the opposition of the group to the results of the 20th Congress—was exceedingly shaky, and nothing intelligible was said about it throughout the plenum. G. K. Zhukov's speech, which immediately followed Suslov's account of what had occurred in the Presidium, lent the necessary tone to the plenum. He raised the question of Stalin's repressions and the direct participation in them of Malenkov, Molotov, and Kaganovich. This theme dominated the plenum, and the troika could do nothing to defend itself. The horrific numbers of arrests and shootings, conducted with the direct sanction of Stalin and his closest comrades, were mentioned for the first time at the plenum. Aristov revealed that 353,074 people had been shot in 1937 alone.[34]

The plenum dropped the issue of Khrushchev's alleged misbehavior as not worthy of serious consideration. Any such criticism was taken to be an attack on the political course set by the 20th Party Congress. Malenkov, Molotov, and Kaganovich quickly understood that they had lost. Although counteraccusations against Khrushchev would have had plenty of foundation, they would only have worsened their own position, which could easily have been turned into a criminal matter. All the participants in the plot, and there was undoubtedly a plot, quickly resigned their positions, repented of their mistakes, and, with the exception of Molotov, voted for the decisions of the plenum.

Khrushchev concluded the plenum by accusing his opponents of an attempt to split the party leadership. He depicted Beria, Malenkov, Molotov, and Kaganovich as responsible, together with Stalin, for the repressions. Specifically, Khrushchev said, "Kaganovich and Molotov, along with Beria and Malenkov, tried to realize their heinous intentions through Stalin. Stalin held off, backed away, but given Stalin's distance from everything, from the party and the people, conditions arose in which Stalin himself eventually set off down the road toward repression. And now they want to pin it all on Stalin."[35]

The plenum condemned the "factional activity" of Malenkov, Kaganovich, and Molotov, and of Shepilov, who "sided" with them; it dismissed the four from all posts and from the Central Committee. (By 1962 they were all excluded from the party.) Despite repenting, other participants in the opposition were not forgiven either. One after the other, Saburov, Bulganin, Voroshilov, and Pervukhin left the Presidium. Of the "Stalinist" leadership, Khrushchev kept only Mikoyan.

The intraparty struggle of June 1957 attests to the fact that the party leadership had assimilated Stalin's methods of resolving political problems. Even so, those methods were not carried to the extreme of physical reprisal. The plenum was right to support Khrushchev, but it essentially precluded criticism of him, thereby neglecting the danger of one-person rule. The opportunity was lost to inhibit the development of Khrushchev's voluntarism and arrogance and to define collectively a realistic and considered political course. On the contrary, all his actions received a priori, unconditional approval; he was given full freedom of action—which, as we know, he later failed to use in the best possible way.

Soon Khrushchev achieved his lifelong goal. In March 1958 the USSR Supreme Soviet named him chairman of the Council of Ministers. No one had yet combined the following four jobs in one person: first secretary of the Central Committee, chairman of the Central Committee's Bureau for the RSFSR (formed in 1956), chairman of the Council of Ministers, and member of the Presidium of the USSR Supreme Soviet.

Having assumed supreme leadership, Khrushchev had to define the state's long-range goals and its path toward the future. "To speak figuratively," Khrushchev stated at the 20th Congress, "we have ascended so high a mountain that we can plainly see broad horizons on the way to our final goal—a communist society." These horizons had to be shown to the entire party and and the citizenry in order to mobilize their constructive forces with an inspirational vision. The 20th Party Congress resolved that a new party program—a plan for Communist construction—should be prepared.

As chairman of the Program Commission, Khrushchev followed the preparation of materials carefully from the very beginning. He expressed the desire that the program be a "clear, precise, inspirational document—a poem, but also timely, vital, with a broad perspective."[36]

On June 19, 1961, a draft program was considered at a Central Committee plenum. In his speech, Khrushchev summarized its various provisions in the following terms: "As a result of the implementation of this general outline, an economy of communism will for the most part be created. At the base of this economy, social relations will be transformed. This will mean that in the course of twenty years, Communism will for the most part be built. . . . The Soviet Union will ascend to such a height that, in comparison, the principal capitalist countries will remain far below."[37] On October 31, 1961, the 22nd Party Congress unanimously adopted the new party program.

Alongside his canonical conception of communism, which remained unshakable, Khrushchev also possessed a purely pragmatic, everyday understanding of Communist society, in which the good of human beings must stand at the forefront. He perceived communism not so much as a theoretical abstraction as a practical realization of human potential. "What is the main thing in Communist society?" Khrushchev asked. "Man. And all physical and mental efforts, all material means must therefore be directed toward better satisfaction of human needs and those of Communist society as a whole. This must be said."[38] And it was said.

A sincere, burning desire to achieve a better life for the Soviet people was the fertile soil for Khrushchev's Communist illusions. He passionately wanted to lead the country to the "shining heights of communism." His Communist dream simply did not pan out; it turned out to be a utopia, as has happened before in history. Khrushchev is not to blame for this; he was no more than a link in the chain of believers in the Communist idea, which in reality turned out to be far from communism. The new party program included the classic transition from socialism to communism, even though the socialism from which one could make that transition was lacking.

The 22nd Party Congress and the new party program became the apogee of Khrushchev's political leadership. The program seemed to push Stalinist socialism into the past. The stage of "Khrushchevite communism" took its place. The need for Stalin, the theoretician and builder of socialism, fell away. His body could now be removed from the mausoleum; doing so would glorify Khrushchev and his own personality cult. The objective processes of social development could not be denied, however, and Khrushchev's triumph, together with his Communist euphoria, turned out to be very short-lived.

The echo of the ovation honoring the new party program had barely died away when confidence in its successful completion began to subside. Economics demanded its due. The effectiveness of production, return on investment, and labor productivity began to decline. For the first time in its history, the country was forced to buy foreign grain. A drop in the rate of economic growth meant, ironically, that although incomes were rising, there were not enough consumer goods to buy with the money. Retail prices rose, food shortages appeared, and social tension grew.

The events in Novocherkassk, Russia, in June 1962 were the first sign of serious trouble.[39] An increase in the prices of meat and dairy products, along with decreases in labor wages, sparked a spontaneous protest of workers making economic demands that turned into a mass demonstration. The demonstration was harshly suppressed with the help of the armed forces; there were many casualties.

Such demonstrations occurred in other cities as well. The reasons for them went beyond the increase in prices (which in fact was not that significant): faith in the ability of the party, the state, and ultimately Khrushchev himself to improve the well-being of the people had been undermined. The disillusionment and dissatisfaction of the masses were exacerbated by the sharp contrast between the recent promise of imminent paradise and the reality of existence.[40]

Convinced of the omnipotence of administrative and organizational measures, Khrushchev made convulsive attempts to rebuild and reorganize, all on his own initiative, without gathering advice, without serious forethought. Organs of economic administration and planning, and of leadership in industry, science, and technology, were endlessly refashioned. The Seven Year Plan having faltered, five-year planning had been revived. Khrushchev soon demanded a return to seven-year planning, however, because party program goals were not being realized.

New administrative organs were created in the countryside: kolkhoz-sovkhoz (or sovkhoz-kolkhoz) administrations. In his April 13, 1964, memorandum on the intensification of agriculture, Khrushchev remarked that modern collective and state farms were huge productive enterprises, which made it possible to replace the "anarchy" of kolkhoz production with more effective administration of agriculture. "Until now," the memorandum continues, "we could not distance ourselves from the legacy of the consumer, small-peasant economy. Now there

are all sorts of opportunities to move the peasants to an industrial production basis, which will free them from the need to keep a cow, chick-
ens, and so on."[41]

Khrushchev advocated the eventual "de-peasantization" of the village, essentially the transformation of collective farmers into agricultural workers. Developing the idea of specialization, his memorandum
of July 18, 1964, proposed transferring agricultural management directly to the provinces, where new specialized organs would answer directly to union republic administrations for production of each agricultural product.[42] That fall, Khrushchev set out on a extensive trip
around the country. Everywhere he presented the new reorganization
as a done deal, even though a plenum on the question was not scheduled until November 17.

At the end of the summer of 1962, "with the goal of concretizing
economic management," Khrushchev proposed dividing party and
other social organizations along industrial and agricultural lines. Many
(admittedly rather timid) objections were sent to the Central Committee. As P. E. Shelest, the Ukrainian first secretary, later said, "Many Central Committee members and republic and local party workers expressed doubt about the wisdom of the proposed reorganization."[43] I
happened to attend the November 1962 plenum where this question
was decided. As a "guest" (journalist), I naturally spent most of my time
in the corridors, the smoking room, and the cafeteria, where a free exchange of opinions took place. I did not hear one good word about this
new reorganization, only bewilderment and outright rejection. When
the vote came, however, it was "adopted unanimously," with "stormy
applause," as is expected in a system of party-command democracy.

Some say that by dividing the party into industrial and agricultural
wings, Khrushchev took a step toward a multiparty, democratic society.
I consider this mistaken. Khrushchev was a consistent (I would say genetic) adherent of a single-party system, of the "leading role of the
CPSU." His main goal in the 1962 reform was to strengthen the management of industry and agriculture. The actual effect was to splinter
the party, further concentrating power in its central organs and thus
bolstering not democracy but autocracy. Khrushchev became even
more independent—not only of the party but of its Presidium and of
the USSR Council of Ministers. What had been becoming an authoritarian regime of corporate leadership began to be displaced by a dictatorial regime of personal power.

A relatively late development in the sequence of events that led to the finale was the Central Committee plenum held on July 11, 1964, the agenda of which contained only organizational questions.[44] Khrushchev unexpectedly delivered a long, impromptu speech containing pointed attacks against local party organs and kolkhoz-sovkhoz administrations, which he blamed for the failures in agriculture. Venting his anger at the All-Union Academy of Agricultural Sciences, Khrushchev demanded that it be expelled from Moscow and instead be "planted in the earth"; he even questioned whether the USSR Academy of Sciences ought to exist. His entire speech was a peremptory barking out of categorical judgments and homilies. Both the content and the tone of the speech provoked confusion from the plenum participants, as well as an alarmed expectation of new and unforeseen changes. An extremely tense situation was created.

I have been trying to emphasize the complex and contradictory political and economic situation as it had evolved toward the fall of 1964. The Soviet authoritarian system was in a crisis. But any retreat from that system, any attempt to go beyond organizational restructuring to embrace free, competitive market relations, was foreign to Khrushchev. Even when he was retired, Khrushchev continued to believe that central planning was essential for a socialist society. Resort to market mechanisms meant capitalism, plain and simple.

Tension grew in Khrushchev's relations with his Kremlin colleagues. Khrushchev ignored collegiality; he did not believe he had any comrades whose opinions were worthy of consideration. Instead, he constantly dispatched personal memoranda, which gradually became directives that were not to be questioned. His activities took on a more and more egocentric character; his self-glorification reached hypertrophic proportions. General fatigue undoubtedly played a role as well. The very idea of further rounds of organizational innovations, whatever their content, provoked resistance.

In the end, the Presidium decided to prevent the next ill-considered reorganization. If the November 1964 Central Committee plenum on agriculture had taken place in the Kremlin with Khrushchev still in office, all his proposals would probably have been adopted. For the Presidium was not prepared to offer concrete alternatives, nor did its members have the civic courage to battle the party and government leader, with all his authority and power, at a regular Central Committee meeting. Instead, keeping in mind the lessons of the failed coup attempt in

June 1957, they decided to dismiss Khrushchev from all his posts and only then to convene the Central Committee.

Carrying out this plan demanded thorough preparation, which naturally proceeded behind Khrushchev's back. It was not entirely conspiratorial, however. A rather broad circle of the leading party and government figures was in the know. G. I. Voronov, then chairman of the RSFSR Council of Ministers, states that the removal of Khrushchev was "in preparation for about a year."[45] V. N. Novikov, a member of the USSR Council of Ministers, writes that in September 1964 D. F. Ustinov (first deputy chairman of the USSR Council of Ministers) assigned him the task of preparing criticism of Khrushchev for the coming plenum of the Central Committee.[46] Central Committee secretary A. N. Shelepin, KGB chairman V. E. Semichastnyi, and Moscow first secretary N. G. Egorychev explained in conversations with the author that Khrushchev's dismissal was not a sudden action and related how it was prepared.[47]

Nor were these preparations a secret from Khrushchev. He did not undertake any countermeasures, however, although he had both the time and the opportunity to do so. He still hoped to avoid a showdown, but he also understood that any attempt to avert one would probably be unsuccessful.

Khrushchev was summoned back from his vacation; on October 13, he flew to Moscow along with Mikoyan. From the airport they went straight to the Kremlin for a Presidium session, at which, as always, Khrushchev took the chairman's spot. All full and candidate members of the Presidium, as well as all secretaries of the Central Committee, spoke. Khrushchev's political leadership was subjected to sharp and far-reaching criticism. Khrushchev responded very briefly to some critical comments, agreeing with some and not with others. In his speech he offered, in my view, a highly candid appraisal of the situation: "I am now suffering, but at the same time I am glad, since a time has arrived in which Presidium members have begun to control the activity of the first secretary and to speak their mind. . . . Today's session . . . is a victory for the party. I have long thought that it is time for me to step down. But life is a tenacious thing. I myself see that I am not handling things well, that I don't even meet with any of you. I have lost contact with you. You have resoundingly criticized me for that, and I myself have suffered because of it."[48]

On October 14, 1964, a special Central Committee plcnum was held.[49] L. I. Brezhnev reported that the Presidium had discussed "fundamental questions of our domestic and foreign policy, on the practice of our leadership, on the carrying out of party policies, on the incorrect and defective style and methods of leadership . . . of Comrade Khrushchev." Suslov added that Khrushchev had done a great deal for the good of the party and the country, especially in the first years of his tenure.

Given the Presidium's substantive discussion and the broad support of its proposals in the Central Committee, it was decided not to open debate. The plenum granted Khrushchev's request to be released from his duties as first secretary and member of the Presidium, as well as chairman of the USSR Council of Ministers. The plenum elected Brezhnev first secretary. On October 15 the Presidium of the USSR Supreme Soviet appointed A. N. Kosygin chairman of the USSR Council of Ministers.

The paradox or, conversely, the logic of the times is that Khrushchev attained supreme power precisely when that power lost its support both from below (as daily life became worse and worse, people lost their Communist illusions and, with them, faith in Khrushchev) and from above (when Khrushchev stopped reckoning with the nomenklatura elite and started taking everything upon himself). Khrushchev exhausted himself struggling against these two forces. That which had to happen, happened: "The Moor has done his duty, the Moor may go." The move against him was prepared at an enlarged session of the Presidium in which Khrushchev himself took part and where all members of the party and state leadership, more than twenty people, spoke. The fact that his departure was not discussed openly and widely in advance does not in itself indicate a "plot," for this was standard procedure. Changing the leader was the prerogative of the Central Committee and the Presidium of the Supreme Soviet. Recall that Malenkov and Bulganin were dismissed as chairmen of the Council of Ministers by just such a maneuver. Khrushchev himself never complained about the procedure, although the fact of his dismissal wounded him deeply.

Despite all his shortcomings, the name of Nikita Sergeevich Khrushchev is forever connected with the historic feat of denouncing Stalin's personality cult, with the beginning of the liquidation of the consequences of Stalin's repressive regime, with the liberation of hundreds of thousands of innocent people from prisons and camps and the restoration of their rights as citizens and their good names, and with a sincere concern for the good of the people.

But the Thaw of the 1950s did not become a real spring. Neither the country nor Khrushchev himself, for all his good intentions, was ready for such a decisive step. He himself admitted as much:

> We did not feel entirely positive about the Thaw. On one hand, we did actually allow a certain leniency; we weakened control, and the people began to express themselves more freely both in conversations and in the press. . . . People in the leadership, including me, promoted this Thaw; we undertook it consciously, and we were consciously a bit afraid of that Thaw. Because from that Thaw there might have emerged a flood, which would have overcome us and with which it would have been hard to cope. But that is possible in any political affair. We therefore restrained the Thaw to some extent. . . . We feared that the leadership might not be able to manage or direct the creative powers of the people into a Soviet channel, so that the fruits of those creative forces would contribute to the strengthening of socialism.[50]

Khrushchev dreamed of creating a society of genuine freedom, social equality, national brotherhood, and common welfare, where labor would be a means not just for the achievement of wealth but for the realization of creative individual potential. This task turned out to be beyond his strength, and in fact the path itself was mistaken. But the creation of such a society (no matter what it is called) inevitably remains in people's thoughts. To the question of how to build such a society and what paths lead there, history will eventually find an answer. And on the pages of that history, the name of Nikita Sergeevich Khrushchev will always have a place.

3

The Rivalry with Malenkov

ELENA ZUBKOVA

Traditionally, Soviet history of the 1950s and 1960s has been closely connected with the activity of Nikita Khrushchev, and it is perfectly natural that he should appear as a central figure in all studies of the period. At the same time, representations of Khrushchev as the sole leader of the reformist wing in the party are one-sided. Khrushchev's personal contribution to developing the reformist path may be gauged only on the basis of a comparative analysis of the views and positions of other politicians, and a determination of the influence each of them had on the course of political decision-making. Another circumstance mandates a deeper investigation into the question at hand: many of the most constructive decisions, from discrediting Stalin to drawing up new approaches to agrarian policy, occurred when Khrushchev had not yet achieved predominance, at a time when he was still forced to share power with Stalin's other former comrades-in-arms or to compromise with the opposition within the Presidium of the Central Committee.

Recent historical works have discussed two possible alternatives to Khrushchev: G. M. Malenkov and L. P. Beria. The attempt to present the history of the reforms in a much wider context indisputably deserves attention. But if such a preoccupation with alternatives leads only to the proclamation of the next Messiah, that would have little in common with historical analysis. If one is to approach the problem of leadership during the Thaw in truly analytical fashion, the aim should be to answer a broader question: to what extent did the struggle for the leadership and the distribution of forces in the highest echelon of power determine the content and development of concrete policy?

The resolution of the crisis of governance caused by the death of Stalin, which ended in the establishment of Khrushchev as the sole leader, went through four stages: (1) March–June 1953, when leading positions were occupied by Beria and Malenkov; (2) June 1953–January 1955, the period of Malenkov's formal leadership; (3) February 1955–June 1957, when Khrushchev became the key figure in the "collective leadership"; and (4) June 1957–October 1964, characterized by Khrushchev's personal leadership and the formation of opposition within the apparat.

It is possible to talk about Khrushchev's policies in pure form only from the second half of 1957, when he began to act as an individual leader. That period allows us to see more precisely both the personal potential and the limits of Khrushchev as a reformer. Before 1957, and particularly during the first two years after Stalin's death, one must be extremely cautious in gauging how decisive Khrushchev's role was in influencing policy decisions.

Stalin's death opened the road to reform. Elements of society, and even of the leadership itself, felt the need for reform directly after the end of World War II, but reform probably was not possible during the Stalin's lifetime. By the time Stalin died in March 1953, the internal economic and political situation, as well as the development of the Cold War in the international arena, created a series of pivotal problems which any leaders would have to try to solve one way or another.

The first set of problems involved the machinery of repression. By the end of the 1940s, the security organs—the Ministry of Internal Affairs (MVD) and the Ministry of State Security (MGB)—had become a special system of totalitarian control, encompassing practically all spheres of social life and all levels of society, from the bottom to the highest echelon of the leadership. After Stalin's death, the law of self-preservation required that his successors introduce certain modifications into this system so as to avoid becoming prey to another round of purges. Another problem, whose solution also required a reform of the security organs, was posed by the gulag system; its preservation in unchanged form not only did not meet the needs of economic efficiency but also threatened political stability. Stalin's death stirred the gulag up: MVD memorandums reported "mass insubordination," "rebellions," and "uprisings" in the camps and colonies. The most important uprisings were at Special Camp No. 2 (Norilsk) in the summer of 1953, Special Camp No. 6 (Vorkuta) in May and June of 1954, and Special Camp No. 4 (Karaganda province), the "Kengirsk uprising" of May 1954.[1]

An alteration of repressive practices could not be limited simply to a change of regime in the camps and colonies, or to a partial reshuffling of personnel in the security organs. Ultimately, the possibility of liberalizing the political regime as a whole had to be considered, although the question of how far this liberalization should go remained open.

No less important were problems in agrarian policy that required an immediate solution. After 1945, not only did villages not achieve pre-war levels of production, but many were on the verge of complete ruin. Twice during the postwar period, in 1948 and in 1952, the agricultural tax was increased. The process of amalgamating collective farms at a forced pace created many problems for villagers. The postwar wave of repressions also was a major blow to the collective farms. As a result, by the beginning of the 1950s, despite the use of internal passports to limit migration into the cities, flight from the villages had become a frequent occurrence. Between 1948 and 1953, the number of able-bodied collective farmers (not taking into account the western provinces) had dropped by 3.3 million.[2] The situation in the villages was so catastrophic that a draft plan for raising the agricultural tax in 1952 to realize forty billion rubles was not adopted because it was clearly absurd. Even after Stalin's death, the basic principles of agrarian policy remained unchanged and were followed even by leaders who initiated agrarian reforms.

The state of affairs in the western republics of Belorussia and Ukraine, as well as in Latvia, Lithuania, and Estonia, created serious problems for the Moscow leadership. The policy of Sovietization there was still meeting with resistance, although opposition was not as active as it had been immediately after the war. Finally, there was a set of foreign policy questions that had to be decided by the new leaders, whoever they turned out to be, for neither Moscow's dictatorial control over Eastern Europe nor its open confrontation with the West was increasing the prestige of the Soviet regime.

For these reasons, the directions of possible post-Stalinist change were in a way already determined when Stalin died. In this case, the interest of the ruling stratum coincided with the interest of the people at large. As a result, the realization of reforms promised to produce not only practical gains but also good propaganda, which would increase the prestige of the new government both at home and abroad. However—and this is extremely important—only the general direction of policy was established. The main questions—in what ways and how consistently the new political course would be carried out, and how its concrete contents and pace of realization would be determined—depended on the distribution of forces in the leadership and on the identity of the leader (or group of leaders). In a situation when reforms are implemented from the top, the personal factor is bound to play a key role.

The lengthy duration of the governance crisis in 1953, and the prolonged struggle for leadership among Stalin's former comrades-in-arms, resulted from the absence of a clear successor who possessed real power. It was no accident that the first redistribution of roles in the top leadership in March 1953 did not decide the question. Power was divided among Beria, Malenkov, and to some degree Khrushchev, who headed the three key institutions in the Soviet hierarchy of power: the organs of the MVD and MGB (Beria), the Council of Ministers (Malenkov), and the party Central Committee (Khrushchev). Khrushchev had an obviously subordinate role, and until Beria's arrest the ruling duumvirate consisted of Beria and Malenkov. It was they who proposed the new party and government leadership line-up in March 1953, as well a general reorganization of administrative structures. The other members of the Presidium had no choice but to accept their proposals.[3]

At the time of Stalin's death, power was concentrated in the hands of three generations of party officials. Following the purges of the 1920s and 1930s, the "elders," people with prerevolutionary party service behind them, ceased to play a significant role in the party and economic bureaucracy. The essential positions in the government were occupied by representatives of the middle generation, those who entered the Communist Party immediately after the Revolution or in the 1920s, and the so-called young generation, which moved up during the war and immediately afterward. In 1953, power at the top mostly belonged to the middle generation, which was noticeably pushing aside elders like Molotov, Kaganovich, Mikoyan, Voroshilov, and others.

Khrushchev and Malenkov belonged to this middle generation, whose genealogy is connected with the Revolution and the Civil War. Almost all representatives of this generation owed their ascent to the personnel purges of the 1920s and 1930s. They formed the backbone of the Stalinist guard, and the elite of the new structure of party nomenklatura. Their common origin and path of professional advancement not only shaped their special status but also led to common ways of thinking and acting. Whereas elder, prerevolutionary Bolsheviks had begun their activities during a period of party pluralism, the middle generation entered the Bolshevik party when it had already established a monopoly on power. Non-Bolshevik political groups were liquidated, and later various groups within the Bolshevik party were also destroyed. For those who remained in its ranks, the principles of absolute party rule and hostility to any kind of opposition had become axiomatic. The middle generation of party leaders adopted this model of organizing power because they knew no other. People of their life experience could not produce fundamental movement in the direction of democracy, despite the fact that they truly believed they were acting for the common good, understood as the interests of socialism.

The future careers of these party and state leaders in March 1953 were determined by two factors: formal authority (their place in the hierarchy of Stalin's comrades-in-arms) and the actual power of the position they held, that is, the capacity to control one or another sphere of activity. From the perspective of formal authority, Malenkov had the strongest position. He had delivered a report on behalf of the Central Committee at the last party congress in 1952. In Stalin's absence, he chaired meetings of the Presidium and the Council of Ministers and placed his signature next to Stalin's on the more important government resolutions. After Stalin's death, Malenkov inherited the post of chairman of the Council of Ministers. For Stalin, the authority of the position had been symbolic, since he controlled all three levers of the government (MVD, Council of Ministers, and Central Committee), whereas Malenkov had virtually no possibility of triple control, as he shared power with Beria and Khrushchev. Meanwhile, Malenkov's position ultimately turned out to be weaker than those of Khrushchev and Beria when it came to potential influence on policy as a whole

Khrushchev's chances seemed least favorable in March 1953. Unlike Beria, he did not have a force like the MVD and MGB supporting him, and he lacked Malenkov's experience in the highest echelon of the leadership. Malenkov had worked directly with Stalin since the end of the 1930s; Khrushchev joined the inner circle only in December 1949, when he was made first secretary of the Moscow party committee and secretary of the Central Committee.

In accordance with the postwar practice of distributing responsibilities among the Central Committee secretaries and Politburo members, each of them was put in charge of some division or branch. Malenkov was given agriculture; Beria, the organs of state security and internal affairs, as well as the development of atomic weapons; Molotov, foreign policy. Khrushchev, who was busy directing the Moscow party organization, did not have any of these branch responsibilities. Narrow specialization was also enforced by the way decisions were made in the highest echelon of leadership: from 1948 on, there had been practically no meetings of the Politburo, and most decisions were made without discussion, by sending a document around for each leader's signature. After the redistribution of jobs in March 1953, Khrushchev again ended up without a sphere specifically set aside for him, where he could display his talents concretely. As a secretary of the Central Committee, his initial responsibilities were too abstract, and his jurisdiction too unclear, to allow him to act resolutely.

Khrushchev adopted a wait-and-see attitude, leaving the initiative to Beria. Between March and June 1953, Beria put forward a series of proposals, the most important of which were directed toward reforming the MVD-MGB system. Beria proposed transferring prison camps and colonies from the MVD to the Ministry of Justice (except for certain camps for political prisoners), limiting the use of forced labor in the economy, abandoning unprofitable "great construction projects of communism," reviewing fabricated convictions, abolishing torture in the conduct of investigations, and proclaiming a wide amnesty (which would not affect prisoners condemned for political motives).

In May and June, Beria presented three memorandums on nationality policies to the Central Committee Presidium: "Issues regarding the Lithuanian SSR," "Issues regarding the western provinces of the Ukrainian SSR," and "Issues regarding the Belorussian SSR." He proposed changes, including abolishing forced Russification and promoting local cadres to leadership posts. In this case, Beria acted within the limits of his jurisdiction, inasmuch as his proposals on cadres mostly involved replacing top officials of the organs of internal affairs and state security. Later on, after Beria's arrest, his stance on the issue of nationalities policies would become one of the main accusations against him.

Efforts to review procedures for promoting national cadres in the republics had been mounted even before 1953. However, the practice in existence since 1936, according to which any appointment to a nomenklatura position presupposed obligatory confirmation through the organs of state security, doomed these early efforts. In the western provinces of Ukraine and Belorussia, or in the Baltic states, it was difficult to find a person with a record that seemed clean to the NKVD (predecessor of the MVD), that is, someone who had not lived on occupied territory or did not have relatives abroad. In February 1952 the Central Committee Secretariat specifically discussed this issue in connection with a report on the work of the Vilnius province committee of the Lithuanian Communist party.[4] Malenkov, chairing this meeting, addressed the need to change the policy on national cadres and most of all the fact that "bandits trust each other more than MGB personnel trust our own cadres."[5]

Beria's memorandums were based on decisions adopted back in 1952, but he expanded upon them and made the suggestions more concrete. His initiative on the nationality issue clearly promised large political dividends. Attempting to act in the spirit of the time and to expand his own personal popularity and influence, Khrushchev supported Beria's proposals. In June 1953, following Beria's example, Khrushchev prepared a memorandum for the Presidium, "On the state of affairs in the Latvian SSR," and a draft Central Committee resolution on the same question.[6] A comparison of Beria's memorandums on Ukraine, Belorussia, and Lithuania with Khrushchev's memorandum on Latvia not only indicates the common approach of both leaders but also proves that Khrushchev, in preparing his memo, was directly guided by Beria's and may even have used his materials.

At the July 1953 Central Committee plenum on the "Beria affair," not only was Khrushchev's initiative not mentioned, but Khrushchev spoke of Beria as the sole author of all memorandums on the issue of nationality policies, including Latvia.[7] Another curious fact is that the first secretaries of the Communist parties of Ukraine, Belorussia, and Lithuania also spoke at the plenum, denouncing Beria's nationality proposals. The leaders of the Latvian Communist party did not denounce Beria.

This episode is characteristic of a time when the fate of initiatives, even fundamentally progressive ones, depended on the outcome of the struggle for political power. Of course, the new government incurred its own costs with regard to nationality policies: for example, Russian speakers in non-Russian republics complained about the restrictions of their rights. Beria's proposals, however, were not rejected for that reason, but because they were directly linked with Beria's name. It is possible that Khrushchev was inconsistent in conducting agrarian policy in 1953 for this same personal reason. Although he participated directly in implementing agrarian policy, many in society, and especially the peasants, regarded the policy as Malenkov's idea. According to people who were close to Khrushchev, the Soviet leader was not devoid of vanity and was sensitive to the problem of primacy. Molotov, for example, remembered that after Malenkov's speech on his agrarian program in August 1953, Khrushchev was literally outraged: he, Khrushchev, should have been the first to speak.[8]

Khrushchev's fears of losing his chance for primacy apparently played a vital role in the removal of Beria. Certain documents from Khrushchev's Secretariat show that he kept a careful eye on the balance of power and that he carefully monitored any strengthening of the positions of other members of the Presidium, particularly Beria and Malenkov. One such document was a radiogram by one of the leaders of the national underground in Ukraine (OUN), V. Kuk, which was received via wiretap and sent to Khrushchev for his information. The author of the radiogram described the state of Moscow leadership in June 1953: "Beria is far from being the boss in the Kremlin. He is forced to share his power with Malenkov and others, and was even forced to relinquish primacy to him. . . . We must expect various additional revelations in coming personnel changes; they will continue for a long time, until the time when a 'wise leader' again appears for the whole USSR. Who will this be? I think that it will not be Malenkov, but Lavrentii [Beria], because he holds concrete and reliable power in his hands, and that is the strongest legal argument in any political situation."[9]

The last sentence of the text was underlined, either by Khrushchev himself or for him, precisely because it contains the essence of the report: the naming of the main contender for top leader. Khrushchev was not even mentioned among the contenders. Moreover, this evaluation of the situation in the Moscow leadership seemed accurate. Khrushchev began the struggle for power in the least favorable position—at least on paper—of any of the top contenders.

However, the authority of his office and of his personality allowed Khrushchev ultimately to emerge victorious from this struggle. There is little basis to assert that he pursued only his own self-interest and sought only personal gain. On the contrary, Khrushchev seemed truly convinced that in entering the fight, he was acting on behalf of the social good, first and foremost. But Khrushchev was also convinced that he was the best person to determine what was beneficial for society and what was not. In this, he differed little from his comrades-in-arms, including Malenkov. Why couldn't Malenkov and Khrushchev come to an agrecmcnt? This question relates not only to the fates of both leaders but also to the fate of the reforms begun after Stalin's death.

All the necessary conditions appeared to exist for such a duo: not only were the two men drawn together by the nature of earlier activities and personal relations, but their dissimilarity could have been complementary. Khrushchev and Malenkov had worked together closely from about 1931, when Khrushchev was secretary of one of the Moscow district party committees and Malenkov was the manager of the organization-instruction department of the Moscow city committee. Furthermore, during the same Moscow period, Khrushchev helped Malenkov out of a difficult situation. In 1937, when Khrushchev was already Moscow first secretary and Malenkov headed a department of the Central Committee, the Moscow city party conference considered candidates for membership in the Moscow party committee. In defending his own candidacy, Malenkov talked about the period of the Civil War and mentioned the city of Orenburg, where he had joined the Red Army. At that point, one of the audience members posed a question: "Were there Whites in Orenburg at the time?" "Yes, there were Whites in Orenburg," Malenkov replied, and he immediately heard: "That means that you were with them!"[10] Unexpectedly, Khrushchev came to his aid: "Comrades, I think that such questions can lead our conference astray. The Whites may have been in Orenburg at the time, but Comrade Malenkov was not on their side."[11] In a sense, Khrushchev was simply coming to the defense of a "proven" person from the Central Committee who found himself under fire, but at a time of mass purges, support of this kind had great meaning, at least for the development of personal contacts.

In addition to personal relations, however, which were friendly enough until much later, there were other elements that brought Khrushchev and Malenkov together and fostered a mutual understanding between them. Both men came from the party apparat. Whereas Khrushchev was a particularly practical person, who had worked at all lower levels of the party and headed large party organizations in Ukraine and Moscow, Malenkov spent a large part of his life in the Central Committee apparat. Khrushchev had greater experience in independent decision making, while Malenkov's earlier activities had constrained his initiative to a considerable degree. Malenkov was a typical apparatchik, whereas Khrushchev was more of a party functionary; but both belonged to the same generation of Stalinist political leaders. Their professional skills consisted first and foremost of the ability to carry out the will of the supreme leader, Stalin. The habit of "absolutizing" the organization, which became a trait of the collective psychology of this layer of the party elite, undoubtedly influenced their reform policies later on: both Khrushchev and Malenkov saw a well-adjusted system of party responsibility and discipline as the main mechanism for implementing reform.

When it came to leadership potential, Malenkov was not self-sufficient. He did not have the appropriate personality, as he himself apparently understood, and he willingly shared power with others. He could play the role of number one while remaining in essence number two; this was how his relations with Beria worked out and how a partnership with Khrushchev could have developed. Malenkov needed Khrushchev, and Malenkov understood this. But he was also necessary to Khrushchev, and this Khrushchev could not or did not want to understand. Malenkov, a man of compromise, could have counterbalanced the impulsive and brusque Khrushchev. But Khrushchev's advancement to personal leadership was the product not only of his personality but of circumstances as well. The whole structure of power, as before, gravitated towards one-man leadership. Khrushchev took advantage of this tendency, but in overtaking Malenkov, he ultimately undermined himself.

It is difficult to compare the scope of Khrushchev's and Malenkov's activities as leaders: the former was in power for a "remarkable decade," the latter for a little over a year. But there is plenty of material to help us judge the approaches and potential of each.

Traditionally, when Khrushchev's merits are enumerated, his rehabilitation of political prisoners is usually mentioned first, followed by his new agrarian policy. When one speaks of Khrushchev's mistakes, agrarian policy comes first again. This paradox is explained by Khrushchev's inconsistency, but this does not settle the issue. Rather, it raises the question of the reasons for such inconsistency, which are difficult to attribute solely to Khrushchev's character. Actually, there were several other reasons, although the personal aspect also played a role.

We need to remember that the agrarian reforms of 1953 were not initially linked to Khrushchev's name. When Khrushchev addressed agrarian problems at the September 1953 Central Committee plenum, he did not speak as the initiator of a new course but as its transmitter. New approaches to agriculture were first developed in the Council of Ministers, through Malenkov's apparat. In March 1953 the Ministry of Finance drafted a report for Malenkov on tax policy in the countryside. Calculating the profitability of peasant farms in relation to the growth of taxes between 1949 and 1953, the report cited the appearance of "a disproportion stemming from an economically unfounded increase of taxes on peasants."[12] This conclusion was substantiated in a report that the minister of agriculture and state procurement, A. Kozlov, sent to Malenkov in July 1953. That report can be considered the foundation of both Malenkov's speech at the August 1953 USSR Supreme Soviet session and Khrushchev's speech at the Central Committee plenum a month later.

Kozlov's report was analytical in character, summarizing the shortcomings of agrarian policy and suggesting concrete measures for leading agriculture out of a crisis (although the term "crisis" was not used). Many of the problems facing Russian villages were brought to light for the first time, for example, the severe decline in the standard of living for collective farmers after the war and the mass flight from villages.[13] The main thesis of the report was the need to take into account the material interests of the peasant. The proposals of the Ministry of Agriculture and State Procurement for lowering taxes and mandatory deliveries of agricultural products, and for forgiving debts of collective farmers, were afterward ratified by the USSR Supreme Soviet.

Malenkov presented the main report at the Supreme Soviet session. His speech was programmatic in nature, though with a series of innovative suggestions.[14] He spoke of changing priorities in domestic policy and about turning the economy's face to the people. With this in mind, he suggested reviewing the relative rates of growth of heavy industry versus production that directly affected the needs of the population and launching social programs, which would include the development of housing construction, trade, and public health. At that same session of the Supreme Soviet, a new law was adopted on the agricultural tax, constituting a significant reform of the taxation system that had existed since 1930.[15]

After his August 1953 speeches, Malenkov's name became very popular, particularly among peasants. Newspapers containing Malenkov's Supreme Soviet speech were "avidly read in the village," and the ordinary poor peasant said, "This guy—he's for us!" as we see in one of the letters sent to the CPSU Central Committee.[16] It was at this time that a saying arose that is still remembered in rural Russia: "Malenkov came by, and we ate some bliny."

In 1953 Khrushchev could hardly be considered the initiator of agrarian reform for another reason: he had already been burned on the agricultural question when he wrote his famous 1951 article, "On the construction and provision of public services and amenities on collective farms."[17] This article helped prompt the Central Committee's "secret letter" of April 2, 1951, which severely criticized Khrushchev for, among other things, underestimating the importance of individual peasant plots for village residents.[18] This episode seriously damaged Khrushchev's reputation as an agrarian. Malenkov, on the other hand, had headed agriculture in the postwar period. In his memoirs, Khrushchev characterizes Malenkov's competence in agricultural issues in very unflattering terms, citing Stalin's opinion as proof.[19] However, during the seven years from 1945 and 1952 (with a break in 1946), Malenkov took care of agrarian problems, toeing the Stalinist line. Naturally, this policy was very different from the one that Malenkov adopted in 1953, when he had the opportunity to act independently.

Malenkov by no means acted alone in devising a new agricultural course; the new line was supported by the Presidium. The troubles in agriculture were evident from the beginning of the 1950s to anyone who had the slightest notion of conditions in the countryside. That is why attempts to reexamine agrarian policies were undertaken even during Stalin's lifetime. In February 1953 a draft resolution was prepared, "On measures for the future development of livestock farming on collective farms," which foresaw the need to raise state procurement prices so as to increase the material incentive of the collective farmers. The resolution, however, was not adopted.[20] On the basis of currently available documents, there is no evidence that any high-ranking leaders opposed a reexamination of agrarian policies after Stalin's death; certainly neither Khrushchev nor Malenkov did. The cause of their conflict lies not in conceptual disagreements (of which there were none, even on the question of developing the Virgin Lands) but in personal competition, which Khrushchev initiated.

At the January 1955 Central Committee plenum, when Malenkov's fate as the leader of the state was being decided, his speech at the August 1953 Supreme Soviet session was cited against him. In fact,

Malenkov would never have made such a speech without majority support in the Presidium. Before the session, he showed the text of his report to his comrades, including Khrushchev, without meeting any objections.[21] Malenkov himself elucidated the nature of the conflict at the January 1955 plenum: "Although this speech was made with the agreement and knowledge of Presidium members," Malenkov admitted, "it ought to have been done on the basis of party decisions. . . . In other words, these questions should first have been decided at a Central Committee plenum."[22] In 1953 an extremely atypical occurrence in Soviet policymaking took place: the Central Committee approved a change in agrarian policy after the main tenets of this policy had been promulgated at the session of the Supreme Soviet. There was more to it, however, than this breach of the customary sequence: the real issue was that Malenkov was responsible for the decisions of the session, whereas Khrushchev addressed the plenum.

Malenkov had outstripped Khrushchev on this question in 1953. It was no accident, therefore, that Khrushchev accused Malenkov at the January 1955 plenum of striving for "cheap personal fame" and even of "dictatorial tendencies."[23] Such tendencies were visible in that after being elected chairman of the Council of Ministers, Malenkov had suggested that all documents submitted to the Central Committee and the Council of Ministers be addressed to himself and Khrushchev. Khrushchev charged that although it might seem that Malenkov was "sharing power with others, in fact he wants to take everything into his own hands. This is not a political or professional quality, but a dictatorial tendency."[24] As soon as Khrushchev, with the help of other Presidium members, obtained Malenkov's resignation, however, he immediately began to exhibit the same tendencies himself. Beginning in 1955, all joint party-government decisions took the form of resolutions of the Central Committee and the Council of Ministers, although previously they had been signed in the reverse order: as resolutions of the Council of Ministers and the Central Committee. Earlier, Stalin had signed resolutions in the name of the Council of Ministers, and Malenkov did so for those from the Central Committee. After Stalin's death the old practice was at first maintained, with Malenkov, as the chairman of the Council of Ministers, and Khrushchev, as the secretary of the CPSU Central Committee, signing the joint resolutions. Malenkov would seem formally to have taken Stalin's place. Khrushchev ended this continuity: it is not coincidental that the change in the order of signing official documents came at the same time as Malenkov's dismissal.

The personal rivalry between Khrushchev and Malenkov affected far more serious matters than the order in which documents were signed. Although for all intents and purposes Malenkov was removed from power, Khrushchev still mistrusted the agrarian initiative of 1953, even though it was now called "the September plenum" policy. In Khrushchev's mind (and for the majority of the nation), the agrarian policy was still linked to Malenkov's name. Perhaps this explains the gradual curtailment of the 1953 agrarian policy, first and foremost in the development of subsidiary peasant plots. The decisions of 1953 remained in effect only until about 1957–1958. The period from 1954 to 1958 is therefore considered the most successful in the whole history of the Soviet countryside. Gross agricultural production for those years increased 35.3 percent relative to the prior Five-Year Plan. This figure was achieved for the most part on account of the increase in the productivity of individual plots.[25]

A change in policy toward individual plots occurred in 1956, when a resolution was adopted by the Central Committee and the Council of Ministers, "On regulating the agricultural artel and the further development of initiatives of collective farmers in the organization of collective farm production and the managing of the affairs of the artel." This resolution barred expanding such plots at the expense of public land and even recommended that plots be reduced in size.[26] Thus the principle of requiring limits on the number of animals held as the property of collective farmers was strengthened, "taking into consideration the local conditions."[27]

Along with decisions that limited individual plots (which, by the way, can only provisionally be called "subsidiary"),[28] opposite measures were adopted that encouraged them. Beginning on January 1, 1958 (and further developing the decisions of September 1953), obligatory deliveries of certain types of agricultural produce from individual plots were eliminated, and procurement prices on them were raised to the level of prices fixed for collective farms.[29] In reality, though, the new rules were not always followed; some representatives of local government, attempting to fulfill the plan for government procurement at all costs, forced collective farmers to turn over the output of their personal plots to fulfill collective farm requirements. At one of the conferences of the Central Committee the statement was made, "Conducting agrarian policy in this way only angers people."[30] Perhaps if policy on individual plots had been more consistent, abuses like this might have been eliminated. As early as the end of 1958, however, another idea was gaining a stranglehold over central government policy: that individual plots would die out in a socialist system. This line of reasoning is clearly evident in resolutions of two Central Committee plenums, in December 1958 and December 1959.[31]

Starting in 1959, many collective farms suspended distribution of fodder as payment for a workday and began to forbid collective farmers to use public reserves for their own livestock.[32] As a result of such policies, peasants were forced to limit the total livestock in their plots; by the end of 1960, the number of peasant homesteads with cows had fallen practically to the 1950 level.[33]

Of course, Khrushchev intended no "harm" toward individual plots. He was truly convinced that large collective farming is more effective than individual farming, and that the public economy was capable of satisfying not only the state's demand for foodstuffs and raw materials but also the needs of rural people. Such an optimistic evaluation, however, was not realistic.

The personal competition inside the Presidium after Stalin's death influenced not only the new agrarian policy but also the development of foreign policy during the 1950s and 1960s. The first question that split the ranks of the "collective leadership" was policy toward Germany. In the spring of 1953, Beria, with Malenkov's support, attempted to get the policy of building socialism in East Germany reexamined. The East German question was placed before the Presidium of the Council of Ministers, where Beria and Malenkov expected majority support. But the discussion turned into what Khrushchev recalled as "a huge fight," leaving Beria and Malenkov in the minority.[34] Beria's position on the German question can be explained not by any particularly liberal tendencies but primarily by the fact that he was well informed about the developing political crisis in East Germany. The June 1953 uprising in East Berlin not only displayed the inability of the East German leaders to solve their internal problems with dispatch but also revealed the miscalculation of Soviet leadership.[35]

Another conflict between Khrushchev and Malenkov (or rather between Malenkov and the majority of the party Presidium) was produced by Malenkov's statement about the inevitable demise of world civilization in the event of a third world war. A resolution of the January 1955

plenum declared Malenkov's statement "theoretically harmful and politically erroneous," favorable "only to imperialistic warmongers, who
seek to frighten the Russian nation with their 'atomic' blackmail."[36]
Khrushchev was the most decisive opponent of Malenkov on this question, but only in theory. In the event, it was to be Khrushchev himself
who fundamentally altered the priorities of Soviet foreign policy by ad-
vocating a series of initiatives aimed at reducing international tension
and developing a dialogue with Western countries.

When he was already retired in the 1970s, Malenkov wrote an essay
that includes a section entitled "On the harmful deeds of N. Khrushchev." In the essay, he devoted substantial space to criticizing Khrushchev's foreign policy. The most serious accusation that Malenkov
lodged against Khrushchev was bringing about a rapprochement between the Soviet Union and the United States, which Malenkov regarded as a "concession to imperialism." According to Malenkov, "the
whole enormous growth of the aggressive policy of the United States,
its creation of dangerous hotbeds of war, the transfer of thermonuclear
arms to military bases in various parts of the world, all this posed a real
threat of the sudden use of thermonuclear weapons. But Khrushchev
and others employing similar opportunistic propaganda sowed illusions and fed the relaxed mood about the struggle with the instigators
of war."[37]

It is paradoxical that Khrushchev, who reproached Malenkov for excessive mildness in foreign policy, was the first to undertake concrete
efforts toward a rapprochement with the West, whereas Malenkov, who
urged a return to the principle of peaceful coexistence and detente, as-
sessed Khrushchev's steps, taken precisely in this direction, as too opportunistic. Upon closer analysis, however, the paradox disappears and
the approaches of both leaders turn out to be not so different after all
(witness Khrushchev's many well-known attacks against the "imperialists"). In contrast to Malenkov, who rapidly became an observer, Khrushchev was forced to act in concrete situations and to make decisions
based on actual circumstances, without relying solely on personal convictions.

Khrushchev was more pragmatic than Malenkov and Stalin's other
former comrades (with the exception of Beria). It was this personality
trait that allowed him to raise the question of Stalin's "personality cult."
The decision to do so was made collectively, and when giving his secret
speech about Stalin at the 20th Party Congress, Khrushchev relied on

the views and support of both the Presidium and the Central Committee. Before that congress, on February 13, 1956, a Central Committee plenum discussed the special report on the personality cult and decided that it would be presented at a closed session of the congress. According to Khrushchev, the text of the secret speech was still being prepared on February 13.[38] The plenum instructed Khrushchev to make the speech.[38] On the eve of the closed session, the text of the report was sent to Presidium members, who approved and adopted it with minor editorial corrections.[40]

Despite the collegiality of this decision, the country's leaders never had a unified view on the Stalin question, which was extremely delicate for all of them. Malenkov, for example, viewed the personality cult primarily as a moral problem. He wrote much later, "What has come to be called the 'personality cult' includes first of all the assertion by the leader and others of his infallibility, regardless of whether his behavior and actions are correct or faulty and mistaken."[41] He spoke of Stalin's personality cult but never linked the problem to Stalin's personality. Khrushchev, by contrast, took the path of personification in an effort to assuage public opinion. However, public reaction to the public discrediting of Stalin and what was termed "the consequences of the personality cult" came as a complete surprise to everyone, and the resulting turmoil surpassed what the leaders considered permissible limits. Despite their different approaches to the personality cult, the leaders were more or less unanimous on the main thing: to them, the cult was an internal party problem, a problem for the Central Committee to resolve, a problem of which the public could be informed—but no more than that.

Strictly speaking, the term "Khrushchev's reforms" is as arbitrary a designation as the term "Malenkov's reforms." Reform is a program of consecutive actions directed toward changing existing political and economic structures or toward their complete replacement. It is difficult to view the actions of leaders in the Thaw period as coherent and systematic. Malenkov and Khrushchev each approached the question of defining and implementing reforms distinctively. Malenkov was more of an evolutionist, a supporter of gradual, carefully considered actions. Khrushchev placed his bet on quick returns from reorganization, on measures that would lead to an immediate and substantial result.

Despite their different approaches, however, both men basically tripped over principles they shared: state socialism as applied both to thinking and to practical policy, the unique role of the state and the unconditional priority of state ownership, traditional paternalism in designing social programs, and the inadmissibility of private interest and pluralism in any sphere of activity.

Both Khrushchev and Malenkov regarded the existing system as the "right" one, in need only of improvement and development but not of complete overhaul. The leaders of the Thaw were as remote from the idea of fundamental changes as they were from the slightest doubt about the socialist nature of the Soviet social system. That is why Malenkov's promising idea about a social reorientation of the economy could transcend neither the dispute over the priorities to be attached to heavy and light industry nor the attempt to solve the most pressing day-to-day problems. Nor was Khrushchev less set in his way of thinking, although he harshly criticized Malenkov.

The main directions of what are generally referred to as "Khrushchev's reforms," which were outlined in the decisions of 1953–1954, were not so much the result of the benevolence of any leader as they were an answer to the challenge of the time. Both Khrushchev and Malenkov belonged to the reformist wing of the party and were equally disposed toward changes, despite their well-known differences on a variety of questions. Personal rivalry between them not only did not contribute to the development of reformist policy but also led to a course correction that must be considered unfortunate.

4
Repression and Rehabilitation

VLADIMIR NAUMOV

While the life and political activities of Nikita Khrushchev continue to be admired and respected by some, they have been harshly and passionately criticized by others. This ambivalence is connected with Khrushchev's reformist activities of the 1950s and 1960s and primarily with his speech at the 20th Party Congress, which turned all Soviet history upside down, opened a new stage in its development, and ultimately led to the collapse of the Communist regime.

Whatever Khrushchev's intentions may have been, his act is still denounced by orthodox Communists, be they covert or overt Stalinists, and greatly admired by their opponents, the democrats and anti-Stalinists. The events of this seemingly long-ago time still remain an object of fierce contention in Russia. To use V. I. Kliuchevskii's phrase, they are a banner for some but a target for others.

Historians, politicians, and journalists look at Khrushchev's participation in the mass repressions of the 1930s primarily through the prism of his secret speech at the 20th Party Congress. Khrushchev's opponents and adversaries use his involvement in mass political repressions to question his moral right to give a speech exposing Stalin's crimes. They portray his exposure of Stalin as an important instrument in the struggle for personal power. They interpret all Khrushchev's initiatives as a departure from the principles of Marxism-Leninism, a betrayal of the interests of the party. They ask why he did not mention his own participation in the mass repressions of the 1930s. It is true that he did not mention his own role, but he also avoided mentioning the role in those crimes of his Presidium colleagues, who sat in full complement behind him during his speech at the 20th Congress. And at no time did any of them raise the issue of their own guilt or publicly repent of their criminal actions.

Khrushchev's silence, as well as that of his Presidium colleagues, can be explained not merely by a fear of being held responsible for those actions. The point of Khrushchev's speech was to expose Stalin's crimes and to reveal him as the organizer of the repressions. In all the Presidium's discussions of the personality cult and of the speech itself, the personal responsibility of Presidium members and their participation in the repressions never came up, even though conversations did touch on possible consequences for them. And measures were therefore taken to prevent any discussion of the speech at the Congress.

The question of personal responsibility was first approached a year later, at the June 1957 Central Committee plenum, when Central Committee members exposed Viacheslav Molotov, Lazar Kaganovich, and Georgii Malenkov as participants in the bloody events of the 1930s. Only those Presidium members who had come out against Khrushchev were accused; he and Anastas Mikoyan seemed to have had no connection with the repressions. Khrushchev avoided answering Kaganovich's direct question about his participation.

Speaking at the same plenum, G. K. Zhukov did address in a general way the need to carefully expose everyone involved in the repressions. "It must be," he said, "that other comrades, former Politburo members, are guilty as well. I think, comrades, that you know whom I'm talking about, but you know that these comrades, through their honest work and forthrightness, have earned the trust of the Central Committee and of the entire party, and I am sure that we will henceforth recognize them as leaders for their forthrightness and their sincere acknowledgment."[1]

Of course, Khrushchev participated directly in the repressions that occurred in Moscow and Ukraine between 1936 and 1939. And in exposing others, Khrushchev should have mentioned himself. Yet these facts do not in any way diminish the importance of his role in exposing the Stalin phenomenon, condemning the Stalin personality cult, and revealing the crimes and overall arbitrariness that occurred on Stalin's orders.

The question of Khrushchev and repression should not be restricted to determining Khrushchev's role in the 1930s. Repressions were undertaken by the Communist regime before that time, and they unfortunately did not end with the 20th Party Congress. The party formally condemned the repressions of the 1930s, but it did not repent before the innumerable victims of its regime. Hence we must evaluate as fully and objectively as possible Khrushchev's actions to rehabilitate

victims and to liberate them from prisons, camps, and exile. These issues cannot be considered outside the historical context in which Khrushchev was politically formed and in which he worked between the
1930s and early 1960s. Khrushchev did not represent either the entire
party or the entire party apparat, but he simply could not avoid coming
to terms with them. We must also understand how Khrushchev was
limited by his own convictions and his own view of the party's role in
society, and of his own historic mission as its leader.

A turning point in Khrushchev's political career came in the early
1930s. This was the time of the first five-year plans, which were supposed to be fulfilled ahead of schedule, and of the great leap in the country's economic development. By the early 1930s, there were no longer
any open opposition groups. Stalin's political opponents had been si-
lenced. But Stalin was not satisfied with victory over groups in the party
that had come out against his leadership. He determined on a purge of
those party members and functionaries who hesitated or were disposed
to be conciliatory toward former oppositionists, or assumed that once
ideological disagreements were resolved, peace and accord would necessarily come to pass in the party.

Aggressiveness, toughness, and eagerness to achieve results by any
means regardless of consequences were what Stalin demanded of new
recruits at all levels of party-state power—not intellect or competence.
The most important criteria were decisiveness and unwillingness to
compromise. Loyalty to the great leader was demanded from skilled
party workers as well. Among those belonging to this new Stalinist generation of the upper party leaders were K. Ia. Bauman, A. V. Kosarev,
N. I. Ezhov, Ia. B. Gamarnik, P. P. Postyshev, S. I. Syrtsov, and R. I.
Eikhe, all of whom perished in the Great Terror. Only two persons were
able to consolidate their position at the highest level of power: A. A.
Zhdanov and N. S. Khrushchev.

The ranks of the leadership were replenished by people who
reached the very top when mass repressions were already in decline.
Among them was Khrushchev. He had not a shadow of a doubt regarding the correctness of Stalin's actions. He was transported and be-
witched by Stalin's genius and wisdom; his very proximity to the leader
had a huge impact on such an emotional nature as Khrushchev's. I
think even his feeling of personal gratitude for the attention Stalin
showed him was overshadowed by his profound euphoria at being involved in the great events happening in the country under Stalin's lead-

ership. The view that Stalin was resolving the grandiose problems of the era was skillfully created, in part by masterfully manipulating public consciousness, but we cannot deny there were huge social achievements. Stalin's name inspired the enthusiasm and heroism of millions of Soviet citizens. This is a fact, and Khrushchev reflected moods prevalent in a significant portion of society.

Under these circumstances, Stalin's mistakes and even his terror found justifications. Any departure from the official propaganda line was attributed to the intrigue of internal and external counterrevolutionary forces and regarded as a betrayal of revolutionary ideals and the Soviet system. Naturally, "enemies of the people" had to be subject to punishment that might be extremely severe.[2] Khrushchev, too, believed he was acting in the interests of the party and the laboring masses to preserve the achievements of the Revolution.

Between 1936 and 1937 Khrushchev served as the first secretary of the Moscow province and city party committees. Stalin and the Politburo saw to it that the capital's party organization was a model for all party organizations in the country, especially in an area as important as the eradication of "enemies of the people." The first secretary of Moscow's party organization took part in directing this work. Every morning the secretaries of Moscow district committees met with Khrushchev. He relayed the instructions he had received from Stalin the night before, first and foremost increasing vigilance and strengthening the struggle with the enemies of the party. Lazar Kaganovich often attended these conferences.

Kaganovich's role was as the Politburo's supervisor of the Moscow organization. He was personally responsible to Stalin for his recruit, Khrushchev. Kaganovich frequently attended meetings of Moscow party activists, delivering concrete directives from the Politburo. Up until Khrushchev's departure for Ukraine, Kaganovich remained his patron, master, and mentor.

The secretary of Moscow's Sverdlovsk district party committee, K. P. Chudinova, recalls that Kaganovich once attended a conference of the Moscow committee at which the subject was getting the population to buy state bonds: "At the time peasants were pouring into Moscow to earn some money," Chudinova remembers:

> Village life was no good, money was scarce, and those arriving in the
> capital saved every kopeck in order to send something to their family.

It was very difficult to rouse such workers with propaganda. An agitator would approach with a sign-up sheet for bonds, and they would say right to his face, "What are you robbing me for, my family is going hungry in the village, but you want to take our money right here and now; I don't have any money!" They categorically refused. Having heard this report, Kaganovich proposed, "Give them a couple whacks, they'll get the idea." I couldn't hold back and said, "What's all this about hitting them; after all, we're the most civilized country in the world. Yet all of a sudden, instead of persuading, we let our fists do the talking?" Kaganovich answered, "Comrade Stalin says that's the way to do it. After all, the fascists beat our people, so what are we supposed to do? Pat them on the head? The country needs money, and the plan for bonds must be fulfilled, whatever it takes."

Khrushchev took such words from a Politburo member as a direct order, and he fully adopted them in his own actions. In a May 1937 speech to Moscow city and province party delegates, Khrushchev said: "Over at the first factory, some dithering yes-man, or some Trotskyite started yammering. . . . The Communists took care of him and gave him one right in the kisser. A few people immediately called the Moscow committee, asking, 'How could they beat him up like that?' And I replied, 'Good job, beating him up like that. Good job.'"[3]

Mutual suspicion and a willingness to inform on others spread throughout the party and the country, encouraged by various means. At morning conferences of the Moscow committee, Khrushchev praised those active in unmasking and criticized those who were "falling behind." The situation changed dramatically after the February–March 1937 Central Committee plenum. Increasing vigilance immediately became even more important, and a lack of it came to be regarded as "treason." More and more people volunteered their services.

District party committee bureaus met nearly every day to consider cases of Communists accused of counterrevolutionary activity or of friendship or other ties with those arrested. Province and city committee bureaus met just as often on personal cases of party members. At first, provincial and city committees had to expel supporters from the party before they could be arrested, but by the spring of 1937 such expulsions became a formality. Members were arrested still holding their party tickets, and the NKVD later informed the district committee, sending along the confiscated party cards. Only then did the district committee automatically expel members. No doubts about the grounds for arrest ever arose. On the contrary, district committee bureaus would immediately level charges against people who had worked with those arrested, and thus new cases would arise.

Khrushchev's approval can generally be found on arrest orders for prominent functionaries. In the KGB archive, documentary materials have been preserved that attest to Khrushchev's involvement in mass repressions in Moscow and Moscow province. In particular, he personally initialed documents proposing the arrest of leading officials of the Moscow Soviet and the Moscow province party committee. By early 1938, a significant percentage of Moscow party activists had been arrested by organs of the NKVD. Of the thirty-eight province and city party secretaries who served between 1935 and 1937, only three avoided repression. Of 146 secretaries of city and district committees, 136 were also arrested, as well as many leading soviet and trade union workers, enterprise managers, specialists, and figures in science and culture.[4]

As the first secretary of the Moscow province and city party organizations, Khrushchev not only organized mass repressions within his region but must have been directly involved in them as well. Stalin came up with many forms that such direct participation could take. The first secretary of a province or territorial committee, or of a union republic central committee had personally to sign the NKVD's arrest order and subsequent sentence for any member of the nomenklatura under him. The first secretary headed the so-called troikas created by the Politburo. His personal order was required for the arrest of leading officials of the province, territory, or republic.

If we consider only cases prepared by the Moscow directorate of the NKVD, 55,741 people were repressed in Moscow in 1936 and 1937. The total number of those arrested is much higher. In accordance with a June 2, 1937, Politburo decision "On anti-Soviet elements," a quota of 35,000 was set for the repression of persons from Moscow and Moscow province, of whom 5,000 were to pay the supreme penalty: death by shooting. In a document sent to the Central Committee and Stalin on July 10, Khrushchev requested that 2,000 former kulaks, who according to NKVD data had taken up residence in Moscow, be shot in fulfillment of the quota.[5]

Regional leaders carrying out repressions were themselves fearful, however. No one was immune to Stalin's retribution. Khrushchev probably feared that his measures against enemies of the people were insufficiently energetic. Swift and merciless punishment already hung over him like the sword of Damocles, if only because he had briefly supported local Trotskyites during internal party discussions of 1923. Khrushchev either knew or guessed that during interrogations, the NKVD had collected other material against him as well. Khrushchev's entire secretariat was arrested, and each of his people was worked over to get testimony against him.

Khrushchev did not exclude the possibility of his own arrest. K. P. Chudinova tells that when she learned of the arrest of her ex-husband, she wrote Khrushchev, seeking an opportunity to meet with NKVD agents in order to prove that her former spouse was an honest Communist who had been incorrectly detained. "Nikita Sergeevich," she relates, "took my letter, read it, tore it up into little bits, and threw them into several different wastebaskets. I understood that he himself was afraid."

Starting in January 1938, Khrushchev headed the Ukrainian party organization. Under his leadership, the last wave of the Great Terror was implemented in Ukraine. In May and June 1938, the entire Ukrainian government was replaced. Between February and June 1938, all twelve province party first secretaries were removed from their posts, as were most of the second secretaries. Of the 86 full and candidate members elected to the Ukrainian Central Committee at the 14th Party Congress in June 1938, only three remained from the previous Central Committee, which had been elected only one year earlier. Not one of the new Politburo and Secretariat members had performed similar work before.

In 1938 in Ukraine, 106,119 persons were arrested; nor did the repressions cease in subsequent years. Around 12,000 were arrested in 1939, and around 50,000 in 1940. Altogether 167,565 persons were arrested in Ukraine from 1938 to 1940. The NKVD attributed the intensification of repression in Ukraine in 1938 to the fact that the Trotskyist counterrevolutionary activities increased noticeably with the arrival of Khrushchev. Khrushchev personally sanctioned the repression of a few hundred individuals who were suspected of organizing a terrorist act against him.[6]

In the summer of 1938, with Khrushchev's agreement and sanction, a large group of leading party, soviet, and economic officials was arrested, including the deputy chairman of the Ukrainian Soviet of People's Commissars, other people's commissars, deputy people's commissars, and province party committee secretaries. All were sentenced to either the "highest measure of punishment" or extended prison terms. According to lists sent by the NKVD to the Politburo, approval was granted to repress 2,140 Ukrainian party and soviet activists in 1938 alone.

Through this system of merciless repression, all-encompassing political investigation, and government-induced informing, as well as through ideological influence, Stalinism tried to smother any "human" qualities remaining in the public consciousness. Whoever tried to develop independent political or economic attitudes was threatened with physical destruction. Manifestations of mercy or human feeling provoked confrontations with the punitive organs, which led to a readiness to carry out any order without argument, to accept any lie coming from the authorities without reflection. Deceitfulness, apathy, cynicism, and disdain for the individual abounded. The Stalinist system reared more than one generation of people prepared at any time to demonstrate their loyalty and devotion to the great leader, to anathematize and demand the deaths of those disagreeing with them.

Khrushchev was not a prime organizer of the repressions, but he actively carried them out. Not only did he fully implement directives, but he tried to distinguish himself by significantly overfulfilling arrest orders handed down from above. The system demanded no less from its nomenklatura, especially of such a high rank. In order to keep one's position, let alone move ahead, one had to demonstrate the qualities of a party organizer and an economic manager, and to be uncompromising with enemies of the party.

After the liberation of Ukraine from the Nazis, Khrushchev again concentrated on his work in the Ukrainian Central Committee. The main industrial centers of the republic had been destroyed during the war. Agriculture had suffered tremendously; cities and population centers faced an extremely difficult situation as the result of the cruel destruction of both housing stock and the infrastructure of light industry and food production. In addition, after the liberation of western Ukrainian lands from German troops, Ukrainian nationalist resistance to Soviet power grew rapidly. Initially, neither internal security troops nor army and police units could destroy the nationalist guerrillas. Harsh repression rained down on the civilian population, on those who aided the nationalists or were suspected of doing so. Khrushchev personally monitored the struggle with the nationalist underground; he personally gave the orders to destroy their leaders.

The first postwar years were also a time of repression of former Soviet prisoners of war, Soviet citizens deported by the Germans to Germany, individuals accused of cooperation with the occupying forces,
and Vlasovites—followers of Soviet general A. A. Vlasov, who, having
been captured by the Germans, tried to create an army of Soviet prisoners of war on the Nazi side. All these made up a majority of new political prisoners in the gulag. Several hundred thousand Vlasovites and
around two million former POWs and internees were sent to the camps
and special settlements. The first postwar years were also a time of
fierce struggle with nationalists in the Baltic republics.

In February 1948, Khrushchev approached the Politburo with a proposal to repress "harmful elements in the Ukrainian countryside." It is
difficult to say whether this was a personal initiative of his or part of a
planned struggle with the nationalist movement in the western
provinces of Ukraine worked out in the Politburo and the MGB. Khrushchev's letter may have been only the formal trigger for a plan that was
supposed to be implemented "at the request of the toilers of Ukraine."

Khrushchev's proposal was received by the Politburo on February
10, and the following resolution was adopted:

> 30. Comrade Khrushchev's Question. A Commission is to be formed
> consisting of Comrades Beria (convening member), Khrushchev,
> Suslov, A. Kuznetsov, Abakumov, Kruglov, Vershinin, and Safonov to
> work out questions of resettled individuals, administrative exiles and
> deportees, of the organization of special prisons and camps for espe-
> cially dangerous criminals, including spies, and also the question of
> exiling from Ukraine harmful rural elements, and to present its pro-
> posals to the Bureau of the USSR Council of Ministers.[7]

A corresponding decision was adopted by the Council of Ministers on
February 21. Additional documents regulated in detail the activities of
all services participating in the deportation, all the way down to the soldiers taking part. On June 2, 1948, the provisions of the resolution
adopted in accordance with Khrushchev's letter were distributed to the
western regions of Belorussia, the Baltic republics, and Moldavia.

Dry official statistics bear witness to the scale of this action. On January 1, 1949, 2,300,223 specially resettled persons were on the books.
Between 1949 and 1952, more than 200,000 people (primarily former
kulaks) were released from special settlements. Nevertheless, the population of the special settlements actually grew by more than 650,000

to 2,750,356. The overall number of those exiled by this decision alone approaches one million. Hundreds of thousands from western Ukraine, the Baltic republics, western Belorussia, and Moldavia, the overwhelming majority of them innocent, were torn from their native soil and sent by convoy to special settlements in Siberia, where they were deprived of their freedom. Many perished en route; many more died in their new settlements. An awful story, it is akin to the harsh punishments of whole peoples deported in 1944 and 1945.[8]

How are we to understand and explain Khrushchev's actions, actions of which he remains guilty even if we assume they were ordered by Stalin or the Politburo? Perhaps the example of one person who crossed Khrushchev's path several times during the 1950s and 1960s can help us understand Khrushchev's ambivalent attitude.

During the early 1950s a discussion on economic questions took place in the Central Committee. The discussion was secret; Stalin personally decided who would be invited to this restricted forum, basing his decisions primarily on his advisers' knowledge and level of professionalism. L. D. Iaroshenko, a Gosplan economist, a longtime party member, and a participant in the Civil War and World War II, was among those invited. Iaroshenko naively imagined that he could express his thoughts freely, that he could criticize anyone during the discussion as long as such criticism was objective.

Iaroshenko did speak critically about the draft of a textbook on political economy, expressing some unflattering judgments about the state of economics in the Soviet Union. Stalin was offended by this criticism, and he answered Iaroshenko. Afterward, Iaroshenko sent a letter to the Politburo in which he tried to defend his position. Soon enough, however, he was given to understand what the correct position was, and who held it. Whereupon, in a letter to Malenkov, Iaroshenko identified his own errors:

> In my letter to the members of the Politburo, I made a grossly serious error; on the question of the basic economic law of our society, I set forth a point of view at variance with that of Comrade Stalin. This is undoubtedly a gross error. For every party member, the opinion of Comrade Stalin is and must be an unbreakable law. . . . The organizer and director of the construction of socialist society, the inspirer of all our victories, embodies in his thoughts and actions all the theories and practices of our life necessary for the sole correct resolution of any and all questions. This was a ill-considered step on my part, a real mistake.

By way of explanation I can say that I made this error under the impression of the recently held discussion, although this of course is no excuse. Please forgive me this error.

The Central Committee turned Iaroshenko's action over to the Moscow city committee, which Khrushchev once again headed after his return from Ukraine in late 1949. Khrushchev lit into Iaroshenko for daring to express an opinion that did not agree with Stalin's view. Summing up a discussion of Iaroshenko's case at a party meeting, however, Khrushchev stated, "We are a strong, unified party. We will be magnanimous. We will not impose any penalties on Comrade Iaroshenko, but we will propose to the TsSU [Statistical Control Administration] that they employ Comrade Iaroshenko somewhere in eastern Siberia."

This resolution was adopted, and when Iaroshenko asked E. A. Furtseva the next day what he should tell the party organization at his new place of work, she told him that his errors had been discussed at the bureau of the Moscow committee and that no penalties had been imposed. With that Iaroshenko departed for Irkutsk. When he arrived there, however, the province party authorities acquainted him with a different version of the Moscow city committee's decision: he had long held hostile Bukharinist-Bogdanovist views on questions of political economy; he had expounded those views in a letter to the members of the Politburo; he had concealed his accomplices; he failed to aid the unmasking of the Bukharinite gang. These formulations of the Moscow committee, adopted after Iaroshenko had left the capital, foreshadowed harsh repression, and it soon followed. He was summoned back to Moscow, where in Khrushchev's presence he was exposed as involved in anti-Soviet and anti-party actions. After this "conversation," Iaroshenko was immediately arrested. Not only he himself was punished; so were his brother, who had no relationship whatsoever to economics, and his wife. His whole family was exiled from Moscow.

What does this episode tell us? That the Central Committee seriously scolded Khrushchev for his liberalism in the case. A quick comparison between the proposal he made at the Moscow committee bureau session and the new charges made after the Central Committee's intervention is enough to show how different Khrushchev's stand was from the Politburo's.

Iaroshenko was released from imprisonment at the end of December 1953, reenrolled in the party, and returned to work in his own field.

In a speech at a party meeting on the results of the 20th Party Congress, however, he condemned Stalin's personality cult in far sharper terms than Khrushchev had used in his speech. As a result, the Central Committee secretariat, including Khrushchev, voted to expel Iarshenko from the party again and to dismiss him from work. Under Stalin, Khrushchev had treated Iaroshenko's critical comments leniently, behavior that earned him a reprimand from the Central Committee and forced him to change his decision fundamentally, but in 1956 he sanctioned Iaroshenko's exclusion from the party for a similar speech. Nor does the intersection of Khrushchev's and Iaroshenko's fates end here. After the 22nd Party Congress in 1961, Iaroshenko was readmitted to the party yet again. By then he could no longer work and was in retirement, but there is no doubt that he could not have been restored without Khrushchev's assent.

The death of Stalin did not put an end to repression. Of course the post-Stalin pattern fell far short of the monstrous scale of Stalin's day, but the party leadership considered repression just and necessary—a natural condition, as it were. It was a vital part of the administrative system established after October 1917. All of Stalin's close associates fully shared his views on repression as essential. They fully accepted his so-called theory that the class struggle intensifies over time, and believed in the need to destroy the enemies of the party. To them, the unity of party and people meant complete obedience. They saw their main task as preserving their monopoly of power at any price. This task was accomplished not only through organizational work and the high art of conditioning the masses ideologically, but also by violence against disobedient and subversive elements.

Arrests, exile, confinement in prisons and in camps, and the destruction of millions of people—Stalin's associates did not necessarily agree with terror on this scale, but they did not protest against it either. Both rank-and-file party members and individual leaders began to doubt the legitimacy of the waves of repressions that periodically swept across the country. And with Stalin's death, this evolving awareness of the criminal actions being committed in the country accelerated significantly. But it did not immediately manifest itself in concrete actions.

Paradoxically, it was Beria, the party leader most involved in the repression under Stalin, who tried to position himself as opposed to violations of legality. Immediately after swearing allegiance to the fallen leader on Red Square, Beria called for observing legality and order. Only a few days later, he began criticizing Stalin within a small circle, and then to a broader audience.

One of Beria's first steps as minister of internal affairs was to expose the recent falsified case against prominent figures in Soviet medicine. He undertook to rehabilitate in a very public manner a small number of persons convicted under Stalin. Beria issued an order prohibiting the torture of suspects during the course of an investigation and established strict punishments for the falsification of investigations. Beria not only informed the senior party leadership of crimes committed by organs of state security but tried to distribute information about those facts as widely as he could in the party. On this basis, both native and foreign historians have come to see Beria as the first post-Stalin reformer, one who undertook the mass rehabilitation of victims of political repression.

Why did Beria do this? How are we to explain his position? Some say he was maneuvering to achieve supreme power, to increase his authority in society by all available means. For the sake of objectivity, let us assume that he was not the only one with such goals. It was just this struggle for power that caused the clash of opposing forces that lasted until 1957.

Beria was more mixed up in the crimes of the Stalin period than any other member of the Presidium. He headed the punitive organs for many years, personally participated in the torture of prisoners and the falsification of major political trials, and was personally guilty of destroying major party figures. It is precisely for this reason that he sought to escape responsibility, to erase the image of a butcher, a strangler of freedom, a torturer, and a bloody criminal. All Beria's acts were directed toward showing the party that Stalin personally controlled all punitive actions and that everyone else simply carried out Stalin's will: either you participated in bloody repressions or you would be destroyed.

Beria published the report of the Ministry of Internal Affairs on the falsified Doctors' Plot without the Presidium's consent. On his order, documents exposing the falsified Mingrelian affair (allegedly involving an attempt to overthrow Soviet power in Georgia by conspirators from the region of Mingrelia) were given to local party committees. His order prohibiting torture and false accusations was distributed to all republic, territorial, and province subparty organs.[9]

A few weeks after Stalin's death, Beria condemned the personality cult that had arisen in the party. Malenkov criticized the cult in general terms, without mentioning Stalin, but Beria framed the question in a starker and more clearly defined manner. Having toppled the idol, Beria planned to replace him. But Beria cannot be put in the same category as the other pretenders to leadership. He held in his hands a compromising dossier on every member of the Presidium, with the help of which he could have destroyed them all. He controlled an experienced apparat, bound to him by years of cooperation in bloody crimes. Most of the senior leadership of the MGB was entirely beholden to him, and its functionaries were overjoyed at his return to the post of minister of the MGB.

Beria strove to shift the entire responsibility for mass repressions to Stalin alone. After Beria's ouster, his former colleagues not only attempted to place this same responsibility on Beria; they also went to great lengths to excuse Stalin's actions as resulting from Beria's criminal behavior. In the spring of 1954, Leningrad party activists demanded that former state security chief V. S. Abakumov be prosecuted in Leningrad. In response, Khrushchev said he was not opposed, but he feared that Abakumov would place all the blame on the "old man," who could not defend himself. When Abakumov's trial took place, the state prosecutor presiding over the proceedings deprived him and his codefendants of the right to speak as soon as they tried to point in Stalin's direction. Although Abakumov was ready to expose Stalin's role in the Leningrad affair, the Doctors' Plot, and the affair of the Jewish antifascist committee, he was not allowed to do so.

It was very difficult for the Presidium to protect Stalin for long, however. As political prisoners were released, an enormous number of requests from relatives of former highly placed persons convicted in the years of the Great Terror poured into the Central Committee. Along with its Party Control Committee, the Central Committee was compelled to consider more and more applications for rehabilitation and generally to affirm them. Despite the increase in the scale of rehabilitation, however, the Presidium did not initially reconsider its overall attitude toward mass repressions. It was a only matter of rendering justice to certain individuals.

K. B. Bogomolova-Gamarnik was the sister of the purged Red Army general Ia. B. Gamarnik and had known Khrushchev in Kiev, where she had been a secretary of the party city committee. Having been deprived of her freedom for seventeen years, she appealed to Khrushchev in early 1955 to release her from exile. The request was delivered to Khrushchev, but the Central Committee refused her, explaining that the sister of an "enemy of the people" should serve her entire sentence.[10]

The Presidium also considered the case of a former Soviet ambassador to Great Britain, I. M. Maiskii, who was arrested several times between 1953 and 1955. A former foreign ministry associate had slandered Maiskii, which led to his arrest. In May 1953 the MVD established that all accusations against Maiskii were false, but he was not released. Considering Beria's support for the May reinvestigation of Maiskii's case, the new leadership of the MVD considered him one of Beria's protégés. In June 1955 the Presidium created a special commission on the Maiskii affair under the chairmanship of M. A. Suslov. The commission determined that Maiskii's alleged espionage had not been proven, but it also proposed sentencing him to six-to-eight years of exile without applying the March 27, 1953, amnesty to his case. A June 3, 1955, note to the Presidium signed by Suslov recommended that the court sentence Maiskii in connection with a full range of crimes, including his Menshevik activities during the years of the Revolution and Civil War. On June 13, Maiskii was sentenced to six years of exile by the Military Collegium of the Supreme Court.[11] A month later, however, on July 16, the Presidium decided to grant Maiskii mercy, releasing him from imprisonment and exile, and suspending the Military Collegium's June 13 sentence.[12]

In July 1955 a Central Committee plenum decided to begin active preparation began for the 20th Party Congress. One of the most important matters to be resolved before the congress was how to address the question of mass political repressions. In the fall of 1955, state security organs stepped up their reexamination of cases involving party and state officials convicted between 1936 and 1939. Gross falsifications of cases and methods used to coerce confessions were uncovered. As the wave of revealing materials rose higher, the Presidium was forced to actively consider falsified cases and to rehabilitate those who were innocent. In the fall and winter of 1955–56, extended and acrimonious discussions took place in the Presidium about how to inform the party congress of Stalin's crimes and abuses of power. By that time it was impossible to avoid the issue. But discussions were still confined to a narrow circle of party leaders.

Presidium members' attitudes toward Stalin changed noticeably as the congress drew near. On November 5, 1955, party leaders discussed the celebration of the coming anniversary of the October Revolution.[13] The question of whether or not to celebrate Stalin's birthday at the end of December also came up. In previous years, December 21 had been marked with ceremonial assemblies. This time, the Presidium opted only to note Stalin's birthday in the press.

At a December 31 Presidium session, a contentious discussion took place on the repressions of the 1930s, including the fate of delegates to the 17th Party Congress and of Central Committee members elected at that congress. A commission was created, chaired by P. N. Pospelov and including Central Committee secretary A. B. Aristov, trade union chairman N. M. Shvernik, and deputy chairman of the Central Committee Party Control Committee P. D. Komarov, to study the repression of Central Committee members elected at the congress, as well as that of other Soviet citizens between 1935 and 1940.[14]

Pospelov's commission completed its work toward the beginning of February 1956 and presented to the Presidium a report of approximately seventy typed pages that was heard at a Presidium session on February 9.[15] On the basis of the documents, the commission stated categorically that the cases of anti-Soviet organizations, blocs, and various centers allegedly uncovered by the NKVD were fabricated by investigators, who tortured prisoners. The commission's report also established that torture was personally sanctioned by Stalin, who had planned the terror against party activists and Central Committee members. A. I. Mikoyan recalls, "The facts were so terrifying, that while he [Pospelov] spoke, especially on particularly painful incidents, tears appeared in his eyes and his voice shook. We were all devastated; although we knew much of it, we of course did not know everything that the commission reported, and it was now all checked and proven with documents."[16]

Khrushchev put the question before his colleagues: "Will we find the courage to tell the truth?" Molotov, Kaganovich, and Voroshilov did not dispute the commission's findings but, considering it necessary to preserve Stalin's authority, opposed discussing the Pospelov commission's conclusions at the 20th Congress. Both at Presidium sessions and at the congress (and in Khrushchev's secret speech at the congress) he and other leaders claimed not to have known the full extent of the repressions, the methods of investigation, and the full role of Stalin, and a majority of party members accepted that claim. It represented a sort of collective guarantee for party members. Using this formula, each Communist could rehabilitate himself in his own heart and consider himself innocent of the bloody bacchanalia that shook the party and the country in the 1930s and 1940s.

In view of all the circumstances, Khrushchev's position on Stalin and Stalinism at the 20th Party Congress was an act of high civil courage. His secret speech, no matter what occasioned it, represents an unprecedented act of repentance for crimes committed by the leader of the party. Documents confirm both bitter Presidium disputes about Khrushchev's speech and ultimate agreement with Khrushchev's proposal. But no matter how high the level of collective responsibility may have been, no matter on whose behalf Khrushchev spoke, he was most responsible. It was difficult to predict the eventual outcome, but if it were unfavorable, he risked not only his political career but also his freedom and perhaps even his life.

Khrushchev may have been right not to speak of his own involvement in mass repressions in February 1956, especially considering that other Politburo members, more deeply involved in Stalin's crimes than he was, did not. A discussion of the role of those individual leaders might have distracted attention from the main purpose of the speech: to condemn Stalinism. But the party leadership feared the reaction of rank-and-file members to the facts and conclusions of Khrushchev' speech, and not without reason. The February 19, 1956, draft of Khrushchev's speech stipulated that the issue of the personality cult must not go beyond the party congress. His speech at the secret session of February 25 announced that discussions of the personality cult must not be allowed beyond the limits of the party as a whole, let alone in the press.

In fact, the party was not prepared for such revelations. For the majority of Communists, Khrushchev's admissions were unexpected. Since, moreover, nothing forced the leaders to admit Stalin's sins, why did they agree to have Khrushchev do so? According to A. I. Mikoyan's memoirs, Presidium members feared being held responsible for the crimes and were concerned that the congress could ask each of them what role he had played. Mikoyan therefore concluded that it would be better for the Presidium itself to discuss the repressions than to wait for someone else to bring the matter up. A speech on that subject, Mikoyan believed, could demonstrate to congress delegates that Presidium members had learned the whole truth of Stalin's crimes just before the congress, and only as the result of a special study by a commission they themselves had formed. That way, they could remove from themselves at least a portion of the responsibility for the terror of the 1930s.

Although the same sort of reasoning can be found in Khrushchev's memoirs, it would be a mistake to assume that only subjective motives determined his behavior and that of other Presidium members. In 1953 Soviet society found itself on the eve of a social explosion. Official propaganda clichés about the unbounded power and authority of the party, and the selfless devotion to it of the country's citizens, could no longer conceal the truth. Many millions of people had endured incredible privations and sacrifices for many years. The limit to their patience was approaching. The bulk of the population had already lost faith in the "shining future" promised by the party.

This process of disillusionment had accelerated during World War II. Even amidst war and destruction, life in the European countries was better than in the Soviet Union. The living standard of the defeated Germans was higher than that of the victorious Soviets. People could compare the achievements of Western civilization with Soviet reality. The participation of the Western allies along with the Soviet Union in a war against fascism began to pull aside the curtain concealing the rest of the world from ordinary Soviet people. Soldiers returned home from the front with a feeling of internal freedom. At the front, where party leadership was reduced to a minimum, they had greater freedom of action, including the opportunity to demonstrate personal initiative. Such conditions engendered freedom of thought, which could extend to judging the actions of the senior party-state leadership.

The Soviet system was based on Stalin's authority, on repression, on the fear that he so mercilessly and cruelly inspired. His death evoked an ambivalent response in society. On one hand, the loss of a seemingly eternal, deified leader created confusion, grief, and sympathy. On the other, Stalin's death weakened fear of the government. As a result, the system began to falter, and the population began to express dissatisfaction with existing conditions: the difficult material circumstances, the low standard of living, the severe housing crisis. The new leadership that came to power after Stalin's death realized that it could no longer run the country and preserve the regime with the former methods.

After Stalin's death, the crisis of Stalinism also gripped the countries of the so-called Soviet bloc. Soviet troops suppressed disturbances in East Berlin in June 1953. Major prison uprisings that flared up in the years 1953–1955 shook the whole gulag system. Army units and tanks were thrown against insurrectionists. Yet even after a broad amnesty granted in March 1953, more than 1,360,000 prisoners remained in the gulag on April 1, 1954. Some 448,000 were serving sentences for "counterrevolutionary crimes," and around 680,000 were incarcerated for serious felonies. Almost 28 percent of the prisoners consisted of young people under age twenty-five.[17] If and when these prisoners gained their freedom, the result could be huge social shocks. The Soviet Union needed fundamental reforms to preserve the essence of the existing regime. That was one of the most important reasons why party leaders undertook criticism of Stalin and Stalinism.

Wasn't Khrushchev also pursuing personal power when he denounced Stalin's personality cult? Certainly, Presidium members suspected that Beria would do so, that he would destroy documents attesting to his own personal crimes and collect materials demonstrating other Politburo members' misdeeds. And in fact Beria did not reveal details of the cases that the MVD was reviewing; he merely informed his colleagues of the results, which he tried to publish independently rather than under the name of the Central Committee and its Presidium.

After Beria was shot, Presidium members, by mutual agreement, immediately destroyed all the documents in his safe. Khrushchev claimed not even to have read the documents. Perhaps not, but there is no doubt that his assistants, in particular Ivan Serov, carefully studied them. Of all the Presidium members, Khrushchev was the only one who had a direct entrée into the Ministry of State Security, via its chief, Serov. It has been charged that while in power, Khrushchev oversaw the destruction of all or part of archival materials testifying to his own role in repressions. But explaining the circumstances under which the Moscow city and province archives were "cleansed" turns out to be very complicated. Several versions of what happened exist, all of them linked with Khrushchev in one way or another. But no one I talked to could document his or her version.

Did Beria really intend to use this information incriminating his colleagues in his struggle for power, or were Molotov, Kaganovich, Malenkov, Khrushchev, and Mikoyan alarmed about nothing? To judge by documents that have been preserved in archives, Beria had not yet taken any such action. But the possibility that he would do so was so great and so threatening that Presidium members had good reason for their fear. Beria was not the only one who could use Presidium mem-

bers' complicity in Stalin's misdeeds in the struggle for power. A. I.
Adzhubei, editor of *Izvestiia* and Khrushchev's son-in-law, admits that
"elements of the power struggle" were involved in the process of exposing Stalin's crimes.[18] But although personal ambition helped determine Khrushchev's actions, more fundamental was his overall attitude toward Stalin's abuse of power and mass political terror, an
attitude that was reflected in the way he set about liquidating the consequences of Stalinism, liberating Stalin's victims from the camps and
prisons, and restoring their honor and dignity.

On Khrushchev's insistence, the Central Committee took extraordinary measures to accelerate the release of political prisoners from
camps and exile. On March 24, 1956, the Presidium of the Supreme Soviet adopted a decree "On the consideration of cases of individuals serving sentences for political, work-related and economic crimes." Special
commissions of the Supreme Soviet Presidium and the Central Committee were then formed, each of which was assigned to visit one of the
camps and to release then and there those convicted without foundation. Each commission included one of the old Bolsheviks, drawn for
the most part from those recently rehabilitated. Each commission was
authorized to acquaint itself with each prisoner's case and to check the
charges against their personal explanations.

K. P. Chudinova describes the work of the commission in the Kar-
gopolsk camp, where 383 political prisoners were confined: "Among
those convicted under Article 58 were former German police collabo-
rators, participants in punitive brigades, and participants in gangs that
armed themselves in territories freed from Hitler's troops and killed
Communists and Soviet workers. But there were also many convicted
only for the aid they were forced to render the *banderovtsy* [followers of
the Ukrainian nationalist leader Stepan Bandera] or other nationalists,
who were not in essence enemies of Soviet power."

The camp also held those convicted of anti-Soviet agitation during
the postwar years. The fifty-year-old Shargorodskii got ten years: his
poem dedicated to Stalin contained the line "He alone does not sleep,
and his pipe has gone out." The extinguished pipe was interpreted as
indicating a negative attitude and a slander against Stalin. The metalworker Sibirev got ten years "for praising foreign technology." Fedosov
got the same sentence for the same thing. Bashirovogly was convicted
of terrorism when, in 1946, he wrote a letter to Stalin criticizing the
leader of Azerbaidzhan, M. D. Bagirov, for his rude attitude toward

workers. The case of Cherkashin, a Komsomol member and petty officer on a navy cutter, is characteristic. During his studies in a political circle, he asked a question about relations with Yugoslavia. For that he was charged with "justification of the treacherous policies of Tito, slandering one of the Soviet leaders, discrediting measures of Soviet power designed to construct Communism." In the case of Loginov, convicted by a special assembly in 1950 for anti-Soviet agitation, there was no evidence at all confirming any accusation, but he got ten years. "As a result of the reexamination," Chudinova concluded, "our commission liberated 251 individuals. None of those convicted in 1937–38 remained in the camp."

Similar work was conducted by all the other commissions, and as a result, in a short time, hundreds of thousands of political prisoners were released and returned to their homes. Alexander Solzhenitsyn, who himself was in a camp, credited Khrushchev with having a profound spiritual impulse that led him to release so many from the camps. His action did indeed bear witness to the sincerity and depth of his attempts to expiate the authorities' guilt for Stalin's crimes.

From the very beginning, however, the rehabilitation of victims of political repression was not popular among the nomenklatura and some party members. This was especially true of those who in the recent past had been actively "unmasking" their comrades at work or writing slanderous denunciations, either under pressure from state security workers or of their own free will. With hundreds of thousands of people returning from the camps and exile, Anna Akhmatova tried to imagine how the two Russias would meet each other—the one that had done the imprisoning and the one that had been imprisoned—and how they would look each other in the eye.[19]

I think the great poet was referring to encounters not only between individuals but also between that mass of former prisoners who had survived the camps and the power that had sent them off to torments and suffering. That power might now be represented by different functionaries, but it remained in essence the same and resented the pressure from above that forced the liberation of two camps. It did not take much time for these new functionaries to show the face of the old power, the face of the old rulers.

From the very beginning of the process of rehabilitating victims, the party apparat put up active resistance. Correspondence between KGB Chairman Ivan Serov and General Prosecutor R. A. Rudenko, dating from April 1957, is revealing. Serov explains to the prosecutor that it is impossible to check on the correctness of the sentences of people repressed in the 1920s and the first half of the 1930s:

> If we proceed from the formal circumstances (lack of necessary evidence that was not collected during the investigation), then in resolving questions about these cases, we might make a gross error by rehabilitating actual criminals.
>
> All this might lead to a series of undesirable consequences of a political, legal, and economic nature. First of all, actual enemies of the Soviet state might be rehabilitated, and along with them other individuals who committed crimes but were brought to justice on related grounds. Second, incorrectly rehabilitated individuals (those who remain living or relatives of the deceased) will undoubtedly develop a certain viewpoint about those around them. Third, wrongly rehabilitated individuals will illegally receive compensation from the state for the value of their confiscated property and all corresponding rights associated with the fact of rehabilitation.
>
> The need for a mass reexamination of archival-investigative cases from the years 1937–38 has been occasioned by the established fact of the violation of Soviet legality in investigative work. We do not have such data at our disposal about cases from the 1920s and early 1930s, and we therefore have no basis for reexamining these cases on a mass scale.

As a result of this correspondence between Serov and Rudenko, the question of rehabilitating victims of the 1920s and first half of the 1930s was struck from the agenda by the prosecutor's office and the KGB as late as April 1957.[20]

Many limitations on the rehabilitation of victims of political repression in the 1930s were established by party organs. In its summary for 1956, the Party Control Committee noted that its reconsideration of cases had identified people who had spoken against the party in defense of the opposition during the period of bitter struggle with the Trotskyites and right opportunists. There had been no basis for bringing these people to trial, but at the time they were correctly expelled from the party. The Control Committee refused to accept such individuals back into the party, and they consequently did not receive full rehabilitation.[21]

In the bitter atmosphere of 1956, an attempt was made to put the brakes on the whole process of rehabilitation. This came about when Khrushchev's speech denouncing Stalin sparked harsh criticism of the party at party meetings. Speakers demanded the removal of monuments of Stalin, the renaming of cities and streets, and the punishment of those guilty in the mass repressions, including leaders who had worked closely with Stalin. Confronted with this turmoil, the Central Committee resorted to harsh measures in order to regain control of the situation. On April 5, 1956, the Presidium adopted a resolution "On hostile statements about the results of the 20th Party Congress at the meeting of the party organization of the USSR Academy of Sciences Thermal Technical Laboratory." At that meeting, the young scientist Iu. F. Orlov had called for democratic transformations in the country; three people supported him, and their presentation was greeted with applause. When the presidium of the meeting demanded that their statements be condemned, more than a third of those in attendance voted against the proposal. The Central Committee expelled the offending speakers from the party, disbanded the laboratory's party organization, and assigned the district party committee the task of re-registering party members, retaining "in the ranks of the party only those who are in practice capable of conducting the general line of the party and struggling for the execution of the decisions of the congress."[22]

In June 1956 the Central Committee published another resolution, "On the personality cult and its consequences," establishing strict limits for criticism of Stalin and Stalinism. In July of the same year, the Central Committee sent a confidential letter to all party organs and primary party organizations informing them of repressive measures including the prosecution of individual Communists and party organizations for "incorrect" discussion of the decisions of the 20th Congress.[23] The letter warned that "some Communists . . . are not able to determine when freedom of discussion exceeds the limits of *partiinost'*, and the criticism turns into slander." The party did not need such "Communists."

The June 30, 1956, Central Committee resolution raised the question of party leaders' personal responsibility for mass repressions: "Why did no one in the upper leadership try to remove Stalin and put an end to the terror?" According to the letter, no one could have opposed Stalin since "whoever had opposed Stalin in those conditions would not have received support among the people." The confusion and dismay of those in power is evident in this awkward self-justification by Stalin's former comrades. As if it had ever occurred to them to oppose Stalin!

The system of power that existed in the country was shaken as soon as the slightest freedom of speech was allowed in the party (but not in society as a whole), and members of society thought of trying to gain their democratic rights, which were formally guaranteed in the constitution. On December 19, 1956, the Presidium adopted the text of a letter to party organizations, "On strengthening the political work of party organizations among the masses and ending the attacks of hostile anti-Soviet elements."[24] The Stalinist argumentation used in the letter testifies to the Presidium's position and the mood of its members. The letter ends with well-defined instructions: "The Central Committee emphasizes with special force that we cannot have two opinions about how to struggle with hostile elements. The dictatorship of the proletariat must be merciless to anti-Soviet elements. Communists in the organs of the prosecutor's office, the courts, and state security must keep a sharp eye on the interests of our socialist state. They must be vigilant in searching for hostile elements and, in accordance with the laws of Soviet power, must put an end to criminal actions in a timely manner."

These instructions were carried out without delay by the punitive organs, the courts, and the prosecutor's office. Party leaders themselves offered an example. Within two weeks after the 20th Party Congress, Central Committee secretary Shepilov gave a speech at the Central Committee Academy of Social Sciences on the results of the congress. During the discussion, some Communists went too far in criticizing the Stalin personality cult. Shepilov sent a memo about these comments to the Presidium and the Secretariat.[25] Appropriate measures were quickly adopted. Professor B. M. Kedrov (subsequently an academician) was expelled from the Academy, and philosophy instructor I. S. Sharikov, an invalid from the war and a party member since 1931, not only was expelled from the Academy but spent several years in a camp for political prisoners. And this occurred within an institution that was an extension of the Central Committee itself.

In 1956 a discussion group of young Leningraders, headed by Revolt Pimenov, was arrested and convicted, as was a group of young instructors and graduate students at Moscow State University, headed by Lev Krasnopevtsev, a year later. In 1958 it was the turn of S. Pirogov's Moscow group, and in 1960 the editor of the journal *Sintaksis*, Aleksandr Ginzburg, was arrested. And there were more.

After the Central Committee's December 19, 1956, letter was distributed, a wave of arrests and harsh sentences swept the country, in which Communists and non-party members lost their freedom for "slandering" Soviet reality and for "revisionism." In the first months of 1957 alone, several hundred people were convicted as criminals, and the arrests continued throughout the following years. Not all those arrested were sent to prison. A no less miserable experience awaited those who were not: the psychiatric hospital. In February 1964 General Piotr Grigorenko was arrested for speaking out at a party meeting and for distributing leaflets that offered his view of current events. After his arrest, he was subjected to medical "evaluation" and declared psychiatrically not responsible for his actions. Grigorenko spent six and a half years in psychiatric hospitals. He was kept in special isolation units of the KGB under the guard of officers from Lefortovo Prison.[26]

Grigorenko was arrested for distributing "fabrications" insulting the Soviet state and social order that he knew to be false. These charges, like those made against thousands of other Soviet citizens, were totally trumped up, but those so accused were nevertheless subjected to harsh punishments. The Party Control Committee expelled from the party P. I. Gudzinskii, a Bolshevik since 1919 and a senior engineer. During a party meeting following the 20th Congress, he "slanderously asserted that the party and the country, over the course of 30 years, have undergone a very dark period, that this history was not condemned at the 20th Party Congress, and that the speech on the personality cult at the 20th Party Congress 'did not teach anything to the party.'" In fact, Gudzinskii's "slanderous" statement repeated almost verbatim the conclusions reached by Pospelov's commission on the eve of the 20th Congress: "in the half-century history of our party, there have been pages of great suffering, but there was no more difficult and bitter page than the mass repressions of the years 1937–38, which nothing can justify."[27]

After the 20th Congress, repression likewise fell upon those who had only recently been released from the camps. According to the December 19, 1956, Central Committee letter, "among those returning, there are some maliciously disposed against Soviet power, especially among former Trotskyites, right opportunists, and bourgeois nationalists. They gather anti-Soviet elements and politically unstable individuals around themselves and try to renew their hostile anti-Soviet activities."[28] In carrying out instructions from the Central Committee, local party organizations and judicial and punitive organs dealt harshly with people who had previously been imprisoned for many years. According to the Leningrad party leader Frol Kozlov, a group of newly rehabilitated former political convicts was expelled from the party once again and exiled from Leningrad.

Unfortunately, party and punitive organs moved from repressing individuals to mercilessly shooting peaceful demonstrators. Blood flowed in Tbilisi right after the 20th Party Congress, where some inhabitants participated in a meeting dedicated to Stalin's memory on the third anniversary of his death. Troops opened fire on the participants. Dozens of people were killed and hundreds injured, and a large group arrested. Criminal proceedings were brought against them, with many being convicted and sentenced to one to ten years in prison.[29]

It was not only in Tbilisi that military force was used. An even greater tragedy played itself out in Novocherkassk. In connection with an increase in the wholesale and retail prices for meat and dairy products, a strike spontaneously broke out in early June 1962 among workers of the Novocherkassk Electric Locomotive Factory. In a demonstration before the factory administration, the workers demanded, "Meat, milk, increase in salary." The next day, workers and members of their families marched in a column toward the center of the city to express their complaints to Central Committee Presidium members who had arrived in the city. It was a peaceful demonstration with red flags at the head of the main column. People bore portraits of Lenin and fresh flowers. On the way downtown, a large group of young people joined the demonstrators. When the thousands-strong crowd approached party headquarters, Presidium members Kozlov, Kirilenko, and Mikoyan, who were in the building, related the situation to Khrushchev in Moscow and requested permission to give an order through the defense minister to break up the demonstration with the help of the military. As soon as the demonstrators reached the building, an order was given to open fire on the unarmed people. Shots rang out.[30]

Twenty people were killed on the spot, including two women. Eighty-seven people were hospitalized with wounds; three of them died. The fearful lesson taught by the authorities in Novocherkassk did not end with this, however. Mass arrests of so-called "disorder ringleaders" began. In all, 116 people were held responsible for the Novocherkassk turmoil. Seven were shot, and many others were sentenced to extended prison terms, from ten to fifteen years.

Afterward, a meeting took place between the personnel of the Novocherkassk garrison and the subunits of the internal troops and

Frol Kozlov, now a Presidium member and Central Committee secretary. In the name of the Central Committee, the Soviet government, and Khrushchev personally, he gave high marks to personnel that took part in dispersing the demonstrators and expressed gratitude to the troops for the courage they showed.

The events in Novocherkassk were a watershed moment in punishing any popular manifestations of dissatisfaction with living conditions, including severe food shortages. Harsh suppressions of worker demonstrations took place in other cities, including Aleksandrov, Murom in Vladimir province, and Temirtau, where troops put down protests mounted by workers and other residents. Conditions became more severe for political prisoners as well. In 1962, all camps were switched from a standard regime to an "intensified" one, and in the fall of the same year, they were switched to a "strict" regime, making camp life even more severe.

Thus a two-tiered process developed in relation to political repressions. On one hand, victims of the 1930s and 1940s were rehabilitated. On the other hand, camps for political prisoners filled up with more and more new faces; and in certain cases, courts handed down capital sentences, with the Presidium's agreement. These two contradictory processes could not exist simultaneously. One of them had to collapse. Sure enough, the process of rehabilitation began to wind down. After many thousands of cases had been considered in the Party Control Committee in the years 1956 and 1957, the number of rehabilitation cases decreased sharply. In 1962, only 117 cases were examined. In addition, 25 percent were refused rehabilitation or restoration to the party.[31] In 1963, fifty-five cases were considered, of which seven were refused.[32] Active rehabilitation thus lasted for eight years, from 1954 to 1962, and it ceased completely in 1965. The process of intensive rehabilitation was renewed only a quarter of a century later, toward the end of 1987.

After the October 1964 Central Committee plenum, which ousted Khrushchev from office, the Party Control Committee examined forty-eight cases that had arisen earlier for political reasons. "It was established while examining these applications that certain Communists, in their speeches at party meetings or more frequently in letters addressed to the Central Committee and local party organs, had expressed their dissatisfaction with the leadership of Comrade N. S. Khrushchev. All these expressions were evaluated as anti-party at the time, and the extreme form of party punishment was applied to them: exclusion from the ranks of the CPSU." Having examined these cases, the Central Committee restored to the party all those who had made such statements.[33]

In the early 1980s, the Politburo restored V. M. Molotov to the party. He was rehabilitated on all counts, was personally received by the general secretary of the party, and was allowed to publish in the press. Such gestures of forgiveness or rehabilitation were not made toward Khrushchev. By an irony of history, it was Khrushchev, not Molotov, who ended up an anti-party figure in the eyes of the Central Committee.

5

Khrushchev and the Countryside

ANATOLII STRELIANYI

In March 1953, immediately after the death of Stalin, Nikita Khrushchev became one of the secretaries of the CPSU Central Committee. In September, he was already proposing a plan for improving the condition of the countryside that would have done honor to any Communist functionary of the time. Simply recognizing the miserable condition of the countryside constituted a revolutionary step. Khrushchev was the first to say what everyone knew but no one even dared think: that people in the villages lived badly, in abject poverty; that they were even worse off than people in the cities; that they were worn out by practically unpaid labor, taxes, and extortion; that they did not want to live on the collective farms; that they were actually fleeing them in all directions, despite the fact that collective farmers were required to remain on the land and were deprived of internal passports.

The measures Khrushchev announced were simple and understandable to everyone: pay collective farmers more, reduce taxes, write off back taxes, and increase the size of individual peasant plots. Some of these measures were included in Georgii Malenkov's speech at the August 1953 session of the Supreme Soviet. The people were also promised that the development of light industry would be accelerated. The economic decisions of 1953 were among the most important of those taken during the period of "collective leadership" between 1953 and 1957.

The results of these simple but quite practical measures, which did not question the basis of socialist agriculture, were felt immediately. By 1956 agriculture had achieved unprecedented rates of development. Before Khrushchev, increases in the yield of milk were measured in kilograms. Under Khrushchev, the figures in many places rose to centners (one hundred kilograms). In Ukraine in one winter (1955–56) the yield of milk doubled compared with the previous winter and increased by 65 percent in the country as a whole.[1] "Soviet power has never seen such growth in the production of milk in all its history," rejoiced Khrushchev.[2] Over these three years thousands of collective and state farms increased the production of milk and meat by a factor of two or even three.

With a vindictive feeling Khrushchev recalled his recent battles with such people as Molotov, who believed that a lessening of pressure on the countryside would provoke a drop in discipline and thus in production. His plans had seemed impractical to Malenkov as well. "What can be said now to those friends?" Khrushchev later gloated. "Who looks like a fool? They look like fools."[3]

He decided that it would be possible to achieve even more. To do so, he thought it necessary to introduce corn everywhere. Khrushchev declared corn cultivation to be the party's most important task.[4] He shook his finger at those who applauded in response to his hymns about corn but planted it sparingly, merely in order not to stand out, as if saying, "Just leave us alone!"[5] And he began stubbornly extending the border of the corn belt to the north of the old line of Kiev-Sumi-Kharkov-Rostov. First it was raised to Orel, then to Moscow, and then even farther. "This year we will definitely grow corn in Yakutia, and maybe even in Chukotka. Will potatoes grow there? They will. It seems to me that even corn will grow."[6] When at his command the corn belt took over the zone of the white nights as well, Khrushchev decided that everything would now be in order as far as fodder was concerned, and he cast his glance in the direction of the United States.

When Khrushchev announced the Soviet Union had "entered into a competition with the world's richest capitalist country," something about "impractical Red schemes" appeared in Western newspapers. Wounded by this, Khrushchev ordered his economists to figure out exactly when the United States might be overtaken. The economists responded: 1975. In that year, the Soviet Union, moving at the then-current rate, would have increased the production of meat by 3.2 times and would have achieved the same level as the Americans. But for the moment, the year was still 1957.[7]

Around the country, however, corn was already making good progress. It was planted in Udmurtii and Chita, in Arkhangelsk and Vologda; mighty stalks of the "queen of the fields" were brought to Moscow to show to Khrushchev. Khrushchev presumed that all this promised mountains of feed for livestock, so he decided to throw down a challenge to his cautious economists. They had referred to 1975; in response he used words that terrified the ten people in the country who understood them: "In the next few years."

At a well-attended agricultural gathering in Leningrad, he talked about those economists who "presented a paper and affixed their stamp," to the effect that catching up to the Americans earlier than 1975 was out of the question.[8] The hall erupted in laughter. In it were several hundred of the best specialists, the stars of the Russian northwest who "seemed to agree" with Khrushchev that there was reason to laugh. To carry out collectivization in two to three years, and industrialization in ten, but then to spend twenty years catching up with the United States in meat production? Those economists are simply illiterate, the people in the hall probably thought. No, "from the point of view of arithmetic, there is no mistake here," said Khrushchev, "everything is proven. But, comrades, it is necessary to understand what kind of forces have built up among our people . . . . After all, you see that many collective farms have in literally two to three years increased production by several times. What sort of arithmetic calculations can be applied to this? This is politics, this is a political phenomenon. . . . The power of the collective farm system, the patriotism of the Soviet people, and socialist competition will allow us to decide this task in the next few years."[9]

His decision to abolish mandatory deliveries of produce from collective farmers' private plots after January 1958, a decision that he had made in haste, met with applause in the hall and with jubilation across the whole country.[10] In the life of the rural family this decision caused great changes. Getting rid of the burden of payments in kind immediately gave such families greater freedom in their financial decisions; at least on their own plots of land, people became more or less their own master.

Thus did the task of catching up with the United States within the next few years in per-capita stock-raising become an official economic and political task for the country. All collective and state farms were supposed to publish their plans on this topic. Khrushchev took particular care to see that there would be no shortage of patriotic zeal in the population. Without getting fancy, he created an image of the enemy, using the typical colors, emphasizing only the fact that Uncle Sam was terribly alarmed by the agricultural plans of the Soviet Union.

At the end of 1959 Khrushchev announced at a Central Committee plenum that state purchases of meat from collective and state farms had increased by 36 percent.[11] Did he know where this growth was coming from? Many farms bought up animals from the population; also, without thinking about tomorrow and urged on by the party apparat, they slaughtered underfed young animals and sometimes even nursing cows. If he did not yet know about this, he would soon. But for the time being he welcomed the successes: in Riazan province, for example, where 100,000 tons of meat had been sold to the state instead of the planned 50,000 and the people had committed themselves to fulfill three plans within the next year; and in Tula and Lipetsk provinces. And he criticized those lagging behind. Briansk province, for example, promised to sell 51,000 tons but sold 21,000, less than in the previous year.[12] There were many such provinces. If things were to go that way everywhere, he warned, "not only will we not provide the country with agricultural products, we will eat up everything that we have."[13] He read aloud letters from the Far East, where meat had appeared in stores in anticipation of his visit, only to disappear again after he left, and he spoke about the worsening supply of milk and meat to Kharkov, Dnepropetrovsk, Gomel, Rostov, and Cheliabinsk provinces, as well as to Georgia and Kazakhstan.[14]

Here for the first time he urged, although not very loudly, that impossible promises not be made.[15] He was almost afraid to acknowledge that practically all the targets had been and would continue to be fashioned out of thin air. After all, they would otherwise not be so high, yet he was the first to demand that they be raised.

The tone in which he talked about corn began to change and become erratic. Khrushchev already knew that for the district and provincial party authorities, only one thing was important: that the corn be planted. Whether or not it would grow and could be harvested was unimportant. There wasn't enough money or labor for the struggle with weeds and for getting in the harvest. Vast experience in fakery and peasant savvy was put to use. Corn that had died beneath the weeds began to show up in reports as having been used as feed for grazing animals. More and more frequently, Khrushchev read the riot act to sycophants, smart alecks, and loafers from the commanding ranks of the party, but just as before, there was not enough grain in the country, grass yields did not increase as expected, and the fodder base for livestock remained low. Where could they get grain? Since 1954, the Virgin Lands had been cultivated in Kazakhstan, Siberia and in the Altai region, but that had not solved the problem. He called a meeting of leaders of East European socialist countries and ordered them flat out not to depend on the Soviet Union for feed grain, to moderate their demands, and to rely more on their own resources.[16] Denying them fodder, he advised them to plant more corn, as the United States and Soviet Union were doing: "Corn is the most powerful, the strongest resource in the improvement of animal husbandry."[17] He urged them not to stand on ceremony with the conservative-minded peasant: "We have acted for the most part by convincing the people; we have demonstrated the benefit of this crop with concrete examples. But when we have to, then here and there we have compelled people to grow corn."[18]

Khrushchev persistently and probably nervously sought out reserves of feed production. Again and again he looked closely at Ukraine.[19] Ukraine planted ten million hectares of corn, but that made little sense. Something else had to be done. But what? "It would be good to make an appeal on behalf of the party and the government to collective farmers, workers on state farms, equipment operators and specialists in this area, so that the best people can undertake the cultivation of corn."[20] The reliance on patriotism, on propaganda, and on educational work with people was typical.

Khrushchev turned his attention to some six million hectares of fallow lands in humid areas of the country. No one was utilizing them properly; they were just empty. They had to be plowed and planted with corn. In the east, in an area of inadequate moisture, there were another six million hectares of fallow land. Agronomists argued that these lands had to remain fallow, so that they could accumulate moisture. Khrushchev did not agree with them. If the fields were planted with a vetch-oats blend, or with corn, then "it would be possible to obtain a great mass of feed for livestock."[21]

The year 1960 dealt the most serious blow to Khrushchev's plans since 1953. In a number of republics, the production of meat actually declined. In October he wrote a note to the Presidium of the Central Committee, warning that "if necessary measures are not taken, then we may regress to the situation in which we found ourselves in 1953."[22]

The population was dissatisfied with the food supply. It was now impossible to ignore mass fakery in the deliveries of meat and dairy products. Not long ago, Khrushchev had congratulated Riazan province for fulfilling three years' worth of plans: he held it up as an example for the others and awarded the Gold Star to the party first secretary, Larionov. Khrushchev did not want to admit that he had been dealing with a big-time fraud and swindler. People had been warning that not everything was "clean" there, and now it was clear that tripling output was a fantasy.[23] Finally Khrushchev demanded that such warnings be checked out, and "resolutely condemned instances when certain workers recklessly make up obligations, trumpeting them with all their might."[24] He exclaimed sadly, "Why should we resurrect the worst that we had before?"[25] Nor were things going well in the Virgin Lands or Kazakhstan; the total amount of livestock was not growing, animals were not gaining weight—and officials were pleading a shortage of feed. There was a massive decline in the number of sheep in the country. "Sheep are literally dying before our eyes on many collective and state farms. . . . A disgraceful state of affairs!"[26] Georgia had lost one of every ten sheep. Milk yields were falling, cows were slaughtered for meat, "young animals were rapaciously cut down."

The whole autumn Khrushchev prepared his report for the Central Committee plenum, which was to take place in January 1961. Nothing occurred to console him or others; no miracle happened. He called provincial party authorities and summoned the first secretaries. They could say nothing reassuring and asked that he slip them feed—as if he had been growing the stuff himself! "Leaders of the republics, regions, and provinces are explaining why their commitments have been unsatisfactorily fulfilled. Explanations can be found for the bureaucrat, but not for the population."[27]

The fact that they, leaders of all ranks, were beginning to speak more and more boldly about the unfulfillable tasks that he had set them alarmed and bothered him almost more than the failures. "If someone tries to prove that there is no possibility of a drastic improvement in animal husbandry and of meeting the needs of the population of the Soviet Union for those products, then he is an unfit leader."[28] Struggling with defeatism, Khrushchev would revert to extreme measures—he would remove unsuitable leaders. "Given our natural conditions, our expanse of lands, and, most important, our economic possibilities, only the politically bankrupt can claim we can't provide meat and dairy products for the entire country."[29] Officials like that should resign; the party was strong, and there was no shortage of people; "Young leaders will show their capabilities."[30]

Khrushchev kept searching for crops and technical innovations that would help young leaders do what the old leaders had not managed to do. He turned his attention to beets. The chairman of the collective farm in his native Kalinovka in Kursk province told him it was easier to get four hundred centners of sugar beets per hectare than two hundred centners of potatoes. And four hundred centners of beets constituted 14,400 fodder units, whereas two hundred centners of potatoes was only 6,000 units. Then came peas, and then beans; he discovered the great value of all of them.

Khrushchev also outlined measures to rectify the financial and economic situation of agriculture. In 1958, at his initiative, the Machine Tractor Stations (MTS) were liquidated. These were state enterprises that had been performing basic mechanized field work, regulated by contracts with collective farms. The collective farms compensated them in kind—with grain and other agricultural goods. But on the face of one earth, as brave publicists wrote, there existed two masters with contradictory interests. The collective farm was interested in harvesting crops and in minimizing its own expenses for the harvest. The MTS was interested in completing as much work as possible and receiving as much grain as possible for it. The prices set by the state for the services of the MTS were extremely high, so many collective farms ended up indebted to the MTS. The liquidation of the MTS could have corrected the problem, but their machines that were sold to collective farms were priced very high, and collective farms had to pay for them over exceedingly short periods of time. They were made to do this by none other than Khrushchev: the state needed resources, and the damage done to the nation's budget from the liquidation of the MTS had to be compensated. Immediately after the liquidation of the MTS, high prices were set for new machines, spare parts, and motor fuel for collective farms.

The situation on collective farms began to worsen noticeably. Indirectly acknowledging the causal connection with MTS reform, Khrushchev outlined a series of serious measures: reduced prices on spare parts, gasoline, and automobiles; lower taxes; the granting of repayment extensions to those who still had not paid for machines purchased from the MTS; and a reduction of credit rates.

In a harsh and candid report at the January 1961 Central Committee plenum, Khrushchev remembered to mention the United States. The Soviet Union had to catch up with America, and it would do so despite all difficulties and obstacles. That same January he said, "Some of you may wonder why we are talking today about the possibility of catching up with America in the per capita production of meat. . . . No, comrades, we must talk about this; the Communist Party of the Soviet Union, and all of our people, are certain not only that we will catch up with America but that we will surpass it."[31] As for the decline in agricultural production over the past two years, it had occurred "not because opportunities were lacking, but because certain leaders got a swelled head. And a swelled head is a great evil. . . . Cheats, fakers, irresponsible chatterboxes—these are the most evil enemies."[32] They must be contrasted with friends of all that is new and progressive, those who make up the avant garde of the struggle for meat and milk. Perhaps a "Golden Book" or a "Book of Universal Honor" should be established, which would include those who are catching up with America.[33]

Khrushchev took no weekends or holidays off during all of 1961 but traveled around the country, working as if it were wartime, sending urgent messages to headquarters, to the Central Committee Presidium. In the winter he was supposed to go to a meeting of agricultural workers in Voronezh. Learning of their lofty guest's impending visit, the people there began to take the usual measures. Just before his departure from Moscow, he received a letter from a railroad worker about what sort of measures they were. It turned out that in the region where an atomic energy station was being built, there was a lot of corn left unharvested. With the help of the head of the railroad station, a state farm official hooked a rail up to a tractor and began to flatten the field, so that the corn standing unharvested in the field would not be visible from the road leading to the atomic energy station. The railroad worker's letter was checked and confirmed. Upon his arrival in Voronezh, Khrushchev demanded an explanation from the first secretary of the provincial party committee, Khitrov, who answered that such was their method of cleaning up the stalks of corn.[34]

"Can it really be true that we can't find people to decide this question correctly?" Khrushchev had exclaimed several years previously at another meeting, depressed by the fact that people continued to dislike corn. "Whoever does not agree can get up and express his point of view."[35] No one stood up in his presence, either then or later, but one voice was heard nevertheless. When Khrushchev spoke with particular indignation about the neglect of corn in the most blessed places in the country—on the Don, in the northern Caucasus, in Ukraine—someone shouted: "They are afraid of crops that require weeding between the rows!" These were the sort of words that Khrushchev should not have hurried to answer, but hurry he did.[36]

There was not one person in the hall who did not understand the terrible truth of these words. Beets, sunflowers, potatoes, and corn were among the crops that required such weeding. In contrast to cereals, such crops had to be protected from weeds all summer; otherwise there would be no harvest. They could be weeded with herbicides, by machine, or by hand, with special chopping knives. But there were no herbicides, there were few machines, and millions of hectares could not be handled with chopping knives. As for corn, in many places there was nothing with which to plant it, and harvesting it was difficult; there were not enough combines. Under such conditions, crops like these were a great risk, and it was no wonder that collective farm chairmen sought in every way to avoid them. To the person who yelled, "They are afraid of crops that require weeding between the rows!" Khrushchev responded instantly and in such a manner that subsequently no one dared to speak up. He said that only bad Communists were afraid of such crops—those who thought of themselves and not of the needs of the country.[37]

Khrushchev ordered that detailed information be prepared for him upon his return to Moscow. First of all, he wanted to know how matters actually stood in the fields: it turned out that however much it was sown, corn remained unharvested all around the country. Second, what was going on with the machinery? Several years before, he had quietly asked Gosplan about this; someone there had reassured him: agricultural machinery was completely sufficient. And since it was sufficient, he had not objected when Gosplan began to close agricultural machine-building factories, one after another. The Zaporozhe combine factory had been transformed into one manufacturing second-rate light machinery.

In Moscow he immediately sat down to read over the prepared information. The picture was gloomier then he could have expected. In 1957, 55,000 corn combines had been produced, but in 1960 only 13,000. Nothing had been demanded, nothing had been checked, and therefore nothing had been done. He had asked that corn cultivation be expanded—and so, creakingly, it had been. He had always been certain that he personally was managing agriculture, but the information showed that for all these years, each person had gone his own way. Even corn, despite all his pressure, had been neglected. In Kostroma province, oats, and grasses made up 54 percent of all crops, while corn constituted less than 2 percent. In Moscow province, which Khrushchev knew inside out, they had also done as they wished. In 1958, hoping to get more grain from the east, Khrushchev released Moscow and all the other non-chernozem regions from the obligation of submitting grain to the state. Let their grain remain on the collective and state farms as fodder, he thought. It worked out differently. The non-chernozem zone immediately cut back the production of grain. In Moscow province the sowing of grain was reduced by 42 percent as compared with 1953, and they stopped planting buckwheat. Instead of those crops they began to plant annual grasses that required no work or worry. The area devoted to them increased fourfold but yielded a paltry quantity of hay: nine centners per hectare.

It was agony for Khrushchev to read this information. It showed that he had been too hasty when, soon after increasing investment in agriculture, he had reduced the value of these investments by raising prices and taxes. The order to make these increases had been neither written nor spoken, but it had been fulfilled better than anything in writing. He now undertook a series of meetings with various provincial leaders. Their changed attitudes were strikingly clear. Two consecutive years of failures had sobered them noticeably and had forced them to be braver. Up to that point, they had been certain that the most important thing demanded of them was big promises and individual examples of well-managed affairs; that Moscow, in the form of Khrushchev, did not expect real results; that he and they were performing a kind of propaganda show, intended in part for domestic consumption but basically designed for the West.

But to Khrushchev himself, this was no show, but actual work; not a game of "catching up with and overtaking America," but a real effort to do so. Now Soviet officials experienced bewilderment and resentment. The 1961 plans they received from Moscow for the obligatory sale of agricultural products to the government required them to make up the shortage of the last two years; Khrushchev himself insisted that this be done. Everybody understood that the game was up. It was necessary to work; but at the same time, hard as one tried, such a plan could not be fulfilled. An unfulfilled plan, however, would mean that their careers were over. They complained that he was asking the impossible of them, and he responded: "We must struggle not to preserve the existing level of production, but for its universal improvement. Anyone who does not understand that doesn't understand anything of the policy of our party."[38]

Even as the top man in the country, Khrushchev looked at things from the perspective of the people, as if he were the most typical, ordinary collective farmer: the bosses were to blame for everything, and he experienced genuinely hostile feelings toward them. The idea came to him of moving the Ministry of Agriculture out of Moscow and into a nearby village—from the asphalt to the earth.

During his vacation in the south, Khrushchev by chance found out that the system of payment in kind for collective farm labor had ended, a system to which the collective farmers had grown accustomed under Stalin. At that time it had been the only system, and it existed for awhile under Khrushchev as well. Then it changed all by itself. Required sale of agricultural products to the government got so high that collective farm leaders were forced to reduce their spending on "internal economic needs." Khrushchev reacted in one of his memos to the Presidium: "We must never ever convince collective farmers to refuse additional [i.e., in kind] payment and to receive money instead of goods. One must conduct oneself honestly; one must strengthen the trust of the collective farmers. We must live not only for today."[39] Even in this text, which was not intended for publication, he did not call a spade a spade, but he pretended to believe that someone was persuading collective farmers to receive money instead of products. After seeming to reestablish payment in kind with one hand, he then and there withdrew his generous offer: "Of course, if collective farmers voluntarily opt to receive additional payments in cash, then they should be given them in cash."[40] The end result was that collective farmers expressed that "voluntary" wish all the way to the liquidation of the Soviet Communist party.

Khrushchev realized that under his tolerant regime, the technical basis for agriculture had been undermined, and that he had placed too much faith in agricultural propaganda: "If all we do is call on people to cultivate corn and sugar beets, and to go over the 'herringbone system' of milking cows [an approach to group mechanical milking of cows, which Khrushchev also actively propagandized], but we do not arrange to produce corn- and beet-harvesting combines, and milking and other machines, then we will wind up being simply windbags. One cannot call for high labor productivity and cut down corn with axes."[41] He was no longer pleased by people who promised in a fanatical and obliging

way to expand the sowing of corn endlessly: "I cannot object to this as-
piration, but I would like to give you some advice—first of all, learn to
reap the biggest harvest from every hectare."[42]

On the other hand, he could not reconcile himself to the fact that after eight years of persistent effort, despite an unheard of propaganda
campaign on behalf of corn, people continued to prefer grasses. He
seemed to understand that the reason lay in the shortage of machinery,
but at the same time he felt that peasant conservatism was involved,
along with scientific dogmatism. He had in mind the so-called grassland system of farming of the Stalinist academician V. R. Williams,
which was introduced under Stalin; it represented a shoddy imitation
of certain extensive systems of virtually medieval farming, against
which the most prominent scientific specialists in the area of farming,
such as N. M. Tulaikov, had struggled—and paid for their efforts with
their lives.

Williams taught that half of the plowed land should be set aside for
perennial grasses, and that only spring grains should be sown. But
Khrushchev worked for thirteen years in Ukraine, where, from time
immemorial, spring crops did not grow as well as winter ones. It was
only with great effort that he managed to restore winter crops there. He
had nothing against Williams ("That was a man close to us," Khrushchev said about him),[43] but he needed grain, he needed reliable and
large harvests. Explaining his approach, he cited the Ukrainian saying:
"We are poor people, we are uneducated people, just tell us what we
need to know to make some dough." The ideological defeat of the grassland system, on behalf of which the print media, radio and television,
film and theater were all mobilized, was accomplished in several weeks;
it seemed complete and definitive, and the term "grasslander" became
a bad word.

Now the struggle could be transferred to the fields. Here Khrushchev displayed the caution that he had forgotten when he introduced
corn. He said that farmers could not just plow up all the grass un-
thinkingly. In order to use the earth languishing beneath pure fallow
lands and grass, collective and state farms would have to be equipped
with more technology. But provincial and regional party leaders undertook to destroy the sowing of grasses just as zealously as they undertook to do anything recommended by Moscow that did not demand
a lot of work and that could be accomplished by decree and crude pressure.

All these years Khrushchev had wanted to bring order to the fields and to the farms, to rationalize the collection of cultivated crops, and to introduce more livestock. This signified, however, nothing less than an effort to create a new and unprecedented kind of agriculture: to replace one civilization, the civilization of grass and fallow lands, with another, immeasurably greater one, the civilization of corn and other similar crops; to do this starting from practically nothing, without the necessary machines, fertilization, and herbicides, without roads, without dependable backup in terms of storage and supply facilities or production of feed mix; and most important, to create it on a command basis. Notes of harsh self-criticism (even though he said not "I" but "we") sounded in his speeches in the 1960s (which for him, as we know, consisted of not quite four years), but he never expressed the slightest doubt about the feasibility of this task under these conditions and with these capabilities.

At the start of the 1960s he reconsidered his opinion on mineral fertilizers. He discovered that the West Germans used one ton per hectare and the Americans more than one and a half centners, whereas the Soviet Union was scattering a mere handful, and not even correctly at that. Until that point, however, he had taught his cadres that mineral fertilizers were expensive, that it took a long time to establish their production, and that it was therefore necessary to gamble on expanding the sowing of corn. He put together a fantastic set of economic relationships. Instead of mineral fertilizers, corn. The quantity of livestock would quickly be increased with corn. And "with the increase in livestock, the accumulation of manure will grow. And this route to increasing fertilizer production is much easier and cheaper than the construction of factories for the production of mineral fertilizers. Moreover, nitric and other mineral fertilizers can in no way substitute for organic fertilizers."[44]

Khrushchev's well-known American farmer friend Roswell Garst was no longer paying attention to manure, however; it was a lot of trouble for little benefit in comparison with artificial fertilizer. When they told him that Khrushchev had introduced corn without fertilizer, he flatly refused to believe it. Even when he saw it with his own eyes in the Kuban region, he did not believe that it was happening with Khrushchev's knowledge. "What are you doing?" he screamed at everyone in the field, trying to stop the seeding machines. "I am going to complain to Khrushchev! You cannot plant corn without fertilizer!"[45] This outburst made an impression on Khrushchev. After thinking for a minute, the Soviet leader began to explain himself: he had always understood the role of mineral fertilizers, or so he said, but the country did not have the resources to build chemical factories.

The more Khrushchev traveled around the country, and the more he tried to draw the people and the party cadres into undertaking great tasks, the greater the lying, servility, and irresponsibility grew. He paid no attention to the obvious cause: the tasks that he was putting before agriculture were not feasible under the given sociopolitical conditions and the given system. Khrushchev did try to institute a program of managerial reorganization in March 1962. The goal remained the same—the construction of communism; that had just been included in the new party program. As a result, the task of catching up with the United States in per capita production of basic products was not removed from the agenda. He calculated that in order to do so, it was necessary to produce seventy-five tons of meat per hundred hectares of plowed land and sixteen tons per hundred hectares of arable land. According to him, the most important thing, which had so far been insufficiently achieved, was the concrete, knowledgeable management of production. He reached that conclusion as the result of his disappointment with cadres. "The time will come when we will train leaders such as comrades V. M. Kavun, G. E. Burkatskaia, and I. M. Semenov in all collective and state farms. [Kavun, Gurkatskaia, and Semenov were famous, truly talented collective farm chairmen.] Then the functions of management will change fundamentally. It will clearly boil down to working out general patterns, and to giving orders for the production of products which the country and our people need. Right now such a situation does not exist. Right now you look at one person and are pleased, but you try to bring someone else around and get nowhere."[46] (Characteristic of Khrushchev's administrative-utopian thinking is the conception that the center can, without difficulty, determine the volume and structure of consumption and "give orders" to agriculture).

Here we approach an issue that historians and journalists have evaluated in a way that Khrushchev would not have liked. The key feature of the reorganization of agricultural management he undertook was that managerial structures were created that were supposed to bypass district party committees. As Khrushchev described his plan, the new structure would not be "a district level organ, but will be invested with the substantial authority of province, region, or republic organizations."[47] It was supposed to be called a "production administration," and it would itself have a small party committee. The territory that it covered would, as a rule, be larger than a district. Districts, consequently, were subject to enlargement, and district party committees to liquidation. Previously, district party committees had directly managed all life on the territory they governed—primarily agriculture, of course, if it was an agricultural locality. Khrushchev decided that this combination of a political and an economic-managerial role was no longer rational. The separation of these roles should be expressed in the development of a new governmental organ—a so-called production administration. It was through this organ that the party would henceforth implement this line.

Until that point, the vertical structure looked like this: the CPSU Central Committee Presidium→the CPSU Central Committee→the presidiums and central committees of the republics→the province party committees→and, finally, district party committees, which dealt directly with the collective and state farms. Now instead of the district committees there appeared these production administrations, whose staff consisted exclusively of agricultural specialists, to each of whom was assigned one or several collective or state farms.

Khrushchev's current well-wishers see this reorganization as an effort by the Soviet leader to weaken party authority in relation to the countryside, so as to pave the way to democracy. But this was not the case. In fact, the idea was really to "improve" command or, as Khrushchev persistently emphasized, to render party (that is, his) leadership more concrete and businesslike. The vertical structure of Presidium→Central Committee→province committee→district committee broke down (as had been the case from Lenin's time on) in its approach to any enterprise, be it a collective or state farm or a factory enterprise. The enterprise was directed not by the party committee but by its own director, in accordance with the principle of one-man management. (On the collective farm the position of chairman was formally an elected one.) It had not occurred to anyone, however, to suspect Lenin of intending to weaken the leading role of the party in the society building communism through such a breach in the vertical structure.

At the same time that Khrushchev was reorganizing the management of agriculture, it became necessary to raise the price of meat. The people were outraged, and in Novocherkassk workers took to the streets and were fired upon; not only this crime, but the very existence of the disturbances was carefully covered up.[48] It is unlikely that a person could really take such steps if, in the depths of his soul, he did not want a further strengthening of the power of the party, and consequently of its apparat.

In October 1961 the new party program was adopted, accompanied by an extremely intensive propaganda campaign, in which the party solemnly proclaimed that the current generation of Soviet people would live under communism. It was this very idea that justified the further strengthening of the party's leading role in society. For an ideological person, for a convinced Communist like Khrushchev, such assertions in the party program could not be just empty words. Moreover, in October 1961, at the 22nd Party Congress, Khrushchev and delegates prompted by him attacked Stalin and Stalinism with greater force and passion than in 1956 at the 20th congress. And one of their most serious accusations, which had been leveled against Stalin in 1956 and was repeated again now, was that he had reduced the role of the party and had placed state punitive organs above the party. (Incidentally, it did not occur to anyone that that was the way it should be, in a certain sense, in a government based on law).

The same applies to Khrushchev's November 1962 division of provincial party committees into industrial and agricultural branches. There is no reason to detect any motives or goals other than those which he himself had so frequently expounded. The division of provincial committees was one of the last efforts, not to weaken, but to strengthen the party's supervision of agriculture. The creation of provincial party committees exclusively for agriculture was merely implementing the idea of specialization in Soviet terms. Khrushchev wanted the party's agricultural branch to focus harder on village affairs than ever before. We should remember as well under what conditions this whole reorganization was undertaken. Agriculture was in a deplorable state; all the ideas and programs, all the "panaceas" Khrushchev had supposed would raise agriculture to American heights, had met with failure. He had focused entirely on technology and the organization of production—not on politics, the political struggle, or political problems. To put it even more narrowly, he had reduced matters to what to cultivate, and how.

So circumscribed had been his thinking that he had no room for concern over the party's extreme authoritarianism. Nothing in his field of vision told him that the party was taking on too much, that it was rendering any initiative of the lower classes impossible, and that it was not allowing, for example, trade-money relations to develop. On the contrary, he thought that the party was taking on too little, providing only general guidance, and that it was spreading itself too thin when it should be concentrating on the resolution of very concrete economic and technological problems. "How many and what kinds of crops should be sown on 100 hectares of plowed land in order to receive 150 centners of meat? . . . 8 hectares of corn for a harvest of 500 centners, 3 hectares of sugar beets for a harvest of 250 centners, 2 hectares of peas for a harvest of 30 centners, 2 hectares of fodder beans for a harvest of 200 centners of silage mass."[49] This is what occupied his mind while at work, on the road, or on vacation.

It is true that Khrushchev demonstrated the ability to reconsider some of his opinions, but which ones? It turned out that corn could not be queen of the fields everywhere. "In the arid regions of southern Ukraine and in certain other republics, we must carefully determine which grain is more beneficial to cultivate: winter wheat or corn. . . . We did not swear forever by one particular crop, we do not intend to bow down to it. . . . The crop that gives the greatest harvest and better rewards the work that has been invested in the conditions of a particular zone should be considered crop number one."[50]

Khrushchev's reformism consisted both of a rejection of the Stalinist terror and at the same time the assertion that this terror had contradicted Marxist-Leninist teaching. For a person whose entire political life had been spent under Stalin and who had himself been a part of the highest—terrorist!—leadership, this was an enormous step forward, from which began the death throes of communism on a worldwide scale. Yet to Khrushchev's current well-wishers this does not seem like much, so they ascribe to him intentions that exceed even those of Gorbachev.

It is worth looking closely at the widely held view that Khrushchev consciously picked a fight with the party-state apparat, a stance that, so the argument goes, ultimately defeated him. The people who subscribe to this view are influenced by Khrushchev's frequent blunt statements about bureaucratism and bureaucrats and his general distaste for bureaucracy, which he frequently, and in a colloquially rude manner, contrasted with the "toilers." But in criticizing bureaucratism and contrasting bureaucrats with the working classes, Khrushchev was not original. He was following a tradition established under Lenin and firmly entrenched under Stalin. Just as Mao would do, Stalin thoroughly frightened the bureaucracy from time to time and, when he felt it was necessary, moved from words to action without hesitation. Khrushchev actively participated in one such episode after the war, namely, the repression of members of the lower party-state apparat, of bureaucrats who saw to their own personal supply of products while taking care of business on collective farms. This form of collective farm–state farm "hospitality" exists to the present day. If Khrushchev later distinguished himself with his attacks on the apparat when he was in power, his attacks were less severe than Stalin's. Usually he restricted himself to verbal reprimands and relatively inoffensive practical measures.

Immediately after Stalin's death, the "collective leadership" (in which Khrushchev did not yet have a deciding voice) launched a struggle against bureaucratism. The initiator of the struggle "until a complete victory has been won" was none other than Malenkov, recalls one of the apparatchiks, F. Burlatskii. Malenkov was highly belligerent; he called for the rebirth of a part of the state apparat, while condemning the party apparatchiks' "complete scorn for the needs of the people." Burlatskii describes the great assembly in the Central Committee at which Malenkov said such things. The representatives of the apparat were crushed. It was then that Burlatskii heard the "lively and, it seemed to me, merry voice of Khrushchev: 'All this is, of course, true, Georgii Maksimilianovich. But the apparat is our fulcrum.' And only then did friendly applause break out, which did not quiet down for some time."[51]

The Bolsheviks were practical people (if one does not consider their belief in such an impractical thing as communism), and they knew how to get things done. In 1953 Khrushchev saw to the weakening of administrative pressure on the countryside, and he encouraged discussions about planning from below; something along those lines even took place. But even then he did not hesitate to use coercion, that is, to use the apparat in an overt manner to advance the very same corn we have been talking about or his other technological ideas and innovations—nor did he hesitate to share his experience with the leaders of the Eastern European countries. Khrushchev's relations with and attitude toward the apparat depended directly on the successes of agriculture. While things were not going too badly, relatively speaking, he had no particular complaints about the apparat, and he gave the countryside considerable room for initiatives and independence. But as soon as failures occurred, Khrushchev stopped playing at democracy. One recalls, for example, how he took away the non-chernozem regions' freedom to choose whether or not to produce grain. And one notes a curious dialectic that was completely natural for Khrushchev: the failures in the countryside set him against the apparat and bureaucratism and at the same time against the independence of collective and state farms. He strengthened simultaneously his criticism of the apparat and its role in agriculture.

In 1963, when it was no longer possible to conceal from himself, from the country, or from the world that the attempt to lift agriculture to the American level in just a few years had failed. Khrushchev began to prepare a special Central Committee and governmental decree. "In this decree," he announced before it was even promulgated, "the 'administrationism' and corruption of previously adopted decisions on the planning of agriculture are condemned."[52] He and everyone else knew what that meant. During Khrushchev's years in power, many decrees were indeed adopted that formally provided for a great deal of economic democracy. But the apparat was not and could not be governed by them in practice; otherwise, it would not have been in a position to implement any of Khrushchev's decisions, instructions, or wishes. It is impossible even to say that Khrushchev tried to transfer the blame from himself to the apparat. There was no need to do so: it went without saying that he was primarily trying to understand and somehow correct his own mistakes while using the corresponding speech formulas and techniques that had been developed over the years of Soviet power.

In contrast to Khrushchev's contemporaries, historians do not always understand this correctly. Some, for example, take literally his words about apparat resistance to his reforms, particularly in the area of agriculture, and the apparat's corruption of his plans. But the truth is that such resistance was insignificant and almost subconscious. Both Khrushchev and the mechanisms and traditions he inherited were such that they would not have endured any perceptible opposition.

Just what was the apparat? It included the Central Committee, union-republic central committees, and regional, provincial, and district party committees. It was also the regional committees of the trade unions and the Komsomol, plus government ministries with their local subunits—for the ministries of agriculture, of agricultural deliveries, of agricultural machine-building, etc. How was their resistance expressed? Did they really hinder Khrushchev from extending the sowing of corn up to the White Sea in the north and to Iakutia in the northeast?

No, they did not hinder it; it was the corn itself that did not want to grow there, whereas all these apparats pretended as best they could that it was growing well. Did they hinder Khrushchev from liquidating district party committees and splitting provincial committees? Again, no. With great reluctance they undertook to fulfill one of the last of his decisions—the liquidation of fallow lands and the reduction of the grassland; but even in this, they ultimately outdid themselves. The apparat even dealt with such difficult and dangerous things as the destruction of villagers' private plots.

Historians confuse "active resistance" and "frame of mind." There was not and could not be real apparat resistance to Khrushchev's policies regarding the countryside; on the contrary, the apparat demonstrated all kinds of zeal, and often the apparat's initiative was the real key. As for the frame of mind, over time it indeed became increasingly critical and gloomy, not only in the apparat but in all strata of society. Perhaps the apparat became somewhat more angry than other groups because of its impotence; despite all its wishes, it was not capable of achieving what Khrushchev needed, and therefore winning his favor. But lack of love for Khrushchev did not keep the majority of apparatchiks from being in agreement with all his attacks on and measures against the truly oppositionally minded sector of the intelligentsia.

Lest one sin against logic and facts, it must be said that the apparat's loyalty to Khrushchev is confirmed primarily by the agricultural failures and the fall in the output of food products. If the apparat had delayed in carrying out such decisions as the liquidation of fallow lands, the harvests would have been greater. Nor can it be said that there occurred any large-scale or deliberate reductio ad absurdum of Khrushchev's ideas. Overall it was the opposite: so far as was possible, the apparat, in particular the lower part, adapted them to real conditions; otherwise the results would have been even more deplorable. We must not forget for a moment that the leaders and specialists of collective and state farms constituted the most important part of the bureaucratic, managerial, party-state (call it what you will) apparatus. Innumerable facts attest that at least this part of the apparat acted in a well-defined way; it willingly adopted and implemented any sensible undertaking by Khrushchev, and, as much as it could, it slowed down everything irrational, smoothed it over, and adapted it to the demands of common sense. There are not the slightest grounds for supposing that this remained a secret to those in the district or provincial committee, or to the

Central Committee members, or that it could be done without their agreement.

Khrushchev gave many examples in his speeches of apparat or bureaucratic bungling. In Dnepropetrovsk province the first functionaries to come along, often completely insignificant people, were put in charge of growing corn. A certain supplier named Osipov came to a collective farm, ordered the corn, which had not yet reached milky ripeness, to be cut down, and took off. When asked what he had done, Osipov calmly explained: "They told me in the province to go to the collective farm and to force them to cut the corn for silage. And that's what I did."[53] But there were many more—or at least no fewer—facts of another kind, when administrators and bureaucrats of all ranks, and particularly district and farm leaders, demonstrated a sensible, creative approach, which often required courage and ingenuity. The press wrote a great deal about them after the removal of Khrushchev, but everyone connected with agriculture knew all about this even in his time. Not only were failures and the real reasons for them hidden from Khrushchev, but intelligent people did not dwell at great length on the real reasons for their successes in his presence. When Khrushchev praised the young, talented, collective farm chairman Vasilii Kavun for the fact that he was able to grow peas, which supported high levels of meat-milk production, it did not even occur to him that, in addition to the peas, Kavun was able to grow the grasses that the Central Committee's first secretary hated so much and store them "underground"; corn and beans were sown along the road, but out beyond the range of vision were the grasses.

Although he thought he was disappointed in the apparat, Khrushchev was actually disappointed in the creative possibilities of what under Gorbachev would be called the command-administrative system. The model Khrushchev proposed for agriculture resembled a good factory and a good military unit. Having heard enough about the disorder in the Virgin Lands and about the barbarous relations to technology there, he quickly and easily outlined a project resembling a paramilitary phalanstery: "We must secure technology for the brigades, secure land for them. . . . The whole structure of work in the brigade, as well as agrotechnology, must be developed by the agronomist with the participation of the brigade. The established order of work in the brigade must be law. No one can violate this order. With such an organization of affairs we can guarantee a good harvest." At the end of 1961 he continued to stand by his ideas: "You know, when an attack is being prepared, first of all the people are trained. . . . Generals and officers must teach the soldiers the solution to the task at hand. . . . When the battle has begun, success is decided by the soldiers who have entered the battle with the enemy. That's how it is with agriculture, too."[54] If such was the case with agriculture, then the most important thing was the selection of cadres for training and management of collective-state farmers, first and foremost the chairmen of collective farms and directors of state farms.

Some historians maintain that Khrushchev was defeated in a one-on-one struggle with the apparat after being abandoned by the people. But this is not so. Rather, his removal was the practical result of a classic feature of the Soviet system, of the inevitable failure of noneconomic methods applied by the powers-that-be in their relations with agriculture. The difference was only that this practical result was experienced for the first time by the leader of the country. Toward the end of Khrushchev's rule, so much farm produce was being requisitioned through coercion and "administrationism," the personification of which was Khrushchev, that output could not grow unless requisitioning was at least partly replaced by a tax in kind. I am not resorting by chance to these terms from the days of NEP, the "new economic policy" of the 1920s. I remember well how often the term "tax in kind" (*prodnalog*) was heard in secret conversations of collective farm chairmen, and of district and provincial party secretaries in Khrushchev's last year, and how often it cropped up in letters to the Central Committee and the editors of central newspapers. Immediately after Khrushchev's removal, measures were adopted that did not amount to a tax in kind, that is, a transition to the primarily economic methods of managing agriculture, but moved in that direction. And these measures ripened under Khrushchev in the innermost depths of the apparat—just like those which Khrushchev himself had adopted when he first came to power. Leonid Brezhnev, replacing Khrushchev, basically did what Khrushchev had done when replacing Stalin: he began by liberalizing economic life.

The question arises: could Khrushchev (already seventy years old) have moved along this path if he had remained in power? The answer might seem to be: why not? After all, he had done this ten years earlier. At that time it was none other than he who proclaimed with such force the NEP principle of material interest. Nevertheless, we probably have to answer the question in the negative. It is noteworthy that after these ten years, he did not once recall NEP, even in the most difficult moments. From the perspective of an orthodox Communist, NEP was an equivocal era in Soviet history, which Khrushchev probably did not allow himself to remember. Some revisionist-minded economists carefully but persistently argued that Lenin had not considered NEP a deviation, that his characterization of NEP as "serious and long-lasting" signified "forever," that NEP principles (the permitting of private property and particularly of trade-money relations—that is, of major elements of the "market") should be used right up until the victory of communism. These people could lead others astray, but not Khrushchev, who had experienced NEP himself. For Khrushchev, NEP was a retreat, a policy from which movement was possible in one direction only—that of Communism.

Khrushchev was an honest person with a developed feeling of responsibility. The party promised communism to the people when it seized power in 1917, and in adopting the new party program, it established a definitive period of time for the fulfillment of that promise: twenty years. To return to NEP would have signified a rejection of that goal and a violation of the new program, yet loyalty to the program, as was written in the statutes, was a mandatory condition of party membership. Khrushchev treated his own membership in the party seriously. If he had rejected the construction of communism—that is, if he had ordered that this theme be removed from the agenda in ideological work, or if he had even moderated his resolve to work "in the Communist way," to plant the sprouts of communism, even without expecting the completion of the structure—he would not have been removed, and he could have ruled for as long as he wanted. As Brezhnev did.

Brezhnev and Kosygin, heads of the new "collective leadership," accused Khrushchev of subjectivism, voluntarism, despotism, self-praise, and other things. None of these words had anything to do with reality. Only one accusation would have been accurate—that Khrushchev preserved his loyalty to Communist ideals and in complete seriousness wanted to build communism, to build it together with Brezhnev and Kosygin, with all the "collective leadership," with the party-state apparat, with all of the Soviet people, with the moral support of all progressive humankind. This was the essence of Khrushchev's conflict with the apparat. Using all his strength, Khrushchev forced the apparat to build communism (to put an end to village inhabitants' private plots, for example, as Lenin had requested back in 1919); but it was not that the apparat was not willing to do it, just that it did not work out. The apparat felt the frightening resistance of life, but what could Khrushchev have advised or ordered?

"The most important thing is that party organizations are not working to learn the condition of the cadres and to replace worthless, backward leaders. Right now these cadres are drying up the collective and state farms." This was how he explained at the very end the fact that many collective and state farms had not moved an inch during the entire ten years of his work. "Let's select the Davydovs [men like the hero of M. Sholokhov's book *Virgin Soil Upturned*, a Communist worker who became a good chairman of a collective farm], the Grachevs [like the chairman of a collective farm in Kalinovka, Khrushchev's native village]. If we do, I am certain that in one to two years the collective farms will be transformed."[55] This was his response to the apparat's question, What is to be done? The entire country was asking the same question at that time.

The word "nomenklatura," introduced into Western languages partly thanks to M. Voslensky, signifies the party-state bureaucracy in the countries of the socialist camp.[56] It contains not only an evaluation (a negative one) of the bureaucracy but also a sort of explanation of the plagues and crimes of socialism in these countries. Such use of these words, emphasizing the nomenklatura in the study and interpretation of Soviet reality, contributed of course to the undermining of the unproductive and inhumane social system. But in essence this was the same "struggle with bureaucratism" that Lenin fervently pursued, as did Khrushchev, in a more intensified form. "If anything will destroy Soviet power," Lenin wrote, "it will be bureaucratism." Following the leader, all those who were not indifferent to the issue of socialism and communism repeated this phrase, people all the way up to Gorbachev.

Bureaucratism, bureaucracy, the apparat, the nomenklatura, officialdom—this was how the Leninist party, and the masses following it, explained all the failures on the path they were exploring. For the masses, it goes without saying, someone was to blame—whether an individual enemy, or a whole class, or a social stratum—for everything bad; it was not so difficult to understand and accept the Leninist explanation. The latter prevented or blocked doubts about the Communist ideal itself, about the very possibility of building a classless, noncommercial, and at the same time flourishing society. When Western propaganda, relying on Western Sovietology, aroused in the Soviet person ill feelings toward the apparat and the apparatchiks, toward bureaucracy and bureaucrats, toward the nomenklatura and *nomenklaturisty*, to a certain extent it followed the channel of Soviet internal propaganda. The influence of both these currents of propaganda is still felt in the attitude of certain historians, journalists, and memoir-writers and, probably, in the general view of Nikita Sergeevich Khrushchev and his era.

6

Industrial Management and Economic Reform under Khrushchev

WILLIAM J. TOMPSON

For a generation after Nikita Khrushchev's removal from power, the conventional wisdom among Western—and, much later, Russian—scholars regarding Khrushchev's handling of industrial management and economic policy was relatively simple: the Khrushchev period was all but a dead loss as far as economic reform was concerned; the failure to undertake reforms was largely the result of Khrushchev's lack of enthusiasm for, if not outright hostility toward, such ideas; and this failure to introduce more economically rational forms of management must be regarded as a lost opportunity.[1] Abraham Katz's assessment of the period accurately reflects this viewpoint. Summing up the Khrushchev years, he writes that "the principal contribution was undoubtedly the flowering of economic thought, which was partially the result of destalinization and the end of the terror, partially fostered deliberately by the leadership itself." He goes on to mention, among other secondary "achievements," the fact that Khrushchev, by his failures, discredited once and for all solutions based on party activism, administrative reorganization, and "direct voluntaristic action," which had been "an inherent tendency in the system since war communism." By setting unrealistically ambitious economic targets, he argues, Khrushchev inadvertently intensified the search for new economic solutions.[2]

The conventional wisdom is half right. There was no serious attempt at economic reform in the Soviet Union until after Khrushchev's forced retirement, and Khrushchev himself was largely responsible for this. Where the conventional wisdom has gone wrong is in the belief that this omission was necessarily something to be regretted. The failure of subsequent attempts to create a reformed communism and the collapse of communism in Europe attest to the dangers of trying to graft elements of the market onto a command economy. Far from offering the best of both systems, the resulting hybrids proved neither success-ful nor stable. Khrushchev's reluctance to set out down the reform Communist path must be seen somewhat more charitably in this light.

Why No Reform under Khrushchev?

At first glance, Khrushchev's failure to undertake some sort of eco-nomic reform is somewhat surprising. He was, after all, an innovator by both temperament and conviction. During his eleven years in power, he demonstrated a willingness to experiment in almost every sphere of policy, from agriculture to education to foreign affairs. The results of his innovations were decidedly mixed, but his willingness to adopt new approaches to the problems facing the Soviet Union set him apart from both his contemporaries in the post-Stalin leadership and his immedi-ate successors. This openness to innovation was all the more remark-able for having survived the ideological rigidity of the late Stalin period, when new thinking could be politically, if not physically, dangerous.[3] It might appear surprising, therefore, that the first real attempt at eco-nomic reform in the Soviet Union had to await his downfall.

To say that there was no economic reform under Khrushchev is not to say that economic policy was stagnant: there were significant changes in industrial administration, investment priorities, and plan-ning. What was missing was an attempt to enhance the role of specifi-cally economic levers, such as price and profit, either in drafting state plans or in regulating enterprise behavior—an attempt to change not simply economic priorities but the very rules by which the system op-erated. This failure is all the more surprising given that these issues were widely discussed in the 1950s and early 1960s in academic insti-tutes and specialist journals, at Central Committee plenums, and even in the popular press.[4] Indeed, even before 1953 economists such as Ev-sei Liberman had sought to build on the wartime experience of simpli-fied planning and the use of incentive schemes to enhance the role of profitability in guiding enterprise behavior.[5] This was the one field of economic thought that had not stagnated in the 1940s, chiefly because its aim was to strengthen enterprise self-finance (*khozraschet*), an ac-ceptable theme even under Stalin.[6]

Although proposals for planning reform do not appear to have made much headway politically, microeconomic (enterprise) reform was discussed at the highest levels, and a number of Khrushchev's colleagues in the leadership publicly supported it.[7] Khrushchev himself addressed the issue rarely, but his comments suggested that he was at least open to the idea.[8] Moreover, he was clearly concerned in the early 1960s with the very issues that the reformers sought to address: productivity,[9] technical innovation,[10] improved quality,[11] and the elimination of the stultifying effects of excessive bureaucracy and inflexibility in economic administration.[12] Ironically, all these priorities reflected the fact that as the Soviet Union grew richer, resource constraints—and hence the need to improve efficiency and productivity—were becoming more rather than less important. This reflected the shift from "extensive" growth, based on the mobilization of additional factors of production (land, labor, and capital), to "intensive" growth, based on improving the efficiency with which these factors were employed. This shift led to a heightened concern with concepts such as relative scarcity and opportunity.[13]

The question, then, remains to be answered: Why was there no enterprise reform under Khrushchev? It might be suggested there was significant political opposition to the idea and that the Soviet leader was unable to overcome that resistance. However, Khrushchev never hinted at such opposition—in contrast to his robust attacks on the "steeleaters" and others who resisted his pet schemes—and those of his colleagues who addressed the issue in public seem to have been more strongly in favor of it than he was. He spoke to the issue only rarely, and then without the enthusiasm characteristic of his pronouncements on matters close to his heart. The evidence suggests that he came to accept the need for some sort of enterprise reform but never really threw his weight behind it. This is not surprising. Khrushchev's political interests and his convictions inclined him toward policies which—whether he realized it or not—were fundamentally at odds with the kind of reforms advocated by economists like Liberman and favored by many industrial managers. The point is not so much that Khrushchev was hostile to reformist ideas as that he regarded them as secondary to his more direct attacks on various economic problems. They therefore fell victim to his pursuit of other priorities.

Political Imperatives

Khrushchev's political strategy during 1953–1957 effectively precluded any pursuit of enterprise reform, an issue of which he was probably only vaguely aware in any case. As first secretary of the Communist Party of the Soviet Union, his top priorities were to strengthen his grip on the party apparatus and to bolster its position vis-à-vis the other major institutions of the regime. Moves to expand the power of party officials and, in particular, of the territorial party apparatus allowed Khrushchev to achieve both aims simultaneously, while eroding the power of those institutions dominated by his rivals. Since by the end of the Stalin era the party's role in industrial management was quite limited, Khrushchev initially focused his attention on other issues, chiefly agriculture. However, he soon began to develop a two-pronged campaign to strengthen the party's role in industry and at the same time to undermine the economic ministries that formed the power base of his rival, Georgii Malenkov. The first line of attack was a press campaign exhorting party officials to adopt a broader understanding of the concept of party *kontrol* (oversight) of nonparty institutions, particularly economic enterprises.[14] This was accompanied by attacks on the work of the ministries for their alleged "bureaucratism."[15] The kontrol campaign and the attacks on the ministries remained major themes of Khrushchev's speeches and party propaganda even after Malenkov's demotion in early 1955. On balance this was bad news for advocates of enterprise reform, as it was an explicit call for party officials to meddle in industrial management.

At the 20th Party Congress, Khrushchev took his commitment to party activism to its logical extreme, telling delegates: "The work of a party official should be evaluated primarily by those results attained in the development of the economy for which he is responsible. Officials who refuse to understand this or who are unable to lead the struggle for economic growth must be replaced in good time. . . . Evidently it is necessary, comrades, to raise the material responsibility of officials for the jobs entrusted to them. If the plan is fulfilled or overfulfilled—more pay; if it is not fulfilled, earnings should be reduced."[16]

This went further than Khrushchev's colleagues wished to go. It is unlikely that the territorial bosses who made up so much of Khrushchev's power base in the Central Committee were any more enamored of the idea than the country's industrial managers. The proposal never surfaced again.

The second prong of Khrushchev's strategy was an emphasis on territorial decentralization of economic authority. A host of all-union ministries were reorganized as union-republican structures,[17] and the ad-

ministrative and budgetary powers of the union republics were broadened.[18] On the face of it, this emphasis on territorial decentralization
was not necessarily incompatible with reducing the number of performance indicators, devolving authority to enterprise managers and allowing such factors as profit and price a greater role in governing enterprise behavior. There was scope for both sorts of measures in the
hypercentralized system of 1953. Ultimately, however, the two approaches reflected different aspects of the problem. The enterprise-
autonomy strain of thought, if taken far enough, represented a real
departure from existing methods of economic management, while regional decentralization simply altered the distribution of administrative authority in what remained essentially a command economy. The
former approach also involved an inevitable surrender of power by the
politicians, for any attempt to establish "objective" economic criteria
that could help guide planners or managers would, if implemented, re-
strict political leaders' freedom of action in economic policy.[19]

The theme of territorial decentralization found its most radical expression in Khrushchev's 1957 *sovnarkhoz* reform, when the central
ministries were abolished and replaced by territorial "councils of the
national economy" (*sovnarkhozy*), which were responsible for running
all branches of industry within their jurisdictions. Khrushchev may
well have believed his claims that the new system would do away with
the "interdepartmental barriers" and ministerial pursuit of autarky that
had characterized the ministerial system. There is little doubt, however,
that the reorganization, which was advanced by Khrushchev as his personal initiative,[20] was motivated chiefly by political considerations.
The destruction of the ministries suited the political interests of Khrushchev, who thereby deprived his rivals of a political base, and of his
supporters in the territorial party apparatus, who had long resented and
complained about the power of the central ministries and who now took
over control of economic administration. Moreover, the problems
which the reform was supposed to address were scarcely on the political agenda until Khrushchev put them there with his proposals. "Departmentalism" was nothing new, and there was nothing in the specialist or popular Soviet press in late 1956 or early 1957 to suggest that
it had reached crisis proportions; enterprise reform, not the defects of
the ministerial system, dominated specialist discussions.[21] In any case,
the economic significance of the reform paled alongside its political importance. The essential features of the system were left unchanged:

central planning, the lack of enterprise autonomy, and so on. Even some Soviet observers noted that the reform would merely shift departmentalist practices down the administrative hierarchy, from central ministries and their *glavki* (main branches in the localities) to sovnarkhozy and their branch administrations.[22] Other Soviet critics of the plan rightly pointed to the economically adverse consequences of small economic regions and the danger of autarkic tendencies ("localism").[23]

The evolution of the plan from Khrushchev's initial proposals into the legislation adopted by the Supreme Soviet six weeks later confirms the impression that politics, rather than economics, was driving the reform. Khrushchev's initial proposals were followed by a remarkably frank, month-long press discussion, which included a fair amount of only thinly veiled criticism of the plan. The sovnarkhoz law adopted at the end of this discussion was a much more radically decentralizing measure than what Khrushchev had proposed in March, and all the major changes represented concessions to the interests of regional and republican party leaders, who had pressed for the greatest possible control over the new structures.[24] Khrushchev, locked in conflict with his Presidium colleagues, was clearly prepared to pay a high price to secure the support of territorial party officials, whose backing for him was critical during the "anti-party group" crisis the following month. By contrast, managers' concerns about how the sovnarkhozy would supervise them, and their warnings that the new councils must not exercise "petty tutelage" over them, went unheeded, as did their calls for greater enterprise autonomy. Enterprise directors were the sharpest critics of the new plan, and, significantly, not one spoke at the Supreme Soviet session that adopted it. Several stressed that greater enterprise autonomy was essential to prevent the pursuit of autarky by the sovnarkhozy.[25]

The irony here is that Khrushchev remained committed to central control of the pace and direction of economic activity. His initial proposals represented only a limited decentralization of decision making, and his stated aim was to increase the role of the union republics in economic administration while concentrating the center's directing role in a strong, operationally powerful Gosplan. Even the revised sovnarkhoz scheme adopted in May is more accurately characterized as a "territorialization" of administration than a decentralization of decision making. Khrushchev's vision involved a combination of central decision making and active local implementation, which would do away with the rigidity and bureaucratic inertia of the ministerial system.[26] The speed with which Khrushchev began to reconcentrate economic power in Moscow once his political supremacy was safely established reinforces the sense that the decentralizing elements of the reorganization were a political expedient rather than a reflection of Khrushchev's priorities in economic policy. From 1958 on, the powers and rights of the sovnarkhozy were steadily eroded as Gosplan's powers expanded and numerous new central bodies were created, including all-union state committees for key sectors, a USSR Sovnarkhoz, a USSR Supreme Sovnarkhoz, and so on.[27] The sovnarkhozy themselves were amalgamated and reorganized, and by the time of Khrushchev's fall, centralized branch administration of industry had been revived in everything but name.

In Khrushchev's mind, party guidance of industry and territorial devolution were closely linked, as he interpreted the party's role in management chiefly in terms of the territorial apparatus. As a political strategy, this was a smashing success, strengthening the apparatus's role in the political system as a whole and winning Khrushchev the overwhelming support of territorial party officials, who identified him with the post-1953 decentralization of administration.[28] When Khrushchev's showdown with his opponents took place in June 1957, the support of republican and provincial officials in the Central Committee was critical to his success in overturning the opposition's "arithmetic majority" in the Presidium. Clearly, however, this strategy left little room for enterprise autonomy or for a loosening of administrative controls over enterprises and greater reliance on economic mechanisms.

Reforms Sidetracked

Advocates of wider managerial powers, who seem to have included Malenkov's successor as premier, Nikolai Bulganin, were not idle in the mid-1950s. At the May 1955 all-union conference on industry, Bulganin and the enterprise directors in attendance recommended increased reliance on material incentives, including the use of prices to generate incentives for enterprises to improve and innovate, and greater enterprise autonomy. Leading directors called for less detailed plans and reporting requirements, more supply flexibility, greater power over enterprise operations, and protection from sudden changes in plans and orders from above.[29] Bulganin returned to these themes at the Central Committee plenum on industry two months later.[30] Khrushchev, clearly pursuing his political agenda, turned the managers' criticisms of the system against the ministries and ministerial officials generally but failed to acknowledge (or perhaps even to grasp) the *economic* significance of what they were saying. His speech stressed the importance of territorial decentralization and regional planning and the responsibility of local party organs for raising productivity.[31]

The crisis in capital investments that derailed the overambitious Sixth Five-Year Plan at the end of 1956 triggered renewed discussion of price formation, profit, and the role of the "law of value" in a planned economy. Between December 1956 and January 1958 there were four conferences on these and related subjects at the Institute of Economics of the USSR Academy of Sciences and a fifth at Moscow State University. There was also an upsurge in press articles on the subject.[32]

In practice, however, the reformers achieved little. The July 1955 plenum resolution contained only a single sentence about the need to enhance enterprise directors' rights. Territorial decentralization and party guidance of industry, by contrast, were dealt with at length.[33] In August the government issued a decree that involved a limited extension of enterprise directors' powers over pricing, the sale of surplus equipment and output, the organization of staff, and the drafting of the enterprise's *tekhpromfinplan* (technical industrial financial plan).[34] However, the decree was often ignored in practice: although it stipulated that enterprises would henceforth be subject only to an overall annual plan broken down by quarters, detailed monthly plans were still being imposed on most enterprises as a matter of course a decade later.[35] It could hardly have been otherwise, given that the pressures which caused higher-level administrators to engage in perpetual plan revision—chiefly the need to deal with local shortages and bottlenecks—remained unchanged. The macro-level demands of the system did not permit individual production units to enjoy immunity to administrative interference from above.

The December 1956 crisis held out greater promise for advocates of enterprise autonomy, not least because Khrushchev himself was briefly cut off from economic policymaking. However, he quickly turned the tables on his opponents, and by mid-1957 the sovnarkhoz reorganization had rendered much of the reform discussions irrelevant. Khrushchev acknowledged the debate over enterprise autonomy but said only that the matter should be studied and "the wisest solutions found"—scarcely a ringing endorsement of the reformist agenda.[36] In practice, the sovnarkhozy replicated virtually all of the failings of the old system, including departmentalism, while greatly aggravating the problem of localism (*mestnichestvo*) and increasing the "petty tutelage" to which enterprises were subjected by their administrative overlords. Enterprise managers voiced such complaints throughout the sovnarkhoz period.[37]

Although the sovnarkhoz reform represented a major setback for proponents of economic reform, it did present them with certain opportunities. A sovnarkhoz overseeing a large number of branches of industry could not "think" in physical units to the same extent as a single-commodity branch ministry. This increased the role of money in the system, as the sovnarkhozy had to pay greater attention to money comparisons when making choices about factor use. The role of money would have expanded still further if the promised shift to planning from "macroeconomic aggregates down" (rather than from "branch targets up") had been implemented. Taken together, these developments would have increased the need for price reform.[38] One western economist noted at the time that the sovnarkhozy had more difficulty supporting chronically loss-making enterprises than had the ministries. Given that the alternative to closing such enterprises (impossible) or continuing to subsidize them indefinitely (undesirable) was to cut costs and raise prices, this might over time have pushed the sovnarkhozy toward more economically rational pricing. This would have been possible, in principle at least, because the power to set prices on many goods had been devolved to the union republics.[39]

In short, the sovnarkhozy were an even less effective substitute for the market than the ministries, and their weaknesses thus strengthened the case for more fundamental reform. However, Khrushchev, as ever, resorted to bureaucratic rather than economic solutions. Central bodies multiplied, as did decrees restricting the freedom of the sovnarkhozy and punishing officials for localism and other such sins. The result was an unwieldy bureaucratic leviathan and a system of economic and administrative law that was riddled with ambiguities and contradictions. By 1964 there were nearly a hundred officials of ministerial rank. Never before had there been so many, and never before had their powers been so ill-defined.

The Convictions of a Party Activist

It would be a mistake to explain Khrushchev's commitments to party guidance of industry and territorial decentralization solely in terms of political expediency. These themes clearly served his political interests during the factional struggles of 1953–57, but the evidence suggests that Khrushchev genuinely believed in them. Of course, this may in part have been because he had a political incentive to do so—genuine conviction and political necessity doubtless reinforced one another—but his own career background also inclined him to favor these approaches.

By the time of Stalin's death, Khrushchev had been working in the party apparatus almost without interruption for more than thirty years, nearly always in the territorial apparatus. He better understood the perspective of the party's territorial bosses than any other member of the top leadership and was aware of the frustration they felt when bombarded with overly specific orders from an often ill-informed center. He later recalled of his time as party chief in Ukraine, "We were forever receiving from the ministry memos and directives that almost invariably ran counter to our understanding of what should be done."[40] Shortly after the sovnarkhoz reform, he told one Western journalist, "The main force was administrative action, from one center, all over the country. It was really incredible! A minister used to be higher than God, . . . the party, the trade unions and the members of the Young Communist League were only like auxiliaries."[41]

Moreover, Khrushchev himself had adopted a hands-on approach to economic affairs wherever he had been posted. As a lower party official in Ukraine in the mid-1920s, he had made economic tasks his primary concern, immersing himself in the most trivial aspects of economic work.[42] The picture he painted of his work as a district party secretary in 1925 could well have been a description of the kind of party official he sought in the 1950s and 1960s: rather than using his position to escape the mud, the frost, and the summer heat in favor of a comfortable, desk-bound style of administration, he moved constantly about his little domain, criticizing, questioning, encouraging, assisting in the fields, the mines, the factories.[43] Even during the intense intraparty battles of the 1920s, when the rhetoric of ideological struggle dominated party meetings, Khrushchev seems to have placed economic work ahead of witch hunts directed against various right and left "deviations."[44]

He carried such attitudes to subsequent postings. Serving in Kiev in 1929, he stressed the importance of day-to-day economic work to the party's struggle against Trotskyites, criticizing party workers who debated theoretical issues rather than concrete economic tasks and who failed to take responsibility for the performance of enterprises in their jurisdictions.[45] Running Moscow in the 1930s, Khrushchev immersed himself in every aspect of the reconstruction of the capital then under way, in some cases overruling specialists and taking technical decisions that he was in no sense qualified to make.[46] Khrushchev continually exhorted his subordinates to involve themselves more deeply in the running of industry, arguing that the party ought to give detailed instructions to every worker, shop foreman, and supervisor.[47] These attitudes remained unchanged during his eleven years governing Ukraine[48] and his four years serving a second stint as Moscow party chief.[49]

After 1953, then, Nikita Sergeevich quite naturally saw the solution to the bureaucratism and inflexibility of the Stalinist system in the selection of motivated, energetic party cadres with the organizational talent required to motivate (and discipline) workers and managers, "mobilize hidden reserves," and ensure plan fulfillment. This party activist line was a direct throwback to the heady days of collectivization and the First Five-Year Plan. Khrushchev no doubt saw the achievements of this period, and indeed his own achievements, as a vindication of this approach. Proud of the work he had done and of the heights he had scaled in his career, he could scarcely be expected not to believe that his understanding of party work had been the correct one. Moreover, now that the period of revolution and radical social transformation was over, Khrushchev understood the necessity of finding the party a new role, one that would involve it more closely than ever in the technical and economic aspects of "Communist construction." If the party did not play a central role in economic management, it would soon become an irrelevance. Thus, the first secretary told the 22nd Party Congress:

> Now, when the country possesses enormous material possibilities and a highly developed science and technology, when the initiative of the masses flows like a mighty flood, the speed of our advance depends chiefly on the correct pursuit of the political line set forth locally and nationwide, on the correct and effective functioning of the entire system of state and public organizations and on their ability to make good use of the advantages of the socialist system. From this there follows a need to heighten the directing and organizing role of the party in the period of full-scale Communist construction.[50]

Khrushchev's faith in the capacity of party leaders to play the role in which he wished to cast them may well have been bolstered by the fact that, arguably, the regime no longer faced the choice between "expert" and "Red" which had confronted it in its early years: far more party officials had technical qualifications. Ironically, this was largely a reflection of the fact that engineers and other production specialists had been among the most vulnerable groups during the upheavals of the late 1920s and 1930s, from Shakhty through the Great Terror. The pressures and dangers of being a production specialist led many graduates with technical educations to flee production as rapidly as possible (or even to avoid it altogether) by moving into party work, economic administration, research, or teaching.[51] This was the path taken by many of Khrushchev's younger colleagues and associates, including his eventual successors, Leonid Brezhnev and Aleksei Kosygin.[52]

At the time of the sovnarkhoz reform, moreover, Khrushchev oversaw a restructuring of the curriculum of the party schools that trained up-and-coming party officials. The term of study in the schools was doubled from two to four years, with a new curriculum emphasizing "practical" economic subjects far more than "theoretical" political ones. Fully 1,800 hours of instruction were devoted to topics such as bookkeeping, production methods, and even animal husbandry, while only 1,400 hours were devoted to political economy, dialectical materialism, and related political subjects.[53] The first secretary harshly criticized those party functionaries who resisted the new demands, seeing party work as something separate from economic work and failing to "direct the economy concretely."[54]

Khrushchev's emphasis on party activism in industrial management, like his commitment to territorial decentralization, served his political interests well during the factional battles of 1953–1957. By the end of 1957, however, Khrushchev's supremacy in the Presidium was unchallenged, and his attention shifted from securing the loyal support of the party apparatus against his opponents to securing its active cooperation in the implementation of his ambitious plans for economic development. Here the party apparatus let him down, showing itself to be as resistant to change and vulnerable to bureaucratism as the old ministries had been. Khrushchev's public statements from the beginning of 1958 on reveal growing evidence of his frustration with the failure of regional and local party bosses to fulfill his hopes.[55] None of this apparently undermined Khrushchev's basic conviction that improving economic performance depended chiefly on better organizational work and that the party was the institution best able to perform that function. He seemed to believe that things would work out, if only his party officials would labor as he had done. The result was, in the first instance, an increasing—and politically damaging—reliance on cadres policy to achieve his ends. By 1964 there was a dangerously large number of (mainly party) officials in the Central Committee who had lost their posts under Khrushchev, and many more who resented the environment of insecurity and constant pressure from above in which they worked. Khrushchev had dismantled almost all the central economic ministries and to a great extent emasculated the Ministry of Agriculture, leaving him in mid-1957 with little alternative but to govern through the territorial party organs. The reconstruction of central economic institutions from 1958 was thus in part an attempt by Khrushchev to reduce his reliance on the party apparatus, which was not achieving the desired results.

Khrushchev's continuing determination to make party guidance of production work found its last and fullest expression in his ill-advised scheme to split the lower levels of the party hierarchy in two, with separate organs looking after the management of industry and agriculture. Under the proposals that Khrushchev presented to the November 1962 Central Committee plenum, central committee bureaus were to be established for industry and construction, on one hand, and agriculture, on the other, in each union and autonomous republic. *Obkomy* and *kraikomy* were to be divided completely, so that there were parallel committees for industry and agriculture in each region and territory. Most areas would thus end up with two separate party organizations headed by two first secretaries. The reorganization was less radical at the higher levels of the party hierarchy, but the creation of a Central Committee Bureau for Chemical and Light Industries and of a powerful Party-State Control Committee with closer ties to the former than the latter further expanded the party bureaucracy's ability to intervene in the state economic machine. [56]

Khrushchev's publicly stated objective in undertaking the bifurcation of the party apparatus was to rectify what he perceived as a conflict between the party's involvement in agriculture and its role in the management of industry. Party officials were unable to give continuing close attention to both sectors, with the result that industry was being neglected in favor of agriculture. A further problem was that this double responsibility led to a "campaign style" of party work, with one issue or another becoming the focus of intensive concern and activity for a short period, only to be forgotten when attention shifted to the next campaign, which might affect an altogether different sector.[57] There was some truth to both of these complaints. Ironically, both problems were to a great extent products of Khrushchev's own leadership style, which kept local officials under constant pressure to devote time and energy to his latest agricultural schemes. Earlier in 1962, he had gone out of his way to stress their personal responsibility for agricultural production.[58] It was also the case that the educational backgrounds and abilities of the incumbent first secretaries were better suited to running agricultural campaigns than to managing industrial plants. Not surprisingly, therefore, the great bulk of sitting *obkom* bosses became heads of agricultural party organs after the November plenum. The newcomers appointed at that time were on the whole younger and better educated, and they were generally put in charge of industrial party organs.[59]

The potentially far-reaching political implications of the bifurcation have been widely discussed and need not be recounted in detail here.[60] It is enough to note that the party apparatus was hostile to it; that it was never implemented in many areas—fully one third of obkomy and kraikomy never split; and that it was widely, and with good reason, feared that the appointment of so many new regional officials was intended as a prelude to a purge of the old ones. Such a move would have been wholly consistent with Khrushchev's desire to fashion an activist and managerially competent party apparatus. Political considerations were probably at least as important as economic ones in prompting Khrushchev to pursue a scheme that was probably his greatest single contribution to his own downfall.

The adoption of the bifurcation scheme represented a clear defeat for proponents of enterprise reform, just at the time when it appeared that there would be real progress in the direction advocated by Liberman and his colleagues. The press discussion of Liberman's proposals had been renewed on September 9, when *Pravda* carried an article by Liberman himself calling for a broad debate on the role of profits and profitability in the economy, and lasted until the November plenum.[61] No clear plans were advanced at this stage; the reformers were simply pressing for a fresh approach to management, which would reduce the role of administrative fiat and allow purely economic levers to play a role in the direction of economic activity. Nevertheless, the prominence given to reformist ideas in the course of the autumn raised hopes that reform in this area, long awaited and twice deferred, would soon be forthcoming. The beginning of the reform discussion, however, coincided with Khrushchev's first proposals to the Presidium on the subject of the bifurcation.[62]

The two approaches were clearly incompatible. Liberman and his supporters (who included Kosygin, then first deputy premier) wished to reduce bureaucratic interference in the operations of enterprises, while Khrushchev's scheme was intended to tighten the party hierarchy's grip on the day-to-day management of industry. Tatu argued that Khrushchev was opposed to Libermanism,[63] but it would probably be more accurate to say that he was uninterested in it at that stage. His few public statements on the subject of economic reform were broadly favorable to the expansion of enterprise autonomy, the use of material incentives, and the acceptance of a role for profit in the management of individual enterprises.[64] Caution, rather than hostility, would seem to have characterized Khrushchev's handling of Libermanism. He was content to allow the discussions and experiments to go forward, and he appears to have accepted the need for some sort of enterprise reform. Without his active support, however, enterprise reform had little chance of becoming a reality, for it threatened the interests of planners, state economic administrators, and party functionaries, all of whom would have suffered a loss of power of economic enterprises but who could expect nevertheless to continue to be held accountable for the enterprises' performance.

Khrushchev's Economics

To a great extent, then, the cause of economic reform fell victim not to Khrushchev's hostility but to his indifference. His pursuit of political survival in the years immediately following Stalin's death and his steadfast commitment to the centrality of the party's role in economic management effectively precluded the pursuit of genuine economic reform, despite his apparent openness to some of the reformers' ideas. As Katz observed of the sovnarkhoz reform, "the notion of decentralization to the enterprise level was, as it were, almost an innocent victim of the major political battle and was never attacked directly."[65] Much the same might be said of the bifurcation. Nevertheless, insofar as it is possible to judge Khrushchev's economic views from his public statements and actions, it appears that he would have had many reasons to approach enterprise reform with great caution. Had he understood the full implications of the Liberman debates, he probably would have been far less open to reformist proposals than he was.

In the first place, the use of profits to guide enterprise behavior would have required a meaningful price reform; otherwise, enterprises would be responding to financial indicators that in no way reflected relative scarcity. Liberman's critics were not unaware of this; one pointedly observed that his proposals led to the conclusion that prices in a planned socialist economy should be prices of production, as in a capitalist economy.[66] After all, if prices did not reflect costs, then the concept of profit had no meaning. There had already been lengthy debates on the role of the "law of value" in a socialist economy and on various other proposals to adopt, if not market pricing, then at least some system of price formation that had an economic basis.[67] The reformers wanted price to reflect the "value" of expended labor, possibly including "stored-up" labor (that is, capital).

This threatened, however, to constrain the politicians' freedom to establish economic priorities, because a genuine price reform would make the true costs of politicians' and planners' choices known. Such a course would, ipso facto, have raised the political costs of certain decisions, even if the leadership formally retained full authority over resource allocation. In particular, it would have exposed the full extent of the favored position of heavy industry relative to other sectors: using the existing prices, data on net material product by sector of origin tended to understate heavy industry's share. Price reform would likewise have exposed the true relationship between investment and consumption. In other words, the existing pricing system provided a hidden subsidy to certain sectors and final demand end-uses (chiefly heavy industry and investment) at the expense of others. Reforming it would have reduced the redistributive function of prices and increased that of the state budget, making the hidden subsidy visible.

There is little doubt that such a constraint would have been unacceptable to Khrushchev, who valued his freedom to channel investment resources into sectors and projects that he favored, whether agriculture, rockets, or chemicals. It is not clear to what extent Khrushchev understood the implications of price reform, but at the November 1962 plenum he did at least mention the link between khozraschet and the "abnormal situation . . . in setting prices for industrial products."[68] At the same time, he rejected the notion that the law of value functioned "spontaneously" in a socialist economy, and reaffirmed his belief in the principle of planned proportionate development, including the priority of heavy industry. The clear implication was that it was up to the political leaders and planners to determine the relevant proportions.[69] The economist L. Gatovskii, quoting Khrushchev, rejected the views of those who believed that national economic proportions should be determined by directing investment to industries where profits were highest.[70]

Khrushchev's views on the subject of investment priorities changed over the course of his eleven years in power. They were often unclear—sometimes deliberately so. He began as a staunch supporter of the Stalinist dogma of the priority of heavy industry but later shifted to the view that priority should be given to those sectors of heavy industry which produced the means of production for the light and food industries and for agriculture.[71] There is no evidence, however, that he ever wavered in his belief that the party (meaning the party leadership) must have the final say in the matter. Moreover, although Khrushchev moved some way from his dogmatic Stalinist position of 1954–1955 on the issue of investment priorities (in particular by giving a greater share of investment to agriculture), he never abandoned the priority given to "production of the means of production" in favor of a pro-consumer line. His priority sectors were not the same as Stalin's, and he definitely gave households a better deal than his predecessor had done, but his focus remained on investment rather than consumption and on increasing production of capital (rather than consumer) goods.

It is largely for this reason that the efforts of mathematical economists to revive proposals for optimal planning (first debated under Stalin) failed to make any real impact on policy. Relying on input/output analysis and linear programming, they sought to resurrect efficiency prices, opportunity costs, marginal costing, and interest rates (albeit all under different, more ideologically acceptable names) in an effort to make reformed prices and khozraschet indicators into "weapons of the plan." Mathematically determined plans would serve as a surrogate for the market.[72] Even actual price reform could be avoided by using "shadow prices" in the planning process and leaving actual prices (and hence official data on economic activity) unchanged. Nevertheless, the mathematical school's proposals, if implemented, would have provided planners with economic criteria for judging the relative desirability of various investment alternatives, thereby impinging on the politicians' freedom to determine the country's economic objectives.

It is unclear to what extent Khrushchev grasped the implications of the reform debates. Much of the discussion may well have meant little to him—and interested him less. He was, however, a shrewd-enough politician to resist policies that threatened to undermine his power, and he seems at some level to have grasped that many of the reformers' ideas could do exactly that. This seems to be at least part of the reason for the distinction Khrushchev drew between the role of profit at the level of the individual enterprise and its role in the wider economy. He stated that profit could be useful as an indicator of an enterprise's efficiency but denied that it had a positive role in a socialist economy as a whole, since that would imply that production was undertaken for profit.[73] In other words, profit might be employed to encourage workers and managers to do a better job executing plan tasks, but it could *not* play a role in the allocation of resources between sectors—that is, in determining *what those tasks should be*. This, moreover, was the position that seems to have emerged from the deliberations of the scientific council to which the Liberman discussion was referred after the November 1962 plenum.[74]

This was arguably an untenable position, since a reform limited to the enterprise level was never likely to achieve much. But the reformers could hope for no more, given that a wider reform would have represented unacceptable constraints on political decisionmakers. Economically, too, it is difficult to see why Khrushchev and his colleagues would have risked a more extensive economic reform. The system in the early 1960s was still performing relatively well, and it would, from Khrushchev's perspective, have been economically foolish as well as politically inexpedient to tamper too much with the economic mechanism.

The reformers' proposals were anyway unlikely to excite a man of Khrushchev's outlook, for several reasons. First, his behavior in virtually every area of policy suggests that he had little time for formal, as opposed to substantive, rationality. If he wanted, for example, to increase chemical production, then he pushed through a crash program of investment in the chemicals industry; after all, he had the power to do it, and what else was that power for, if not to be used? The notion of creating a structure of incentives that would induce economic actors to do voluntarily what he could order them to do anyway must have seemed unnecessarily roundabout to a man accustomed to achieving his aims by administrative fiat. Moreover, Khrushchev's belief in the omnicompetence of the party official was such that he did not limit his concerns to assignment of the most general tasks. He was quite willing to involve himself in detailed technical decisions about how things were to be done, and he clearly believed that lower party officials should be similarly immersed in "practical work." The first secretary's own propensity to meddle in technical questions that he was ill-qualified to address expressed itself most evidently in agriculture, but this disposition no doubt reinforced his belief that party officials should be deeply involved in the resolution of technical questions in industry too.

Second, Khrushchev's leadership style was characterized by a combination of impatience and borderline utopianism which sat uneasily with the economic reform agenda. The impatience was partly political. George Breslauer has argued persuasively that Khrushchev's rhetoric on a number of issues consistently created a sense of crisis designed to foster dependence of the party elite on himself. The implicit message was that unless the authorities took rapid and decisive action on a given issue, they would face the threat of popular unrest and social upheaval.[75] There appears, however, to have been more to this rhetoric than an attempt to manipulate elite fears of the masses. Khrushchev may truly have feared the possibility of what Popov calls "a crisis of the Hungarian type."[76] Whether the fear was genuine or not, the impatience Khrushchev expressed was real: he was impatient with both subordinates and policy initiatives, quickly replacing or amending them if they did not produce the desired results. This tendency, which seems if anything to have been even more pronounced after 1960, made Khrushchev an unlikely Libermanite. The measures being proposed by the economic reformers were indirect and incremental, and they would have been most unlikely to produce the quick, dramatic results which Khrushchev wanted—and which, by the early 1960s, he probably needed. The evidence suggests that Khrushchev accepted some of their ideas, but it is doubtful that he expected too much of them or saw them as the primary thrust of a new approach to economic policy.

The utopianism was reflected in the first secretary's unrealistically ambitious goals for economic development, particularly those found in the Sixth Five-Year Plan, the Seven-Year Plan, and the Third Party Program. These targets were an expression of the voluntarist streak in Khrushchev's character, his belief that the party could, given sufficient zeal and organizational skill, achieve whatever goals it set for itself. This was the Khrushchev of the "Three Plans a Year" campaign in agriculture, the Khrushchev who from the 1930s on repeatedly expressed his contempt for those who cited "objective conditions" as an impediment to plan fulfillment.[77] Yet the further Khrushchev went in embracing economic rationality, the further he had to go in accepting the constraints of those very "objective conditions" to which he so steadfastly refused to bow. Enterprise reform might be palatable if limited to the enterprise level, but price reform, the acceptance of a role for profit in the economy as a whole, the use of surrogate interest rates to decide between investment proposals, and other more fundamental reforms were all unthinkable. They would have forced Khrushchev, a leader whose ambition was to transform his country economically in a very short period, into an incrementalist straitjacket.

Historical What-Ifs

It has been argued that Khrushchev by 1964 had come to accept the need for some type of economic reform along the lines of the Kosygin reforms adopted the following year and that only his removal prevented him from seeing the reforms through.[78] There is indeed some evidence for this view, not least the speed with which they were adopted after he fell, which suggests that the preparatory work was well under way by October 1964. Even at the November 1962 plenum, where the bifurcation scheme seemingly scotched the reformers' plans, Khrushchev called (not for the first time) for careful study of reformist proposals and for the organization of experiments in industry, and the plenum resolution called for the adoption of a Law on the Socialist Enterprise, "keeping in mind the further expansion of the powers of enterprise directors."[79] The council designated to consider the Liberman proposals after the plenum clearly accepted the need for some sort of reform, albeit limited to the enterprise level. In 1963–1964, Khrushchev picked up another reformist theme, stressing the need to establish a system in which enterprises were accountable to their customers for the quality of their output and had a direct interest in raising quality.[80]

In July 1964 an experiment was begun with two clothing firms, Bolshevichka in Moscow and Mayak in Gorkii, which were to plan production and deliveries on the basis of orders from specified retail outlets.[81] They were also to experiment with the use of profit as the primary success indicator for management. Shortly thereafter, the Liberman discussion, which had been largely banished to specialist journals after November 1962, resumed in the central press. Discussion of the role of profit as the main performance indicator was accompanied by proposals for price reform, the use of surrogate interest rates, negotiated prices, and differential rent payments.[82] Significantly, no conservative opposition to the proposals was expressed in the major papers; thus, as Abraham Katz has observed, the Khrushchev era ended with an unopposed affirmation of the need for reform on the enterprise level.[83] All this might suggest that the Kosygin reforms could well have been adopted even had Khrushchev remained in power.

Against this, however, is the evidence that Khrushchev was at best lukewarm in his support for Libermanism. The referral of the Liberman debate to a scientific commission for over a year at the end of 1962 looks more like a delaying tactic than a reflection of serious interest on his part, particularly given Khrushchev's often impetuous leadership style. Indeed, his handling of other issues suggests that he would have pushed for the rapid and widespread adoption of Liberman's proposals had he embraced them. The fact that a leader as verbose and forthright as Khrushchev spoke so little and so cautiously about enterprise reform reinforces the impression that he had no real enthusiasm for it. By late 1964 he appears to have accepted the need for some cautious steps toward price reform and greater use of profit as an indicator of enterprise performance, but he was far from being a champion of the Libermanist cause. At the same time, Khrushchev was in late 1964 moving in the direction of further centralization of economic administration. In July he proposed reorganizing agricultural administration vertically along branch lines (as industry had been run before 1957).[84] The historian Nikolai Barsukov has claimed that Khrushchev also intended to return to vertical management in industry.[85] These were scarcely the initiatives of a convinced reformer.

There is good reason to doubt whether matters would have been significantly different under any other leader. None of Khrushchev's rivals in the Presidium would have accepted an economic reform that allowed economic forces a significant role in determining investment priorities or growth rates, and any leader prepared to contemplate such a radical reform would have found himself in conflict with most of the regime's major institutions, including the ministries, the party apparatus, Gosplan, and (if the priority of heavy industry were threatened) the military.

Moreover, although enterprise directors were understandably united in support of greater managerial autonomy, any reforms that raised the prospect of a shift in investment patterns could be expected to provoke the opposition of managers in those sectors threatened with declining resources, chiefly defense and heavy industry.

At most, then, the reform agenda would still have been limited to changes at the enterprise level designed to strengthen khozraschet. Such a reform could never have achieved much and would arguably have been counterproductive. The failure of the 1965 Kosygin reforms, of which little remained by 1970, highlighted the difficulty of limiting change to the enterprise level—that is, of trying to alter the incentives facing enterprises without undermining the authority of the administrative and political institutions above them.[86] Indeed, it may be that this was for the best, as the 1965 reforms, if fully implemented, might well have made things worse. Vladimir Kontorovich has argued persuasively that the ministerial and other officials who resisted the implementation of the Kosygin reforms were in fact acting in the best interests of the system by defending what was a coherent, if not particularly good, system against reforms that would have rendered it incoherent and made it function even less well.[87]

Ultimately, "within-system" reform of a centrally planned economy may well have been a recipe for disaster.[88] Enhancing enterprise autonomy and giving profit a greater role in enterprise behavior would have required price reform. Since central planners could not in the end have arrived at scarcity prices, this would logically have led to price decontrol and to allowing enterprises to set their own output targets in response to price signals and to find their own customers and suppliers. Such market socialism would, however, have run into the problem of the "soft budget constraint," with enterprises expecting state subsidies, wasting resources, failing to pursue new technologies, and so on—until the authorities opted for privatization as the only way of forcing them to function effectively. Certainly the experience of the Gorbachev leadership and of Communist reformers in Central Europe in the 1980s suggests that the path of within-system reform was a dead-end. Their story should perhaps lead to a more sympathetic evaluation of Khrushchev's record. Historians may well need to transfer Khrushchev's failure to pursue economic reform from the debit to the credit side of the balance sheet.

7

Cultural Codes of the Thaw

NANCY CONDEE

The Kinship System

In our time there is no father-and-sons problem in the form in which it existed in the days of Turgenev. For we live in an entirely different period in history, a period that has its own pattern of human relationships.—Nikita Khrushchev, speech of March 8, 1963[1]

The story of Thaw politics is about culture. The story of Thaw culture is about politics. Neither can be told without the other. Culture provides the conceptual nomenclature for the Thaw in prose writer Ilya Ehrenburg's 1954 novel.[2] Politics provides the four crucial dates, a kind of pulse that drives and accentuates the cultural events: 1953, 1956, 1961, 1964.

In between these four dates lie the three major episodes of the cultural Thaw. In the first episode, set in motion by Stalin's death, the key figures are the writers Olga Berggolts, Vladimir Pomerantsev, Leonid Zorin, and Ehrenburg himself.[3] Their thematic concerns—lyricism, sincerity, generational differences, corrupt bureaucrats—form a cluster of issues that remain at the very center of Thaw culture.[4] A casualty, albeit a temporary one, of this first episode is Aleksandr Tvardovskii, who was forced to resign the editorship of the thick journal *Novyi mir* to Konstantin Simonov on August 11, 1954.

The second episode is signaled by the events of the 20th Party Congress and marked by the ceremony of Nikita Khrushchev's "secret speech" of February 25, 1956. The central texts of this episode are Vladimir Dudintsev's novel *Not By Bread Alone* (*Ne khlebom edinym*, 1956) and Book Two of the collection *Literary Moscow* (*Literaturnaia Moskva*, 1956).[5] The best-known casualty of this episode is the poet Boris Pasternak, who completed the novel *Doctor Zhivago* in 1955 and published it abroad in 1957.

The third episode is marked by the 22nd Party Congress and consecrated by the removal of Joseph Stalin's body from the mausoleum on Red Square. Key texts include the literary collection *Pages from Tarusa* (*Tarusskie stranitsy*, 1961), Aleksandr Solzhenitsyn's short story *One Day of Ivan Denisovich* (*Odin den' Ivana Denisovicha*, 1962), and Yevgeny Yevtushenko's poems "Babi Yar" (1961) and "Heirs of Stalin" ("Nasledniki Stalina," 1962).[6] This episode reaches its climax in the Manège exhibit "Thirty Years of the Moscow Artists' Union" in December 1962. Its end is marked by a series of casualties, including the arrest and trial of the poet Josef Brodsky (arrest January; trial February 1964); of writers Andrei Siniavskii/Abram Terts and Iulii Daniel/Nikolai Arzhak (arrests September 8 and 12, 1965; trial February 1966); and of dissident Iurii Galanskov (arrest January 1967; trial January 1968), followed on August 21, 1968, by the invasion of Czechoslovakia, beyond which point it is impossible to speak about the existence of the Thaw.

The logocentrism—or literocentrism, to be more precise—of this brief synopsis is intentional, insofar as literature constituted the primary cultural field within which the party leadership most publicly engaged the liberal intelligentsia. Secondary cultural fields were provided by painting and cinema—that is, visual representation with extensive international exposure that could be "read" (after its own fashion and for its own purposes, of course) by the party and cultural administration.

Literature had long overtaken cinema's leading role in the Leninist cultural hierarchy of the 1920s and had become, under Stalin, the crown jewel of Soviet culture, whose citizens were, as a party slogan put it, the "most reading people." While literary production had indeed withered by the late 1940s and early 1950s, cinema—its erstwhile competitor—had virtually disappeared.[7] The fact that cultural literacy was first and foremost *literary* literacy provided the potential to marshal both the liberal and the conservative intelligentsia around literary confrontations in a fashion unattainable by the other arts. Hence, the subsequent arrests of Siniavskii and Daniel in 1965 provoked a broad, interdisciplinary response within culture at both extremes of the political spectrum, including the ensuing demonstration on December 5, 1965, widely regarded by those within the dissident community as the birth of the human-rights movement.[8] The "dissident interdisciplinarity" of the late 1960s and the 1970s has its beginnings precisely in that literocentric culture of the Thaw period and looked to the short story, the poem, and the memoir as key elements of its genesis tale.[9]

In certain cultural arenas other than literature, the Thaw story continues beyond Khrushchev's fall for nearly four years. To understand the internal logic of these cultural processes, one must of course acknowledge that the end of the Thaw is a function of (1) the particulars of production within the individual culture industries, (2) the industries' positions within (or vis-à-vis) the ideological hierarchies of official culture, and (3) the very different time frames within which a cultural text is produced. Were we tempted to insist that cultural experimentation came to an end in October 1964 with Khrushchev's fall, we might well recall that the same year marked the opening of the Taganka Theater and the revival of official interest in the Meyerhold lineage. The significance of the Taganka in the 1970s as a rare bright light on the otherwise dreary panorama of stagnation is due in large measure to its attenuated relationship with Thaw culture, a star that had since died.

Two other interesting, but dissimilar, examples of this post-Khrushchev thaw are cinema and jazz. The first—a highly institutionalized, bureaucratic medium occupying a central place in official culture—required considerable time and resources from beginning to finished product, whether we are speaking of the filmmaker's cinematic text or the filmmaker as such. The second—a highly improvisational medium on the fringes (at best!) of accepted culture—required few conditions for the production of the cultural text other than the musical instrument itself.

Yet, despite their differences, both cinema and jazz underwent an extraordinarily productive period extending well beyond Khrushchev's ouster.[10] Cinema's productivity continued until the crushing of film director Grigorii Chukhrai's experimental studio, in connection with the 1967 celebration of the fiftieth anniversary of the October Revolution[11]. Jazz enjoyed the closest thing to mass popularity in the festival movement of 1965–1967.[12]

Thus, although the literary Thaw is coterminous with Nikita Khrushchev's governance, in most other cultural spheres this is by no means the case.[13] Nevertheless, his removal on October 14, 1964, marks the end of a set of cultural codes that could not be sustained without the peculiar position that Khrushchev had staked out on the cultural landscape.

That position might best be described as avuncular, bearing the authority of the elder relative who is not the father and thereby disavows direct, historical responsibility for the past. A key text here is the Secret Speech, the document that exposes the crimes of Stalin and signals a lateral shift in the dynastic pattern, marking the innocence of the uncle in the sins of the father. This oblique stance (and its accompanying oblique vision) acquiesces in authority while stepping aside from lineage, a pattern played out again and again in the culture of the Thaw period. It neither begins with Khrushchev nor is explicitly sanctioned by him as a story available to other storytellers. Nevertheless, his enactment of this role in the Secret Speech and elsewhere is a powerful statement about the legitimate signifying practices of authority—including narrative authority—in the late 1950s and early 1960s.

Thus, however much cinema, jazz, and other cultural phenomena may have negotiated ways temporarily to sustain their particular liberal tendencies until as late as August 1968, already by the early 1960s the political liabilities of Khrushchev's stance were clear to his imminent successors: Khrushchev had debunked the father but was unwilling (or, depending on the storyteller, unable) to take the father's place, leaving unresolved many key questions of legitimate authority and its lineage. For nearly a decade, in the "struggle between the new and the old, and the inevitable victory of the new,"[14] Khrushchev managed to reject the authority of the false past because he embodied the authority of the present, which contained within itself the true past. His ability to be critical of authority while not losing authority could not, however, be maintained indefinitely, nor could he indefinitely escape the unresolved issue of political succession. Into the familiar story of "fathers and sons" he had introduced a destabilizing variant: uncles and nephews. It was destabilizing because the limitations of kinship authority were all too evident.

Thus, while it could be persuasively argued that the indeterminacy of the Thaw's end—did it end in 1964? in 1966? in 1967? in 1968?— is itself a legacy of the Thaw's own greater tolerance of diversity, ambiguity, particularity, and difference, it more compellingly reflects the uncertainty on the part of Khrushchev's own successors about how to reconstruct a family tree whose patriarchal lineage had been so publicly and officially lopped off a decade earlier. Khrushchev's successors failed to credibly reinvent legitimate lineage, and the crisis engendered by the Secret Speech of 1956 was one from which Soviet culture, as it had been variously constituted since the late 1920s, never recovered.

Studied Deviance

> In wintertime our hangout was the Dynamo skating rink. We teenage "style-
> hounds" (*stiliagi*) went there because they played jazz over the PA. I even
> signed up for some kind of special lessons in order to have a pass for that
> rink. We would skate out in full regalia, in suit and tie just as we did for
> dances. And with nothing on our heads. . . . We wore high-topped skates
> and skated all together, against the flow, slipping in and out among the cou-
> ples in their heavy outfits and hats.—Aleksei Kozlov[15]

Why does the Thaw story matter? The story is, among other things,
the Lutheranism of the socialist experiment. It is a story about the limits of socialism; about how the Third Wave was formed; about the birth
of modern-day human rights and samizdat;[16] about the youthful formation of the leaders of perestroika, the so-called Sixties generation or
shestidesiatniki, born between the great divide of 1928–1929 and the
outbreak of the Great Fatherland War in 1941.

Although it is possible to speak of any generation in terms of a
unique collective experience, the Sixties generation is the one from
which all three subsequent generations—seeking their separate identity—have been forced to distinguish themselves. The Sixties generation was composed of "last idealists," those who were born "not in time
for the front," "Romantics who never fought,"[17] "would-be Decem-
brists whom no one summoned to Senate Square."[18] Indeed, of the
many generational differences between Khrushchev and his young interlocutors in the creative and scholarly intelligentsia, a striking contrast is afforded precisely by the presence or absence of militarism as a
trope lending coherence to the verbal confrontations, crises, and con-
flicts of the Thaw period. For Khrushchev, the language of militarism
made sense; it was the language of his generation and the language of
the state. For his young interlocutors in the liberal intelligentsia, military metaphors were more complex.

Moreover, while peaceful coexistence in foreign policy dictated a
move away from militarism toward less dangerous forms of competition (principally in economic and cultural affairs), culture itself—situ-
ated for Khrushchev and the party in the ideological sphere—could
tolerate no peaceful coexistence, which would be tantamount to anti-
communism. As Khrushchev spelled out most unequivocally in his key
speech of March 8, 1963: "We should like our principles to be understood well by all, and especially by those who would foist on us peace-

ful coexistence in the sphere of ideology. . . . He who preaches peaceful coexistence in ideology is objectively slithering into the positions of anti-communism. The enemies of communism would like to see us ideologically disarmed. And they are trying to achieve this insidious purpose of theirs through propaganda of the peaceful coexistence of ideologies, the 'Trojan horse' which they would be happy to sneak in to us."[19]

Before the enemies of communism sneak the horse of peaceful co-existence any further into the citadel of Russian culture, let me add that military metaphors are in no sense new to the rhetoric of Marxism-Leninism. They take on, however, a different ritual significance for Thaw culture, given a foreign policy that specifically distances itself from militarism and a youthful creative intelligentsia too young to have fought in the Great Fatherland War but old enough to have lost their fathers in it. Here Khrushchev's cultural politics could be seen as a kind of internalization of war into the ideological arena of peacetime culture—one of its many similarities with the First Five-Year Plan—where it is acted out symbolically in the restricted combat of official speech, scholarly debate, paper, stage, and celluloid, engaging the metaphors of militarism to make sense of the cultural process: "warriors on the ideological front," "standard-bearers," etc.[20]

The Sixties generation, who had no direct combat experience but knew war only through their own oblique vision—absent fathers and older brothers—responded with its own lateral shift. In a kind of isomorphic parallelism to Khrushchev's stance, they produced fictional heroes who were courageous but not heroic, brave but not epic. Their challenge to Khrushchev's deviance was the creation of their own forms of collective deviance: the *geroi-neudachnik* (hero-loser) and the *nikchemnyi chelovechishka* (good-for-nothing small-fry) of Bulat Okudzhava's songs and stories; the first-person narrative divergent from collective memory, subjective stream of consciousness, and dialogic monologues of Vasilii Aksenov's stories; the fractured forms and fractured consciousness of Andrei Voznesenskii's poetry; the views of the child or adolescent in stories by Sergei Antonov and Vera Panova, as well as Andrei Tarkovskii's cinema; the poet Yevgeny Yevtushenko's "Precocious Autobiography," whose deviant vision is signaled by developmental immaturity, as if provoking kinship's authority to counsel and intervene, instruct and insist. The *bezotsovshchina* (fatherlessness) of postwar (and, symbolically, post-1956) youth compounded the urgency of avuncular intercession in response to the symptoms of deviance.[21]

This youthful "skating all together against the flow" was Thaw culture's most characteristic deviant response to Khrushchev's own deviationism. Even the mass spectacle was seized and redefined as a mass youthful deviance (official, of course, in all respects): the mass poetry readings at Luzhniki Stadium in the 1950s; the World Youth Festival of 1957; the Winter Stadium jazz festival of 1966 in Leningrad, to name the best known. In no sense did Khrushchev lead this tendency; rather, he accentuated it by giving it official shape.

By 1961 the youthful skaters had left the rink and headed off for the Baltic region; as Dimka in Vasilii Aksenov's story "Starry Ticket" (*Zvezdnyi bilet*) puts it, "I'd rather be a tramp and suffer privation than spend my life as a little boy doing what other people want me to do." The pain of fatherlessness had been transformed into a celebratory enactment of homeless privation.

Ritual Combat

Since the early years of Khrushchev's rule, the containment of conflict was of paramount concern to cultural producers, for reasons both internal and external to the realm of culture: most evidently, the bloody solutions of the Stalin years, the devastation of the Great Fatherland War, and the idiotic efforts—largely but not exclusively confined to the immediate postwar years—to achieve a culture of "conflictlessness." The artistic strategy of "no conflict"—or, more precisely, the conflict between "excellent" and "even better"—had played itself out in all its ghastly glory through such novels as Semen Babaevskii's *Knight of the Golden Star* (*Kavaler Zolotoi Zvezdy*, 1947–1948) and *Light Over the Land* (*Svet nad zemlei*, 1949–1950), such plays as Anatolii Sofronov's *Moscow Character* (*Moskovskii kharakter*, 1950), Ivan Pyrev's classic film *Kuban Cossacks* (*Kubanskie kazaki*, 1948).

From the early 1950s onward—indeed, even before Khrushchev's emergence as leader—scholarly efforts by I. I. Chicherin, V. Ia. Grechnev, and others undertook to reconstruct the boundaries of conflict: its legitimate participants, its appropriate issues, loci, media, risks, liabilities, and limits. The theory of conflictlessness was explicitly rejected at the Second Congress of Soviet Writers in 1954.[22]

To the extent that the collective farm had previously been the frequent site of conflictless culture—a kind of ultimate totalitarian utopia, simultaneously harmonious with nature *and* party, with spontaneity *and* consciousness—much of the literary scholarship of this era, from G. A. Mogilevskaia[23] to D. F. Ivanov[24], returned to the collective farm to find the mechanics of a reconceptualized paradigm of conflict.[25] Other studies of this period, such as the work of the literary theorist V. Ozerov, focused on lengthy jesuitical distinctions between "true conflict" and "false conflict."

Khrushchev's contribution to this debate was the realignment of conflict along a temporal axis—the old and the new. Khrushchev's old and new divided at 1956 and was most often a distinction between old and new abstractions,[26] that is to say, between symbols, objects, and activities but not between people: "We must . . . discard all that is old and rusty, equip ourselves with new and better weapons, and clear the road of all obstructions, all that is dead and useless. In the life of our Soviet state, the period after Stalin's death was just such a period. . . . We did so to get rid of unhealthy and dangerous practices of the past."[27] In this fashion, his temporal axis contained an escape clause: in a conflict of old and new ideas, the new should emerge as stronger; in a conflict of post-1956 elders and youth, the elders should emerge as stronger—as long as they were the correct elders.[28]

It could be argued that this totemic conflict of old and new, which seeks specifically not to annihilate either but to hold their unequal strengths up as an object of contemplation, is expressed most articulately in the architecture of the Thaw period, which pits its modern monuments in stark visual contrast against the ancient monuments of Russian churches: the Kremlin Palace of Congresses (1959–1961), the Hotel Rossiia (1964–1969), and the beginning of Kalinin Prospect (1964–1969) at Vorovskii Street are all set off ostentatiously against such (comparatively) modest architectural examples of the ancient ideology.

This temporal old/new axis had faded from prominence since the 1920s, when the year 1917 had served as a historical and political division between demonic and sacred rule. Stalin's realignment of conflict had emphasized a spatial axis (foreign, Western, and capitalist enemy versus patriotic, Soviet, and socialist comrade), yet increasingly in the 1930s it became a system without fixed temporal or spatial coordinates. As so often within paranoid conceptual systems, fixed coordinates were continually suspect, subverted, and circumvented, such that only within the symbolic universe of culture (and most particularly in the terrarium of the fictional or celluloid kolkhoz) could there be found an imaginary safe haven. Outside, an uncontrollable mitosis raged: a "them" versus an "us" that continually subdivided into more arcane and camouflaged variants of "them."

Khrushchev, drawing the line at 1956 with near-biblical clarity, attempted to situate himself in so doing in a kind of "third space" that is the new post-Stalin, *older* generation. Within this third space of an otherwise unreformed diarchy, he attempted to alter the signifying practices of conflict, to contain them within the definitions of "us" and "them" that are self-regulating and self-restraining *because* they are self-contradictory: new, but not young; elder, but not answerable.[29]

This third space for Khrushchev, a critical element of his destalinization campaign, corresponds in many ways to the third space of inner freedom, private life, moral ambiguity, neutrality, indifference, or sincere feelings that is an essential feature of Thaw culture. An explicit example would be Ehrenburg's work on Stendhal and the ensuing controversy over inner freedom, implicitly a different truth from party truth.[30]

Seeking to be Stalin's successor but refusing to be Stalin's heir, Khrushchev found a self-authenticating stance that relied not on dynastic patterns of legitimation but rather on the contradictory interplay of deviance and continuity, confounding established distinctions between state and intelligentsia. That paradigm of mutual exclusivity falls apart to reveal the complicity of the intelligentsia in enacting cultural gestures similar to those of the state.[31]

Whether we are speaking of the representations of official culture, tolerated culture, or unofficial culture, the unifying concern of the era was studied deviance, a self-conscious and stylized set of codes that were ostensibly concerned with notions of norm and deviance but were equally eloquent in their anxiety about the containment of conflict, because the subject position of the norm had itself been weakened by the knowledge of its own deviance. The language of deviance was by no means invented by Khrushchev, but its state recognition in 1956 was a momentous change in Soviet cultural rhetoric.

If Khrushchev could never fully disentangle himself from the sins of Stalin and reinvent himself as innocent, neither could he succeed in arguing to the younger generation a philosophy of obedience, which he himself had so brilliantly violated. The Thaw, then, is not about the less-ening of conflict. Coming out of an era of extreme, forced solutions—the social carnage of the late 1930s, the wartime toll of the 1940s, the false solution of cultural conflictlessness—the Thaw is about the rhetoric of conflict: its rules, tropes, and gestures. It is fueled by a knowledge of complicity of the so-called new in the wrongs of the so-called old.

Khrushchev as Cultural Critic

[The painting] consisted of some messy yellow lines which looked . . . as though some child had done his business on the canvas when his mother was away and then spread it around with his hands.—Khrushchev[32]

And I called out to him: "Whose ship?" and he who was on her answered: "Thine."—Archpriest Avvakum[33]

To speak of the Thaw as synonymous with Khrushchev is mislead-ing and confusing. Khrushchev's antipathy to the term was well known, expressed most clearly in his March 8, 1963, speech to an assembly of writers and artists at the Kremlin. This antipathy had a number of ex-planations. Foremost was Khrushchev's personal dislike of Ehrenburg, which stemmed most explicitly from Ehrenburg's perceived distor-tions of Lenin's position on left art and from Ehrenburg's position as an outside observer to the Revolution.[34] Ehrenburg's oblique vision made him an unwelcome competitor, an uncle whose bad habits threat-ened to wield more influence over the younger generation than Khru-shchev's own. Yevtushenko in this respect might be seen as a youth caught between competing uncles.[35]

Khrushchev saw a number of other shortcomings in the metaphor of a thaw. Associated with the concept of thaw is the notion of instabil-ity, impermanence, incompleteness, of temperature fluctuations in na-ture, when it is hard to foresee what turn the weather will take. While the untutored student of the Thaw might argue that these qualities were precisely characteristic of the historical period, such was not the view of the critic Khrushchev ("such a literary image cannot convey a correct impression of the fundamental changes that have taken place since Stalin's death in the social, political, economic, and spiritual life of So-viet society").[36]

Although it might seem strange at first to consider the views of

Khrushchev as critic of Soviet culture, that was, in a sense, his most characteristic role. After all, whether we are speaking of Ehrenburg's story or of Leninism-Stalinism's story, the story had already appeared by 1956; Khrushchev's crucial contribution in the years that followed was his textual critique. Moreover, Khrushchev's personal vision of art, his likes and dislikes, were, given his position, not without relevance to the Thaw.

Indeed, more is known about Khrushchev's views on culture than those of any Soviet leader before or since. We know, for instance, that Khrushchev did not care for jazz but admired the early work of the songwriter Isaak Dunaevskii and the singer Leonid Utesov. He liked the "humanity" of the painter Aleksandr Laktenov and detested the "dirty daubs" of Boris Zhutovskii, an artist involved in the Manège affair. He cared neither for the cinematic extravaganzas of Ivan Pyrev nor for the "twisted and wrong" images of film director Mikhail Romm—who, like Ehrenburg, was a misguided uncle. He had no time for the cubist sculptor V. P. Kaviladze but admired the work of N. V. Tomskii and L. I. Kerbel, whose statue of Karl Marx in central Moscow had been awarded a Lenin Prize. He found architect Konstantin Melnikov's Rusakov Club in Sokolniki to be a "repulsive-looking, inconvenient structure"; nor did he like Karo Alabian and Vasilii Simbirtsev, architects of the Central Theater of the Red Army, "the most irrational building there is." He loved to hear violinist David Oistrakh perform. He was an admirer of the nineteenth-century composer Mikhail Glinka but also enjoyed songs in the revolutionary tradition, such as "Victim of Dire Bondage" ("Vy zhertvoiu pali"), "Whirlwinds of Danger" ("Vikhri vrazhdebnye," also known as "Varshavianka" or "Warsovienne"), the "Internationale," as well as the songs of Dmitrii and Daniil Pokrass, Vasilii Solovyev-Sedoi (composer of "Moscow Nights") and Eduard Kolmanovskii (best remembered for his 1961 setting of Yevtushenko's poem "Do the Russians Want War?"). He had strong views on the can-can and loved the verses of the worker-poet Pantelei Makhinia, a friend who had been killed in the Civil War. He loved the verses of Ivan Nikitin. Are these views, one might argue, less worthy of attention than those of any other cultural critic who has wielded enormous and arbitrary power in the art world?

What emerges from this seemingly haphazard assortment of preferences is unquestionably cultural conservatism, but also—unintentionally, perhaps—something more complex, namely a twentieth-century antipathy toward modernism, whether early twentieth century or the neo-modernism permitted as a result of Khrushchev's own liberalizing efforts. This antipathy constitutes the central paradox of Khrushchev: in providing the political conditions for a tentative reemergence of modernist values—whose overlapping characteristics include radical novelty, an impulse to extreme individuation, and the valorization of inaccessibility—Khrushchev's extended polemics at the Manège exhibit and elsewhere embodied a kind of state postmodernism, anticipating many of the stylistic and thematic concerns of his cultural decedents, whether we are speaking of the sentimental, improvisational musings of Dmitrii Prigov's poems, the kitchen dialogues of painter Ilya Kabakov's canvas, or the defecatory infantilism of Vladimir Sorokin's prose. Dialogic, ephemeral, and self-interrupting, Khrushchev's official utterances were an ideological nightmare for his speechwriters and aides, since, as opposed to Stalin's speeches, no canonical text could be predictably defended. And although the speeches are marked by an extreme distaste for modernism's innovation, eccentricity, and incomprehensibility, they are not a reiteration of Stalinist positions. Instead, they exhibit a public and official love of the improvisational, the extemporaneous, the profane, and the essayistic, a mixing of cultural styles and levels that defy established hierarchies and cultural codes.

The 1962 Manège exhibit was, in this sense, really two exhibits: the artists' neomodernist painting and Khrushchev's postmodernist prose. Central Committee Secretary Leonid Ilichev and his Stalinist cohorts, who accompanied Khrushchev to the Manège, were irrelevant to this central cultural conflict. That conflict was only superficially between liberal artists and the conservative state; at a more significant level, it was between the artists' own outmoded aesthetics and Khrushchev's rancorous postmodernism.

Casting aside Stalin's cultural authority as "great scholar" (*bol'shoi uchenyi*), Khrushchev embraced the identity of the cultural essayist of his time. His literary style was occasional, journalistic, a *critique du jour* deriving from Lenin's *Party Organization and Party Literature*. Yet his style was closer still to two literary-political ancestors of Russian history who otherwise had little in common with him. These are Ivan IV and Avvakum, whose personalizing tone reached across the boundaries of state and ecclesiastic cultural models and violated the norms of institutional anonymity to inscribe a "faced literature." Their "emancipation of the personality," as Dmitrii Likhachev has described it, is—like Khrushchev's own—a kind of thinking out loud, a series of diary entries.[37]

However dissimilar in other respects to the tyrant Ivan and the Schismatic Avvakum, Khrushchev resembles these two figures in his efforts to break through the established codes of speech in the communication of state policy, and he personalizes that policy in anecdotal form. He "narrativizes" politics through a series of literary asides, reminiscences, and anecdotes, most often as a response to the initial narrative of his interlocutor. Hence he is not an author in any pure sense (any more than were Ivan and Avvakum), but rather an essayist whose occasional writings polemicize with a prior text. As in Ivan IV's letters and Avvakum's autobiography, Khrushchev's speeches take on a kind of internalized dialogue, in which he assumes the stance of his interlocutor, mimics the voice that is not his, and masquerades as—and, ultimately, unmasks—his enemy-listener. Elsewhere, as in a speech delivered September 19, 1959, at the Twentieth-Century Fox Studios, the very temple of masquerade, Khrushchev addresses the American movie moguls, marshaling the same alternating codes of self-abasement and bombast so consciously exploited by Ivan and Avvakum:

> I was in the Red Army when we beat the white Guards and drove them into the Black Sea. My unit was stationed in the Kuban region, and I was quartered in the house of an educated family. . . . I remember the landlady asking me, "Tell me, what do you know about the ballet? You're a simple miner, aren't you?" To tell the truth, I didn't really know anything about ballet at that time, because I had never seen one, and, moreover, had never seen a ballerina. I had no idea what it was all about, so to speak. But I said to her, just wait, we're going to have everything, and ballet, too. . . . And now I wish to ask you: in what country is the art of the ballet most highly developed? Would it be your country? No.[38]

Pitting what the cultural theorist Boris Groys would term his "aesthetico-political will to power"[39] against his interlocutors, Khrushchev calls into play the same implicit contradiction as Ivan had exploited: common speech and conversational tone spoken by the very subject who embodies state power.

Khrushchev's polemics with prior texts address virtually all major issues of domestic and foreign policy. In response to the question of Stalin's mistakes in agricultural policy, there is the story of his cousin's apple orchard; to the question of literary battles within the intelligentsia, there are his memories of the pitched battles between men of Kursk and Orel provinces; to the question of foreign travel, there is the story of ballerina Maya Plisetskaia ("The human psyche is a terribly fragile thing. . . . I'm proud of my decision to let Maya Plisetskaya travel abroad."); to the story of foreign residence, there is the story of the pianist Vladimir Ashkenazi ("What's wrong with him living in London? . . . After all, he's a musician, and that's a free profession.")[40]

To Yevtushenko's poem "Babi Yar" Khrushchev responds with two stories: about the Jewish fitter Iakov Isaakovich Kutikov, who supervised Khrushchev's work in Iuzovka; and about his Jewish friend Comrade Vinokur, party secretary of a creamery in the Baumann district when Khrushchev was secretary of the district party committee. Although ostensibly the topic of conversation is the existence of a "Jewish question," it is at the same time a battle of narratives—Babi Yar's Jews versus Iakov Kutikov and Comrade Vinokur. The more credible story will serve as the answer to the Jewish question.[41]

It is of no small interest, therefore, how Khrushchev viewed the term "Thaw" and which counternarratives he marshaled in response. Apart from the insight it gives into the biographical Khrushchev, his disagreements with the term are worth considering because the two concepts—"Khrushchev" and "Thaw"—exist in a much more complex and antagonistic relationship with each other than their accustomed interchangeability would suggest.

Khrushchev had his own set of metaphors for the cultural process, the social changes, and the intellectuals debates of his tenure. Of the five I will mention here, the most common (and the least surprising) metaphor for the cultural process is conflict, expressed most articulately in the vocabulary of battle: "The press and radio, literature, art, music, the cinema and theater are a sharp ideological weapon of our Party. And the Party sees to it that that weapon should be kept ready for action at all times and strike telling blows at our enemies."[42]

Elsewhere, Khrushchev conceives of the contemporary political entity as an orchestra, in which the artists must learn to play in time with the cultural gestures of the party: "Just as a conductor sees to it that all the instruments in his orchestra shall sound in harmonious accord, so in sociopolitical life the Party directs the efforts of all Soviet men and women towards the attainment of a single goal."[43]

Sometimes these two metaphors fuse, producing the military orchestra. Initially an attack on the "cacophony" of jazz, this extended metaphor becomes an attack on all alternate systems to Leninist policy: "Well, we flatly reject this cacophony in music. Our people cannot accept this rubbish in their ideological arsenal. . . . When a soldier goes into battle he takes with him what he needs. The orchestra is one thing he never leaves behind. On the march the orchestra inspires him. . . . Our policy in art, a policy of irreconcilable opposition to abstract art, formalism, and every other bourgeois aberration in art, is the Leninist policy we have ever unwaveringly followed and will continue to follow."[44]

A third metaphor, which employs the ancient tradition of ship as society, stresses the same motifs of leadership evoked by both battle and orchestra: "But that is not to say that now that . . . guidance has been slackened, the ship of society drifts at the will of the waves, and everyone can behave arbitrarily in any way he pleases. No, the party has steered and will firmly and consistently continue to steer its Leninist course."[45]

A fourth metaphor for the cultural process of the Thaw period is the thunderstorm, a metaphor that rivals Ehrenburg's own. Here the unstable "fluctuations in nature, when it is hard to foresee what turn the weather will take," do not bother Khrushchev. Indeed, in this continually improvised universe, contradictions are resolved not by the imposition of consistency but by the very impermanence of the political moment. In his speech of July 17, 1960, Khrushchev's memory of an actual thunderstorm grows in magnitude to become an extended metaphor for the entire country undergoing destalinization:

> It was well that the lightning flashed. Those flashes threw a bright light into every nook and cranny of which timid people were afraid. The peals of thunder helped those who were hard of hearing to awaken, and to see and understand the remarkable new changes that had occurred in our country since the Twentieth Congress of the C.P.S.U. The downpour washed away all the extraneous matter that prevented certain ideologically immature people from seeing reality in its true light. The result was that people felt freshened up, and found that it had become easier to breathe, fight and create.[46]

Khrushchev's thunderstorm is his counterstory to his rival uncle. Unlike Ehrenburg's model of lessening rigidity and gradual warmth, Khrushchev's is one of meteorological chaos, conflict, crisis, and resolution, resulting in a kind of rebirth, a resurgence of energy and life forces. It is not surprising, therefore, that a final metaphor to which

Khrushchev returns periodically to describe the cultural process is the *bania*, the Russian rural steam bath. Here the scope of the metaphor is more modest, describing only the literary process, and the metaphor does not open up in the same fashion to consume the entire society, yet the diction is remarkably similar to the thunderstorm: "A competent critic can do a good deal even for the most prominent writer. An intelligent critical article is like a bunch of birch twigs for anyone who enjoys a steam bath—he lashes himself with the twigs as he takes the bath, or if he doesn't want to do it himself, someone else does it for him. A steam bath complete with birch twigs is not a bad thing, because it opens your pores and makes breathing freer and life easier."[47]

Thus, within the closed, symbolic space of the bania and by means of the birch twigs (*venik*) of literary criticism, the literary process imposes its hygienic discipline on the kinfolk of writers and artists. I would argue that, given the bland conventionality of the first three metaphors (battle, orchestra, ship) in the rhetoric of authority, it is the thunderstorm and bania, whose similarities of diction are so striking, that constitute the core discourse of Khrushchev's version of the Thaw.

Clearly, Ehrenburg won. Not even I would propose that we refer to 1953–1968 as the Bania. That term would, however, more accurately describe the centrality of ritualized aggression, sublimated conflict within a circumscribed arena, and health-driven thrashing of the body of culture, in order to make it "come clean," as the literary critic Vladimir Pomerantsev had advocated, in his own fashion, in his signal Thaw essay "On Sincerity in Literature."[48]

> In the history of art, there is one very important trait: the inheritance of seniority passes not from the father to the eldest son, but from the uncle to the nephew.—Viktor Shklovskii, "On Cinema"[49]

I began this essay with the notion that the stories of Thaw politics and culture are inextricably intertwined, and I would like to conclude by returning to that idea. Espousing peaceful coexistence in international politics, the state waged war in culture, but it was, compared to the Stalinist nightmare, a war more of words than of deeds. In this symbolic conflict, the word could be called upon to stand in for or symbolize the deed of the state but must still be answerable to the deed, because—like paper money—it stood *in the place of* the deed, using its discourse and substituting for its potential violence.

By Siniavskii's trial in 1966, Khrushchev was already fifteen months out of power. Siniavskii's comment that "the word is not a deed, but a word; the author is not identical to the hero" confronted a crucial dilemma for this era.[50] What Siniavskii had in mind was autonomy both of the word from its object and of the author from his creation; that is to say, in political terms, the literary protagonist's views, deemed anti-Soviet by the state, did not implicate the author. Pushing to the extreme the disjuncture between word and deed, Siniavskii forced the state to face the question of whether, in fact, the two were identical. In Siniavskii's case by 1966, it turned out, they were.

Of the substantial and excellent work done by such cultural theorists as Evgenii Dobrenko, Mikhail Epshtein, Boris Groys, and Mark Lipovetskii on the historical trajectory from modernism to Russian postmodernism (including Siniavskii's own work), little has dealt with the Khrushchev era—and the role of Khrushchev himself—as a pivotal moment in the emergence of postmodernism. His era was one in which private and individual—though not autonomous—worlds became once again possible; in which established hierarchies were called into question; in which rigid binarisms opened out into a third space; and in which the story of socialism's world order ceased to be central. This is the beginning of a different article, but an article that must be written around the text of Khrushchev's Secret Speech if it is to make any sense of contemporary culture.

8

Popular Responses to Khrushchev

IURII AKSIUTIN

For a host of reasons, the serious study of interrelationships between the people and the elite, between the masses and the leaders, has long been difficult, if not impossible, in Russia. Only quite recently have historians been able to turn their attention to the destruction, restoration, and new downfall of the imperial mentality, the sociopolitical preconditions for the Stalin cult, the split between mass consciousness and the behavior of Soviet citizens, the dulling of the collective intellect and internal resistance to the regime, and individual rejection of that regime.[1]

Shifts in public consciousness after the death of Stalin, especially after Khrushchev's exposure of his crimes, are also being examined. Such contradictory tendencies in contemporary public opinion as the genesis of the *shestidesiatniki* (Sixties generation), the "Hungarian syndrome," and the personification of the idea of reformation of society in popular, everyday consciousness are being more and more carefully analyzed.[2]

This chapter attempts to illuminate one such question, the common people's perception of the image of the reformer, Nikita Khrushchev, by tracing the evolution of views of the leader's activities. The character and, in many respects, the limits of this inquiry are determined by the existing source base, which has its own peculiarities. After all, genuine public opinion, in all its diversity and various manifestations, was not directly expressed back then, for the media, which were under the complete control of the party propaganda apparatus, did not offer anything but the official point of view and its approval by "all toilers." No manner of sociological sounding of public opinion was carried out. Nevertheless, there was a need for the higher-ups to know what the lower classes were whispering, and covertly they kept tabs on the situation virtually from the first days of Soviet power, through both party committees and the security police. Their actions were documented in summaries sent to the General Department of the Communist party (CPSU) Central Committee, of reactions to certain decisions of party and state organs, information about electoral campaigns, and lists of the most typical questions asked in various meetings in production collectives.

It is true that all these documents can do no more than give the impression that certain public moods existed at that time. They cannot determine which of those moods predominated at any given point. As a rule, no less than two-thirds, and sometimes the entire document, consisted of a series of statements from those who "completely and fully" approved of and praised the good deeds of the regime. But often, at the end, there was an admission that "along with these, there were individual unhealthy and even at times anti-Soviet statements." Information about concrete manifestations of moods and actions hostile to the authorities and the system, which the organs of state security and local authorities considered essential to share with the higher leadership, was exceptional. Furthermore, it is impossible to be absolutely sure not only that the facts included in these documents exemplify a pattern and were not chosen arbitrarily, but also that they were not simply fabricated or falsified.

In fact, the absence of authentic, trustworthy data makes a strictly scholarly study of public opinion in a totalitarian state impossible at this time. Nevertheless, despite lack of better sources of evidence, the material we have been able to unearth in the archive of the CPSU Central Committee (now the Center for the Preservation of Contemporary Documentation) does reflect to a considerable degree the public moods of the 1950s and 1960s and thus provides some semblance of the "voice of the people."

Nikita Khrushchev did not become the unquestioned leader of the party and the state immediately after Stalin's death. But the common people's reaction to the leader's passing clearly demonstrated the condition of Soviet society, which some of the deceased dictator's successors apparently intended to reform. Both official and private documents from March 1953, as well as subsequent reminiscences, are unanimous in their judgment that mourning in the Soviet Union, except perhaps for western Ukraine and the Baltic states, was nearly ubiquitous, and that the passing of the generalissimo was considered a tragedy by virtually everyone. This is not surprising; after all, it was no mere "great leader and teacher" that had passed on but a living god. The hysteria that the media had just whipped up in connection with the so-called Doctors' Plot undoubtedly played a role as well.

A letter to Khrushchev as CPSU Central Committee secretary from a Communist who did not name herself is characteristic. She maintained that 90 percent of party members did not believe that Stalin died a natural death. "The people consider," she continued, "that this is the work of despicable killers, who have done their wicked deed so skillfully that even medical experts could not discover anything." In this connection, she insisted that Jews be removed from the government: "Antisemitism is foreign to the majority of our people, but the activity of the majority of Jews automatically provokes outrage; to deny this means to shut one's eyes to the facts, which is not an option for party leaders of the Stalinist type."[3]

The CPSU Central Committee, the USSR Council of Ministers, and the Presidium of the USSR Supreme Soviet were swamped with resolutions from party organizations and worker collectives, as well as letters from individual citizens, with suggestions on how best to perpetuate the Stalin's memory. They suggested attaching his name to Moscow State University, the Leningrad Polytechnic Institute, the Bezhetsk Steel Mill, the Kaluga Turbine Factory, the Onega Machine-Building Factory, the Kupavin Light Fabric Factory, and the Kalinin Artificial Fiber Combine. A certain M. D. Momotov wanted to change the name of the Georgian Soviet Socialist Republic to the Georgian Soviet Stalinist Republic, while B. Kozlov wanted the abbreviation USSR to stand for Union of Soviet Stalinist Republics. M. Gorodilov, M. S. Kramer, and Likhachev considered it necessary to change the Order of Lenin to the Order of Lenin-Stalin, while M. T. Iakhin and F. A. Silchenko insisted on the establishment of a special Order of Stalin to reward "progressive people." Officers E. P. Pavlov and G. K. Li proposed the more modest idea of establishing a "Memory of Stalin" medal but of awarding it to all party members or even to all toilers of the Soviet Union.[4]

Muscovite N. V. Kritskov donated a month's pay for the construction of a mausoleum for Stalin.[5] Another Muscovite, Iakov Abramovich Barshtein, a colonel in the reserve guards, sent to the burial commission his two Orders of the Red Banner, his Order of Alexander Nevsky, and four medals: "I ask you to accept and place these government awards, given to us thanks to the great wisdom of his leadership, on the tomb of the Leader of all the toilers of the entire world, our own father and teacher, who led us to the heights of communism, the inspirer and organizer of the great historic victories of the Soviet Army and the entire Soviet people in the Great Patriotic War of the Soviet Union—the greatest commander in the world and the head of the Soviet state and of our Communist Party—the Generalissimo of the Soviet Union—comrade Iosif Vissarionovich Stalin."[6]

One can, of course, doubt the sincerity of such circumlocutions and seek their motivations not so much in love and adoration as in fear for one's own life—after all, this particular correspondent was a Jew—and in the effort to give clear evidence of one's loyalty. There is no doubt, however, that they reflected to a significant degree the mood of the masses at the time. Apprehension about the future and fear in the face of the impending unknown dominated. The poet Sergei Mikhalkov, one of the authors of the Soviet national anthem, recalled that although he, unlike many others, "did not cry and did not feel a sense of there being no escape," he nevertheless "was simply in shock: what will happen now, after Stalin?"[7]

Nevertheless, the country continued "to believe blindly," although not quite so absolutely as before. Many were confused as to why Molotov did not become head of the government (since he was still considered Stalin's right hand) rather than Malenkov, who until recently had been little known. Rumors flew that the latter was a temporary figure, that soon Beria would be installed. Increased attention to this rumor, if not its popularity, was encouraged by an announcement of the Beria-led Ministry of Internal Affairs that the doctors who had been accused of poisoning Soviet leaders on behalf of foreign intelligence services would be freed. Published on April 4, 1953, it was read that same day in worker collectives.

"Comrades, I congratulate you; the honor of the white coat has been restored!" joyfully cried Doctor Livshits of the children's polyclinic of the Sverdlovsk district. "We can now look boldly into the eyes of our patients," Doctor Tolchinskaia, of the medical-sanitary group no. 12, replied to her. "A black mark has been removed from all medical personnel," added Doctor Spesivtseva, of the therapeutic clinic of the First Medical Institute.[8] "We must give Beria, who exposed the harmful machinations of the former Ministry of State Security workers, his due," the metalworker Chilikin said at factory no. 45, after the MVD statement was read to him and his comrades at his shop. The engineer-inspector of factory no. 118 expressed the hope that "comrade Beria, as an experienced chekist, will bring order to the work of the organs of state security and will direct their activities toward the exposure of genuine enemies of the people."[9]

By no means everyone believed in the Kremlin doctors' innocence, however. Some workers of the Second Clock Factory could not understand why those accused had condemned themselves and called themselves saboteurs: "No kind of torture can force you to admit something of which you are not guilty." Brynova and Myshlenkova, workers in the disinfectant department of the Sanitary Epidemiological Station no. 8, reasoned thus: "Has not a mistake been allowed to happen? Why did Oleg Koshevoi[10] firmly stick to his opinions when they tortured him, while, according to the announcement, a 'false confession was forced' from these people?" Kotireva, a laboratory worker at the Krasnyi Bogatyr factory, also had her doubts: "Even before the arrests of these people, there were many discussions about sabotage in medicine, and where there's smoke, there's fire. We must look into this very carefully; someone may have helped the guilty ones get out of it." At another factory, a cry went up after the collective reading of the announcement: "Wrong! We will write to the government that they were incorrectly released. They will poison once again!"[11]

Certain female workers of the Krasin Pencil Factory in Moscow were also confused: "What does this mean? While Iosif Vissarionovich was alive, they were all recognized as guilty. . . . But now that Stalin has died, all the materials turn out to be incorrect?" People also wanted to know whether the doctors were released under American pressure. and also "why this announcement came not from the Council of Ministers, but from the Ministry of Internal Affairs?"[12]

As we now know, some members of the party Presidium were intrigued by the same question, and they drew the appropriate conclusions. On June 26, 1953, Lavrentii Beria was arrested, and from June 2 to June 7 his case was discussed in a plenum of the Central Committee, as the country was informed on June 10. Many believed the accusations made against him. Those few who knew something about and feared the "reformist" plans of yesterday's ober-butcher breathed a sigh of relief, while those who were beginning to have terrible doubts could discard them, on the grounds that it was now clear who was guilty of everything.

On August 8, 1953, Georgii Malenkov, the chairman of the Council
of Ministers, promised at a session of the USSR Supreme Soviet "to
raise dramatically the level of food and industrial goods available to the
population—meat . . . fish . . . soap, sugar, sweets, clothing, footwear,
dishware, furniture—over the course of two to three years."[13] Such
generous promises had frequently been made in the past, but since they
never came true, the population was accustomed to greeting them with
restrained enthusiasm. Concrete measures to relieve difficult conditions in the countryside were a different story, however. From now on,
announced Malenkov, the size of mandatory state purchases of grain
and other crops would be determined by the actual harvest, not by the
potential yield, which state workers established before any harvesting
had actually begun and which did not take unavoidable losses into account. Purchase prices on meat, milk, wool, potatoes, and vegetables
were also raised, while the norms for mandatory deliveries from private
plots were significantly reduced. Back agricultural taxes were completely forgiven, and the tax itself was cut roughly in half. Such unexpected bounty was bound to attract the grateful attention of the rural
part of the country.

But Malenkov's star was not destined to dominate in the political
sky for long. The mass media, including newly arrived television, in-
culcated in the public consciousness, at first subliminally and then
more and more openly, the idea that even though the new Soviet leadership was "collective," the lead singer in the nine-member chorus was
Khrushchev, who was elected first secretary of the Central Committee
in September 1953. Impressions of his public speeches and personal
"appearances among the people" were rather contradictory. The majority liked the ways he differed markedly from previous leaders: his accessibility, unpretentious nature, cheerful bearing, and ability to speak
simply and lucidly without notes. He shocked part of the intelligentsia
with his peasant crudeness, his intentional rudeness, which became
offensive boorishness in moments of dissatisfaction, and his obvious
grammatical errors.

Khrushchev himself considered the arrest of Beria his greatest accomplishment, comparable to a heroic feat. For historians, however, he
has remained primarily the muckraker, the one who exposed Stalin's
crimes. His so-called secret speech "On the personality cult and its consequences," delivered at a closed session of the 20th Party Congress on
February 25, 1956, was soon distributed to seven million Communists

and eighteen million Komsomol members. Although people were not supposed to discuss it, they did. In Tbilisi, from March 5 to March 7, heated discussions took place at organized meetings of students intending to lay wreaths at Stalin's monument. On the fourth day, a crowd of 8,000–10,000 besieged the Georgian Central Committee building and demanded that flags and portraits of Stalin be hung in the city, and that materials about his life and activities be published in newspapers. The frightened republic authorities acceded to these demands.

On March 9, at a demonstration of 80,000 in the center of the city, speakers demanded that the party's decisions be reconsidered, and one of them, R. B. Kipiani, called for the rehabilitation of Beria and the dismissal of Khrushchev. Demands were heard for the secession of Georgia from the Soviet Union as well. But attempts to broadcast the declaration adopted at the demonstration over the radio led to a confrontation with the guard at Communications House, during which seven people were killed and fifteen injured. (Two more died later, when motorized infantry and armed escorts dispersed the demonstration.) Tanks entered the city. The KGB arrested thirty-eight people, of whom twenty were sentenced to various terms of imprisonment, not under anti-Soviet articles but for "hooliganism," "participation in mass disorders," and "fomenting interethnic conflict," which was expressed in the cries,"The Russian dogs are killing our brothers!" The maximum sentence, ten years, was given to Kipiani.[14]

Directly contradictory signals came from Leningrad. An academic fellow of the USSR Academy of Sciences Russian Language Institute, I. A. Alekseev, a party member since 1920, wrote to Khrushchev on March 9, proposing that "the question of whether Stalin is a state criminal should be specially considered in all party organizations." In his opinion, "the majority of the party, at least its healthy part, at least all honest party members who have not made themselves over, will come out and say, 'Yes, he is a criminal against humanity, who ideologically inspired the murders committed by Beria's gang and his forerunners in bloody terror.'" A few days later, at a meeting of party activists of the Vasilii Island region, another Alekseev said: "With his speech, Comrade Khrushchev has accomplished the kind of turnaround in our party life that our party must support. . . . The Spanish Inquisition pales in comparison to what happened here. . . . What can compare with the monstrous feudal exploitation that took place during Stalin's dissembling rule? The collective farms are on the verge of poverty." During the discussion that followed, Alekseev introduced a proposal to "judge Stalin posthumously in the court of the party." Only four of the 750 attendees supported him, however.[15]

In Vladimir province, Syromiatnikov, the chairman of the Lenin's Path collective farm (Kerzhachskii region), proposed to party activists on March 13 that they write a resolution saying that the Central Committee had correctly condemned the personality cult but had done so too late. He favored requesting that the Central Committee undertake measures to exclude any other personality cult in the future. No one supported him, however. Furthermore, various speakers expressed the view that "it would not do to subject the question of the personality cult to so broad a discussion; we should instead undertake gradual and careful measures to overcome the consequences."[16] Bolder questions were raised in notes sent to the presidium of the meeting: "Why couldn't Comrades Khrushchev, Molotov, Voroshilov. and other members of the party oppose this arbitrariness? Why did they place Stalin on a level with Lenin? . . . How are we to understand Khrushchev's proposal to the congress to honor the memory of Stalin? What measures were taken by the Central Committee to prevent various adventurists and two-faced types from using the party to pursue goals of self-aggrandizement, as happened under Stalin? Will there be any instructions concerning the portraits of I. V. Stalin?"[17]

Notes of a similar sort were submitted at a meeting of Sverdlovsk province party activists on March 12: "What kind of memory are we to preserve of I. V. Stalin? What do we do about the visual propaganda (murals, portraits, busts, posters, etc.) dedicated to Stalin? Would it be correct to remove the portraits of Stalin quietly and replace them with others?"[18]

Here and there people hurried to change this visual propaganda without awaiting instructions from the center. Thus, while speaking to the republic activists about the congress, Iakut provincial committee first secretary S. Z. Borisov announced that "instead of the banner of Marx, Engels, Lenin, and Stalin, there will now be the banner of Leninism." He pointed to the banner at the back of the stage that included a bas-relief of all four leaders of the world proletariat and said, "Certain provincial committee workers incorrectly allowed such a display." Then, during the first break in the session, the banner was replaced by a portrait of Lenin alone. Moscow got wind of this incident, and the Central Committee department for RSFSR party organs "corrected comrade Borisov."[19]

It cannot be said that the party activists greeted Khrushchev's speech on the personality cult with enthusiasm. The chairman of the Stalin collective farm (Balaklei region, Stalingrad province) Zadaev expressed his doubts this way: "A certain heavy impression hangs over my soul. I had to conduct meetings in the kolkhozes during the days of Stalin's death, and I saw how the kolkhoz workers suffered through that difficult loss with tears in their eyes. And now we go to the kolkhoz workers and say the opposite. I don't know about other people, but will I have the strength to get this across to them? It's a difficult question."[20]

At the Agryz regional party group in Tataria, Communist Nazarov stated, "We cannot throw Stalin out of history, for Stalin performed certain services in the past, and he has entered the consciousness of the Soviet people forever." Alekseev and Tokmianin did not agree with him: "There are various ways of entering history," they replied. "Stalin allowed the completely unjustified destruction of the party cadres, and this cannot be forgiven."[21]

A still greater difference of opinion arose at other party meetings. "Stalin severely corrected Comrade Khrushchev in the matter of the creation of links and agro-cities. Is this not a kind of revenge?" wondered people in Vologda province.[22] P. S. Derkach, commander of a tank unit of the 23rd guard mechanized division (Moscow military district), said to other officers, "Why was all this published? They should have put all this away in the archives so that people's souls would not be disturbed or devastated."[23] S. I. Konovalchik, engineer-colonel of the Design-Technical Administration of Soviet army communication troops, stated, "After this speech you don't know whom to believe. . . . There is now no guarantee that other leaders will not go and do something similar. Aren't there some mistakes here in the rejection of Stalin's work?"[24] Retired colonel Chursin added, "And where was Khrushchev himself? Why did he keep quiet back then, but begin to pour all this muck on Stalin now that he's dead? I somehow do not trust all the facts that are laid out in the secret letter. . . . Stalin raised me on his ideas from my childhood, and I will not reject those ideas now. I had and will have the highest opinion of Stalin."[25]

Major Taratin, chief of headquarters of the 75th training battalion, had a different opinion: "Stalin's actions regarding members of the party cannot be fitted into any kind of frame, and there is no room for him in our land; he must be taken away somewhere and discarded beyond the borders of the USSR."[26] But Igor Chkalov, senior engineer-lieutenant of the 9th fighter air division and son of the famous "Stalin's Falcon" Valerii Chkalov, said, "It is good that I did not enter the ranks of the party earlier, since now you can't figure out whom to believe: either Comrade Stalin, or Comrades Khrushchev's and Bulganin's line." He went on to explain: "It is still not clear what the policies of Khrushchev and Bulganin will lead to, or how rank-and-file members of the party will look upon them. There will be those who will give up their party cards to mark their disagreement with this line."[27]

This did not happen, as far as we know. But here and there "isolated rotten elements," as a *Pravda* editorial defined them, did appear, elements that "under the guise of condemning the personality cult try to cast doubt on the correctness of the party's policies."[28] There were not too many such cases, but there were some, especially in intelligentsia circles. Academics, with their weakness for analysis, allowed themselves not only to doubt the figure of Stalin but also to question some failings of the Soviet system itself. The historian, academician, and Central Committee member A. M. Pankratova, while reporting on the results of a trip to Leningrad, where she gave lectures and speeches on the 20th Party Congress, presented some of the 825 notes she had received from audience members:

> Isn't the blaming of all mistakes on Comrade Stalin itself a personality cult? . . . Isn't the opinion that Stalin could, alone, break the will of the majority of the party (or impose incorrect resolutions of various questions upon the party) a tribute to the personality cult? . . . Was it correct to rally the Central Committee around one individual at any historical stage? . . . Weren't there socioeconomic and sociopsychological preconditions in Russian life for the fantastic flowering of the personality cult? . . . Where does the material basis for the personality cult lie? Perhaps in the monopolistic condition of industry and agriculture, which do not face any competition and therefore do not have external stimuli to strive for perfection? . . . Why isn't his [Stalin's] behavior explained as a reflection of the interests of a particular social stratum, one that has grown up, let's say, from the soil of Soviet bureaucracy? . . . What has our state been over the course of almost thirty years: a democratic republic or a totalitarian state? . . . Doesn't single-party status and the almost complete overlap of government and party organs facilitate the personality cult?[29]

Clearly these questions went far beyond the explanation for the personality cult contained in Khrushchev's speech and bore witness to its unsatisfactory nature. Wherever silent obedience, against the orders of the Central Committee, was suddenly replaced by discussion, people turned up who tried to advance their own personal view of the problem. This occurred particularly dramatically at a party meeting at the USSR Academy of Sciences Thermal Technical Laboratory at Dubna on March 23 and 26, 1956. Expressing confusion about why Khrushchev's speech "wasn't discussed 'in a serious manner' at the Congress," technician G. I. Shedrin added, "We are now continuing the personality cult by exalting Khrushchev." As for the alleged "strength of the party and the power of the people," he stated categorically, "This didn't and doesn't exist. With Stalin we would have accepted fascism." Junior academic fellow R. G. Avalov expressed similar views: "The people are powerless; a small group of people was therefore able to establish their dictatorship." But Iu. F. Orlov, a junior academic fellow, went farther than anyone: "Our situation is such that property belongs to the people. But power belongs to some heap of scoundrels. . . . Our party is shot through with the spirit of slavery. . . . In the name of state security we have raised a child who hits us in the face." The attempts of the presidium of the meeting to break up the discussion met with resistance: a proposal to condemn these speeches as politically in error and slanderous to the party gained only two more votes than another proposal that essentially supported them.[30]

The higher party leadership, having received news about this meeting, regarded it as an attack on its monopolistic right to expound the truth and reacted accordingly. As early as April 3, it ordered that Orlov's and his comrades' party membership be examined, and that further discussion in party organizations of the conclusions of the congress be held in such a way that such hostile attacks would not be allowed. Here and there, however, the situation occasionally slipped out of control.

V. Churaev, deputy head of the Central Committee department on RSFSR party organs, noted with alarm on April 16, 1956, that "demogogic and even harmful speeches are taking place at meetings of various party organizations, and they do not always receive a decisive rebuff and political evaluation." As an example, he cited the Gorkii Institute of World Literature of the USSR Academy of Sciences, where literary scholar Bialik explained the appearance of the personality cult this way: "It seems to me that, for historical reasons, there existed in the party and state apparat a layer of people for whom the personality cult was advantageous, who used it as a vehicle. They now make lofty pronouncements and figure out ways to maintain themselves in that situation. . . . There have been those who led thousands of people to their death, and there have been those who saw it. . . . If all these people remain in place, if nothing happens to them, if the execution of the 20th Congress's decisions is entrusted to them, then this will be a self-deception on our part."

In spite of such "demogogic pronouncements," Churaev pointed out that "not one of the Communists of the party organization said anything about these speeches. And only Comrade Rumiantsev, member of the editorial committee of the journal *Kommunist*, criticized the non-party and revisionist judgments that were made at the meeting. His correct remarks were met by certain Communists with cries of protest. The meeting did not give a party evaluation of the speeches of Bialik, Gei, and Kuznetsov."[31]

At the Institute for Eastern Studies of the USSR Academy of Sciences, academic fellow Mordvinov, a member of the party since 1918 and a former chekist, having complained that there were "too many emotions and personal conclusions" in Khrushchev's speech, stated, "Members of the Politburo bear responsibility for the condition that has arisen in the party. . . . They answer for the shootings." Furthermore, he reproached Mikoyan and Molotov for insincerity and accused Khrushchev of cowardice. A graduate student, Shastitko, criticized the latter as well: "I do not like Khrushchev's behavior in some cases. When someone is speaking, Comrade Khrushchev often interrupts him with retorts and confuses him." But he really had it in for the so-called "representative" organs of power: "Elections to our councils are a farce; the soviets do not play any role and are not popular organizations; many deputies in them do not work at all. The Supreme Soviet does not work on anything substantive." When the secretary of the institute's party bureau, Ivanova, proposed condemning both these speeches as "politically harmful," the gathering disagreed, and the first secretary of the Kuibyshev regional committee, Ogurtsov, who was in attendance, failed to support this proposal and said nothing. Only two of nine bureau members voted for Mordvinov's exclusion from the party, and only one voted to exclude Shastitko; as a result both received only reprimands. V. Churaev and G. Drozdov, the head of another Central Committee department (of administrative organs), reported on this meeting to their bosses, urging that "the Moscow party committee conduct another meeting to debunk the anti-party attacks of Mordvinov and Shastitko, to decide the question of their party membership, and to strengthen the party bureau."[32]

The personal concerns of Communists who "did not correctly understand the party line on the question of the personality cult" began to be considered in other party organizations as well. Reprimands and exclusions from the party occurred, accompanied by dismissals from work. The election of B. A. Kedrov, a professor of philosophy, member of the party since 1918, and son of a prominent Soviet public figure repressed in 1941, to corresponding member of the USSR Academy of Sciences was postponed for four full years. His sin was to have contended that Khrushchev's speech barely scratched the surface in portraying the personality cult as the personal tragedy of Stalin: "What kind of tragedy is that? Now take the tragedy of the party and the people—that's a tragedy!"[33]

The party organization at the Thermal Technical Laboratory of the USSR Academy of Sciences was disbanded.[34] N. N. Semenov, a geophysicist from Leningrad and a Stalin Prize laureate, was diagnosed as mentally ill and sent to a special psychiatric clinic; he had written a letter to the Central Committee demanding that Stalin's crimes be exposed more consistently.[35]

Churaev, in the previously mentioned note of April 16, 1956, called attention to "cases in which various party organizations show political carelessness, which hostile elements are using." He described an instance that took place in the Verkhov Forest Preparation Point of the Plesets region of Arkhangelsk province. Generozov, a 25-year-old electrical station mechanic and Komsomol member who had not finished his higher education, "started down the path of anti-Soviet actions." What he allegedly did was conduct "harmful oral propaganda among workers" and distribute typed pamphlets that contained "slanderous attacks against the Soviet government, calls for the abolition of the CPSU and for prosecuting its Central Committee." At his arrest by state security organs, three such pamphlets were found on him, as well as a typewriter and the following letter, which, according to his own testimony, he intended to send to Khrushchev upon gaining the approval of the workers:

> Nikita Sergeevich! We, the workers of the Verkhov Forest Point, are grateful to you for finding in yourself the courage to tell the entire people the truth and to communicate facts that give reason not to trust you

or the government. We solemnly honor Lenin. . . . and consider that,
in the situation that has arisen, we must act as Lenin taught: all power
to the soviets, i.e. to the local soviets of the toilers' deputies. . . . If your
announcement and high regard for Lenin are not hypocritical, then
you will send us governmental guarantees that police and state security personnel will not touch our delegates and agitators. Otherwise
there may arise incidents, and perhaps even bloodshed, for which you
will be held responsible.[36]

Churaev's same note included an utterly different example: on April
11 in Vologda, in the main department store, a handwritten pamphlet
was posted with the following declaration: "It's all nonsense—Stalin is
with us." The declaration was signed "VLKSM"—the All-Union Lenin
Communist League of Youth, or Komsomol.[37]

To repeat, there were few such Stalinists among the intelligentsia.
There were many more people who, like the theater director Georgii
Tovstonogov, a two-time Stalin laureate, experienced a "feeling of satisfied justice." Along with Mikhail Zoshchenko and Anna Akhmatova,
the writer Iurii German was subjected to harsh attacks in 1946 by then
chief ideologue Andrei Zhdanov. German called a friend in Moscow
from Leningrad and cried, "We are finally entering the family of European nations. And I am entering the party."[38]

Such unbridled optimists did not, however, typify public opinion at
the time. Akhmatova, the widow of a poet who was shot and the mother
of an arrested historian-ethnographer, said in March 1956, "Now the ar-
restees will return, and two Russias will look each other in the eye: the
one which sent people off to the camps, and the one which was sent off."[39]

Few of those who did the sending turned out to be capable of repentance. "The 20th Congress was a catastrophe for us," admitted
L. A. Fotieva, who in her time had turned over to Stalin the secret political testament of Lenin, for whom she had worked as a personal secretary. Now she tried to justify her unbecoming behavior of long ago:
"Stalin was the authority for us. We loved Stalin. He was a great man."[40]
And who in the political elite could have sworn that they had turned no
one in, had demanded the crucifixion of no one? This is why the elite
perceived the speech on the personality cult ambivalently. While remaining Stalinists at heart, many of the representatives of the nomenklatura (perhaps even a majority) supported Khrushchev's exposure of
the Stalin's crimes—not only for the sake of party discipline and a
servile, hypocritical willingness to please, but because they also felt in

their bones, even if they did not fully understand it, how shaky and un-
sure their position had been under Stalin, how much their life and
death had depended on the caprices of one person, even if he was
"beloved beyond measure." From now on, they were promised stability. For the sake of that, they managed to change their beliefs. As King
Henry of Navarre said in a similar situation, "Paris is worth a mass."

The common people were another story. It still is believed that exposure of the Stalin cult met with their understanding and approval.
But the entire policy of the Communist party over the following three
decades, and the silent majority's reaction to it, raise doubts about such
an assumption. The latest data to fall into historians' hands suggest a
completely different conclusion, namely, that the majority of the people, unlike the intelligentsia, neither understood nor approved of the
sharp reversal from praise and deification to the denunciation of the
"great leader and teacher."

Rumors circulated that at the same closed session of the congress
at which Khrushchev gave his speech on the personality cult, Molotov
took the floor and allegedly said, "Despite the information this congress has received, I continue to believe that Stalin has brilliantly continued Lenin's work."[41] Molotov's name became popular once again in
certain circles. Some participants of the demonstration in Tbilisi mentioned above demanded that he be named head of the government.[42]

Recalling the unrest of the winter of 1956–1957, the critic and prose
writer V. Kardin noted, "The inertia of 'cult thinking' overcame us, and
it was problematic whether we would remain under its spell or begin to
invent a new kind of thinking. The issue was resolved not by voting, nor
by calling a general meeting, but by each individual independently.
Alone with himself or herself."[43] The writer Veniamin Kaverin spoke
about the same issue this way: "One can already walk on two legs, but
many are still crawling on all fours."[44] But how many? A. I. Tarasov had
been found guilty in 1948 for allegedly organizing the Moscow group
Democratic Party, and he was freed immediately after the 20th Party
Congress. En route to the Caucasus, he stopped at his parents' house
in Moscow, where he later recalled, "I was amazed by the people's nostalgic love for Stalin. People remembered his grandiose funeral, the sea
of tears shed, the euphoria they experienced from the deadly crush of
the crowd. 'And hundreds of souls of trampled fellow citizens made up
a mournful wedding crown,' some poet was moved to write. From that
time on, I gave up believing the principle that the voice of the people is

the voice of God. I have begun to understand that each people deserves its government."[45]

If this was indeed the "voice of the people," then it becomes easier to understand why Khrushchev, who worked so hard to make sure that the speech on the personality cult was heard at the 20th Party Congress and then made it known to the entire party and the Komsomol as well, suddenly stopped in his tracks and even began to take steps in the opposite direction. It was not so much his Kremlin comrades who got him to reverse his field (he disregarded their views more and more as time went on), nor was it the Chinese nor even his fear that events would get out of control, as they did in Poland and Hungary. It was resistance of a different sort.

Society, at least a significant part of it, had so intoxicated itself with strong, regular doses of totalitarian ideological poison that refusing it or, even worse, attempting to apply an antidote provoked withdrawal symptoms. In such cases, doctors either resolutely and unflinchingly continue the shock therapy, hoping that the patient will bear it and the outcome will not be fatal, or they limit themselves to homeopathic pills and poultices with no guarantee against possible relapse of the chronic ailment. Khrushchev abandoned the first path and turned to the second.

In the fall of 1956 conversations and discussions about the burden of bureaucracy and the need for more freedom intensified in the ranks of the creative intelligentsia. At a October 22 discussion of Vladimir Dudintsev's novel *Not by Bread Alone,* the writer Konstantin Paustovskii spoke of castes and classes in Soviet society, and a tape of his speech was re-recorded many times and distributed by the first enthusiasts of samizdat. The father of the Soviet hydrogen bomb, Andrei Sakharov, asked his colleague Igor Tamm whether he liked Khrushchev, adding, "I like him ever so much! After all, he differs from Stalin!" Tamm answered, "Yes. I like Khrushchev; he is not Stalin. But it would be better if he differed from Stalin even more."[46]

Khrushchev had his limitations, however. Events in Poland and Hungary showed this especially graphically when they ended with Soviet troops invading Hungary. Part of the population reacted very sharply. On October 25, at an evening dedicated to the anniversary of the October Revolution and held at the USSR Ministry of Internal Affairs club, students of the Moscow State Historical Archive Institute met toasts to the Polish and Hungarian revolutions and to the "impending fourth Russian revolution" with applause and cries of "Hurrah!" In the diary of the student who gave these toasts, this short note has been preserved: "The majority sympathize with the Hungarians. I'm with Gomulka [the reformist Polish Communist party chief]." It is true that this majority, if it did exist, quickly dissipated under the influence of the media's reporting on the "crimes" of Hungarian insurrectionists. As early as November 3, literally on the eve of the intervention, the same diary notes: "A majority of students changed their minds on Hungary. Too bad."[47] But not all "came to their senses.""Magyars! Magyars! You are our brothers, I am with you, your Russian brother." The student Iurii Anokhin read these verses of his at the journalism department of Moscow State University. He got four years in the camps for them.[48]

On November 7, during the parade in Yaroslavl celebrating the anniversary of the Bolshevik Revolution, a tenth-grader from high school no. 55, Vitalii Lazariants, and three of his comrades unfurled a huge poster before the tribune on which the entire regional leadership stood: "We demand the withdrawal of Soviet troops from Hungary!" In Sevastopol someone slashed fourteen portraits of "leaders of the party and government" that were exhibited on the wall of a bread factory. The next day the Tula worker S. T. Voronov slashed with a razor a portrait of Khrushchev on the facade of military base no. 44 in Serpukhov. About a thousand anti-Soviet pamphlets were collected by local KGB organs; quite a few were observed in Moscow, Leningrad, Zaporozhe, Barnaul, and Riga.[49]

The academician and physicist Lev Landau lost his temper while arguing with someone who had cited official explanations of the Hungarian events: "Now how can you believe that? Are we supposed to believe butchers? They are butchers after all, vile butchers!"[50] The biologist Aleksandr Liubishchev, also condemning the intervention, characterized the Hungarian revolution as a reaction not only to Stalin's despotism and oligarchic degeneration but also to Khrushchev's secret speech: "He did much more [to bring it about] than all the propaganda speeches of Voice of America and [Radio] Liberty."[51]

In his letter to *Pravda*, Kharkov pensioner Aleksandr Pashkov, a member of the party since the Civil War, gave a different assessment of the Hungarian events and of the role of Khrushchev's secret speech in causing them. Complaining that the Polish press, Yugoslav president Josip Tito, and Italian Communist chief Palmiro Togliatti were not fully backing the Soviet action in Hungary, he noted, "And all this comes from what? From the rubbish that was spouted at the 20th Party Congress about the dirty deeds of Stalin. They weren't smart enough to do it more quietly; they broadcast such muck to the whole world." From his point of view, which he claimed was shared by the Soviet people, not only Hungary but all of Western Europe should have been occupied back in May 1945, "with the red banner planted on the shore of the Bay of Biscay and on the peaks of the Pyrenees." After all, despite the talk about peaceful coexistence, "one must remember that two bears do not live in one den." Pashkov expressed himself no less cynically about the personality cult: "What are you picking on Stalin for, like devils with a poker? You ran off at the mouth. and now you're trying to wriggle your way out of it. . . . Why are you doing all this, when it is perfectly clear that the personality cult is essentially the product of a certain system?"

At the same time—and this is quite curious—Pashkov contended that the overwhelming majority of the party consisted of "sneaks, careerists, sycophants, fellow travelers, never mind the real scoundrels and even criminal elements," an unavoidable result of a one party system "with a lack of democracy in the country." He suggested "restoring the power of the soviets" and selecting deputies from several possible candidates; reducing the party's monopoly on all positions in the state and economic apparatus; replacing the unions with committees of worker self-governance; and granting freedom of the press.[52]

Pravda, naturally, did not publish this letter but sent it to the Central Committee just in case. Judging by notes made there, the letter was studied very attentively—not the proposals about democratization but the views concerning the "chattering that was unleashed at the 20th Party Congress about the dirty deeds of Stalin," for this was precisely the pragmatic position held by D. T. Shepilov, candidate-member of the Presidium and secretary for ideology of the Central Committee. A half-year later, he explained his position on this question: "History will not forgive anyone those transgressions of lawfulness that have been allowed to occur, but it is not in the interests of our party or the world Communist movement to stir up these issues now. . . . When Comrade Chou En-lai visited, we were forced to hear bitter things: that by raising the question of the personality cult in a one-sided way, we are doing obvious harm to our work."[53]

But the genie was already out of the bottle, and forcing it back in was impossible, even though the Central Committee tried to do so. On December 19, 1957, the Central Committee sent out a secret letter "On the intensification of political work of party organizations among the masses and the suppression of attacks by hostile elements." The very fact of this letter—the basis for which were the conclusions of a committee headed by yet another Khrushchev protégé, Leonid Brezhnev—reflected serious concern "on high" about the developing situation. Khrushchev's January 17, 1957, pronouncement at a Chinese embassy reception attended by Chou En-lai reflected this concern: "God grant that every Communist be able to struggle as Stalin struggled!"[54]

Such waverings neither reassured society nor overcame the incipient divisions about the recent past. Directly opposing points of view were expressed at party meetings when the above-mentioned Central Committee secret letter was discussed. Furthermore, "anti-party, demagogic speeches took place" once again, and they "did not receive the requisite rebuff." In the Levobereg region, Zelenov, superintendent of construction of the Kuibyshev Hydroelectric Station and party bureau member, said, "The leaders of the party and the government somehow got mixed up in their criticism of the Stalin personality cult: first they condemned him, but now they have begun to praise him again." The chairman of the meeting, who was at his wits' end, could think of nothing better than to interrupt such speakers with shouts of "Demagogue! Slanderer!" "You should have been fired long ago," he barked at one of them.[55]

At the Yaroslavl automobile factory, construction worker Kisilev complained that "the way the Central Committee letter was read indicated that you either keep quiet or get sent to prison camp." "Could Hungary really teach us nothing?" he shouted. Those gathered at the meeting applauded after he quoted a worker who had come to the Soviet Union from France: "It is better to die than to live the way we live here." Subsequently, by a vote of 21 to 17, with eighteen workers abstaining, a proposal to include in the resolution a clause condemning his speech as anti-party was rejected. When he was dragged over to the party committee to be interrogated, he continued to press his line there too: "The population of the USSR is divided into plebeians and patricians, and our party finds itself at a dangerous age. It has been in power for forty years, but, as is well known, cheats and careerists . . . even now occupy cozy posts. . . . Draw your own conclusions."[56]

M. Petrygin, an engineer from Tuapse, complained to the Central Committee, "Uncertainty and doubt that the Stalin personality cult and its consequences will be liquidated have grown in our country." He thought that Khrushchev's speech at the Chinese embassy was "not appropriate for the first secretary of the CPSU Central Committee, whose authority has grown . . . until today."[57]

Antonina Peterson, a member of the party since 1917, expressed a diametrically opposed view in a letter to Shepilov from Riga: "Do you really not sense how the party awaits from you the rehabilitation of Stalin? How we all grabbed for the *Pravda* in which the Chinese Communists' article on Stalin appeared! But we want to hear the same kind of words from our party's Central Committee. That would remove a great burden from us."[58] Hopes for the restoration of Stalinism had to be put aside after the unsuccessful attempt undertaken in June 1957 by Malenkov, Molotov, and Kaganovich, along with Bulganin and Shepilov, who "joined them," to rid themselves of Khrushchev.

Despite the fact that the subsequent plenum of the Central Committee turned into an apotheosis of the first secretary, the attitude of Communists and non-party members toward Khrushchev was by no means unanimously positive. Questions asked about the June plenum at party meetings in a series of Georgian towns and cities were indicative. In Bolnisi: "Can we conduct a discussion in the party about those questions that divided Malenkov, Molotov, and Kaganovich from the Central Committee?" In Chiaturi: "Against whom did they speak: against the party or against Khrushchev?" In Rustavi: "An individual is not the party, and since Malenkov, Molotov, and Kaganovich spoke against the secretary of the Central Committee, we cannot consider them an anti-party group." In Stalin's birthplace, Gori: "Who gave the order about the shooting of youth in March 1956?" At the Kirov factory in Tbilisi: "Have the guilty parties in the murder of young people during last year's events been made to take responsibility?"[59]

A total of 225 letters and telegrams with reactions to the plenum arrived at the Central Committee departments of party organs of the RSFSR and the union republics. An absolute majority of them demonstrated strong support for those decisions."Long live the great reformer, Comrade Khrushchev!" one anonymous author cried.[60] Disagreement was expressed in only fifteen letters. Thus a group of non-party workers from the Azov Steel Factory in Zhdanov considered "the denunciation of the personality cult of Comrade Stalin incorrect and harmful." Demanding that "more attention be given to the development of light industry and food production," it insisted that "with the goal of clarify-

ing the genuine truth, . . . Malenkov, Kaganovich, Molotov, and Shepilov should be given the opportunity to speak on the radio and at worker
meetings."[61]

Students of the Moscow State Historical Archive Institute and the
All-Union State Institute of Cinematography, while on military training at the Dorogobug camps of the Kovrov division, competed to see
who could tell the most scathing political joke (about corn, the personality cult, the slogan to catch up with and overtake America, etc.), and
one of them cried out to the entire battalion: "Down with Khrushchev
and Mikoyan! Down with the CPSU Central Committee! Down with the
CPSU itself! Isn't it time to take up arms?"[62]

Such outcries and appeals (as opposed to ubiquitous, openly told
jokes that bore witness to how significantly the atmosphere of fear and
suspicion in society had lessened) were heard very rarely. They were not
so much a manifestation of well-formed attitudes as they were a burst
of emotion, a protest against the disorders and injustices which one had
to face in everyday life. Furthermore, it should be admitted that, as a
rule, state security organs distinguished conscious and serious anti-
Sovietism from random anarchic outbursts and preferred in the latter
case to limit themselves to "prophylactic" work by not turning ongoing
investigations into judicial cases.

Among critics of Khrushchev's policies were also people with embryonic civil self-awareness, who perceived their interests fairly well
and who were able to discern among political leaders those who better
reflected their aspirations and hopes. "Our souls are bitter that individuals who are known to us as good Communists and Bolsheviks are
being driven out of the Central Committee," a certain "group of workers" informed the Central Committee Party Control Committee. "Comrade Malenkov was the first to reduce agricultural taxes by 50 percent—
no one will ever forget that. . . . The people believed him before, believe
him now, and will continue to believe him! Comrade Khrushchev
promised workers that he would raise salaries and arrange for a seven-
hour workday, but instead he forgot to even think about adding to
salaries. . . . Until him, there was at least a decrease in prices every year,
but now he has done away with that as well—just try to live on 300–
400 rubles [per month] with a family of three or four people, and there
are millions like us, who have neither an apartment nor money."[63]

In August 1957 the KGB arrested Dmitrii Kisilev, a literary fellow at
the department of letters of the trade union newspaper *Trud*. Kisilev was

forty-six years old, had been a member of the CPSU since 1942, and had graduated from the Moscow province party school. From newspaper pieces about meetings he had copied the names of workers and employees who had spoken approvingly about the cancellation of government loan payments to the population and the exclusion of the "anti-party group" from the Central Committee, discovered their addresses, and sent them anonymous letters reproaching them in various ways for disseminating official lies. He called the discontinuation of drawings for government loans "robbery of the people," who as it was were "starving." Kisilev "called for the removal of party leaders, and for their exclusion from the party." In all, he sent twenty-two such letters. The Moscow city court sentenced him to five years imprisonment.[64]

The fortieth anniversary of the Bolsheviks' coming to power produced further dissatisfaction. According to KGB data, the celebration proceeded everywhere "in an organized fashion and in an atmosphere of great political enthusiasm." Nevertheless, according to the very same data, on November 6, 1957, anti-Soviet pamphlets were discovered in the Palace of Sport at Luzhniki and in the Bauman region of Moscow, while on November 8, at the site of a serious automobile accident, hand-written anti-Soviet pamphlets were found in the wallet of the hospitalized driver. In the Moscow suburb of Elektrostal, someone affixed an anti-Soviet pamphlet to the hood of a police car, and two more on the doors of the police department. Similar "enemy attacks" occurred in Leningrad, Riga, and Ust-Kamenogorsk, and in the Kalinin, Minsk, Brest, Kiev, Stalin, Poltava, Vinnits, and Stanislav provinces.[65]

When someone told the poet Boris Pasternak that people were resisting the repression of their personal opinions and maintained that "the situation now is different than it was ten years ago," he only shook his head skeptically. It seemed to him that things could not go on this way for long, that there would be yet more changes, and not for the better. "They will be frightened by the little bit of freedom that they have given, and they will tighten the screws," he explained to the sculptor Zoia Maslennikova, without hiding his fear that he would become one of the first victims, as he had given over his novel *Doctor Zhivago* to be published abroad.[66]

And indeed, when the novel received the Nobel Prize for Literature in October 1958, the authorities began a real campaign against Pasternak. They accused him of treason and called him "Judas, a renegade, a weed, a frog in the swamp." Pasternak held out for a week. But after

Moscow writers agreed at a meeting to ask the government to deprive him of Soviet citizenship and deport him, he refused the award. "The country was ruled for so long by a madman, a murderer, and now—by a fool and a pig," he said sorrowfully to the young poet Andrei Voznesenskii, one of the few who had the courage not to agree with the majority at that meeting.[67]

The creative intelligentsia developed this theme of "fool and pig" with considerable enthusiasm in their corridor and table conversations. Some references made it onto paper. The poet Ilia Selvinskii, for example, responded quite unexpectedly to Khrushchev's attempt to convince Americans that censorship in the Soviet Union no longer existed: "It is simply not true that books fly into trash cans. Has censorship really ended? Of course it has; Khrushchev, for example, broadcasts uncensored to the entire world."[68]

Yes, the outbursts Khrushchev began to allow himself more and more frequently contrasted sharply with earlier times, when leaders swore only in their own personal circle or when rebuking their subordinates, and they appeared before a large public only on big holidays, smiling broadly and waving affably to those mere mortals who exultantly welcomed these living demi-gods. And now those times seemed to some common people like paradise, so that the comparison they made was not favorable to Khrushchev. To this nostalgic feeling was added the quality common to many Russians of pitying those who are overthrown, those who have suffered or endured mistreatment from the authorities, even if they themselves had been among those authorities the day before. When former premier Nikolai Bulganin's exile to Stavropol was announced, for an entire month "crowds of 150–200 people stood from sunrise to sunset to see the injured one" at the building of the Council of People's Commissars, where he worked as chairman.[69] On November 6, 1959, anonymous Leningrad residents sent holiday greetings to the ambassador to Mongolia, Viacheslav Molotov. Among other warm words were the following: "Your great friend turns 80 this year. We remember him."[70]

Stalin's birthday, December 21, was not marked in 1959 by any official ceremonies. As early as a week later, however, in the Moscow suburb Kuntsevo, not far from Stalin's former dacha, ninety-two pamphlets were found "with hostile attacks against the leaders of the Communist party and the Soviet state."[71]

Khrushchev did not enjoy particular favor among those holding the opposite view of Stalin and Stalinism either. They were not satisfied with his inconsistent policies and halfway measures. They expressed their dissatisfaction, and sometimes their despair, in extremely militant forms. On July 28, 1961, a letter arrived at *Uchitel'skaia gazeta* (Teacher's newspaper) with a threat to carry out a terrorist act against the head of the government. The KGB identified and on September 20 arrested the author of this letter, a 25-year-old non-party worker named Mordvinov. Admitting he had prepared and sent the letter, he explained his step as an effort to change Soviet foreign policy, including on the Berlin question.[72]

Other threats of terror against the Central Committee found their way into "Materials of the August session of the Temporary Communist Union," which were sent by mail on August 20 and 21, 1961, to various party, state, and social organizations. In this document, the official plan for a new party program was criticized for a "departure from Leninism," and a series of measures was proposed to reduce the screaming inequalities in Soviet society, beginning with a halt to the sale of luxury consumer goods (such as light automobiles) and ending with the confiscation of part of the property of the "Soviet bourgeois-wealthy." The author warned that if the Central Committee did not rework its planned program in the direction indicated or allow a broad discussion of it, then the "Provisional Communist Union" would begin terror against those individuals "whose presence in positions of leadership interferes with our people's path to communism." One month later, the author of this document was "found." He turned out to be S. M. Sinev, a 31-year-old, non-party construction engineer in Krasnodar. During his arrest, a typewriter, one copy of the "materials" that had not been sent, and a rough draft were confiscated.[73]

On August 25, 1961, in Kovrov (Vladimirov province) the following inscription appeared on the wall of a building: "We will avenge the residents of Murom!" and on the wall of another, "Down with the Communist regime! (Young guard)."[74] The number of those fleeing abroad increased noticeably—a way of voting with one's feet for another way of life. On September 8, 1961, the first forcible attempt to hijack a passenger plane occurred, which ended in the death of one of the hijackers and a death sentence for two others.[75]

In October 1961 anonymous letters from Stalingrad were sent to a brigade of Communist labor at a factory in Leningrad and to one of the delegates to the 22nd Party Congress from the Leningrad party organization. As the head of state security put it, "filthy slander against one of the leaders of the party and the government" (read: Khrushchev) was raised in them, and they contained "provocative calls to speak out against his work." The KGB eventually determined that the author of these letters was none other than the deputy head of the organization-instruction department of the Kamyshinsk city party committee, A. N. Frolov. Needless to say, he was immediately dismissed from work and expelled from the party.[76]

Longtime party member B. A. Kolumbetov read a speech at the congress by G. I. Voronov, a Presidium candidate member and deputy chairman of the Central Committee Bureau for the RSFSR, whom he had known at one time. According to Voronov, Russia's collective farms "have decided to increase their twenty-year production of milk 2.9 times and of meat nearly 4 times." Kolumbetov sent an indignant letter to him on October 24, 1961, from Kharkov: "We should not, we should not under any circumstances consider the people and the party masses cattle and feed them such rubbish. . . . Three years ago you, like all leaders, could not make allowances for two years ahead, and now without batting an eye you are going for twenty!? . . . Of course it is easier to rattle the bones of Molotov and Kaganovich than to give your long-suffering people food! . . . You have ravished the people; they have understood that everything is a lie and deception, and there is no joy in the future."[77]

Very few people believed in the communism Khrushchev promised by the year 1980. Contemporary folklore bears clear witness to this. Jingles derisive to point of indecency were sung: "An enema burst in my sweetheart's ass; a specter is haunting the shack, the specter of communism."[78] Jokes from "Radio Armenia," which never tired of answering the most diverse and tricky questions, enjoyed a special popularity. For example, referring to Khrushchev's poor grasp of Russian grammar and punctuation: "What contribution did Nikita Sergeevich make to *kommunizm*? He added a soft sign after the letter *z*." The legendary rascal Khodzha Nasreddin was recalled as well: "Why did he promise the emir to teach the donkey to speak in exactly twenty years? Well, because he was smart; by that time, either the emir will have passed on, or the donkey will have dropped dead!"[79]

For that part of Soviet society that considered itself anti-Stalinist, however, the 22nd Party Congress became a celebration of the soul. The same jesting Radio Armenia, when asked how the Congress had ended, answered, "With the removal of the body." Moisei Morgulis, the barber at the Central House of Writers who was famed for his wit, gushed, "Very good! Otherwise Stalin and Lenin would have gone on living together as if in a communal apartment, even though only one of them signed up for it." And there were malicious jokes as well: "Khrushchev was seen in the mausoleum with a cot; he was probably checking the measurements. No, not with a cot, but with his grandson, to whom he was explaining that he would also rest there. And Lenin could barely stand it! When they moved Stalin in with him, he was outraged that the Central Committee had stuck him with such a pig, and now he was upset again, fearing that they would turn the mausoleum into a hotel!"[80]

The ranks of the Stalinists thinned out somewhat, and they themselves were forced to keep quiet under the pressure of the new denunciations being pronounced at the congress. But not everywhere. In Georgia they clung to their previous opinions and did not bother to conceal them. In Zestafoni, when Stalin's coffin was removed from the mausoleum in Moscow, "evil-minded people" destroyed a monument to Lenin. During the holiday parade on November 7, 1961, in Tbilisi, the columns of marchers who marched past government tribunal leaders shouting "Hurrah," in keeping with a long established ritual, included students and teachers of the university who instead maintained a deathly silence. K. M. Kochiashvili, a Bolshevik since 1914, wrote about this to Khrushchev: "The 20th Congress of our party has provoked serious confusion in the minds of the citizens of the Georgian Republic, or to be more precise, a negative attitude from the mass of the population, primarily from the intelligentsia, toward the spirit that reigned at that Congress."[81]

Letters reaching Khrushchev's staff not only noted the moods of the masses but also analyzed the party-state mechanism and suggested its democratization. A letter from Kiev from Nikolai Rudenko, a Communist since 1941, ran to thirty typewritten pages. I will cite only certain places in the text that were marked in the margins by Khrushchev's associates and therefore, one can assume, were read by him:

> The system of governance of our state clashes irreconcilably with the spiritual and material needs of the people. . . . It was constructed screw by screw by Stalin's hands for the consolidation of his unlimited power. . . . Having denounced his personality cult and commanded our descendants that nothing like this should ever happen again, we have left the machine virtually untouched. . . . And now we have a sit-

uation in which the deceased grabs for the legs of the living. . . . Our plenums, even if we call them historic, can only offer temporary relief to agriculture, much as the life-saving injections of a doctor can only offer temporary relief to a patient. Nikita Sergeevich, your arrival in some region or other only serves as first aid. Unfortunately, the effect of any temporary relief measure wears off very soon.[82]

Rudenko proposed beginning a fundamental reconstruction of the entire state machine by ending the situation in which "almost everything here is now done directly through party organs: animals are raised and slaughtered, collective farms are started up and once again relegated to the whirlpool of backwardness." Such a state of affairs impoverished the political role of the party. "We Communists do not have the right to conduct elections in the manner they are now conducted—cutting down the lists of candidates to the point where there is no possibility of choice." For Rudenko it was clear that "a public figure who has managed to do a great deal for the people gains not only supporters but also antagonists," and if his name on an electoral ballot stood next to names that are known to no one, then "passions could be focused right on him," and this would hinder his being elected. "It seems to me that this circumstance forces our leaders to limit themselves to that anti-democratic electoral system that was proposed by Stalin. But then why not return to the Leninist forms of popular power? After all, they precluded such incidents and at the same time gave the people some weapons in the struggle with the bureaucracy. We must simply make voting secret and not reduce the lists. . . . Then the people will have the opportunity to choose."[83]

Rudenko was sure that it was time to democratize and that delaying or postponing a decision would be tantamount to death. "You yourselves have prepared the way and helped the question to mature. . . . During Stalin's time no small amount of blind faith characterized our citizens; I would call it fanaticism. There used to be a kind of inexplicable film on our brains that was difficult for someone to break through from the inside. You have courageously and decisively torn this film asunder; and suddenly people have felt that they are in a position to think and give their own assessment of whatever happened. What used to be hidden behind seven seals has now become evident before our eyes. . . . Any . . . lie in public life has now become intolerable and offensive. There is now not one politically developed person who would not be offended by our elections!"[84]

Referring to conversations often heard on the bus between Kiev and Obukhov, Rudenko stated that not only was the intelligentsia discussing the defects of the system, but workers and peasants were too. Furthermore, they were doing so completely openly and with great indignation. "The majority of them express sympathy for you, for they understand what difficulties you must face, for every one of your good ideas runs up against the blank wall of bureaucracy. Some of them accuse you of indecisiveness, of a lack of willingness to make sense of the root problems that have given rise to bureaucracy and whitewashing, which have today become almost a social norm."[85]

As we see, the letter was composed extremely diplomatically. In trying to open his addressee's eyes to the vital need for democratization, the author sweetens the bitter pill; in suggesting which reforms to start with, he resorts to unconcealed flattery. Having expressed the desire that "our state should be headed by a someone whom history would have the right to place alongside Lenin," he immediately asks forgiveness for suggesting that such qualities had not yet made their appearance. Perhaps, Rudenko adds, this is because people of one generation are used to forms that have already taken root. "It seems to them that, if you throw [these forms] away, everything will fall apart. It is possible, however, that I am completely wrong in this rebuke. It is possible that you are secretly preparing society for this decisive change."[86]

This was one point of view on Khrushchev's works, gently nudging him in a certain direction. A diametrically opposed, sharply negative perspective was expressed by two inhabitants of Chita. One of them prepared seven leaflets in colored pencil and displayed them in the center of the city during the night of December 31, 1961: "Khrushchev's internal policy is rotten! Down with Khrushchev's dictatorship! Windbag Khrushchev, where is your abundance? Comrades, how much longer will we live in hunger and poverty?" The second posted a poetic pamphlet the next night, New Year's Eve, in a different region of the city: "Ilich, Ilich [Lenin], wake up and look into what Khrushchev is doing; vodka costs 27, and there is no lard or meat at all. We'll get to communism and find no cabbage there."[87]

On February 19 and 20, 1962, an unknown person in Moscow mailed a mass of letters to members of the Presidium, secretaries of the Komsomol central committees, provincial party bosses, and government ministers. The letters contained theses for presentation at the CPSU Central Committee plenum on March 5, 1962. They began by addressing Khrushchev: "We remain your old acquaintances who sit alongside you—the ones who already wrote to you in the beginning of your career as the 'leader.' Do you remember that we predicted at that point how you would deal with Molotov, Malenkov, and the others? Our predictions have been fully confirmed. We announce to you that there are now more of us, for in trying to chase us from the apparat of the Central Committee and the Council of Ministers, you have only broadened our circle. We will soon see you, face to face, out in the open."[88]

Converting the official statistical data of the gross grain collection into a per capita count and getting figures of 46 poods (1656 lbs.) for 1913 and 32 poods (1152 lbs.) in 1961, the unknown author sounded an alarm that must have resounded loudly in the ears of the apparat: "In the current situation it is easy to understand that the forthcoming March plenum will 'disclose the guilty parties' in the profound collapse of Khrushchev's agricultural policies. What lies ahead is an unprecedented reprisal against the cadres. . . . There is no limit to Khrushchev's adventurism, and because of the inevitability of the collapse of these adventures, he will always need scapegoats. And this will continue until some generation of secretaries of national, regional, and provincial committees gets together and tosses Khrushchev overboard, using the same method with which they saddled themselves with him in the first place." So that these very secretaries would not hesitate and would make up their minds to mount a coup as soon as possible, another even more terrible prospect was sketched out for them: "The following could also occur: driven to despair, the people, who have so far only engaged in Italian-style sabotage against all Khrushchev's measures, will suddenly rise up and undertake something that will eclipse all Budapests."[89]

As if to confirm that this even more terrible prospect was not out of the question, an incident occurred on February 22, 1962, at a youth discussion club in the central reading room of the Society for the Dissemination of Political and Scientific Knowledge. The subject of the session was, "May there be more of the obsessed" (the obsession of a young builder of communism, of course). Two typeset documents reached the presidium, along with various notes from the auditorium, that were signed "Union of Freedom and Reason" and contained, according to the KGB, "slanderous fabrications on the situation in the country, spiteful attacks on the CPSU and the Soviet government, and also calls to active struggle for altering the social and state order."

An analogous document was discovered at the Institute for Foreign Languages. That same evening and the next morning, someone mailed 130 of these anti-Soviet documents to various cities around the country. Their addressees were Komsomol committees at institutions of higher education and at industrial enterprises, the editorial boards of newspapers and magazines, and party and government organs. In reporting this to the Central Committee, KGB Chairman V. Semichastnyi noted reassuringly that "active measures have been adopted to discover the propagators of these anti-Soviet tendencies."[90] These measures soon produced results. As early as March 2, two Komsomol members were arrested (V. A. Balashev, a photographer at the Fifth Printing Press of the Military Publishing House, and A. G. Murzhenko, a student at the Moscow Financial Institute), from whom twenty envelopes with pamphlets were seized. Under questioning they admitted that they themselves had composed and printed 350 pamphlets, of which around three hundred had already been mailed or distributed in student auditoriums, and that they had recruited several students to help in this distribution. Reporting on this the next day at the Central Committee, Semichastnyi noted that around two hundred pamphlets had already been received by his department. "Work on ferreting out and seizing anti-Soviet documents continues. The investigation into the affair is being conducted with an eye toward finding all participants in the group and those who may have inspired them."[91]

On March 18, 1962, a round of elections for the USSR Supreme Soviet took place. Several pamphlets calling for people not to vote for the candidates for deputy were collected in Moscow, Leningrad, Rostov-na-Donu, Tallinn, Serpukhov, Pskov, Vologda, Ivanov, and Kalinin province. In Tallinn and Kigisepp, six state flags were torn down.[92] In the Kalinin electoral district of Moscow, where Khrushchev was up for election, remarks such as the following were left on many ballots: "Glory to you, you dear, great Russian! . . . I wish our deputy many years of life for the sake of the laboring people. . . . In voting for you, we are sure that together with our party, you will achieve the improvement of agriculture. . . . The very fact that you have burst the swollen grandeur of Stalin is already enough to have won the trust of the people. . . . We thank Nikita Sergeevich for the good, well-built apartments and buildings. . . . I kiss your initials and send a great thank you for my secure old age, Savina." There were also requests and proposals. For example, to raise the salaries for teachers and doctors, to build more kindergartens and preschools, to cancel night shifts in production, to lower the age for pensions for women. There were also remarks expressing "unhealthy, retrograde" moods. For example, "I expect milk from a goat, but from Nikita, kasha made from manna from heaven. . . . For the first time in my life I am voting against Soviet power—it is very difficult to live. . . . I condemn atomic tests. . . . It would be preferable to speak less about the personality cult and about one's self as well. . . . The Jews are burying Russia."[93]

The shooting of workers in Novocherkassk, the Cuban crisis, the further worsening of relations with the Chinese, the division of the party into industrial and agricultural wings, the uproar with the artistic intelligentsia at the Manezh, the drought and poor harvest of 1963—all this still lay ahead. Dissatisfaction grew. The unhappiness of the apparat also grew. On October 14, 1964, it accomplished what certain anonymous parties, whom the KGB never did identify, had called for two and a half years earlier. The party "unanimously" approved the preordained removal of Khrushchev. It could not have been otherwise. No one consulted the people. And what could they have said anyway, if someone had suddenly appealed to them for a verdict?

Shifts in social consciousness are a slow and torturous process. How difficult it was for public opinion in Khrushchev's time to change is suggested by a poll carried out by the Department of History, Politics, and Law of Moscow Pedagogical University between 1994 and 1997. Interviews were conducted with 568 people who had lived through the events of the Khrushchev era. Of these, 220 (38.9 percent) either had not known then about Khrushchev's criticism of the Stalin cult or had had mixed feelings or were indifferent to it. By contrast, 163 people (28.7 percent) had approved of Khrushchev's action, while 185 (32.6 percent) had either not believed Khrushchev or had disapproved.[94] A more recent poll, in-1998, produced similar results. Out of 568 interviewed, 184 (32 percent) could be put in the first group, 180 (31 percent) in the second, and 208 (36 percent) in the third. Data gathered during this poll on responses to the Soviet military intervention in Hungary, which followed Khrushchev's secret speech, are also revealing. Of those interviewed, 173 (30 percent) approved of it and 109 (19 percent) disapproved; of the latter, 56 were people who had supported Khrushchev's attacks on Stalin. Reactions to Khrushchev's dismissal from power in October 1964 also provide food for thought: of the 195 people

(32 percent) who supported his ouster at the time, 92 could be considered Stalinists. Of those interviewed, 123 (21 percent) regretted his dismissal, 129 (22 percent) were indifferent, and 73 (12 percent) had mixed feelings about it.

From the sociological standpoint, of course, these results cannot be viewed as definitive. Nevertheless, they pose an important question: Was Soviet society really ready for destalinization? Were people ready to reject mass repressions, purges, and bloody terror? Were they ready to give up totalitarian and imperial ways of thinking, the icon of which was Stalin? Khrushchev lost out in 1964 not only because the plotters turned out to be smarter, but because the "voice of the people" was not on his side. Removing Stalin's body from the mausoleum was forgiven neither by the Stalinists nor by the crowd whose object of worship Khrushchev had taken away.

9

The Making of Soviet Foreign Policy

OLEG TROYANOVSKY

It has always been my impression that the 1950s and early 1960s were one of the most exciting and fascinating periods in international affairs and East-West relations in particular. In large measure the driving force behind the changes that occurred in that period was Nikita Khrushchev. I became Khrushchev's assistant for foreign affairs in April 1958. I first joined the diplomatic service at the end of 1944. I was a junior diplomat at the Soviet embassy in London, worked as secretary and interpreter for the Soviet judges at the Nuremberg trials, and at the beginning of 1947 joined the secretariat of the foreign minister of the Soviet Union. I left the foreign ministry in 1949 to complete my education, only to return at Foreign Minister Viacheslav Molotov's invitation in April 1953. I served as assistant to the foreign minister under Molotov, then under Dmitri Shepilov, and finally under Andrei Gromyko, before joining Nikita Khrushchev's staff in 1958.

Until March 1953 it was Stalin alone who had the last word on all major foreign policy decisions. Exchanges of views did take place, but his entourage preferred to keep their opinions to themselves when they differed from those of the boss, or *khoziain*, as he used to be called.[1] After Stalin's death the new leaders not only could start using their own heads, but had to. It soon became obvious to them that the legacy they inherited was appalling. The international situation had become so tense that another turn of the screw might have led to disaster. There was a war going on in Korea and another in Indochina; the two superpowers were facing each other with daggers drawn; the arms race was steadily gaining momentum; the German problem hung like a dark cloud over Europe; there was no settlement of the Austrian problem in sight; the Soviet Union had no diplomatic relations with either West Germany or Japan, and thousands of prisoners of war were still in camps in Russia; the Soviet Union was at loggerheads with Tito's Yugoslavia for reasons that remained obscure to ordinary mortals; Turkey had turned to the West because of Soviet territorial and other demands; the situation in some East European countries was becoming more and more disturbing. The inevitability of a major new war was still a part of the Communist doctrine and this, if taken at face value, would have made any attempts to prevent a new conflict meaningless.

During the short briefing that Molotov, back at his old post as foreign minister, gave me as I rejoined the ministry, I sensed that the new leadership was seriously concerned about the state of affairs in the international arena and was contemplating some important steps to ameliorate the situation. His comments also indicated, however, that in his view some degree of caution was called for so that our Western opponents would not take the Soviet Union's new policy as a sign of weakness.

As I settled down in my new position at the Foreign Ministry, it soon became clear that, although there existed a general consensus among the top leaders as to the need for urgent steps, there were sharp differences in regard to tactical approaches to the problems the country faced. Nikita Khrushchev was the driving force behind the effort to move the world away from the edge of the abyss, where it stood at the beginning of 1953. In this he had the active support of Anastas Mikoyan and, up to 1957, Nikolai Bulganin, whereas his main antagonist was Viacheslav Molotov, particularly on such issues as the Austrian treaty and reconciliation with Yugoslavia. The differences were both real and contrived—real, in that some leaders were prepared to go much further and faster to meet the position of the Western powers; contrived, in that there was a great deal of jockeying for position with the consequent blocking or emasculating of each other's proposals.

It did not take long for Khrushchev to emerge as the number-one personality. From my vantage point, he did so immediately after Lavrentii Beria's downfall, of which he was the prime mover. One indication of his predominance was the way the other members of the Soviet leadership deferred to him at any meeting with foreign representatives at which I happened to be present. Moreover, the very fact that Khrushchev was the first secretary of the Central Committee gave him a built-in advantage over all his colleagues.

In the first few weeks after Stalin's death, the Central Committee Politburo, or the Presidium as it was then called, was deliberating how to handle the ominous international situation it was up against. Meanwhile President Dwight D. Eisenhower delivered a speech on April 16, 1953, in which he called upon the new Soviet leaders to seize the "chance for peace" and help "turn the tide of history." Having declared that the United States would "welcome every honest act of peace," he then stated that the "opportunities for such deeds are many," and he went on to specify them: a truce in Korea, an Austrian treaty, the release of World War II prisoners of war, and steps to reduce "the burden of armaments now weighing upon the world."[2] There was no emphasis on Eastern Europe, except for one or two rhetorical references.

Two days later, however, John Foster Dulles followed with a typical Cold War speech, overflowing with rhetoric about the liberation of the nations of Eastern Europe. It was as if the secretary of state were correcting the president.

After a preliminary exchange of views in the Presidium, it was decided to respond to Eisenhower in the form of an unsigned article in *Pravda* instead of through a statement by one of the leaders. That in itself was an indication that at that stage there was no *primus inter pares* in the Kremlin hierarchy. The foreign ministry was instructed to draft the *Pravda* article for approval by the Presidium. Molotov, who considered his original profession to have been journalism, always preferred to draft the more important documents himself. In this case he invited Dmitri Shepilov, the editor-in-chief of *Pravda* (in 1956 he was to replace Molotov as foreign minister), and Yurii Zhukov, *Pravda*'s foremost columnist, to join him in writing the article. Molotov could formulate his thoughts with great precision, but he was a plodder who took his time on every phrase. So the drafting process took three full days.

The final product was less constructive than it might have been given the circumstances. But Molotov was Molotov, and he was not one to rush into anybody's arms without first making sure that there would be someone ready to receive him. And the Dulles speech, in which the position of the new Soviet leadership was rather contemptuously called a "peace defensive," was not one to encourage any precipitous action. Nevertheless, Moscow's reply to Eisenhower was on the whole positive. And the fact that the president's speech was published in the Soviet press was for those times an important indication that it was regarded as an auspicious event.

In any case, the four conditions set forth by Eisenhower, which the Soviet Union was called upon to fulfill as proof of its good intentions, remained firmly imprinted in Khrushchev's memory. In the ensuing years I heard him refer several times to Eisenhower's April 16 speech.

As Khrushchev's star rose in the Soviet firmament, he began to take one step after another to bring about a relaxation of international tensions, including, but not confined to, those set forth by President Eisenhower. In fact, the truce in Korea was among the first to be achieved. The Austrian State Treaty was concluded in 1955, following direct talks between Khrushchev and Austrian chancellor Julius Raab, in spite of Molotov's active resistance. In the same month, during West German chancellor Konrad Adenauer's visit to Moscow, diplomatic relations were established between the Soviet Union and the Federal Republic of Germany, followed by the release of the Germans still detained in the Soviet Union. The next month, diplomatic relations were also established with Japan, and Japanese prisoners of war set free.

These steps responded directly to President Eisenhower's address. But there were others also designed to normalize East-West relations. In 1954 the Soviet Union initiated an international conference on Indochina, which brought about a settlement in that region—a settlement that, unfortunately, broke down a few years later. In those same eventful mid-1950s Khrushchev and Bulganin, who had replaced Malenkov as head of the government, went to Belgrade for a fence-mending session with President Josip Broz Tito of Yugoslavia. The Soviet Union renounced all claims to Turkish territory, which had been advanced by Stalin after the war, and withdrew its demands for military bases in the Dardanelles. Having given up all rights to the naval base at Port Arthur on Chinese territory in 1954, the Soviet government in the next year went on to relinquish all rights to the naval base at Porkkala-Udd in Finland. Diplomatic relations were reestablished with Israel.

And even that was not all. The 20th Party Congress, in February 1956, condemned many of Stalin's policies and adopted substantial amendments to Communist doctrine, namely that a major new war was by no means inevitable and that the transition from a capitalist to a socialist society could take place peacefully and not necessarily through violent means, as had been maintained previously.

Moreover, during that period the new Soviet leaders probably became more approachable to foreigners, including Western journalists, than the leadership group of any other country. They, and Nikita Khrushchev in particular, showed up at numerous receptions, including those held at foreign embassies, where they freely mingled with foreigners. My impression is that Western correspondents who were accredited in Moscow at that time came to regard those years in Moscow as among the most thrilling periods of their careers.

As for American diplomats, restrictions on their exchanging views with Soviet leaders came from Washington rather than from the Kremlin. Charles Bohlen, who was the American ambassador in Moscow from 1953 to 1956, tells a revealing story in his memoirs of an approach he made to Nikolai Bulganin in March 1956, in which he expressed his desire to have a more substantial talk with the Soviet leaders than the frequent but brief encounters he had with them at various receptions. A few days later Bulganin informed him that he could arrange a "heart-to-heart" talk with him and Khrushchev or with any other major Soviet leader at his dacha any time the ambassador wanted one. Bohlen "enthusiastically," as he put it, cabled Dulles about the offer and suggested that President Eisenhower be informed. Dulles never authorized him to take up the offer, however.[3] As a professional diplomat, I find that this story verges on the incredible. The impression in the West has been that Moscow kept Soviet ambassadors on a short leash, yet I cannot imagine a Soviet ambassador not being allowed to meet a leader of a foreign country. In fact, most of them would have seized the opportunity to meet, say, the president of the United States or, for that matter, the leader of any Western nation without even asking Moscow's permission.

It seems odd that as late as 1956, Washington continued to ignore the obvious fact that not only had virtually all the requirements set by Eisenhower in his April 16, 1953, speech been met, but Moscow had gone far beyond them. It might be said that the Kremlin was conducting a completely new foreign policy as compared to that pursued in Stalin's later years.

Yet there was practically no response from Washington to these far-reaching changes. In fact, when in May 1955 the Soviet Union agreed to arms reductions with inspections in Europe, the U.S. delegation was instructed to "place a reservation" on their own position, in effect disavowing it.[4]

It might be pointed out with some justification that the United States, prodded by Britain, did agree to the four-power summit in Geneva in July 1955, whereas two years earlier a proposal to that effect by Winston Churchill was not supported by Washington. But the position taken by President Eisenhower at that conference contained noth-

ing substantially new, except for the Open Skies proposal, which was
unacceptable to the Soviet Union because it amounted to inspection
without disarmament. John Foster Dulles admitted that, as with the
1954–1955 Geneva negotiations, "we did not actually desire to enter
into either negotiation, but felt compelled to do so in order to get our allies to consent to the rearmament of Germany. World opinion demanded that the United States participate in these negotiations with
the Communists."[5]

If this is taken at face value, it means that the negotiations with
Moscow were used as a cover for the rearmament of West Germany and
its integration into the Western military alliance. It was at about that
time that those who had an insider's view of the maneuvering within
the Kremlin, myself included, began to realize that Khrushchev, as the
prime mover of the policy of relaxation of international tensions, was
finding himself in political difficulties for not being able to show anything for all the moves he had initiated to meet the Western position.
Molotov's opposition to the Austrian treaty and to reconciliation with
Yugoslavia became noticeable at the beginning of 1955; it was apparently his view that Khrushchev was giving away the whole game to
Washington. After the 20th Party Congress, signs indicated that opposition to Khrushchev's policies was not restricted to one person but included others in the leadership group. At one point, around the end of
1955, Molotov instructed one of his staff members, Igor Ezhov, to find
among Lenin's writings some reference to the idea that "naivete in foreign policy was tantamount to a crime." Obviously, the idea was to use
such a quotation against Khrushchev, although I do not believe Ezhov
ever found an appropriate quotation. "Appeasement" was another term
that one began to hear from time to time.

It was one of the paradoxes of the Eisenhower years that U.S. policymakers did not show any signs of encouragement to those sectors of
the Soviet political spectrum that stood for better relations with the
West. On the contrary, intentionally or not, they provided grist for the
mill of the hard-liners.

There may have been various explanations for this, but a deep-
seated view in Washington's political and intelligence community
seems to have remained unaltered throughout the 1950s: that the two
social and political systems were locked in a life-and-death struggle in
which there could be but one winner. The Soviet Union's basic hostil-

ity and ultimate expansionist aims were regarded not only as unchanged, but as unchangeable. For instance, the National Intelligence Estimates for 1957–1962 maintained that "none of the changes in Soviet policy suggests any alteration in basic aims or in the concept of an irreconcilable conflict between the Communist and the non-Communist world."[6]

This appears to have been the mirror image of the views held by Molotov and other Soviet doctrinaires. One may well ask: what about Khrushchev and others—were their concepts any different? I believe that they were. True enough, there was still the belief that in the long run the socialist sociopolitical system would prove more viable than the capitalist system and would prevail—not, however, through a world revolution or a world war, but step by step through peaceful means as the people of one country after another would see the light. The messianic vision had gradually faded away to become something resembling the expectation of the Second Coming of Christ in the West: it was still preached, but in actual fact few expected it to transpire.[7]

By 1957 the situation within the Soviet top echelon was close to the boiling point. The group headed by Molotov, Malenkov, and Kaganovich had gained a clear majority in the Presidium and launched an all-out attack on Khrushchev, accusing him of all sorts of mistakes in the domestic sphere and of appeasing the imperialists in general and the United States in particular. The crisis in Hungary and the disturbances in Poland in 1956 were also supposed to be the consequences of his "liberal" policies.

Khrushchev escaped by the skin of his teeth. He received the support of a Central Committee majority mainly because there was fear that if people like Molotov and Kaganovich were to gain the upper hand, they would revert to Stalinist methods of terror and repression. Some years later Aleksei Kosygin, who by that time had become prime minister, told me that during the 1957 crisis he had unhesitatingly backed Khrushchev because had Molotov been victorious, "blood would have flowed again."

But the outcome of that confrontation did not by any means signify that conservative tendencies within the government and party or, for that matter, in the country at large had been totally overcome. Not only many influential individuals but whole segments of society had an interest in preserving the old ways, whether in domestic or foreign policy. This was true of many party cadres, the government bureaucracy, and the military-industrial complex. Even a large part of the general public was still under the influence of conservative conceptions.

By the middle of 1958, soon after I had joined Khrushchev's staff as his assistant for international affairs, it was becoming obvious that considerable changes in Soviet foreign policy were imminent. The various steps that had been taken to relax tensions did draw the world back from the brink of war, but they did not bring about any substantial breakthrough in relations with the West. In some critical respects, the situation was even deteriorating, at least from the Kremlin's point of view: West Germany was arming rapidly and was being drawn ever deeper into the Western alliance; the arms race was gathering steam and spreading into outer space; disarmament negotiations were getting nowhere, with defense expenditures weighing more heavily on the economy; East Germany was isolated and under pressure as before; the Soviet Union was being surrounded by American military bases; new military blocs were being set up in Asia and the Middle East.

This was also the time when divergences between the Soviet Union and China first began to surface. It was no mere coincidence that in August 1958, only a couple of months before the beginning of the Berlin crisis, the Soviet leader had to undertake a trip to Beijing to pour oil on the troubled Chinese-Soviet waters. In fact, voices in the Soviet political and intelligence community were ever more audible, to the effect that if the Soviet Union had to choose between the West and China, preference should be given to the latter.

There was another substantial component in the complicated equation that led to the Berlin crisis, namely, the role played by the leaders of East Germany. The impression in the West has always been that they were pawns moved on the chess board by the hand of Moscow. In reality they were active players, constantly urging Moscow to take a more forceful stand against West Germany and West Berlin. The usual argument was that the German Democratic Republic was a sort of front-line state, and that the open border between East and West Berlin was being used to undermine East Germany, to drain it of its population, and to wreck its financial system. At certain points Moscow was actually being bombarded by messages from East Berlin.[8]

A factor of a different sort that encouraged Khrushchev to turn from a moderate to a more forceful foreign policy was the situation in the space race. In October 1957 the Soviet Union launched its first Sputnik satellite. I was in New York at the time, and I well recall the tremendous impression that the event created in the United States, with people listening to the beeps coming from Sputnik as it flew over various American cities. I also recall accompanying Andrei Gromyko to a meeting with Secretary of State Dulles, who congratulated the Soviet foreign minister on this outstanding achievement. Of course, this was still some distance from intercontinental ballistic missiles, but it did put the Americans at a psychological disadvantage and opened up opportunities for Khrushchev to indulge in some ballistic bluffing.

To illustrate this last point, let me refer to an argument that took place shortly before the Soviet leader's visit to Washington in September 1959. Khrushchev told us, his entourage, that he intended to present Eisenhower with a replica of the sphere that a Soviet rocket had carried to the moon shortly before and that he intended to do so immediately upon setting foot on American soil, that is, during the arrival ceremony at Andrews Air Force Base. He obviously relished the thought of demonstrating before all the television cameras that the Soviet Union had outstripped the United States in space. Several of us protested that it would be a tactless gesture, which would be resented by the president and the American public. After a lengthy discussion, we finally reached a sort of compromise: Khrushchev would present his lunar gift during his first meeting with the president at the White House, but while the news media were still in the room. I had the impression that Eisenhower received the small sphere with a sour look on his face.

What finally impelled Khrushchev to resort to what today might be called shock therapy was information from various sources that serious discussions were proceeding within the North Atlantic Treaty Organization and, in particular, between the United States and West Germany, regarding the possibility of the Bundeswehr's being granted access to atomic weapons in one form or another. It stood to reason that if this were to happen and there were no meaningful response from the Kremlin, Khrushchev's prestige would tumble dramatically. In fact, it is difficult to understand how Washington could even contemplate such a thing.

The U.S. ambassador to Moscow, Llewellyn E. Thompson, hit the nail on the head on November 18, 1958, when he cabled Washington: "Khrushchev is a man in a hurry and considers that time is against him on this issue, particularly in relation to atomic arming of West Germany. Therefore, I believe Western powers should prepare for major showdown within coming months."[9] This was a remarkably prescient piece of analysis, for the showdown came within nine days of the ambassador's warning. Khrushchev had a very high opinion of Ambassador Thompson.[10]

On November 27, 1958, a note was dispatched to the three Western powers and to the two German states proposing to end the occupation of West Berlin and convert it into a free city. The most significant aspects of the proposal were those which provided for demilitarizing the free city and for granting the German Democratic Republic control of the access routes. The Western powers were given until May 27, 1959, to negotiate an agreement on the free-city proposal.

This, certainly, was not an off-the-cuff decision. There were several discussions on the subject in the Presidium of the Central Committee. Khrushchev seldom took foreign policy decisions without consultation with his colleagues. The trouble was that as time went on, and especially after Molotov and Kaganovich were expelled from the Presidium in June 1957, the other members of the leadership group became more and more reluctant to argue with him, particularly regarding his ideas and proposals. There was always some discussion, even if perfunctory, before a formal decision, and I recall being present at a final reading of the note to the Western powers on Berlin after Andrei Gromyko had inserted all the amendments to the original text which had been proposed by the members of the Presidium and Khrushchev himself. But in this case, too, I did not detect any significant objections or even hesitation on the part of anyone, although this was clearly a major move to a much tougher stance that was fraught with risks. During these discussions, Khrushchev, I thought, gave a persuasive set of arguments in support of the new approach. He emphasized that the Western powers did not seem to appreciate moderation and refused to acknowledge the obvious truth that constructive steps by one party required a similar response from the other side. He went on to point out that our Western partners had not made a single substantial move to meet Soviet interests or the interests of the allies. On the contrary, they were pursuing their old policy of building up their alliances, arming West Germany, and surrounding the Soviet Union with military bases. This being the case, Khrushchev proposed that the Soviet Union assume the initiative in the Cold War. The obvious spot to apply pressure was West Berlin, the Achilles' heel of the Western powers.

All this sounded convincing from the point of view of the Soviet Union's national interests. Probably Khrushchev also had in mind his own position within the Kremlin hierarchy. What made the whole scheme less convincing was that there was neither a clear plan of action nor an awareness of the ultimate objective. What was clear was that a major international crisis was about to erupt. When at an opportune moment I pointed that out to Khrushchev, he referred to Lenin's words in 1917, just before the October Revolution, about first getting involved in a battle and then deciding what course of action to adopt. Actually this was a Russian version of Napoleon's saying, "On s'engage et plus on voit."

On January 10, 1959, to keep up the momentum, the Soviet Union presented a draft peace treaty for Germany to the three Western powers and proposed a peace conference for March 1959. Later still, Khrushchev continued to prod the United States, Great Britain, and France by threatening to conclude a separate peace treaty with the German Democratic Republic and thus to leave the Western powers to deal directly with the East German government regarding access routes to West Berlin and various other matters.

It soon became evident that Khrushchev was anxious to have his Berlin lever produce results as soon as possible. As early as December 3, 1958, in a meeting with Hubert Humphrey, he was quite frank in his desire to get some sort of quick response from the White House. Several times he asked the senator, "What are your president and secretary of state thinking? Where are their counterproposals?" The meeting produced some vintage Khrushchev, with black humor injected on both sides. The Soviet leader talked about his desire for peace, yet was all bravado. He insisted that the new Soviet missiles were able to hit any spot on earth and then asked with a sly smile, "What is your home town, Senator?" When Humphrey replied that it was Minneapolis, Khrushchev approached a big map hanging on the wall and drew a thick blue circle around that city, saying, "I will have to remember to have that city spared when the missiles start flying." To this the senator asked what the chairman's home town was and, on hearing that now it was Moscow, said, "Sorry, Mr. Khrushchev, but I can't do the same for you. We can't spare Moscow [Loud laughter]."

As the year ended and the new one began, the feeling grew that the Soviet chairman was at a loss as to what his next move should be. He continued pronouncing Cassandra-like prophecies as to the calamities that would occur unless the Western powers accepted the Soviet demands regarding West Berlin. But in a situation in which there were no specific counterproposals coming from the other side, there was a strong prospect that these demands would become devalued unless backed by action of some sort. And this the Soviet leader was loath to do for fear of stepping onto terra incognita, with unforeseeable consequences.

Nineteen fifty-nine was a particularly hectic year, with threats and counterthreats, feelers and counterfeelers, hints that one side or the other was prepared to enter into serious negotiations. There was Anastas Mikoyan's trip to the United States in January 1959. The main objective was to indicate to the president and the secretary of state that Moscow was maintaining its tough position but was prepared to negotiate, and that the deadline that had been set was not final. This was followed by British prime minister Harold Macmillan's visit to Moscow a month later. With him Khrushchev was rather aggressive and at times even bad-mannered. In general this was the period when, in line with his new, more assertive foreign policy, he assumed a more forceful style of personal behavior.

This was mostly play-acting, but there were times when Khrushchev would overstep the line. I recall, for instance, that in a conversation with President Giovanni Gronchi of Italy, who came on an official visit to Moscow in 1960, Khrushchev became downright rude. Later I ventured to point that out to him. To my surprise he reacted almost sheepishly, saying that the Italian president had provoked him into saying things that he really had not intended to say. It is worth noting, however, that Harold Macmillan returned home from Moscow feeling that he understood the Russian leader better: "He was interesting to me because he was more like the Russians we'd read about in Russian novels than most Russian technocrats are. They all seem to be made in Germany—rather stiff and . . . you couldn't really converse with them. But you could with Khrushchev."[11]

Finally, after the Moscow visits of Vice President Richard Nixon and former American ambassador to the Soviet Union Averell Harriman, and Deputy Prime Minister Frol Kozlov's trip to the United States, the Soviet leader received an invitation from President Eisenhower to visit the United States. This was interpreted in Moscow, not without reason, as a sort of breakthrough and a tangible result of the pressure that had been exerted on the Western powers since the November 27 note about

West Berlin. This, and the fact that the prospect of West Germany's receiving control of nuclear missiles had receded into the background, seemed to lend added weight to Khrushchev's belief that he was on the right track in dealing with the Western powers.

In actual fact, the results of the visit to the United States were by no means as clear-cut as that. Of course, some good will was injected into the relationship between the two powers and the two leaders—the "Spirit of Camp David," as it came to be called. Khrushchev was buoyed by the fact that he was given a grand reception, which seemed a second recognition of Communist Russia by the leading country of the capitalist world. But judging by more specific criteria, the final score was at best even and at worst may have shown a certain advantage for the American side.

During the discussions on the crucial subject of Germany, only the two leaders and their interpreters were present. I believe each man thought he would be better off without anyone sitting at the back of his counterpart. Khrushchev constantly suspected that Eisenhower was being influenced by the hawks and warmongers, while the president and his entourage, as far as I could judge, had the impression that the Soviet leader had a tendency to play to the crowd when surrounded by his associates or that the hard-liners, supposedly represented by Andrei Gromyko, were hanging on his coattails.

But even without onlookers or back-seat drivers, the talks were tough. In fact, from time to time they seemed to become deadlocked, although the tone was proper and respectful throughout. After two days something tangible began to emerge. The Soviet leader conceded that there would be no fixed limit to the negotiations on Berlin, thereby lifting the threat of unilateral action that hung over the Western powers. For his part Eisenhower agreed that the negotiations would not be prolonged indefinitely, a much less specific commitment. An understanding was also reached that, subject to the approval of the other parties directly concerned, a four-power summit would be convened. Finally, the Soviet leader invited the American president to visit the Soviet Union the following spring.

Nikita Khrushchev returned from the United States in high spirits and with a feeling that he had achieved something substantial. Being an emotional person, with a tendency to get carried away by whatever idea dominated him at some particular moment, he began to look upon his American visit as the gateway to some sort of new era in Soviet-U.S.

relations. In particular, he began to expect that the Western powers would come up with concessions on the German problem. The Soviet mass media, with its accolades for the Spirit of Camp David, only encouraged such exaggerated expectations. I must confess that the book *Face to Face with America,* which described in glowing terms the visit to the United States, revealed the same fault. It was written by a group of authors, myself included, who had accompanied Khrushchev on his trip.

Carried away by this euphoria, the Soviet leader in January 1960 proposed to the Supreme Soviet that the armed forces be reduced by 1.2 million men, or one-third of the current total, within two years. He spoke about the clouds of war beginning to disperse. In the nuclear age, he asserted, large standing armies, surface navies, and fleets of bombers were becoming obsolete. Producing nuclear missiles was cheaper than financing large land armies. And these cuts in expenditures could lead to a higher standard of living for the general public.

The generals and admirals did not think much of their leader's ideas. In fact, they thought very little of them. I recall a session of the Defense Council where some of the prominent marshals, among them Marshal Semen Timoshenko, expressed their doubts about Khrushchev's proposals. I was not present and am therefore unaware of his immediate reaction. But I have little doubt that he was taken aback. Later he did at times repeat the well-known saying that generals usually prepare for the last war.

At about the same time Khrushchev went on a short tour, a sort of whistle-stop trip with stopovers at various towns. So there were plenty of opportunities to gauge the sentiment of the public. And according to Grigorii Shuiskii, an aide who traveled with Khrushchev, practically everywhere the prevailing mood was the same: cheers for peace, which seemed so secure now; applause for Comrade Khrushchev and his efforts; hurrah for a better life to come.

One might have thought that the Soviet leader would have been encouraged by this reception, but he was obviously worried. After one of those spontaneous gatherings, he started speaking, or rather thinking aloud: "Are we not creating false hopes among all these people? Are we not encouraging this wishful thinking? And supposing we fail to make good on what they regard as our promises to bring about a better international climate?" He went on in this vein for some time, wondering what could be done to bring people closer to reality.

To make matters worse, by spring East-West relations seemed to be deteriorating. The Kremlin found Under Secretary of State Douglas Dillon's April 20 speech in New York to be particularly provocative, coming as it did shortly before the Paris summit. The prospect of the Bundeswehr's going nuclear was surfacing again. At a press conference on February 3, President Eisenhower uttered a phrase that reverberated through the Kremlin: "I have always been of the belief that we should not deny to our allies what the enemy [here he corrected himself] what our potential enemy already has." He went on to say that it would be in the interests of the United States to make legislation about sharing nuclear secrets "more liberal." One can imagine what impact the possibility of West Germany going nuclear would have had in the Soviet Union, with recollections of the war still so fresh in people's memories.

More and more information was coming in through various channels, including the intelligence service, indicating that the Western powers had no plans to moderate their position on Germany to any substantial degree. The best that could be hoped for was some sort of agreement for a partial ban on nuclear testing. This would leave Khrushchev stranded as far as the German problem was concerned, with the option of either resuming his threats about West Berlin or ignoring the issue altogether for the time being. Neither option could be regarded as satisfactory.

China, too, remained very much in the picture—as always, I might add. Almost immediately upon returning from Washington, Khrushchev flew to Beijing for the tenth-anniversary celebrations of the Chinese People's Republic. This in itself was symbolic of the need to seek a balance between the two international giants. The 1959 visit to China was Khrushchev's last. The coolness between him and Mao was by now plainly visible. The Chinese made no secret of their disapproval of what they regarded as the Soviet leaders' cozying up to Eisenhower. All this talk about the Spirit of Camp David was, of course, anathema to them. Back in Moscow, one could not fail to notice considerable dissatisfaction among some segments of society at the widening of the rift with China.

The nearer that May 16, the date for the Paris summit, approached, the more problematic the summit's outcome appeared to those of us who were doing the preparatory work in Moscow. And it was obvious that our chief was deeply troubled at the prospect of the summit results not measuring up to previous expectations.

But then another factor made itself felt with a bang—the U-2 reconnaissance flights over Soviet territory. They had started on July 4, 1956, and had continued on a regular basis ever since. For several years the Soviet air defense system had been unable to bring those planes down because of their extremely high altitude. Each flight was duly reported to Khrushchev, and each time he objected to any public announcement being made. His argument was that there was no point in publicizing one's impotence or protesting against something that could not be prevented. "That would only highlight our humiliation," he would say. Meanwhile he was pressing our specialists to come up with a new type of antiaircraft missile capable of bringing down the U-2.

Each new flight was not only a humiliation. It provided ammunition for those in the military and the Presidium who were informed about the flights and who had an inbred skepticism about Washington's good intentions. Indeed, it was difficult to understand the rationale for Washington's actions, particularly since we now know that the president understood the gravity of what was being done. General Andrew Goodpaster, his staff secretary, characterized the overflights as "approaching a provocation, a probable cause of war because it was a violation of their territory."[12] From any point of view, was the game worth the candle?

On the evening of May 1, 1960, some time after I returned home from Red Square, where the traditional military review and civilian parade had taken place, there was a phone call from one of Khrushchev's secretaries: "Nikita Sergeevich has phoned and asked you to call him at home."

When I got in touch with Khrushchev, he asked whether I had heard that an American aircraft had been shot down in the region of Sverdlovsk and that the pilot had been captured. I answered that I had, whereupon Khrushchev said he thought that that might wreck the summit conference in Paris. He then told me to summon the "usual crowd," as he put it, for eleven o'clock the next morning to work on a speech he intended to deliver in a few days at the session of the Supreme Soviet. Khrushchev did not usually care exactly who worked on particular text, as long as the job was done. It was for his assistants to decide who was to be invited to participate. But in this case, as far as I recall, in view of the importance of the speech, those taking part were Andrei Gromyko (who did not ordinarily participate in speech drafting), the editors-in-chief of *Pravda* and *Izvestiia* Pavel Satiukov and Aleksei Adzhubei, and a couple of persons from the foreign ministry, probably Valentin Falin, plus Khrushchev's three assistants, Shuiskii, Vladimir Lebedev, and myself.

During the next several days we helped our boss lay a sort of trap for the White House, and Khrushchev did so with relish. We, for our part, had no doubts that our opponents deserved to be taught a lesson, although we never thought they would play into our hands to the extent that they did.

Khrushchev made two or three speeches to the Supreme Soviet, gradually drawing Washington into issuing several public statements, each contradicting the previous one. But still there seemed to be no danger to the Paris summit, as long as the president's involvement was kept out of the picture. For his part, Khrushchev was careful not to make any accusations against Eisenhower directly. Finally, however, the State Department admitted on May 9 that the flights over Soviet territory had been authorized by the president and implied that they would be continued. A couple of days later, Eisenhower himself confirmed at a press conference that he was personally responsible for the flights and pledged to continue them as necessary for national security.

Harold Macmillan wrote in his diary at that time, "Khrushchev has made two very amusing and effective speeches, attacking the Americans for spying incompetently and lying incompetently, too. He may declare the summit off. Or the Americans maybe stung into doing so."[13]

Now that the president himself had taken personal responsibility for the U-2 flights and it was publicly indicated that the flights would continue, many observers contended that a head-on collision between him and Khrushchev was inevitable. And that was our feeling as well. Not only was Khrushchev personally put in an impossible situation, but his country was humiliated as well. There could be no doubt that unless he reacted forcefully enough, the hard-liners in Moscow and in Beijing would have made use of the incident to argue with some validity that here was a person ready to put up with any indignity coming from Washington.

On May 11, when Khrushchev showed up at the public exhibit of the U-2 wreckage, he plainly hinted that President Eisenhower would not be welcome in the Soviet Union and that the scheduled visit would have to be canceled. Nevertheless, the position to be taken by the Soviet

Union in regard to the Paris summit remained in doubt. It seemed that Khrushchev himself could not quite made up his mind.

According to Khrushchev's memoirs, it was only after his plane was in the air heading for Paris that he made up his mind to take a tough stand at the summit. In this case, as in some other instances, his memory failed him. This is not surprising, since he dictated his memoirs many years after the events described, without being able to check the facts.

The final decision was actually made at the airport just before departure for Paris. All of us had already taken our seats in the plane, while Khrushchev, Andrei Gromyko, and the minister of defense, Marshal Rodion Malinovskii, remained behind in the pavilion that was used for the ceremonies during the arrival and departure of distinguished guests. They were having a final exchange of views with the members of the Presidium.

Soon after the aircraft had taken off, Khrushchev invited those who made up his immediate entourage to inform us of the final decision. He would demand that President Eisenhower commit the United States not to violate Soviet air space again, express his regrets for the violations, and punish those directly responsible. He went on to say that it seemed next to impossible that Eisenhower could accept those terms. Consequently, the summit would almost certainly collapse before really starting. "This is unfortunate," declared Khrushchev, "but we have no choice. The U-2 flights are not only a flagrant violation of international law, but they are a gross insult to the Soviet Union."

All this was received in complete silence. I doubt that anyone questioned the correctness of the decision taken. But most, if not all, were upset at the realization that we were sliding back to the worst times of the Cold War and would have to start from square one again. There was a general atmosphere of gloom at the Soviet Embassy on Rue de Grenelle. I recall Deputy Foreign Minister Valerian Zorin, who was not inclined to emotional outbursts, going around the embassy repeating, "What a situation! What a situation!"

Perhaps the only person who was obviously pleased at the way things were going was Marshal Malinovskii. Some publications on the U-2 affair assert that the marshal was assigned by the hard-liners to accompany the Soviet leader in order to ensure that he would maintain a tough stance. This is absurd. By that time Khrushchev had made up his mind to be tough and needed no prodding. If he needed anything, it was a restraining hand to keep him from overplaying the part of a person outraged at the insult suffered. And overact at times he did, particularly at the press conference held immediately after the collapse of the conference, when he lost his cool in the face of the heckling and booing he encountered.

As far as the exchange of invective is concerned, 1960 was perhaps the worst year of the Cold War. It was probably on the basis of his performance that year that Khrushchev earned the reputation of a sort of international bully. He outdid himself in invoking the wrath of heaven upon President Eisenhower for the U-2 affair. As a result, instead of the White House being on the defensive, as was the case at the beginning, public attention turned to the Soviet leader's outbursts. I have the feeling that that posture began to backfire on him in the eyes not only of the international public but also of the public back home. The Russian people prefer their leaders to be dignified and somewhat detached from the angry crowd. But here was their leader, engaged in what looked like a street brawl, and they did not like it.

I am sorry to say that those of us who were in a position to tell our boss that he was going too far very seldom did so and thus bear some responsibility for his indiscretions. I recall an occasion when Nina Petrovna Khrushcheva, hearing her husband mispronounce some word, asked my colleague Vladimir Lebedev and me, "Why don't you correct him? If you aren't going to tell him, who else is going to?"

At that time the Soviet leader had yet another objective in mind: he came to believe that this tactic of attacking the Republican administration for the U-2 affair would hurt Richard Nixon's chances in the 1960 election campaign and help John Kennedy. Nixon continued to be Khrushchev's bête noir, while the Democratic candidate, who expressed in rather vague terms his regret at the U-2 incident, began to look, if not like a knight in shining armor, then at least like someone not tainted by the Soviet-American clashes of the past eight years. At the Vienna summit in 1961, Khrushchev did say to Kennedy that "we voted for you," and the president replied that he was aware of that. But in actual fact, any influence on the election that Soviet propaganda may have had must have been minimal.

It was in that atmosphere of tension and conflict that in September we set off for the General Assembly session of the United Nations. Once it became known that the Soviet leader would be in New York, what originally looked like a routine gathering soon became a three-ring circus.

Leaders from all parts of the world decided to come, including Macmillan, Nehru, Nasser, Castro, Tito, and sundry other presidents and prime ministers, to say nothing of the leaders of the East European countries. Khrushchev regarded that as a sign of the Soviet Union's high standing in the world: its leader's presence at the United Nations was enough to bring out so many other leading international personalities.

This was the time when the old colonial empires were falling apart. Fourteen new nations from Africa and Asia were to sit in the General Assembly as new members. But many others still remained under foreign domination. During the discussions in the Kremlin prior to our departure for New York, it was decided that the Soviet delegation's main initiative would be a resolution calling for the granting of immediate independence to all colonial territories. This was regarded as a very timely proposal that was bound to please the Third World and demonstrate that we were no less anti-imperialist than the Chinese.

There was something puckish in Khrushchev's nature. Judging by some of his remarks, he had an irresistible urge to humiliate the Prince of Darkness, as he had begun to regard Eisenhower, by appearing uninvited at his court. He spent a full month in New York, needling the U.S. administration, warning of the danger of nuclear war, and calling for the liberation of colonial nations. He used every occasion to catch the public eye and to get his views across, whether from the balcony of the Soviet mission to the United Nations, or at UN Headquarters, or in Harlem, where he went to visit Fidel Castro. Another spot for his chats with journalists was the gate of the Glen Cove country house belonging to the Soviet mission.[14]

There were several highlights at that 15th session of the UN General Assembly. But the session will probably be best remembered for that moment when Nikita Khrushchev, to express his displeasure at something said by a member of a delegation from the Philippines, started banging his fists on the table and, finding that insufficient, took off one of his shoes and pounded the desk with it.[15]

I did not go to the General Assembly that day, but I did happen to be in the entrance hall of our mission on Park Avenue when Khrushchev drove up. It was obvious that he was in a jovial mood. He asked whether I had been at the session, and when I answered that I had not, he said, "Oh, you missed so much, it was such fun! You know, the UN is a sort of parliament, and the minority has to make itself heard one way or another. For the time being, we are the minority. But not for long."

That evening we had Janos Kadar, the Hungarian leader, over to the mission for dinner. Kadar, who had a keen sense of humor, apparently thought he had to express his unease somehow. He said, "Comrade Khrushchev, remember shortly after banging the desk with your shoe, you went to the rostrum on a point of order. Well, at that moment our foreign minister, Comrade Sik, turned to me and said, 'Do you think he had time to put his shoe on, or did he go barefoot?'" Most of those at the table started snickering. I had a feeling that at that moment our chairman realized that he may have gone too far.

When we returned to Moscow, Leonid Ilichev, who as secretary of the Central Committee was in charge of ideology and who could be classed as a hard-liner, expressed his bewilderment to us. He said that when the first reports from New York began to come in, the initial reaction was that this was some sort of frame-up by Western propaganda, and some even wondered whether those broadcasts should not be jammed.

Soon after the General Assembly, Khrushchev found himself beset again by the Chinese dilemma, which was constantly on his mind. It was beginning to look like a set pattern: this turning of the head from the East to the West and back again. After the first trip to the United States in 1959, he immediately rushed to Beijing. Now, after the second trip there, an international Conference of Communist Parties was scheduled for November, where the central issue would inevitably be relations between the Soviet and Chinese Communist parties. The relationship between Moscow and Washington having hit rock bottom, the time seemed to be propitious for a new fence-mending effort with Beijing. A Sino-Soviet drafting committee with Mikhail Suslov and Deng Xiaoping heading the two parties had been at work for some time to try to reconcile the existing deep differences and produce a mutually acceptable text. This they finally managed to achieve after much pulling and hauling. Khrushchev did chide Suslov for conceding too much "under the lash of the Chinese," as he put it. Nevertheless, he was jubilant because the split with Beijing had been gnawing at him for the previous couple of years. On that day, solidarity seemed to have triumphed, only to fade away at the first contact with reality.

Soon after the new president settled down in the White House, the sights of the Kremlin turned westward once again.

Khrushchev's assessment of John Kennedy changed with the passage of time and went through at least three phases, with each new phase having a direct, practical impact on Soviet foreign policy. At first there were hopes that the newly elected president would turn over a new leaf in U.S.-Soviet relations and help raise them from the depths to which they had descended during the last years of the Republican administration. There was little specific evidence to nurture those hopes except Kennedy's statement that, if he had been president during the U-2 affair, he would have expressed his regret to the Soviet government. But Khrushchev was willing to indulge in some wishful thinking and ignore evidence to the contrary, such as Kennedy's calls for greater arms outlays to close the nonexistent missile gap. His main worry continued to be the possibility of Richard Nixon's becoming president.

It was not long after Kennedy had become chief executive that these hopes began to evaporate. The new president took a hard line on several issues where American and Soviet interests collided. Kennedy's inaugural address and, particularly, his first statement to Congress were both regarded in Moscow as bellicose. They were followed by the announcement of a crash program of nuclear missile production. Half the B-52 and B-47 nuclear bombers were placed on a fifteen-minute alert. Information began to arrive about a possible invasion of Cuba, and then came the Bay of Pigs invasion itself. Some time was required to sort all this out, to determine what was rhetoric and what was real policy. That was why Khrushchev chose a wait-and-see approach. He preferred not to respond either way to the proposal for a summit meeting received from Kennedy at the end of February.

In mid-April, the U.S.-sponsored invasion of Cuba at the Bay of Pigs was launched, and it ended in total failure. As a result, the impression grew in the Kremlin that incompetence was the hallmark of the American administrations, whether Republican, as evidenced by the U-2 incident, or Democratic, as evidenced by the Bay of Pigs invasion. Soon after, in the beginning of May, the Soviet leader came to the conclusion that the time was ripe for a summit with the American president. A message went off to Washington accepting Kennedy's proposal for a meeting. Khrushchev's reasoning was that having suffered a major humiliation, the president would be handicapped politically and susceptible to various pressures. In fact, he expected the White House to propose a later date when the after-effects of the Cuban fiasco would have worn off. As it was, Kennedy accepted, and the summit was set for June 3 and 4 in Vienna.

By that time a negative impression of Kennedy had formed itself in

Khrushchev's mind, and it would take a major upheaval—the Cuban missile crisis—to change it. I clearly remember the Soviet leader returning from his first encounter with Kennedy at the residence of the U.S. ambassador in Vienna. It was a restricted meeting, with only a few persons present, and those of us who stayed behind waited eagerly for the results. As soon as Khrushchev alighted from his car, we crowded around him, asking for his impressions. "Well," he said, "this man is very inexperienced, very untried. Compared to him Eisenhower is a man of intelligence and vision." And more in the same vein.

As I was present at some of the subsequent Vienna meetings and luncheons, I can say that in my opinion Kennedy was not at his best at that summit. He got himself involved in a discussion on ideological matters, despite the advice to the contrary of some of his counselors, notably Ambassador Thompson. Once started, this discussion dragged on for almost the whole first day of the summit with no prospect of any positive conclusion. It merely soured the atmosphere from the very beginning. Furthermore, Kennedy seems to have been somewhat bewildered by Khrushchev's onslaught on the Berlin problem. And no wonder. Although in this case the Soviet leader was neither discourteous nor bad-mannered, still he went on pushing and pushing, warning his counterpart of various dire consequences unless the Western powers agreed to cooperate with the Soviet Union in seeking a mutually acceptable solution. Kennedy left Vienna with a heavy heart, expecting a major crisis or, as he put it, a cold winter.

But in the long run, one wonders whether it was not Khrushchev rather than Kennedy who got caught in the Berlin trap that he himself had set. By now almost three years had passed since Moscow first issued its ultimatum on West Berlin. Yet the Western position remained practically unchanged. Whereas in the last months of 1958 and in 1959 there had been at least some semblance of movement, now, in 1961, the Western position seemed to have frozen stiff. The Kremlin was faced with a dilemma: either continue verbal pressure or take some practical steps along the access routes to make the Western position in West Berlin untenable. The first option was unlikely to have produced any effect. It seemed that all possible threats and ultimatums had already been pronounced and found wanting. The second option was too risky to try, since it might have led to a local or more general shootout. Anyone who knew anything about Nikita Khrushchev would have guessed that that was the last thing he wanted.

So here he was between the Scylla of losing face and the Charybdis of a possible armed conflict. Meanwhile, the pressures to do something were multiplying, particularly from the East German leaders. They were sounding the alarm ever more vehemently, primarily regarding the human flow from the German Democratic Republic to the West. There was yet another reason for the hue and cry from East Berlin. Thousands of visitors from West Berlin, the Federal Republic, and various foreign countries could exchange deutschmarks for East German currency at a favorable rate of four to one and make profitable purchases of cheap food and consumer goods in the East.

To my knowledge, the notion of building a wall in Berlin originated among the East German leaders. They had been playing around with various ideas of that sort for some time. But now things were fast coming to a head. For Khrushchev the wall was a godsend. It offered him a third possible way out of his predicament without loss of face or armed conflict. But being reluctant to take full responsibility for the final decision upon himself or in the name of the Soviet leadership as a whole, he suggested that the idea of putting up a wall should be discussed at the Warsaw Pact summit schedule to take place in Moscow August 3–5.

Some doubts have arisen as to whether the issue was actually discussed there. The records of the conference contain only a few oblique references to a wall. I do not find that at all surprising. The decision to construct a wall had to remain top secret until the last moment. Any mention of it on paper might have given the game away. As it was, the secret was well kept. When President Kennedy was first informed that Berlin was being partitioned, his reaction was obvious: "How come we didn't know anything about this?"

The GDR archives, which have now been opened, indicate that to Walter Ulbricht, the East German leader, the Berlin Wall was just a prelude to further steps leading to a peace treaty and the settlement of the West Berlin problem in the GDR's favor. In general, throughout that period Moscow had to restrain the East German leadership from taking steps that might have turned the dormant Berlin issue into a real convulsion.

To Khrushchev the Wall meant the virtual end of the Berlin crisis and tacit acknowledgment that it had failed to achieve its main purpose—to compel the Western powers to seek some compromise on the German problem. It is interesting that Kennedy, for his part, had a similar assessment of what the building of the Wall meant. He told his aides, "Why would Khrushchev put up a wall if he really intended to seize West Berlin? There wouldn't be any need of a wall if he occupied the whole city. This is his way out of his predicament. It's not a very nice solution, but a wall is a hell of a lot better than a war."[16]

Of course, heated rhetoric on Berlin continued in one form or another on both sides. It could not have been otherwise, because the problem of Berlin could not just evaporate into thin air. Moscow had somehow to take care of the desires and ambitions of its East German ally. And of course the Kennedy administration had to do some grandstanding to show the West Berliners and the West German public that they had the support of the United States. There was also the need to make good use of the Wall for propaganda purposes against the Soviet Union. Therefore, Vice President Lyndon Johnson was sent to Berlin, and later the president himself went there to pronounce before ecstatic crowds the famous phrase, "Ich bin ein Berliner."

As a result, there were difficulties along the access routes to West Berlin, there were diplomatic exchanges, there were public statements from both sides, some tough, some reasonable, depending on the circumstances. But these were the last receding waves after the storm, and ultimatums and crises were over. At least that is how it looked from our side of the fence. Obviously, Khrushchev could not just switch off the West Berlin problem with the East German leaders looking over his shoulder. But what he was doing was more political shadow boxing than anything else.

There were one or two incidents that in the previous crisis atmosphere might have erupted into a dangerous showdown. One was the confrontation at Checkpoint Charlie at the end of October 1961. After the East German border guards created some difficulties for Western personnel driving into East Berlin, General Lucius Clay ordered three armored personnel carriers and ten American tanks to take up positions at the boundary line. Shortly after that, ten Soviet tanks rolled up to the line. There they stood facing each other for several days. That incident remained in my mind very clearly. It took place while the 22nd Party Congress was in session in Moscow. Marshal Ivan Konev, who was in command of the Soviet troops in Germany, kept reporting to Khrushchev on the situation, and one could sense anxiety in his voice. Khrushchev was perfectly calm about it all. One even had the impression that he did not attach much importance to the whole incident. After a couple of days, he ordered our tanks pulled back, saying that the Americans seem to be at a loss as to what to do next; they could not withdraw their armor as long as Soviet guns were pointing at them. And indeed, as soon as the Soviet tanks were withdrawn, the American tanks were pulled back as well.

A few months later, another crisis started building, a crisis more ominous and dangerous than anything else that occurred throughout the Cold War. Never before or after did the world approach nuclear catastrophe so closely as it did in the autumn of 1962. The idea of deploying nuclear missiles in Cuba was conceived by Nikita Khrushchev himself. It was his brainchild, and he clung to it in spite of all the dangers and warnings.

What prompted him to take such a risky step? It has been assumed that he was moved mainly by the desire to prevent another invasion of Cuba after the Bay of Pigs fiasco of 1961. In his memoirs Khrushchev described that as the sole reason for the Soviet action. Indeed, at that time we were receiving an abundance of information, official and unofficial, indicating that Washington was developing plans for another attack on Cuba to topple the Castro regime. Very likely some of that was deliberate disinformation to keep the Cubans on edge. American policymakers of that period, such as Robert McNamara, deny that there were any such plans. Nevertheless, Soviet leaders had grounds to believe that a serious threat was looming over Cuba.

I had the impression that Khrushchev constantly feared that the United States would compel the Soviet Union and its allies to retreat in some region of the world. Not without reason did he believe that he would be held responsible for that. In conversations he sometimes recalled the words supposedly spoken by Stalin not long before his death: "When I am not around, they will strangle you like kittens." As the years passed, that feeling had grown under the impact of the relentless accusations from Beijing that the Soviet leader was appeasing the imperialists.

But there certainly was another, no less important reason for the deployment of the nuclear-tipped missiles. Khrushchev had the idea that by deploying them in the immediate vicinity of the United States, he would be able, at least partially, to redress the nuclear balance in favor of the Soviet Union, a domain where the United States had an overwhelming superiority. And since the two superpowers were in the throes of Cold War psychology (or even psychosis), many people regarded that superiority as a serious threat to the security of the Soviet Union.

I recall Khrushchev's conversation with Iurii Andropov, who at that time was the Central Committee secretary in charge of relations with socialist countries and therefore involved in everything concerning Cuba. As they discussed the deployment of Soviet missiles on the island, Andropov said, "When that is done, we shall be able to target them at the soft underbelly of the United States." These words sank into my memory because they reminded me of Winston Churchill's words during the world war, when he insisted on launching an offensive through the Balkans, calling it the soft underbelly of Europe.

Furthermore, Castro invariably claimed that the Cuban leadership, in agreeing to have the missiles deployed on the island, had primarily strategic goals in mind. As for the defense of Cuba, they regarded that as a matter to be dealt with by the Cuban people themselves.

Khrushchev possessed a rich imagination, and when some idea took hold of him, he was inclined to see in its implementation an easy solution to a particular problem, in this case defending Castro's regime and partially rectifying the nuclear imbalance. In such instances, he could stretch even a sound idea to the point of absurdity.

I had grave doubts about the whole project from the very beginning, perhaps because I knew more about the United States than some of the others and therefore could envisage more clearly than they what the American reaction would be. On a convenient occasion I mentioned to Khrushchev some arguments against his plan. Incidentally, it did not take a lot of guts to do so because he practically never raised his voice at his immediate subordinates and, if irritated about something, preferred to vent his bad mood on somebody else. Besides, by that time we had established a good relationship. I think he trusted me and I do not think I ever abused that trust.

In this case he listened to my arguments attentively and in reply said that he could not see why we should refrain from actions that were not going beyond what the Americans had already done by encircling the Soviet Union with nuclear weapons along virtually its entire perimeter. He added that they had forfeited the right to refer even to the Monroe Doctrine, which provided not only that European powers should not interfere in the affairs of the Western Hemisphere but also that the United States should renounce any involvement in European affairs.

It was difficult to refute these arguments because from the formal point of view, they were totally justified. What was almost entirely ignored was the mood in the United States and a possible American reaction. It is also beyond my comprehension how, taking into account the tremendous scale of the operation, anyone could seriously hope to keep it secret; and its success hinged entirely on the element of surprise. It was hoped that by the time the Americans learned of the missiles, it would be too late: they would already be installed, operational, and targeted at the United States. And then our opponents would have no option but to reconcile themselves to a radically changed situation.

I discussed that topic with Khrushchev one more time shortly before the finale, somewhere at the end of September. Having received progress reports from the military, Khrushchev said (we were alone in his office), "Soon all hell will break loose." I replied, "Let's hope the boat will not capsize altogether." Khrushchev was lost in thought for a moment and then said, "Now it's too late to change anything." I had the impression that by that time he had come to realize the risks involved.

Events were unfolding with fatal inevitability as if in a Greek tragedy. One October day followed another, and various signs appeared indicating that some sort of a commotion was mounting in Washington. Finally, on October 22 reports began to pour in to the effect that President Kennedy would make a statement on a matter of the utmost importance. There was no doubt what that matter would be. Khrushchev scheduled a meeting of the Presidium of the Central Committee for 10 p.m.

I remember that the first reaction of Khrushchev and the others to Kennedy's speech was one of relief rather than alarm. The "quarantine" of Cuba proclaimed by President Kennedy seemed to leave a great deal of room for political maneuvering. In any case it did not sound like an ultimatum or a direct threat of an attack on Cuba. A more thoughtful analysis, however, should have led to the conclusion that the discovery of the construction of the missile silos on Cuban soil even before the missiles became operational put the Soviet-Cuban side at a disadvantage from the outset. And it should have been realized at that early stage that the Soviet Union eventually would have to give up the plan to deploy nuclear missiles in Cuba, and the issue would boil down to bargaining over what could be gained in exchange for their removal. Of course, it is easy to be wise now. But at that time, in the heat of the confrontation, nobody on either side of the Atlantic was ready to draw that conclusion.

Besides, there was yet another factor of decisive importance. It was that in spite of the Soviet leader's penchant for taking risks, a war with the United States did not enter into his plans under any circumstances. He understood better than anyone else that in the modern world a military clash of the two superpowers would have evolved into a nuclear conflict with disastrous consequences for all humankind.

During that never-to-be-forgotten week, October 22–28, tension rose steadily from day to day and, in the last couple of days, from hour to hour. The story has been told and retold many times. Suffice it to say that there were two or three crucial moments. One was on Wednesday, October 24, when Soviet ships, having approached the quarantine line and facing U.S. warships, stopped on orders from Moscow or even turned back. This was rightly interpreted as signaling the Soviet Union's willingness to avoid a head-on collision.

Another crucial moment came on Friday, October 26, when Khrushchev sent two messages to Kennedy, both indicating that the Soviet Union was willing to seek a political solution to the crisis and containing some compromise suggestions as to how that could be achieved.

The climax occurred on Sunday, October 28, when Kennedy's message arrived, suggesting a solution: the Soviet Union would withdraw all types of weapons that could be used for offensive purposes in exchange for the repeal of the quarantine and a commitment from the United States not to invade Cuba. In view of the fact that there was a distinct possibility of an air strike or even an actual invasion, this offered a dignified way out for both powers—particularly if we add the unofficial assurances given by the White House that the United States intended to withdraw its missiles from Turkey in the near future.

There was a great deal of commotion and nervous tension in Moscow on that last day, with alarming reports coming in from Washington and Havana. Time seemed to be running out. Fortunately, a positive answer to Kennedy's message went out in time. The crisis seemed to have been resolved, although after-effects in relations between Moscow and Washington and between Moscow and Havana were to be long-lasting.

Andrei Gromyko and a number of others in Moscow later claimed that during the crisis there was no threat of nuclear war, that Khrushchev had evaluated all the positive and negative factors beforehand and that his analysis was foolproof. This argument is difficult to accept. Even if we concede that neither government wanted a nuclear war, they still could have been drawn into one against their will, due to some unexpected circumstance or even an accident. And the downing of the

U-2 plane over Cuba at the height of the crisis proves that unexpected circumstances could occur. Furthermore, Khrushchev could not foresee all possible developments. He certainly misjudged the main factor, the scale of the American reaction.

What is important, however, is that when the wheel began to spin and there was a smell of gunpowder in the air, both Kennedy and Khrushchev displayed wisdom, restraint, and real statesmanship. They did not try to drive the opponent into a corner but left him the possibility of extricating himself from a difficult situation. A Chinese sage once said that it is always important to build a golden bridge over which an enemy can retreat. If we disregard the tremendous risks involved, both protagonists to a greater or lesser degree could and did depict the final outcome as being favorable to their side. The Soviet Union was compelled to withdraw its nuclear missiles from Cuba, a big plus for the American side, while the United States pledged not to attack the island, something Moscow for its part could present as a positive result.

But to my mind there was a consequence of the crisis that had a more lasting importance. What happened in October 1962 had a tremendous educational value for both sides and both leaders. It made them realize, for the first time, that nuclear annihilation was a real possibility and consequently that brinkmanship had to be ruled out and a safer and more constructive relationship between the two superpowers designed and pursued.

After the crisis Khrushchev's attitude toward East-West relations underwent a marked change. His pugnacious behavior during the Berlin crisis and the U-2 incident faded into the background. This transformation was facilitated by the fact that by that time he had come to the conclusion that in the foreseeable future it would be impossible to normalize relations with China. As a result, he was no longer exasperated by each critical salvo from Beijing. This gave him much more room to seek an understanding with the United States and the other Western nations, although even then Khrushchev had to keep an eye on the hard-liners, the hawks, the conservatives—call them what you will.

Another important factor was the change in the way the two leaders regarded each other. As far as Khrushchev was concerned, gone was his somewhat condescending attitude toward the American president. He no longer had doubts about Kennedy's statesmanlike qualities or his ability to take the right decisions. Gone too was the suspicion that the president could be or was being manipulated by the so-called forces of reaction.

The period remaining before the Dallas tragedy and Khrushchev's downfall was marked by tangible progress in Soviet-American relations. On June 10, 1963, President Kennedy made a memorable speech at American University in Washington, D.C. He spoke about the catastrophic consequences of nuclear war and the need to review the American attitude toward the Soviet Union, which had been more profoundly ravaged by war than any other country. He stressed Russian achievements in various fields of art and human knowledge. The speech contained a clear-cut appeal to search for ways to put an end to the Cold War.

In that generally improved atmosphere, an agreement was signed in Geneva on June 20 to establish a hotline linking the Kremlin with the White House. August 15 saw the signing of an important agreement on a limited nuclear test ban, which laid the groundwork for moderating the arms race.

It would be wrong to draw too optimistic a picture. The unresolved international problems were numerous, the differences between the two superpowers were vast, and the inertia of the arms race had become great. Yet one seemed to feel a warm breeze in the Cold War atmosphere. Elements of trust between the leaders of the two countries began to develop. Who knows, perhaps if Kennedy had not been assassinated in November 1963 and Khrushchev had not been removed from office a year later, we would have witnessed the coming of a more sensible and rational relationship between the Soviet Union and the United States sooner than it actually happened.

For the Soviet leader Kennedy's assassination came almost as a personal loss. Because of the time difference, he learned of it only late in the evening of November 22. Some authors maintain that he was in Kiev at that time and rushed back to Moscow in case Kennedy's death should have some unexpected political repercussions. That is not correct. Khrushchev was in Moscow when he learned of the assassination. Early the next morning Foreign Minister Andrei Gromyko and his deputy, Vladimir Semenov, came to the Kremlin with a draft message of condolence addressed to the new president and to the widow.

While we were waiting for Khrushchev to arrive, agency dispatches continued to come in about the reaction to the assassination in the United States and abroad, the circumstances of the arrest of Lee Harvey Oswald, and, finally, the report that Oswald had spent a couple of years in Minsk and had a Russian wife. This last piece of news came as a real shock and must have sent shivers down many a spine. It seemed preposterous even to contemplate the possibility of Soviet intelligence having any connection with the events in Dallas. Still, one could imagine Oswald's stay in Minsk being used to stage some sort of frame-up or provocation harmful to the interests of the Soviet Union.

To prepare myself for any questions by Khrushchev, I called up KGB chairman Vladimir Semichastnyi and asked for any information he had about Oswald. Semichastnyi replied that he had heard of Oswald's arrest and had had time to inquire about him. He could definitely say that his agency had no connection with Oswald whatsoever.

Soon Khrushchev arrived, approved the texts of the two messages to Washington, and set the time when he would visit the U.S. Embassy in Moscow to express his condolences. He also inquired about Oswald and seemed relieved when told of the information received from Semichastnyi. Some preliminary discussion took place as to who should represent the Soviet Union at the funeral. Those present came to the conclusion that as titular head of state, Anastas Mikoyan would be best suited for that mission.

Khrushchev was particularly touched a few days later when he received a personal letter from Jacqueline Kennedy. She wrote that this was one of her last nights in the White House and that she wanted to send this message because she knew how much her husband cared about peace and how relations between Khrushchev and him were central in his mind. She went on to say that the late president and Khrushchev were adversaries but were allied in the determination that the world should not be blown up. They respected each other and could deal with each other.

This brings to an end the short but eventful tale of the Khrushchev-Kennedy relationship, which was soon to be followed by the abrupt termination of the Soviet leader's political career. But that is a different story.

The question may well arise as to Nikita Khrushchev's greatest contribution in the field of international relations. My answer would be that there were at least two major contributions. One was that he helped make the public in many countries realize that a nuclear war had to be avoided at all costs, because it would have meant the destruction of civilization and very possibly the extinction of the human race. He constantly hammered at that thought in his public speeches, interviews, and conversations. The other contribution was that despite his various errors in judgment and unjustified risk-taking, Khrushchev did seek a more civilized relationship between nations. To put it more succinctly, he tried to convert peaceful coexistence from a political slogan into practical policy.

10

The Military-Industrial Complex, 1953–1964

SERGEI KHRUSHCHEV

It is difficult to write about one's father. It is a hundred times more difficult to write about such a father as Nikita Khrushchev, whose contradictory character blended pragmatism and the Communist idealism of the twentieth century. Far from everything that happened between 1953 and 1964 was reported or ended up in archival folders, and at times the most valuable things disappeared. But the formation of a new military ideology happened right before my eyes. On the one hand, the name Nikita Khrushchev is associated with the arms race, the Berlin Wall, and the Cuban missile crisis. At the same time, he carried out sharp cutbacks in the army and in the ocean surface fleet, and he began removing troops from foreign territories. While uttering the well-known words, "We will bury you,"[1] he simultaneously reached out to the West through the opening that he had made in the Iron Curtain.

Josef Stalin left an unenviable situation to his successors. The Soviet leadership expected war to break out at any moment and thought that if it did, the United States, being beyond the reach of Soviet strategic forces, would take advantage of its nuclear superiority. In 1952, the year of Dwight D. Eisenhower's election as American president, I became a first-year student at the Electric Power Institute in Moscow. That November none of us doubted that the Americans wanted a general in the White House because an experienced commander-in-chief would be needed in the impending war. Open boxes with ammunition were stacked near the anti-aircraft guns that surrounded Moscow like a wall.

Obsession with the syndrome of 1941 determined many decisions in those years. This was the point of Stalin's decision, produced by fear, to send one hundred thousand troops to the permafrost of Chukotka in order to ward off an imagined American invasion from Alaska,[2] and of the no less absurd decision to produce and scatter throughout the ice fields of the Arctic ten thousand IL-28 combat bombers.[3] To Stalin they represented a counterweight to the American air bases ringing the Soviet Union. It was under these conditions that a transfer of power took place in Moscow in March 1953. It was up to Stalin's heirs to select a new set of policies or to retain the old one.

The latter option did not tempt any of the contemporary contenders for power, not even the ruthless butcher Lavrentii Beria, who had set as his goal not the reform of the country, as it has become fashionable to say in recent times, but the achievement of supreme power. He bombarded the Presidium of the Central Committee with proposals,[4] which, as Beria saw it, would win him the support of leaders of the union republics, perhaps engage the West's interest, and enlist the devil himself in his struggle for absolute power. And then, partially emptied of Stalin's victims, the gulag would begin to fill up with new "guests." Just as it is impossible to refashion Heinrich Himmler into an anti-fascist simply because he sought a deal with the allies in 1945, Beria cannot be re-created as a reformer.

The preservation of the status quo did not suit Georgii Malenkov and Nikita Khrushchev, who were arriving at center stage at the same time. Their reformist capacities in some ways complemented each other. A reformer is only a reformer when he does not lag behind events but unites his comrades and has no fear of clashing with others. As the first to chair the meetings of the Presidium, Malenkov preferred to listen to the opinions of colleagues and then to join the majority. In replacing him, Khrushchev always went first, dispensing his ideas and only then asking: "Does anyone have any comments?" He would ask, "Who says 'Aye'?" Never, "Who says 'Nay'?" In the rivalry between these two leaders, I believe Malenkov was doomed from the very beginning. He surrendered the field of battle to Khrushchev almost without a struggle, laying on the latter's shoulders the burden of reform.

Where did Nikita Khrushchev and his reforms, not only of military but also of economic and political life, come from? Until the end of his life he fervently believed in the worldwide victory of communism, believed as a good Christian believes in heaven. And for him communism was the same as heaven, only it was on earth, where all people would be happy and live in plenitude and satisfaction.

I remember how in the early post-Stalinist years he would frequently say, "Communism is the best life for everyone. So why should we carry it to other countries on bayonets? Sooner or later they will understand and voluntarily follow us." He did not thirst for a "final and decisive battle" for different, purely human reasons. He had lived through two wars, the Russian Civil War and World War II, and he did not accept their destructive essence. Memories of the atrocities of war, the stench of burning villages, ruins, and the endless mountains of corpses made the idea of starting yet another war, even with the "best intentions," unimaginable to him. One small but telling detail is that he could not watch television programs about war, for they awakened memories that were so strong that they kept him awake all night. "Change the channel, find something else," he would ask the family. I have never forgotten his story about the famous World War II tank battle near the village of Prokhorovka, in his native Kursk. In July 1943, twelve hundred tanks clashed there: the Germans, led by the celebrated Heinz Guderian, and the Soviet tank corps, under Lieutenant General Pavel Rotmistrov.

Hundreds of burning tanks were left under the scorching July sun, their crews burning alive inside. Father told us about how several days after the battle, on the way to the front lines, he visited the battlefield. He described the burned-out tanks that had begun to rust, the land strewn with shell fragments, and the smell of rotting human corpses that he would remember for the rest of his life. Russians? Germans? At that point it did not matter. "So many years have gone by," Father would say to me, "but I close my eyes and that overpowering stench overwhelms me."

No less strong were the memories of the first days of the war, when the Red Army found itself confronting the Nazi offensive unarmed. "Forge some lances," suggested Malenkov in response to Father's desperate call to send rifles for the new recruits. "They sent the last rifles to Leningrad."

Another trait exerted a singular influence on Khrushchev's attitude toward war. All his life he preserved the frugality of a peasant son, whose soul could not accept unproductive expenditures. Defense spending belonged to this category, but avoiding expenditures for the production of tanks, planes, cannons, and atom bombs seemed impossible. Khrushchev had to manage his meager budget so as to feed the hungry— hungry in the literal sense—without sacrificing security. He knew about the hungry firsthand: on his way to work he saw lines forming before dawn at the doors of bakeries. And this was in comparatively prosperous Moscow. He knew about the overflowing collective apartments, huts, and basements, whose inhabitants did not dream of a separate apartment. For them, having the entire family in the same room was a piece of great fortune.

To be so prepared for war as to eliminate its very possibility without impoverishing the country was the basis of Khrushchev's military policy. In order to realize it, he had to overcome both the resistance of party ideologues, who professed the inevitability of a cleansing struggle against the imperialist powers, and the resistance of generals, who believed that with the atomic bomb they could defeat any opponent. One simply had to produce more bombs, airplanes, ships, tanks, and guns.

In February 1956 the 20th Party Congress approved new theoretical postulates: "But there is no fatal inevitability of war," that is, war between two opposing worlds.[5] The transition from capitalism to socialism could take place peacefully, without bloodshed. From our current perspective this language seems banal, especially considering that virtually no one in the West intended to make the transition to socialism. But at that time these simple phrases caused fierce battles.

In those years no one could envisage friendship with the United States or Great Britain. But the era of peaceful coexistence had arrived, in which both sides understood that a resolution of contradictions might not necessitate overt struggle but in which they could not yet cooperate. The thesis about peaceful coexistence had something in common with Leon Trotsky's slogan, "Neither peace nor war," set forth at the time of the Brest-Litovsk Treaty. Although neither Communist ideologues nor Western politicians accepted the proposed formula entirely, everyone understood that, as the Russian proverb has it, "a bad peace was better than a good quarrel."

Dealing with the military turned out to be incomparably more complicated, and Khrushchev did not completely succeed in this venture. At the end of the 1950s, I worked with officers from the general staff, who were developing scenarios for a nuclear war. I remember their optimism: they unhesitatingly wrote off millions of human lives as irretrievable losses and argued over technicalities concerning how to land troops on the North American continent. There were not many opponents of such scenarios. I remember only one: Captain Konstantin Konstantinovich Frantz, born into a family of naval officers, who muttered through his teeth, "Do you intend to come ashore in dinghies? And fight with sticks? Come to your senses!" At the time, no one took him seriously.

But among the civilian leadership, Khrushchev was on Frantz's side, and so were Malenkov, Nikolai Bulganin, and a few others. Malenkov was the first to say openly that a nuclear war would turn into a world catastrophe. In the heat of the Kremlin struggle for power, he was criticized more than once for these words and accused of defeatism, but no one actually refuted this "advanced" idea. Khrushchev took a more cautious position; although he could not imagine starting one himself, he did not entirely reject the possibility of war. Many times I heard him warn against backing oneself into a corner with foolish policies, so that there would be no way out other than to start shooting. In all the crises of that tumultuous age—both those that were launched by Khrushchev himself, like the Berlin and Cuban crises, and those that simply happened on his watch, like the Suez and Taiwan crises—he was careful not to back himself into a corner, not to slam shut the last door, the door leading to a possible way out of the situation.

The new leadership found itself with an army of 5,394,038 troops, the legacy of the Stalin era.[6] It likewise inherited an enormously ambitious shipbuilding program, aimed at eventually dominating the world's oceans, and a variety of programs for the creation of strategic arms capable of delivering nuclear warheads up to eight thousand kilometers (five thousand miles) away, thus bringing the United States within range of a retaliatory strike. But they had also to think of the exhausted people of a country whose war wounds were not yet healed.

As Father recalled, Stalin did not allow him, or most other members of the upper leadership of the country, to deal with military matters. Stalin decided them himself, privately. He consulted only those to whom he had entrusted a particular problem. With Beria he discussed missile and nuclear issues; with Malenkov he talked about radar. At that time, information about missiles and other potential innovations was concealed even from generals. After 1953 Khrushchev had not only to resolve issues, but also to learn about them. Capitalism could not be defeated by military means, he reasoned, but by displaying socialism's ability to provide people with a superior way of life. But for this many resources were needed, which had to be gathered crumb by crumb.

Economizing wherever he could, Khrushchev forbade the construction not only of administrative buildings but also of theaters and workers' clubs. Priority was given to five-story housing. He saw the reduction of military spending as yet another potential way to save. But how to approach it? Soviet marshals and generals, like their colleagues elsewhere in the world, believed in balanced armed forces, which required the linked development of mechanized ground troops, combat and strategic aircraft, artillery, the navy, and much more. If even one link were weakened, the whole chain would fall apart.

To support balanced armed forces it was actually necessary to increase defense spending. It was possible, of course, to press the military to eliminate a certain number of divisions. Khrushchev undertook such reductions on August 12, 1955, by signing a party-government decree cutting back forces by 640,000 troops. Until that time, reductions had been made secretly. By January 1956, not quite three years after Stalin's death, the number of troops had decreased by 1,106,216, to 4,406,216.[7]

Nevertheless, it did not appear possible to accomplish a fundamental shift in such a gradual way. Relying on his characteristic common sense, Khrushchev therefore decided to turn the wheel sharply. On April 1, 1954, Viacheslav Malyshev, the deputy premier in charge of the nuclear program, presented a report that convincingly demonstrated the deadly consequences for the entire planet of any mass use of atomic and hydrogen bombs.[8] Reading the document, Khrushchev concluded that nuclear war was impossible. He did not doubt that the American leadership would arrive at a similar conclusion. If so, there might be a way out of a seemingly hopeless situation.

The threat of mutual nuclear destruction allowed the abandonment of a balanced approach to the armed forces and the adoption of an asymmetric arms strategy, one that provided for the concentration of efforts mostly on intercontinental and middle-range nuclear forces, as well as a reduction in the overall size of the military. A risky approach! A mistake threatened serious, perhaps fatal consequences, but Khrushchev felt there was no other choice. Competition in defense spending with the much more powerful American economy would inevitably lead to the collapse of the Soviet economy, which would of course preclude demonstrating to the world the advantages of socialism. Khrushchev therefore set his heart on a fundamental change in defense policy. But what could be abandoned? When and for how long? After all, the means of delivering intercontinental nuclear warheads was not yet operational, and nuclear warheads themselves were few in number.

Khrushchev did not want to wait for the final development of those delivery vehicles. He had to find a solution immediately. Yet he began his reformation carefully and moved step by step, not according to a prepared plan but by gradually producing new, compact, and—most important—relatively inexpensive forces.

The First Encounter

It began with the navy. Stalin had initiated the construction of a deepwater navy in the 1930s. As soon as World War II was over, although the country had been devastated by years of fighting, new heavy cruisers were ordered, as well as battleships, an aircraft carrier, and many smaller ships, including destroyers and submarines. The program was to take ten years. By 1955 the commander-in-chief of the Soviet navy, Admiral Nikolai Kuznetsov, had proposed spending 110–130 billion rubles in the coming decade, a sum that seemed enormous to Khrushchev, particularly given the severe shortage of resources for cultivating the Virgin Lands.[9] That enormous undertaking aimed to reduce grain shortages, at least until a fertilizer industry could be created, without which any significant increase in the harvest would remain a dream. But to spend more than 100 billion rubles on a navy at the same time?

By 1955 Khrushchev had become rather skeptical about the role of the Soviet surface fleet in a hypothetical future war. The surface ships built in the 1930s with such effort hardly participated in the war with Germany, which was decided on land. Khrushchev also thought that a surface fleet would be unable to defend itself from recently developed low-flying cruise missiles, especially those equipped with nuclear warheads. A confidential movie about a new experimental Soviet cruise missile, the air-to-ship Comet (AS-1),[10] made a strong impression on him. During a Black Sea military exercise, a scrapped cruiser broke in half and sank as a result of a direct hit from a cruise missile.[11]

While Khrushchev's doubts grew, the navy pushed ahead. He decided to investigate the problem himself, traveling around the fleets to see the situation with his own eyes and to listen to people on the spot. In October 1954 he visited Beijing in honor of the fifth anniversary of the People's Republic of China. He decided to take advantage of the occasion to visit the Far Eastern navy base of Port Arthur and to inspect the Pacific fleet.

On his visit to Port Arthur, Khrushchev questioned both economic and political aspects of the Soviet military presence on foreign territories. The maintenance of bases abroad cost a fortune, and a decision to bring the troops home would help win the propaganda game. Marshal Georgii Zhukov, now recovered from Stalinist disgrace and serving as minister of defense, believed that in a modern war neither Port Arthur in China nor Porkalla Udd in Finland could substantially influence military outcomes.[12]

Admiral Kuznetsov took the opposite view. He and Zhukov did not get along, and once in the wake of an argument with the obstinate navy commander-in-chief, Zhukov even threatened to put the sailors in infantry boots, as great an insult to navy pride as can be imagined. The trip around the Far East reinforced Khrushchev's doubts. Port Arthur Bay, in which the Japanese had blockaded the Russian Pacific squadron during the war of 1904–1905, seemed to him simply a trap. The coastal artillery there dated back to the beginning of the century, and a close look only increased Khrushchev's suspicion that the Soviet navy was preparing not for a future conflict but for a past war.

Pacific fleet exercises near Vladivostok confirmed Khrushchev's view that current Soviet naval doctrine had been developed in the pre-nuclear, pre-missile, and pre-radar era. Asked how he would defend himself against cruise missile attack, the commander of the cruiser responded, "I don't know." Of the existence of such arms as the Comet cruise missile, he simply had no idea; officers of his rank were not privy to such secrets.[13]

Khrushchev's visit prepared him for a meeting in Moscow dedicated to naval development over the past decade. There the argument was between Khrushchev, who wanted to save money, and Admiral Kuznetsov, who championed the surface fleet. When the meeting reached a deadlock, Khrushchev posed this question: "If the commander-in-chief were to receive all of the ships that he requested, not within ten years, but right away, would he be able to overtake the U.S. Navy in the world ocean?" The admiral thought for only a moment before answering, "No." The meeting ended with this exchange. Khrushchev's doubts were once again confirmed, but he was not yet ready to act. He wanted to see for himself one more time.

In late September 1955 another meeting took place in Sevastopol under the leadership of Khrushchev and Minister of Defense Zhukov. In his report on naval strategy in the event of the war, the representative of the Black Sea fleet promised a successful assault on the Black

Sea straits fortifications and an equally effective entry into the Mediterranean, followed by the landing of troops in North Africa, somewhere in Algeria. But he said not a word about a nuclear counterattack, including possible use of missiles like the Comet.[14] The meeting had to be interrupted owing to lack of preparation. When it reconvened in early October, Khrushchev and Zhukov set the tone. Khrushchev posed a question and asserted his position:

> Given the current possibilities of detection, communication, and [the development of] powerful missiles, can surface ships of such great size fulfill their objectives? Surface ships will become a burden. . . . Because the role of artillery changes with the development of missiles, it is inadvisable to develop artillery ships. . . . Current armor does not protect against missiles. . . . I have faith in submarines. We can make a submarine fleet and naval aviation the main force in the battle at sea. . . . The defense of naval communications demands the creation of aircraft carriers in order to achieve the tasks of the anti-aircraft defense, but this is a task for later on. . . . What is needed are ships for defense against submarines: ships equipped with sonar detection, with anti-submarine missiles.[15]

Marshal Zhukov supported that position:

> We have no need to enter into a quantitative competition in surface ships with a potential foreign adversary. Our opponents depend upon naval transportation. . . . For the disruption of sea and ocean communications a powerful underwater fleet is needed. . . . These tasks cannot be assigned to the surface fleet. It is not sensible to set out to strengthen the surface fleet. . . . New surface ships should be directed toward provisioning an underwater fleet in cooperation with supporting land forces. . . . Our submarines should be powered by atomic energy units and equipped with powerful sea-launched missiles. . . . For open theaters it is necessary to have ships with surface-to-air missiles. It is not necessary to build aircraft carriers in the near future. Our strategic situation is different from that of the potential foreign adversary, for whom aircraft carriers are a vital requirement.[16]

The government rejected the ten-year shipbuilding program. Not only was Admiral Kuznetsov denied funding, but he was demoted to vice-admiral. Neither Khrushchev nor Zhukov could forget the words he had blurted out at the meeting: "History will not forgive you."

Khrushchev characteristically strove to see matters through to the end. The next step was to revise the structure of the existing navy. Cruisers and battleships that were almost ready for deployment were eventually scrapped when Khrushchev learned how incredibly expensive they were. The maneuvers of the Black Sea fleet, for example, alone burned more fuel than was annually designated for the agriculture of Ukraine as a whole.

The decision did not win Khrushchev support among navy officers. Even Khrushchev himself was occasionally overcome with doubt; under pressure from navy men, he several times reopened discussion of the role of the surface fleet, but his position never did change. The last such discussion took place in 1960, the year of the standoff between the Soviet Union and the United States in the Belgian Congo. With an American cruiser squadron along the African coast, Khrushchev summoned the commander in-chief of the navy, Admiral Sergei Gorshkov, and the minister of the shipbuilding industry, Boris Butoma, and asked, "What would it cost to create a similar force?" The answer, received a week later, was, "Five billion rubles and eight years." Khrushchev merely grunted and glumly joked: "For that kind of money the Americans can sail alone."[17]

In the 1960s the surface fleet became a great deal smaller: mostly cruisers of prewar design and those that had been built in the first postwar decade. They were to be modernized and equipped with cruise missiles (a similar cruise missile, designed for coastal defense, was named Sopka, SSC-2B). On one of the Black Sea cruisers, they even replaced large-caliber battle guns with cruise missiles but then got rid of them on grounds of cost.

Anti-submarine warfare ships, ships for coastal defense, cruise missile boats of the 183- and 205-type, eighteen of them equipped with the cruise missile P-15 (SS-N-2A),[19] known in the West as the Styx—these became the basis of the new surface fleet.[20] The production of destroyers was sharply reduced. In the early 1960s the newest 58-type destroyers—with two P35 four-cruise-missile launchers (SS-N-3B),[21] capable of striking a target up to 250 kilometers away—replaced the destroyers of the 56-type (with torpedoes) and the 57-type, which was equipped with a launcher for the cruise missile SS-N-1.[22] Instead of building an entire run of fifty such destroyers, however, it was decided to produce only four of them.

Thereafter submarines became the core of the navy. They were armed with both ballistic missiles for attacking the territory of a potential foreign adversary and cruise missiles, whose task was the destruc-

tion of aircraft carrier group units and communication ties. With the
exception of the latter, however, the Soviet navy was losing the competition with the United States. When the first American nuclear submarine, the *Nautilus,* entered into service in 1953, an analogous Soviet
submarine was just being designed. It appeared only in 1958.

The placing of ballistic missiles on submarines also aroused controversy. In the early 1950s no one was specifically designing them for
the navy. It was decided to adapt the short-range land-based ballistic
missile (SS-1C, SCUD-A) with a range of 80–150 kilometers, which
used nitric acid as an oxidizer. Soviet missile-builders did not yet even
dream of solid rocket fuel. The first launch took place on September 16,
1955, and in 1959 the missile was accepted into service.[23] It was not
placed in the body of the submarine, however, so it had to be squeezed
into the crowded space of the deckhouse. As a result, both the diesel
611-type and the first 629-type missile-launching nuclear submarines
were equipped with only two missiles each.

The fighting capacity of these submarines turned out to be very limited. In order to hit targets, they had to be close to shore, thus entering
a zone in which anti-submarine defense completely dominated. After
the R-11, in 1960, there followed the R-13 (SS-N-4 SARK) with a range
of up to 650 kilometers.[24] After this a new nuclear submarine, the 658-
type, was designed, and the 629 was modernized, increasing the number of missiles to three.[25] In 1963 an underwater launch finally became
possible. For this an R-21 missile was designed (according to the new
fleet register D-4 [SS-N-5 SERB]), but as before it used nitric acid.[26] The
first solid fuel missile, RSM-45 (SS-N-17 SNIPE),[27] similar to the Po-
laris and the Poseidon, appeared only in the 1980s.

This whole leapfrog pattern of development graphically illustrates
the paradox of the absence of vertical planning in a system dominated
by a centralized plan. As a result, whereas the United States developed
only two types of missiles and two types of submarines (with modern-
izations and variations), the Soviet Union, between 1959 and 1980, developed ten types of missiles and four types of submarines, which naturally required corresponding expenditures. This was not a chance
occurrence but the normal pattern. In conditions of extreme concentration of power, the bureaucratic hierarchy loses the ability to engage
in optimally effective long-term planning. Military-industrial development agencies begin to work their will, guided by selfish motives that

are far removed from the real interests of the state. State structures, deprived of a choice due to the absence of competition, fall into complete dependence on such agencies. Thus, in the Soviet Union expenditures for the realization of large-scale plans swelled, and the number of stages of developed models grew, providing a comfortable life for designers and producers of arms.

On the other hand, decision making adequate to the needs of the time depended directly on the leader and his qualifications, biases, and understanding of the question at hand. If the leader was lazy, decisions were made at the next level down the power pyramid. Between 1953 and 1964 Khrushchev characteristically took the reins of the government into his own hands. Under Leonid Brezhnev fundamental decisions in the area of defense were made by Dmitrii Ustinov and Marshal Andrei Grechko.

As a result of abandoning the construction of a carrier fleet, cruise missiles on submarines became the sole weapon capable of striking war ships and transports from afar without entering into direct contact with anti-submarine defenses.

In the Soviet Union the development of cruise missiles was assigned to several design bureaus. Georgii Beriev designed the P-10, Vladimir Iliushin designed the P-20, Artem Mikoyan designed the P-30, and Vladimir Chelomei designed the P-5 (SS-N3C Shaddock).[28] Unlike all the others, his P-5 took off with closed wings, emerged like a bird from a hollow, and only after 1.4 seconds opened its wings in the air with the help of a special hydraulic device and then locked. His missile was the one chosen to begin production.

It was harder for Chelomei than for the others. Just a few days before Stalin's death his design bureau, with all its materials on cruise missiles, was closed. He "got in the way" of the Comet's developers, Artem Mikoyan and, more important, Colonel Sergo Beria, who had become the chief engineer of Design Bureau No. 1.[29] The latter was a behemoth with many thousands of workers, where, under the supervision of engineers brought in from Germany, Soviet scientists reproduced and perfected German projects for guidance systems of various types of anti-aircraft and cruise missiles.

Chelomei, who now found himself out of work, knocked on every door, even Beria's. Beria heard him out but did not hurry to respond. "When you are needed, we will call you" was the best answer the designer managed to get. "I will leave you my home phone number. After all, I no longer have work," Vladimir Chelomei muttered in bewilderment. "No need, those whom we need we find ourselves," came the ominous response. Beria loved to joke like this. Soon he was gone, but Chelomei had no better luck with other leaders, even when he forced his way through to Bulganin, who listened to him inattentively and dismissed his proposal for arming submarines with cruise missiles.

Chelomei had more luck with Khrushchev, who liked the young inventor. In the event of success, the new cruise missile promised to turn the submarine fleet into a threat to the naval communications of an enemy. Khrushchev decided, however, to talk it over with Bulganin. "I'd get rid of him," the latter responded to Khrushchev's ecstatic take on the inventor and his discoveries. "Stalin kicked him out, as he should have. But do as you like." Bulganin could not stand conflict. Chelomei received permission to get the work going again, and he got a small factory in Reutov on the outskirts of Moscow in the bargain.

Chelomei's cruise missiles were included in the architecture of the submarines, and preparation time for launch was thus reduced to minutes. The first to be activated was the P-5 (SS-N-3C), designed to destroy inland targets at a range of up to five hundred kilometers. The 659-type nuclear submarine carried six cruise missiles, quite an achievement considering that the R-11 had only three. After the P-5 came the P-6 (SS-N-3A Shaddock),[30] capable of striking any ship up to 350 kilometers away. The 675-type submarines were equipped with six Shaddocks. P-35s (SS-N-313 SEPAL),[31] designed to take on destroyers, and the coastal defense system Redut (SSC-1B) followed in turn.[32] Thanks to his development of postlaunch opening wings, within a decade Chelomei left the rest of the world behind. In the Soviet navy, cruise missiles occupied the dominant position for a long time before the appearance of the U.S. Navy Tomahawks.

Despite Khrushchev's apparent victory, his conception of making submarines the core of the navy did not outlive him. After his retirement submarines were built in much greater quantities than in the United States—ten times as many as Khrushchev had planned. In addition, however, Brezhnev returned to the Stalinist policy of creating an oceangoing surface fleet, thus placing a heavy burden on the Soviet economy. The ambitions of the admirals were satisfied. Yet, as Admiral Kuznetsov correctly stated in 1955, the Soviet navy never did become a rival to the U.S. Navy in either the Pacific or the Mediterranean, although it was comparable in the overall number of ships.

Strategic Arms: Missiles and Airplanes

The story of the Soviet navy is only one of the episodes in the formation of the asymmetric defense policy of Nikita Khrushchev. Its main component was strategic nuclear forces. What kind of security for the Soviet Union was possible if, in the event of war, its armed forces could not make a retaliatory nuclear strike on the territory of the United States? Khrushchev understood this dilemma well.

The design of missiles and bombers began well before Khrushchev came to power. American carpet bombing of Germany and the nuclear attacks on Hiroshima and Nagasaki changed Stalin's negative opinion of strategic bombing. A key step in this new direction was his order to Andrei Tupolev to produce an exact copy of the American B-29 bomber, based on a B-29 Superfortress with the name "Tramp" painted on its cockpit, which got lost and landed at a Soviet Far Eastern air base soon after the end of the world war. By that time the B-29 represented an old design, but no one dared disobey Stalin's order. It was not very difficult to copy the airframe and the engines, but dealing with the avionic system, instruments, remote-control gun systems, and automation was different. For this an entire branch of the avionic systems industry was created. It would not be an exaggeration to say that in a certain sense Stalin's order forced the Soviet aviation industry to leapfrog an entire era and thus make great strides in catching up with the United States. After all, without different types of avionic systems, the Soviet Union could not even think about contemporary airplanes.

Nevertheless, the main task was not achieved. The TU-4, the B-29's copy, did not succeed as an intercontinental bomber, nor did the TU-16 jet that came after it. Their fighting range was limited to Europe. It is true that under pressure from above, Tupolev undertook the design of the intercontinental TU-95, but he honestly warned his superiors that it would not be able to penetrate the U.S. air defense. His colleague Vladimir Miasishchev was more optimistic, and he promised to create an intercontinental jet bomber.

Work on the design of intercontinental cruise and ballistic missiles began after the first hydrogen bomb was tested, on August 12, 1953. Mi-

asishchev undertook to develop the Buran,[33] an intercontinental sub-
sonic cruise missile with a range of up to 8,000 kilometers. A similar
development was conducted in the United States under the name
SNARK.

Semen Lavochkin, the father of the best Soviet fighters in World
War II and the promoter of ram jets, began to design the Buria cruise
missile.[34] By contemporary standards it had incredible parameters: it
flew three times the speed of sound and at a height of twenty kilometers, and it had a range of 8,000 kilometers. An analogous American
cruise missile was called the Navaho.

Finally, Sergei Korolev, the most energetic among the pioneers of
Soviet rocket science, began the design of his, or more accurately
Mikhail Tikhonravov's, intercontinental ballistic missile, the R-7 (SS-
6),[35] the same type that today takes Russian cosmonauts into orbit.
Tikhonravov and Korolev in fact shared duties, with the former the
brains of the project and the latter the muscle. The decision of the Central Committee and the Council of Ministers to develop the R-7 was
made on May 20, 1954.

The American Atlas rocket could be considered roughly analogous
to the R-7. Its launch weight did not exceed 90 tons, whereas the R-7,
because of the six-ton weight of the three-megaton thermonuclear warhead, weighed in at 270 tons. It was precisely this six-ton payload, as
well as the inability to ignite rocket engines in a vacuum, that compelled
the designers to resort to the then exotic one-and-a-half stage-rocket design.[36]

In 1955–1956 the first phase of strategic arms development was
completed, and the remaining projects, although not yet ready to be
tested, were sufficiently developed so that Khrushchev could decide
which should be pushed further. After a visit to Miasishchev's design
bureau in Fili, Khrushchev decided that Miasishchev's experimental
M-3 "looked good." But all the new ideas and all the latest achievements
of engineering thought that the designer had poured forth turned out
to be too numerous for one airplane. In fact, the airplane never seemed
ready to fly; there was always some problem to be fixed.

Although several air force divisions were equipped with it, the M-3
could not be used to attack the United States. Just as Tupolev had predicted, it could not carry enough fuel for the trip back. It is true that "sor-
cerers" from the Soviet air force proposed a way out of the situation.
One suggestion was that after bombing the main U.S. cities, the planes

should land—in Mexico. Khrushchev was taken aback by such gall but quickly composed himself and morosely joked, "And how will you negotiate this with the Mexicans? Does your mother-in-law live there?" Those present giggled obsequiously.[37] Further conversations with Miasishchev finally convinced Khrushchev that strategic bombers could not be counted on.

That left missiles. In the winter of 1956 Korolev invited Khrushchev and other members of the Presidium to look over his brainchild, the R-7. The demonstration made an impression. Although test flights were still to be done, Korolev promised no unexpected troubles. Khrushchev's visit to Korolev's design bureau coincided with successful tests of his other missile, the R-5M (SS-3), with a range of twelve hundred kilometers. For the first time it was launched, not with an dummy nuclear warhead, but with a real one.

This flight triggered Khrushchev's missile diplomacy. In 1956 he decided to employ the "new arms"[38] in the European diplomatic arena. He began with Great Britain, taking advantage of a state visit in April 1956 to announce that the Soviet Union had enough missiles to wipe any European state off the face of the earth. From that time until the Cuban missile crisis in 1962, he used the thesis of alleged Soviet missile superiority wherever he could, and highly effectively. He bragged left and right about how the Soviet Union produced missiles like sausages. In response to my disbelief (how could he talk about mass production of missiles if you could still count them on your fingers?), Father simply laughed: "If we intended to wage war, then the outcome of the battle would certainly depend on the number of missiles; but since that's not the case, let the Americans rack their brains over how many we actually have. They will avoid starting a war."

For the same reasons, he from time to time shared the latest ideas of the chief designers in interviews with Western journalists—for example, a global missile, a quasi-Sputnik with a nuclear warhead capable at any moment of overcoming any (then hypothetical) anti-missile defense. When I became indignant over the exposure of our ultrasecret projects, Father said that no reasonable politician would allow anyone to release nuclear warheads into orbit. He thought that his interview about the existence of a such a possibility would make his opponent nervous and force him to spend money defending against nonexistent arms. He frightened politicians in the United States so much that they entered into a missile race with a shadow, a race with their own fear.

And . . . they won! They won because the "missile gap" in Soviet favor, which they had feared, did not exist.

What actually happened with the Soviet ICBM buildup? In 1957, after the first successful tests of the R-7 and the launch of the Sputnik satellite, Khrushchev made a final decision: intercontinental ballistic missiles would become the core of the Soviet strategy of containment, making possible a fundamental reduction in the size of the army. Khrushchev dreamed of using the money saved for economic development, to catch up to and overtake the United States in all areas, including standard of living. For a start, however, it was necessary for intercontinental missiles to become an operational reality. Korolev did not succeed in achieving this. His new missile turned out to be too complicated and too costly to maintain. To preserve minimum combat readiness it was necessary to build an oxygen factory works at every launch site. And this was not all. The guidance of the R-7 from a distance was realized, as with the old German V-2, by electrolytic integrators recharged directly before the launch. In addition, to prevent significant flight deviations, it was necessary to set up two radio guidance points, each five hundred kilometers away, for each launch site.

Surprisingly, neither the designers of the R-7 nor the bureaucrats from the Military-Industrial Commission of the Council of Ministers got around to figuring out the cost of operating the missiles. In 1956 even the frugal Khrushchev did not ask this question of Korolev. At that time everyone believed in developing the missile "at any cost." They finally calculated the amount in 1958, when Khrushchev decided, without waiting for the formal conclusion of R-7 test flights, to proceed with deployment. Each R-7 launch site, not counting operational costs, would cost half a billion rubles. And the total number of proposed sites in the Soviet Union ran to several hundred.

Khrushchev was horrified. He summoned Korolev, Deputy Chairman of the Council of Ministers Dmitrii Ustinov, and Defense Minister Rodion Malinovskii. "We don't have the money and we won't. We have to find a different solution," he declared at the very beginning of the conversation. Those present disagreed. Korolev reported that the compounds he had chosen, liquid oxygen and kerosene, were the only ones capable of creating the thrust necessary to launch thermonuclear warheads across the ocean. Malinovskii insisted that the number of missiles could not be decreased. Ustinov complained about the lack of missile production capacity and requested additional investment. In his opinion, if not the R-7, then some other missile would have to be produced in large quantities, and it was necessary to prepare for this.

Finally a compromise was reached. The R-7s were restricted to one additional launch site in Tiura Tam (Baikonur), with four new sites in Plisetsk and one more missile base in Krasnoyarsk province. The Krasnoyarsk project was never undertaken, however; the final total was thus six missiles sites at two bases. Khrushchev asked the designers to think of how spending on missile production could be reduced. Korolev repeated that nothing better could be done on the technical side.

Ustinov's proposal for the construction of new missile factories was not accepted. Khrushchev proposed organizing missile production at existing aircraft factories and beginning construction of the R-7 at the giant Kuibyshev plant, which had traditionally produced Tupolev bombers. Eventually other aircraft productive capacity was also converted to missiles. From now on, aviation would be allotted a subsidiary role in Soviet military doctrine. Long-range bombers were supposed to "clean up" what had not been destroyed by a missile strike (mostly in the European Theater), and their production was considerably reduced. For the time being, short-range combat planes were not to be touched, nor was anti-aircraft defense. Anti-aircraft forces were given a priority comparable only to that of ballistic missiles. The flights of the U-2 surveillance plane over Soviet territory contributed substantially to this policy.

It was not only missiles that crowded out bombers at the factories. Khrushchev wanted to introduce contemporary passenger craft, and Vladimir Iliushin produced a turboprop, the Il-18. Not wishing to be left out, Tupolev quickly reworked his bomber into a passenger prototype. Using the Tu-16 as a foundation, he created the Tu-104; the Tu-95 served as the prototype of the Tu-114.

The shift in priorities affected developments and designs. In 1960 Vladimir Miasishchev completed work on the supersonic bomber of the future, the M-50. Just like the M-3 in its time, it incorporated all the latest achievements of aviation science but, consequently, cost a great deal. Khrushchev decided to halt the work, thus conserving many resources. The military objected but did not succeed in altering the decision. The M-50 was shown at the air show in Tushino, but that was it. Soon the Kremlin decided that it was inadvisable to maintain two design bureaus, Tupolev's and Miasishchev's, for heavy bombers. Tupolev, the father of domestic aircraft, was not touched, but the design bureau in Fili was reoriented to missiles. Vladimir Chelomei replaced Vladimir Miasishchev. It was there, in Fili, that the UR-200 and UR-100 (SS-11) missiles, the well-known Proton space launcher (UR-500), and part of the space station Saliut were designed.[39]

Tupolev's work on bombers was greatly reduced. Plans for the modification of the Tu-16 and the Tu-95 were abandoned. Only two new projects, the long-range heavy interceptor Tu-28–80 and the Tu-22, which was intended as a replacement for the Tu-16, were continued. Rather than develop a new long-range bomber, Khrushchev advised Tupolev to concentrate on the supersonic passenger plane the Tu-144, the rival of the French-British Concorde.

Soon Khrushchev moved in on air force bases. The civilian airline Aeroflot was catastrophically lacking in airfields, and those that did exist were not designed for servicing large airplanes. Either they had to be rebuilt or new ones had to be constructed. But where could they get the resources? Khrushchev decided to transfer to civil aviation a number of military airfields that were located close to large cities. The process began with Sheremetyevo outside of Moscow, where an airfield was built for flights made by high-ranking officials. Other air force bases transferred to Aeroflot were the strategic base in Brovarii outside of Kiev and the anti-aircraft defense base in Sukhumi. In response to objections from the military, Khrushchev replied: "In peace time the airports will serve the people, and if, God forbid, a time of misfortune arrives, we will return them to you." Naturally, such attempts to take over the property of the armed forces did not win him supporters in their ranks.

Work also stopped on intercontinental cruise missiles. Then came the fighters' turn. In 1963 Lavochkin's design bureau lost its independence.[40] The Kremlin thought that four bureaus designing fighters was a bit much, and it was decided to abandon three of them—those of Artem Mikoyan, Aleksandr Yakovlev, and Pavel Sukhoi—and Lavochkin's bureau began to take care of designing lunar spacecraft. The air force generals grumbled, but they did not choose to oppose Khrushchev openly, as Admiral Nikolai Kuznetsov had, at least not for the time being.

Simultaneously with the cutbacks in aviation came comparable cuts in artillery production. It seemed to Khrushchev that all the main tasks assigned to artillery in previous wars—preparing a breakthrough in ground operations, destroying anti-tank fortifications, and taking on planes and tanks—were now more effectively and cheaply handled with missiles. In one factory after another, the production and design of new artillery systems was halted. In 1963 Vasilii Grabin's bureau, which had designed most of the artillery for the Red Army during World War II and in the postwar period, was closed.[41] At chief designer Boris Shchavyrin's famous mortar enterprise in Kolomna, they began to produce anti-tank and tactical missiles instead, including the OKA (OTR-23).[42]

The war in Vietnam showed that the elimination of artillery was premature and that many military tasks remained that could not be accomplished with missiles. Since Khrushchev had been removed from power long before, previous production was restored and new guns were created, as many as the generals' hearts desired.

But let us return to strategic missiles. In 1958–1959 the R-7 had no serious competitors, and Korolev hoped to pressure Khrushchev into authorizing the production and deployment of more of them. But Khrushchev still sought an alternative solution. It came from Ukraine. Mikhail Iangel, the creator of the middle- and intermediate-range ballistic missiles R-12 (SS-4) and R-14 (SS-5),[43] and the chief designer of the "Southern" design bureau, which had been created in 1954, proposed using nitrogen acid components to build the R-16 (SS-7) intercontinental missile.[44] The latter turned out to be not only cheaper and easier to use than the R-7 (SS-6), but also more compact and lighter by more than a hundred tons. Khrushchev strongly supported the new proposal, but he did not rush to make decisions. For him, Korolev's authority was incomparably higher than that of Iangel, and in recent months Korolev had convinced him that such an idea was technically unfeasible: it was one thing to use nitrogen acid to make missiles with a range of two thousand and even four thousand kilometers, and it was quite another to make them with a range of eight thousand kilometers; it would be impossible to design the required engine. Khrushchev had no reason not to trust Korolev, but his instinct told him that it was worth the risk. He decided to double-check and spoke with Valentin Glushko, the designer of most of the Soviet rocket engines, including those placed on the R-7. Glushko supported Iangel's proposals and said that he would take it upon himself to make the necessary engine. (Khrushchev did not know that the disagreement between Korolev and Glushko concerning which components were preferable for rocket flight, liquid oxygen or acid, dated all the way back to the 1930s. Glushko supported the use of acid.)

The decision to design the R-16 was taken on May 13, 1959.[45] That was the day the creation of genuinely strategic arms began. But the R-16 was in no way comparable to the Minuteman missile that was being designed at that time in the United States. The nitrogen acid corroded the missile fuel tanks, which made it impossible for missiles to be kept ready for launch. Several hours of preparation were required, whereas the Minuteman was ready to go, as the name suggests, within minutes. Nevertheless, the R-16 was a step forward from the R-7.

In another decree, dated the same day, permission was given to Sergei Korolev to design his R-9 (SS-8),[46] also an intercontinental missile, which used deep-freeze oxygen developed from the technology of Petr Kapitsa and Vasilii Mishin.[47] The R-9 was similar to the American Atlas.[48] Khrushchev wanted to protect himself from possible failure and therefore decided to bet on both designers. Korolev's R-9 was not widely deployed. The R-16, however, was notable in the history of Soviet strategic missile forces. The deployment of the R-16 began early in 1962, just before the Cuban missile crisis. It was the first missile to go into underground silos in 1963. It thus became the first missile that could ride out an American first strike and then respond, thereby giving the Soviet Union a true deterrent capability.

The New Army

Field demonstrations of new military technology played a significant role in the evolution of Nikita Khrushchev's military worldview. Upon his insistence, it was decided to hold field demonstrations of the latest technology every two years. Generals (of rank no lower than corps commander) and officials responsible for arms development could thus become familiar with those arms that would be used in the event of a nuclear war. Such field demonstrations took place in 1958 and 1960 in Kapustin Yar, in 1959 in Sevastopol, in 1962 in Severomorsk and Arkhangelsk, and in 1964 in Baikonur and in Kubinka, near Moscow.[49] It was in Kapustin Yar in September 1958, in my presence, that the generals literally begged Khrushchev to resume nuclear tests.[50] The last straw was a carefully prepared comparative demonstration of large, cumbersome nuclear warheads and the miniature analogs, which still required testing. The officers insisted that if the Americans were to complete their series of test explosions and the Soviet Union were not to do its own tests, the Soviet military would be left far behind. Khrushchev did not intend to allow that.

Chelomei's design bureau, where I worked, demonstrated its missiles at these field tests. I was present at most of them and I listened to what was discussed at the conclusion of the tests. After 1958 my father constantly returned to the role of the different branches of the armed forces in what he assumed would be a totally destructive nuclear war. Would it end with the death of civilization? He never posed this question to the military officers. It was the business of politicians, not the military, to do everything possible to avoid catastrophes. But what if nuclear war were to break out? How could its outcome be affected by all those planes, helicopters, tanks, guns, and other arms whose production was devouring so much money?

In contrast to Western strategists, Khrushchev did not believe local wars could occur, given the global nuclear opposition of the two great powers. In his opinion any local conflict would ultimately involve Soviet and American forces and escalate into a nuclear encounter between the two powers. Since in Khrushchev's doctrine there was no place for local wars, he did not consider it necessary to produce the arms necessary for them. The generals took a diametrically opposite view.

Did Nikita Khrushchev make a mistake? History would suggest so. But the reverse is also possible: that it was precisely the superabundance of conventional arms, which Khrushchev sought to avoid, that gave rise to local wars.

There is yet another fundamental question on which Khrushchev failed to agree with the generals. He no longer considered the presence of Soviet troops on the territory of the Warsaw Pact allies advisable. "The regimes existing there should rely not on bayonets but on the support of their people. If the people do not support them, then who needs such leaders?" I heard these words from Father more than once. He also did not doubt that the people stood behind socialist governments, just as he was certain of socialism's superiority over capitalism. "But then why give our enemies a reason to assert that local regimes are upheld only by the existence of our troops?" Father asked anxiously.

Furthermore, he simply could not resign himself to the enormous expenditures necessary for the maintenance of troops on foreign territory. Between 1962 and 1964 he more than once returned to the necessity of the Soviet army's departure from Hungary, Poland, and possibly even from East Germany—although withdrawal from the latter could only come after the West's recognition of its independent statehood. Military officers stood their ground, contending that Soviet military bases in Eastern Europe guaranteed the security of the Soviet Union. Khrushchev considered their point of view obsolete and not suited to the realities of nuclear-era confrontation. "Given modern means of transportation and possibilities of deployment," he said, "the outcome of war will not be decided in border battles. From a strategic perspective the existence of Soviet ground troops on western borders is useless, and their withdrawal will provide us with enormous political and economic advantages. Moreover, if necessary, modern means of transportation, including aviation, would allow the rapid return of troops." The issue of withdrawing troops from Eastern Europe, however, was not destined to grow into a conflict between Khrushchev and the generals. The problem was moot after the leaders of Hungary and Poland, Janos Kadar and Wladyslaw Gomulka, spoke out against it.[51]

In March 1963 there was a meeting of the Defense Council at Chelomei's design bureau and, at the same time, an exhibit of prospective arms developments. The goal of the meeting was to choose the better of two proposals, submitted by Mikhail Iangel and Vladimir Chelomei, for the development of a new intercontinental ballistic missile capable of rapid response—in other words, to determine the basis for future nuclear deterrence forces.

The Ministry of Defense and the General Staff insisted on developing tactical nuclear weapons for ground troops, on the same level as mortars, mines, and grenades. The commander of ground forces, Marshal Andrei Grechko, began by discussing plans for modernization of the Luna (FROG-4), a tactical missile launcher. He went on to lobby for mass production of long-range nuclear artillery. Everyone had already heard his main argument: the Americans either had all of this already or would in the near future.

At their tête-à-tête meetings at Camp David in 1959, President Eisenhower had spoken with Khrushchev about the pressure applied to the political leadership by military officers on both sides. Eisenhower even suggested a united front against the expansionist ways of the military-industrial complex. Khrushchev took the words of the American president less as a joke than as a dream. He said noncommitally, "It would be nice . . . ," and then started to talk about other things, about Germany, about disarmament, and so on.[52] After the May 1, 1960, flight of the American U-2 reconnaisance plane and the collapse of the Paris summit, any such hopes turned to dust.

Khrushchev had to deal with the military on his own. Grechko presented the latest information on the U.S. army: "Besides the tactical ballistic missile Honest John, they have equipped their ground troops with long-range artillery capable of firing nuclear shells. Infantry subunits have different types of nuclear mines at their disposal. They are on the verge of considering portable nuclear missiles, virtually hand-held ones." In the Soviet Union, in the words of Grechko, things were in a catastrophic state. Besides the Luna there was practically nothing to rely on. Grechko did not doubt that without tactical atomic warheads, including miniature ones with an equivalent of one to two kilotons, it would be impossible to win a modern battle.[53]

Khrushchev, however, did not favor tactical nuclear arms. For him nuclear weapons served not as an instrument of war but as an argument in political battles, a means of pressure, fear, even blackmail. Ten-, thirty-, and fifty-megaton warheads, too big for use in Europe, had the sort of psychological impact that Khrushchev wanted. Smaller, tactical weapons seemed dangerous to him because they lowered the threshold of fear. Moreover, such devices cost a lot. The Minister of Intermediate Machine-Building, Efim Slavskii, who was in charge of the weapons industry, reported that a 1.5 kiloton warhead for an atomic cannon would cost no less than a megaton warhead for an intercontinental missile. If the equipping of ground troops with atomic arms were taken seriously, tens of thousands of warheads would be required.

The most that Khrushchev would agree to was further design work and the construction of prototypes of a long-barreled nuclear cannon and a nuclear mortar. They were brought out twice a year, during parades on Red Square, but Khrushchev vetoed their mass production. In answer to persistent demands he angrily joked: "What else do you need? Everyone knows, on our side and the American side, that we have them. This pair is enough to satisfy your pride and to frighten the Americans. They will never believe that we have only two guns." With the Luna things were a bit easier. It entered production, although only a few nuclear warheads were produced.

Nor did Khrushchev want to hear about nuclear mines. He was not swayed by references to the Americans. He stuck to his opinion that if you wasted your energy on all these "games," then you would definitely lose. If the Americans wanted to, then let them throw money away. In Khrushchev's opinion, if a nuclear war were to start, there would be no "battlefield."

After the March 1963 Defense Council decision eschewing tactical nuclear weapons, Grechko unsuccessfully tried to bring Khrushchev around to his side.[54] But after Khrushchev was sent into retirement, Brezhnev reversed direction. The number of nuclear warheads, most of them tactical, rose into the thousands, and then it kept on rolling.

The main question facing the March 1963 Defense Council meeting, the selection of an intercontinental nuclear missile, did not take much time. Iangel and Chelomei were heard from, then designers of engines, guidance systems, and launch systems. After a short discussion a missile that had been proposed by Chelomei, the UR-100 (SS-11), was chosen.[55] Like all the previous missiles, it was based on liquid, extremely toxic nitrogen components. By carefully sealing tanks and pipelines, and employing special high-resistance coatings, the missile could stand in the silos for more than ten years, completely ready for launch. The Soviet Union had finally caught up with and even surpassed the Minuteman. But the deployment of UR-100s in silos began only in 1968, six years later than the Minuteman was deployed in the United States.[56]

As it happened, however, the most important development at the Defense Council in Fili was a discussion that spontaneously arose about the role of the different branches of the armed forces in modern war and, as a result, about the future of the Soviet armed forces. I will talk about this in greater detail, since Father spoke about his vision of the future of the Soviet armed forces. By 1963 he had fully formulated the asymmetric scheme for the development of the different branches of the armed forces on which he had been working since 1954.

Defense Minister Malinovskii began the conversation. He had scowled and barely said anything throughout the meeting. In his opinion the army was in bad shape—particularly personnel. In the mid-1960s, young men born during the war were coming up for the draft. But given the low birthrate then, there was no one to draft, and subunits were not achieving the requisite numbers. Malinovskii particularly criticized various privileges that allowed certain individuals to receive a deferment, or to avoid the draft entirely.

Grechko supported Malinovskii. Arguing against student exemptions, he maintained that a student who went through the army would become a real man. Grechko also spoke out against military departments in universities, which turned out reserve officers. He did not like their civilian status and their lack of military experience. Such departments ought to be closed down, with a corresponding increase in military school enrollment. Grechko also opposed reducing the term of service in the army from three to two years, and in the navy from four to three years. Technology was getting more complicated, training took more and more time, and the soldier had hardly begun to serve before it was time for demobilization. He proposed extending the length of service to four years or more in branches equipped with particularly complicated technology. The generals in the hall supported with an approving murmur those who had finally decided to speak the truth.

The military officers present did not actively resent Khrushchev. But as Khrushchev well knew, this kind of spontaneous rumbling, were it not quelled, could develop momentum. He began with a rhetorical question: Who was serving whom? Was the army serving the people or were the people serving the army? The length of service had been reduced not haphazardly but after long consideration. The economy required workers' hands; there were shortages everywhere, and in the meantime young people in the army were consuming but not producing.

"Did you ever consider how many useful things can be produced by those servicemen who leave the army a year early?" Khrushchev asked, shooting a look at Andrei Grechko. He added that, of course, in three years it was possible to learn military matters better than in two, but five years was even better. He recalled that under Tsar Nicholas I men served twenty-five years; this, presumably, was the ideal to which the marshal aspired?

Khrushchev then urged that priority be given to strengthening the country's economy. If it were healthy, then no imperialists could scare us. "It is necessary to think, to think in a new way," he said, smiling for the first time. Grechko began to smile in response. Malinovskii continued to look glumly at the floor. The other generals fidgeted in their chairs, obviously not satisfied.

"As for students," Khrushchev continued, "you simply do not understand! Otherwise you would not raise such a ridiculous question. How can you think that way? We are spending billions of rubles to train these students to become the specialists that we so desperately need, and you want to pull them out of school and ship them off to march and drill!"

"As for military departments in universities, if they are not working satisfactorily, if they are turning out defective officers, we have to act; but to draft students as soldiers amounts to economic sabotage. We stand for the interests of the people, the interests of the state, which needs educated engineers, agronomists, and other specialists, who make our life better. The army is obliged to protect their work. Grechko is trying to turn everything upside down: if everyone were to be drafted into the army, there would be no one to protect and the army would turn out to be unnecessary. We need specialists, and we will teach them in institutes. Army problems," Khrushchev concluded, "cannot be solved at the expense of the people."

The question regarding students was resolved for the time being. But neither Malinovskii nor Grechko considered himself defeated. Again and again they raised the question with Khrushchev, each time unsuccessfully. Only after Khrushchev's retirement was Grechko able to convince the government.

Khrushchev continued to think aloud at the meeting: What should the army be like in the future? For now one could only dream about complete disarmament. But the time had come to approach defense capability in a new way. "Let us take tanks, for example," he told the assembled generals. "During the last war they served as the nucleus of the attack and the core in defense. They were invulnerable to small arms and yielded only to cannons; but just try to escape from inside one. At the end of the war, everything changed; the Germans burned tanks with their bazookas while remaining practically invulnerable. Our advantage at the time was so great that we simply did not feel these changes. And yet even with the bazookas, it was necessary to get right up close. Today antitank missiles destroy armored vehicles from as far away as their range allows, up to several kilometers. Tanks, self-propelled artillery, and armored personnel carriers simply become traps for the crew. And without thinking we are ordering more and more of them? We are wasting billions of rubles."

"Aircraft have also practically lost their former importance. Anti-aircraft missiles sharply reduce their fighting capacity." As for helicopters, Khrushchev was among the skeptics. In his opinion, helicopters would lose the struggle with anti-aircraft missiles. Their clumsiness meant their ruin. "The foundation of defense today is strategic missiles," Khrushchev said. "A few dozen missiles with thermonuclear warheads are enough to deter war."

Khrushchev was now carried away; he was looking ahead to the future. "If missiles are capable of protecting us, then why do we need to maintain such an army?" he repeated. Those present sat silently, obviously displeased. "We can take the resources that today we are wasting on defense," Khrushchev continued, "and put them to good use."

It was necessary, Khrushchev asserted, to review the entire structure of the armed forces and to create a small but highly trained army. The phrase "professional army" was not spoken at that time, nor will I use it, so as not to jump from the 1960s to the 1990s. The nucleus of this army would be strategic missiles, to deter aggression. In addition, small, very mobile ground forces would protect the silos. Its soldiers could live at home, occupy themselves with useful work, and spend some time on military preparation. They would only take up arms if a real danger to the state were to appear.

In the hall there was now a tense silence; there was no support for Khrushchev, but no one took it upon himself to object.

"In this situation there will be no problems with students," he smiled, "and it will not be necessary to increase the length of service. If a person lives and works at home, his military training can continue for as many years as necessary." And, as if remembering suddenly, he added: "Of course, not to the detriment of work."

For the moment these were just ideas, continued Khrushchev, and it was necessary to think them over. Most important, however, such dreams could only be realized after we had enough missiles.

The generals brightened up.

"Incidentally, about missiles," Khrushchev said, turning to Ustinov, "we must think of the future. We do not need an endless supply of them. Several hundred or a thousand. And beyond that? The factories will cease operations? This is not economical. Think, Comrade Ustinov, how they can be transformed so as to benefit the people."

Ustinov nodded his head and wrote something in his notebook.

"Comrade Iangel," said Father, continuing his thought, "has a huge factory. There they produce tractors as well as missiles. But we do not need so many tractors. Maybe they should also master shipbuilding? We have a great need for good river ships."

This statement came like a bolt from the blue. Iangel looked with surprise and fear at Father and tried to say something, in all probability to object, but changed his mind and sat still.

Frol Kozlov interjected that it was necessary to weigh everything carefully.

Khrushchev nodded: "This is the stuff of the future; for now let's make good missiles."[57]

Most of these thoughts remained merely plans or dreams. The time that had been allotted to Khrushchev was running out. For twenty long years no one remembered either about the reorganization of the army or the conversion of missile factories to peaceful production. The asymmetric approach to the construction of armed forces was treated as a frightening heresy. Meanwhile the balanced armed forces ate up more and more resources.

There was a reason why Nikita Khrushchev imagined a militia-based structure for the army. In the 1920s, working in Ukraine as a party executive, he had to supervise the structural reform of the military. After the Civil War the army was sharply reduced and converted from a regular army to a territorial one attached to the place where Red Army soldiers lived and worked. Now in 1963, he reasoned, the time had come to reconsider this experiment in light of the current situation. The conception of a territorial army was not only not developed, it was not even sketched out on paper. Therefore one can only guess what exactly Khrushchev might have come up with.

Khrushchev believed that between two hundred and three hundred missiles would be enough to deter an aggressor, thus making war pointless. If the possibility of war was excluded, then the total number of ground troops might might be around three hundred thousand people and would not exceed five hundred thousand. But military officers simply could not accept that. March 1963 can therefore be considered the point when Khrushchev finally lost the support of the generals, even those who had been his friends for decades.

The postwar history of Khrushchev's relations with military officers was one of steady deterioration, from virtually unconditional support to unconditional enmity.

After the death of Stalin he was the sole member of the highest leadership who not only had good relations with the generals but also enjoyed their respect. The personal relations of party bureaucrats and high military officers largely reflected broader relations between the Communist party and the army. The party never entirely trusted the military, and it strove to place its own man next to every commander of any rank. Victory or defeat in battles depended on the harmonious cooperation of these two people—the commander and the commissar. And Khrushchev, a civilian, was fated to be a commissar in both the Civil War and World War II.

By virtue of his character Khrushchev tried to understand all the particularities of military leadership, but he preferred not to impose his opinion. He protected his comrades on the front from Stalin's wrath as best he could. In 1942, for example, Stalin considered arresting General Rodion Malinovskii, who then commanded the army outside of Stalingrad. Malinovskii's chief commissar, Iu. Larin, had shot himself after sending a mysterious letter to Stalin. Khrushchev was able to persuade Stalin that Malinovskii had nothing to do with this letter. "Then go and sit with him in the army," Stalin snapped in a fit of anger, "and watch out for him." So Khrushchev was demoted from front headquarters and forced to remain at Army Headquarters for several weeks, with no explanation, to the bewilderment of Malinovskii and all his staff.[58]

In 1941–1942 Khrushchev retreated along with the army from the western borders of Ukraine to Stalingrad, participated in the battles of Stalingrad (1942–1943) and Kursk (1943), and left his post as first member of the Front Military Council only after the liberation of Kiev on November 6, 1943. It was then time to see to the restoration of the destroyed cities and villages of Ukraine. At various times he worked side by side with Georgii Zhukov, Semen Budennyi, Semen Timoshenko, Malinovskii, Andrei Eremenko, Ivan Bagramian, Semen Biriuzov, Andrei Grechko, Matvei Zakharov, Kirill Moskalenko, Vasilii Chuikov, and many other generals and marshals who at the end of the 1950s occupied high positions in the armed forces. When post-Stalin political battles began, these men took Khrushchev's side. In June 1953 Zhukov, Moskalenko, and other generals responded with alacrity to the request to help arrest Beria. In 1957, when the so-called anti-party group challenged Khrushchev, the army quietly demonstrated its support for him. And as paradoxical as it may seem, the army even supported him when Zhukov was removed as minister of defense.

The more Khrushchev intervened in the affairs of the armed forces, however, and the more persistently he cut the spending on their upkeep and reduced their size, the more difficult his relations with the generals became and the greater their resistance grew. They gritted their teeth when Khrushchev withdrew troops from Port Arthur, Finland, and Romania and when he reduced the armed forces in 1955 by 640,000 men and women and then again in May 1956 by 1,200,000.[59]

His clash with Admiral Kuznetsov went unnoticed. To the navy the generals reacted with indifferent coldness. They also endured yet another reduction of the army, this time by 300,000 men and women, in January 1958.[60] The cuts in the Air Force provoked a muffled murmur, and one more reduction of the army in 1960 by 1,200,00 provoked ill-concealed outrage.[61] (After all these reductions there remained 2,423,000 military personnel).[62] The conflict was momentarily resolved by the retirement of the chief of the general staff, Vasilii Sokolovskii, and the commander of the ground forces, Ivan Konev, who were replaced by Khrushchev's "loyal front comrades from World War II," Matvei Zakharov and Andrei Grechko. These two, however, did not stay loyal for long. Raised on the dogma of a massive army and accustomed in time of war to fight with huge numbers, they believed the reduction of personnel spelled inevitable catastrophe in a future war. Khrushchev appeared to them not as a reformer but as an agent of destruction. They held their peace until the March 1963 meeting of the Defense Council in Fili. But then Khrushchev's encroachment on that holy of holies, the regular army structure, made him seem a traitor to Soviet national interests.

Throughout 1963 and 1964 the tensions escalated. In September 1964 Nikita Khrushchev burned his bridges with yet another appearance before the army command.[63] I had occasion to attend this meeting too. It took place after the demonstration of the newest weapons of the ground forces in Kubinka outside Moscow, on September 14, 1964. On display were prototypes of future weapons (in many respects laying the foundation for today's Russian army) such as Grad (an unguided, short-range missile), Shilka (an anti-aircraft gun), and the T-72 tank. After the demonstration a conversation once again took place about the future of the army. This is what I wrote upon returning to Moscow:

"To discuss things while they were still fresh in their minds, they gathered in the staff house. Father began with tanks. 'Can these tanks really be compared with those that we had in the war, even the best ones we had? If only we had had them then . . . ,' he said. His audience buzzed approvingly, but father changed the subject. He repeated what he had said at the Defense Council in fili in the spring of 1963: 'We are caught up in the experience of the Second World War, not analyzing it critically. . . . Do we really intend to fight somebody?'"

Father conceded that the weapon designers' work was without a doubt worthy of praise but added that they did what they were "ordered" to do.

"And they're the ones who do the ordering." Father said, jabbing his finger toward the marshals sitting in the front row. "They determine what we need and what we don't. One gets the impression that they need everything."

Father shifted to the nature of modern war. What looked like improvisation a year earlier at fili had grown into certainty: nuclear arms made a war between the Soviet Union and the United States impossible. There could be no winner. The side faced with defeat in conventional fighting would inevitably try to alter the course of events in its favor, or ultimately to take revenge, by reaching for the hydrogen bomb.

"If we exclude the possibility of a conventional war between the Soviet Union and the United States, between the Warsaw Pact and NATO, then why do we need all these arms?" continued Father. "Everything is very nice, very modern, but it costs an enormous amount of money. There is no extra money in the country! Therefore it is necessary to think very seriously about what kind of army we need, and then to decide how to arm it."

"Otherwise you will leave the people without even clothes on their backs." Khrushchev repeated his joke, and to defuse the situation he playfully nudged Malinovskii in the side with his thumb. Malinovskii gave a forced and sour smile. The others were silent. They had not forgotten Khrushchev's speech at the Defense Council in March 1963. His return to this theme promised a new reorganization, and a new reduction of the army. The Soviet generals believed, as so many generals have, that "great states are made glorious by their armies."

From the perspective of the generals the gathering at Kubinka had not been successful. Malinovskii and the others wanted new arms, but they did not get them, at least not then and there. "The commander-in-chief has taken it into his head to make a mess of the army." That was the only way that the marshals could perceive the transition to some kind of mythical territorial militia. A struggle lay ahead.

At that moment neither Khrushchev nor Malinovskii knew that nothing depended any longer upon the commander-in-chief, that his proposals no longer interested anyone, that no one intended to fulfill his orders. Exactly one month remained until "the end."

The plans to oust Khrushchev from his post were kept secret from the military by his political opponents until the very last days of his rule in October 1964. The conspirators' fear of a repeat of the events of 1957 was without foundation. In October 1964 the military, led by Minister of Defense Malinovskii, unanimously supported Nikita Khrushchev's dismissal from power.

Leonid Brezhnev, who next ascended the political Olympus, lived up to the military's expectations. Under him they returned to the customary system of balanced armed forces, and all that they had lost under Khrushchev was restored, including the surface fleet and an abundance of aviation. Tens of thousands of tanks, guns, and nuclear warheads (from multimegaton to very small models) were built, thus bringing the country to the brink of economic ruin—exactly what Khrushchev had cautioned against.

How would the world have changed if Khrushchev had succeeded in his reforms of the army? In what kind of world would we be living right now? There seems little doubt that the United States and the other NATO countries would have followed the Soviet Union's example in the reduction of armed forces and would have felt secure. Or was humanity ready for such radical changes in 1960? Was it accidental that history almost simultaneously removed both reformers from the stage— the chairman of the USSR Council of Ministers, Nikita Khrushchev, and the U.S. president, John F. Kennedy? No answer exists for such questions, and history does not accept conjecture.

11

The Case of Divided Germany, 1953–1964

VLADISLAV ZUBOK

Nikita Khrushchev's personal diplomacy provides a vast range of episodes for his biographers, from triumphs for the policy of peace to "hare-brained schemes" and impulsive, dangerous zigzags.[1] Since the end of the Cold War and the reunification of Germany, some historians have contended that Khrushchev was ahead of his time, a precursor to Gorbachev and the "new political thinking." Yet the Berlin Wall, whose construction was sanctioned by Khrushchev in August 1961, was long a grim emblem of a Europe and Germany torn asunder by the Cold War.

In this chapter I will argue that divided Germany was a grave international problem for Khrushchev. The realities of the German question severely limited his freedom of choice, just as the realities of the party command system crippled his attempts at domestic reforms. An understanding of Khrushchev's diplomacy on the German question makes it easier to answer a larger question: why the Soviet reformer was unable to transcend the legacy of the Cold War that he inherited from Stalin.

The reunification of Germany in 1990 radically increased the availability of documents on the subject of divided Germany. Western collections, particularly on the Berlin crisis (1958–1962), are substantial although not yet complete.[2] On the Soviet/Russian side, the archival records began to appear only a few years ago, but already hundreds of files of documents have become available, particularly in the Archive of Foreign Policy of the Russian Federation. The few memoirs of those dramatic days, though appearing three decades later, are of great value.[3] On this issue history is true to itself: it only begins to speak when it is past.

Stalin's German Headache

Karl Marx, in "The Eighteenth Brumaire of Louis Napoleon," remarked that people, including politicians and statesmen, have to act in circumstances created by others, even against their will. This observation is often misused, but it explains much of Khrushchev's role in the gyrations about the two German states and West Berlin. Khrushchev believed that the German question was urgent, unfinished business. He regarded it, along with the Korean War, as a ticking time bomb left by the dying Stalin for his successors.

In Stalin's reflections on a future war (in his eyes an inevitable outcome of the imperialist structure of international relations), Germany seemed the only force that, in combination with American technological and economic might, could seriously threaten Soviet security in Europe. For him the Marshall Plan of 1947 was a reincarnation of the Dawes Plan (1924) and the Young Plan (1929), directed at re-creating German military potential. The military capabilities of the Federal Republic of Germany (FRG, or West Germany) were not in themselves a threat to a Soviet Union armed with atomic weapons; it was the Anglo-American plan to rearm and integrate West Germany into the anti-Soviet alliance that made all the difference. The agreements of 1952—on coal and steel, the Bonn Convention, and the agreement to set up a European defense community—worried Stalin because they created a huge shift in the European balance of power: the strength of the Bundeswehr (the West German army), trained by experienced former Nazi officers, would now be coupled with American air and naval superiority and supported by the enormous pool of American and German industrial resources.[4]

This ominous development was triggered first and foremost by Kim Il Sung's aggression in Korea. In the West, primarily in the United States, the North Korean attack was seen as part of a plan for the global expansion of communism, and the Truman administration decided to meet it with superior Western force. But Stalin must have viewed the U.S. response to his Far Eastern venture from an opposite angle, as indicating a master plan against the Soviet Union in Europe and Asia. To him it looked as if the Americans were using the Korean War as an excuse to bring this plan to fruition. Therefore, instead of ending the conflict in Korea by an armistice (which the leaders of the People's Republic of China and of North Korea cautiously suggested in 1951–1952), he pushed for a war of attrition. He very likely hoped that, by keeping the Americans tied up in east Asia, he would derail their war preparations in Europe and gain time for his own (allegedly defensive) military buildup.

In September 1951 Stalin decided to start a diplomatic campaign for German reunification in order to thwart the creation of a "European army." In March 1952, somewhat belatedly, he sent a note to the three Western powers—France, England, and the United States—proposing to conclude a peace treaty with Germany. It is highly unlikely, given Stalin's ideas and perceptions, that he regarded German reunification as probable under existing conditions.[5] In any event, Western stonewalling on his March proposal proved that, without more far-reaching Soviet steps to reduce tension in the Far East and elsewhere, diplomatic negotiations on the German question could not be jump-started.

But what is improbable is not necessarily unthinkable. The reunification of Germany, by Stalin's own logic, would have been better for the Soviet Union than its continued division. A reunified Germany, even with its own military forces, was preferable to the Federal Republic's acting in alliance with the Americans, bristling with arms and bent on the reconquest of lost eastern lands. A "loss" of the German Democratic Republic (GDR, or East Germany) therefore could be contemplated in the Kremlin as a realistic tradeoff for the decoupling of the North Atlantic Treaty Organization (NATO), the de facto demise of U.S. dominance in Western Europe, and the recognition by a reunified Germany of the postwar borders and regimes in Eastern Europe—something that the Soviets laconically called "Yalta and Potsdam." Therefore Stalin never foreclosed the option of German reunification and, as recent research indicates, he let Beria in 1952 advocate a "special opinion" in favor of it.[6]

The signing of the Bonn Convention, ending the military occupation of West Germany, was a signal to Stalin and his diplomats and generals that the West was seriously preparing for a future war. As a result, Stalin took the subsequent—and fateful—step toward a conversion of the German Democratic Republic from a provisional establishment to a full-fledged satellite state. He finally agreed with the leaders of the German Socialist Unity party (SED) on a crash program for the "construction of socialism" in East Germany.[7]

During the last months of Stalin's life, a time of dread and uncer-

tainty, Soviet policy in Germany was a shambles. Rapid "industrialization and collectivization" in the GDR dealt a blow to the authority of the
Communist regime there and to the reputation of the Soviet leadership
among those Germans who still hoped for a reunification of their country. This policy further strengthened the government of West German
chancellor Konrad Adenauer, which promoted remilitarization of West
Germany under the aegis of the European Defense Community (EDC).
The division of Germany between the two hostile blocs had been pro-
gressing for six years, but by 1951–1952 it was becoming irreversible.

Khrushchev Comes to Grips with the German Question

Khrushchev was not among the people who helped Stalin formulate his
German policies. In the late-Stalin Politburo (then called the Presidium
of the Central Committee) this circle included Viacheslav Molotov,
Lavrentii Beria, Georgii Malenkov, and Nikolai Bulganin. Of course in
1951–1952 Khrushchev might have received memorandums about the
German situation and possible Soviet responses to the Bonn Convention.[8] But he did belong to a second and larger group that viewed the
German problem not geopolitically but emotionally, as war veterans,
party men, and economic managers. These functionaries of the Soviet
state had a strong gut feeling that a reunification of Germany on a
"bourgeois" foundation would mean the undoing of the great Soviet
victory over nazism and would deal a blow to the international communist idea. They came to regard East Germany as a bastion of the Soviet economy, particularly important for atomic, missile, and other
components of the military-industrial complex.

Khrushchev had seen the fire and blood of the war with the Germans as had no one else in the post-Stalin Politburo, and he had a deep
and emotional veteran's complex. For him to recognize that the future
belonged to Adenauer instead of the socialist GDR would mean that
millions of victims of the Great Patriotic War had died in vain. Always
an admirer of technological progress, Khrushchev also expected a socialist Germany to be a valuable contributor to the economic development of the socialist bloc. As party boss of Ukraine in 1946–1949, he
knew all too well that dismantled German equipment was essential to
the restoration of the Donbass.

Three months after Stalin's death, the members of the new "collective leadership" had to make a choice about German policy that would

cast a long shadow. In the spring of 1953 there was a major crisis in the GDR. The big leap to East German socialism had led to rapid deterioration of the economic situation and a massive flight of people to West Germany—120,000 in only the first four months of 1953. In early April the Soviet leadership for the first time had to give the GDR substantial economic assistance.[9]

Whereas the decision to end the Korean War had unanimous support in the collective leadership, the move to change Stalin's policy in the GDR produced a heated debate and ended in a serious split.

At a Presidium session on May 27, Molotov, who had unquestionable authority in international affairs even before he became foreign minister upon Stalin's death, presented a proposal to abandon the "forced construction of socialism" while continuing to support socialism for the GDR and in principle for Germany as a whole. He proposed to implement a series of measures (some of them had been prepared for Stalin's decision but never approved) to boost the authority of the East German government, possibly even by ending formal Soviet occupational authority there.[10]

It soon became clear that Molotov's proposal provided no new vision on the German question as a whole, left no chance for negotiations with the West, and came too late to bolster the authority of the GDR leadership, as the East Berlin revolt of June 16–17 showed.[11] At the same time his policy had serious implications for the Soviet Union. Instead of pumping resources out of the GDR, the Soviets had to pump their own resources into their satellite country to stabilize it. On the political level, the Molotov line for the first time made Soviet support of the GDR an equal or even higher priority than the ultimate settlement of the German question.

Molotov's proposal was preempted by Lavrentii Beria, who after Stalin's death became the head of all secret police and intelligence structures, including the gulag, and (together with Malenkov) the "tsar" of the huge military-industrial complex. Beria's motives, as well as the substance of his counterproposals, remain obscure and undocumented to this day, although there is no lack of hypotheses. Pavel Sudoplatov, a former KGB lieutenant general and one of Beria's trusted assistants, recently recalled that he got an order from his boss "to prepare top secret intelligence probes to test the feasibility of unifying Germany." According to Sudoplatov, Beria said "that the Kremlin believed that the best way to strengthen our world position would be to create a neutral, unified Germany run by a coalition government. Germany would be the balancing factor between American and Soviet interests in Western Europe. This would mean concessions from us, but the issue could be resolved by compensating the Soviet Union, actually with blackmail money for demoting the Ulbricht government from its central role to a peripheral one. East Germany would become an autonomous province in the new unified Germany."[12]

After Beria's arrest, Molotov, Malenkov, and Khrushchev almost in unison denounced his position on Germany. According to them, Beria believed that the GDR was "not even a state" and could exist only as long as it was supported by Soviet bayonets. During the decisive discussion of the German question in May, Khrushchev, to Molotov's "pleasant surprise," had firmly supported him against Beria. Recalling the episode much later, Molotov attributed Khrushchev's stand on Germany in 1953 to his Russian patriotism and his sense that the Soviet Union had not won the last war to see a "capitalist Germany" resurrected.

Khrushchev was indeed guided primarily by his feelings in this crucial episode; Beria's proposal went too much against his instincts as a war veteran and party man. As to the realpolitik aspect of the issue, Khrushchev did not see how a reunified capitalist Germany could remain neutral in the bipolar Cold War. To the contrary, he argued before the July 1953 Central Committee plenum following Beria's arrest that it would just strengthen American imperialism by putting "18 million Germans" under its "mastery." "If a treaty [of neutrality] is not guaranteed by force, then it is worth nothing, and others will laugh at us and consider us naive."[13]

For the rest of his career as a statesman, Khrushchev remained firmly committed to a socialist Germany, to the GDR of Walter Ulbricht, Wilhelm Pieck, and Otto Grotewohl. His public denunciation of Beria's proposal as "treasonous" no doubt reverberated in his ears a few years later, when he negotiated with the leaders of Western powers about the German question.

The June 16–17 revolt of East German workers against the SED leadership, an uprising that only occupying Soviet troops could put down, also left a deep mark in the memory of Khrushchev and many others in the collective leadership. Information from the GDR after the so-called June events indicated that the SED had "demonstrated it was completely out of touch with the masses" and showed "plain cowardice" in the crisis.[14] But the lesson that the Kremlin leaders drew was the opposite of Beria's: instead of using the Ulbricht regime as an expendable asset in the big diplomatic game, they decided to build it up, to preserve its "monolithic unity" and Ulbricht's leadership in the SED by any and all means.

The crisis in East Germany had another, geostrategic lesson for Khrushchev and others in the Kremlin. The June uprising was interpreted, in the spirit of Stalin's realpolitik, as a planned American action, part of the US rollback strategy in Germany and Korea. Some in Moscow feared that after the "provocation" in Berlin there would be renewed tension in Korea.[15] They regarded support of the Communist regimes in both divided countries as one indivisible aspect of maintaining the defensive perimeter against U.S.-led alliances in the West and in the Far East.

Kim Il Sung in North Korea used this circumstance to manipulate both the Soviet Union and the People's Republic of China and became "a tail that wagged the dog."[16] The case of the GDR was different. The Ulbricht leadership lacked the authority that Kim acquired during the Korean War and never overcame its severe deficit of legitimacy.[17] Yet Soviet leaders were prepared for a long uphill struggle to make the GDR tail look more independent of the Soviet dog. In a word, they expected to develop their East German satellite into a full-fledged ally. "Given a correct political line," said Molotov at the July 1953 plenum, "the German Democratic Republic will become an increasingly reliable friend of the Soviet Union and will turn into a serious obstacle to the fulfillment of imperialist plans in Europe."[18]

Khrushchev soon became a more committed follower of this doctrine than Molotov himself. Around the end of 1954, when West Germany finally became a full-fledged military partner in NATO, the Soviet leadership decided to set up a Warsaw Treaty Organization. Against Molotov's opposition, Khrushchev insisted that the GDR ought to be a member of the organization. Whereas Molotov doubted the Soviet Union should fight for the Germans, Khrushchev wanted the GDR's sovereignty guaranteed and protected by the whole alliance.[19]

This was the second time Khrushchev had come to grips with the German issue as a whole. For Molotov the problem of the transformation of the GDR was a long shot. In January 1944 his deputy, Ivan Maiskii, wrote to him from London that "ideological rearmament of Germany" was a requirement for the peace in Europe, yet it would be the most difficult of all problems. Only "if and when" the German people were "sincerely to embark on the construction of a socialist Germany" might the pressure of occupation, reparations, and international control over them "be lifted altogether." It was, Maiskii wrote, "the music of the future."[20] Skeptical and cool, Molotov must have wondered if recognizing Germans, as well as Hungarians, Poles, and Czechs, as equal members of the socialist alliance system were not still the "music of the future."

But Khrushchev intended to be a conductor of this music. Optimistic and impatient by nature, he believed that eventually all countries, including Germany and the United States, would move toward a progressive, ultimately communist social order. Where Molotov (a perfect match for Stalin) was cautious and conservative, Khrushchev often put horses before carts, in the firm expectation that the future would be on his side. The GDR, he believed, should and would be "a window into socialism" for the rest of Europe.

A prosperous, flourishing East Germany would make possible another goal cherished by Khrushchev: transforming the division of Germany from the main source of tension in Europe into a foundation of European stability. If Soviet diplomacy could get the Western powers to legitimize the division of Germany into two states, it could defang the Cold War in the center of the continent. The realization of this goal, against high odds, became a major strategic aim of Khrushchev's diplomacy from 1955 to 1961.

Optimistic Gambits

In September 1953 Khrushchev became party first secretary and seized the initiative from Malenkov in domestic policy. He then began to look for initiatives in foreign policy. Valentin Falin, then an analyst for the Committee on Information at the Soviet Ministry on Foreign Affairs, recalls rumors of "the competition between Molotov and Khrushchev." "No substantive discussions and coordination, just a tug-of-war," he concluded, was the essence of the Soviet diplomacy after 1953.[21]

This tug-of-war revolved around the question of how to wind down Cold War confrontation and reduce military expenditures. Pursuing this goal, Khrushchev groped for a bold new beginning, for a restructuring of international relations within the Communist world (relations with Tito, Mao, Ho Chi Minh, and others) and with the capitalist powers, particularly in Europe. He chose to begin with the settlement of the Austrian question.

The diplomacy of Stalin and Molotov firmly linked the signing of the Austrian state treaty (formally terminating the state of war with Austria) with the resolution of the German question and the territorial dispute over Trieste. Since the early 1950s the Austrians had feared that their country, like Germany, might be torn apart by the two hostile blocs. So, despite American pressure, they quietly lobbied for talks with Moscow.[22] At the same time some Soviet diplomats, especially those stationed in the FRG, began to push for Austrian neutrality as a means to promote West German neutrality and to thwart a military integration of the Federal Republic with NATO. But Molotov objected to the withdrawal of Soviet troops from Austria. He pointed to the danger of another anschluss and doubted that capitalist Austria could remain neutral. Khrushchev, who in 1953 had been a believer in Molotov's arguments, rejected them outright in early 1955. He now hoped that Austrian neutrality could contribute to a disengagement from bloc confrontation in the heart of Europe.

Yet while Khrushchev changed his positions on specific issues, he did not abandon his deep-seated beliefs. Curiously, he believed in a distinction between Germany, an aggressor in the last war, and Austria, allegedly an early victim of German aggression. Unlike the loss of the GDR, the loss of Austria could not be a threat to the Soviet sphere of influence in Central Europe. Still, he had to ensure that the Austrian Communist party did not object to the withdrawal of Soviet troops.[23]

Over Molotov's dogged opposition. Khrushchev insisted on bilateral talks with the Austrians and, during the preparation of a Soviet negotiating position, on getting rid of Soviet property in Austria (including all Austrian-based Soviet petroleum-industry and other assets). The Presidium minutes are not available, but the records of Molotov's secretariat at the foreign ministry are eloquent enough. Several times Molotov attempted to delay the withdrawal of Soviet troops in Austria, and every time the Politburo, dominated by Khrushchev, rejected those attempts.[24]

The signing of the Austrian state treaty in May 1955, after a four-power conference approved the results of the bilateral Soviet-Austrian talks in Moscow, was a breakthrough for Soviet diplomacy and an important victory for Khrushchev. The treaty cleared the way for a four-power conference in Geneva (July 1955) and the visit of West German chancellor Adenauer to Moscow (September 1955). This was a two-track approach by which the Soviet government expected to overcome the impasse over the German question.[25] After the formal integration of West Germany into NATO and the incorporation of East Germany into the Warsaw Pact, the Soviet leadership finally made a choice: it was time to recognize the existence of two states in Germany as a long-term reality and, on the basis of this recognition, terminate the state of war that still existed with those successors of the defeated Third Reich.

At the Geneva conference of the leaders of the four powers, Khrushchev was the de facto head of the Soviet delegation. He left the summit fully confident that he could stand up to Western leaders and defend Soviet national interests. In September, during the meetings with Adenauer, when discussions took a very unpleasant turn, the cocksure Khrushchev threw his famous tantrums to intimidate his foreign counterpart.

At the same time he was still open to advice and careful to take his initiatives only after (more or less) substantive discussion in the Presidium. One of his most influential advisers was Anastas Mikoyan, among other things a longtime expert on Soviet foreign trade. Both Mikoyan and Khrushchev expected that diplomatic relations with Bonn would open great opportunities for a quick expansion of Soviet influence in the FRG, particularly on the Social Democrats (SPD) and on business circles. Soviet diplomats and experts contributed to those expectations.[26] They hoped that the pressure from those circles on Adenauer would bring about a rapid reopening of West German foreign policy toward the East, a sort of Rapallo agreement (which announced bilateral relations between Weimar Germany and Soviet Russia during the Genoa conference in 1922).

During 1954–1955 Moscow took steps, mostly unpublicized, to establish contacts with leading figures from the SPD and the business community, including Erich Ollenhauer and the Krupp family.[27] In December 1955 Valerian Zorin, the first Soviet ambassador to the FRG, received an instruction "to give necessary attention and support to the Social Democratic party and those bourgeois circles that stood in opposition to the policy of the Adenauer government."[28]

Soviet diplomats and intelligence informed Khrushchev that most Western European politicians paid only lip service to the idea of German reunification. During his sharp exchanges with Adenauer in Moscow, Khrushchev concluded that the West German chancellor clearly preferred the existence of two German states to the uncertainties (especially concerning neutrality) of German reunification.[29] He firmly rejected Adenauer's demand that both sides commit to reunify Germany and reopen the question of East German borders. Clearly Khrushchev expected that a strong Soviet position on the two states, especially in defense of GDR sovereignty, would ultimately force the Federal Republic to give up its revanchist claims.

If Khrushchev had expectations of another Rapallo, they soon went up in smoke: West German political and business circles were not ready to respond with *Ostpolitik* to a new Soviet *Westpolitik*. The Americans were already concerned about Austrian neutrality and alarmed by Adenauer's trip to Moscow.[30] President Dwight D. Eisenhower and Secretary of State John Foster Dulles feared that the FRG could start practicing see-saw diplomacy (*Schaukeldiplomatie*) between the superpowers and were determined to preserve the West German backbone of NATO and keep Adenauer in office. Since any formal recognition of the two states by the West would have undercut the domestic standing of the old chancellor, there was no chance that Eisenhower and Dulles would recognize the GDR. The United States preferred to support the West German official stance on nonrecognition of the GDR and new East German borders. After his trip to Moscow, Adenauer reaffirmed this policy in the so-called Hallstein Doctrine.

Khrushchev's goals were diametrically opposed to American policy. At the 20th Party Congress in February 1956, when the Soviet leader denounced Stalin, he also won approval for the doctrine of "peaceful coexistence"—a formulation that allowed him to reduce the constraints of Stalin and Molotov's diplomacy and make more concessions in the search for international compromises and settlements. After the talks in Moscow, Vienna, and Geneva, the Soviet leader was eager to continue his "peace initiative" and diplomatic blitzes so as to bring about a settlement of the German question on the new, two-states terms and a dismantling of the opposing blocs in Europe.

Unfazed in his optimism, Khrushchev believed that Soviet unilateral concessions would advance Soviet security more than a war of attrition, hot or cold. An international thaw would cause the Western alliance to fall apart from its own inner contradictions. It was in fact this credo that, among other factors, drove Khrushchev's peace initiatives. During a meeting with Danish prime minister Hans-Christian Hansen in the Kremlin on March 3, 1956, Khrushchev said candidly: "NATO was created as the result of a big military psychosis, when some people had painted the Soviet Union in a very unfavorable militaristic light before the peoples of European countries. On our side, we also gave a pretext for that. And so Denmark jumped into the jaws of the Atlantic alliance. We have already proved our peacefulness rather convincingly and will prove it further. Thereby we will loosen up NATO. We will further proceed unilaterally to reduce armed forces so that all see our peacefulness, and then it would be hard for you to preserve NATO, before your public opinion. People would demand even more strongly the policy of peace."[31]

By the end of 1956 the thaw had turned into slush, as destalinization triggered national revolts in Poland and Hungary against the regimes imposed by the Soviet Union. It was the first serious crisis of the new Soviet foreign policy: a forced intervention in Hungary, in particular, seemed to compromise the new image of the USSR gained by the peace initiatives of 1953–1955. The decision to intervene was taken after several agonizing days.[32] But immediately thereafter Soviet foreign policy moved back to a "peace offensive" and capitalized on the British-French fiasco in their war against Egypt. Khrushchev eventually pushed for a withdrawal of Soviet troops from all East European countries (even Poland and Hungary), contending that they were unnecessary for military logistics and costly in economic and political terms. The Soviet group of forces in Germany (GSFG) remained the only force that Khrushchev was not ready to withdraw unilaterally. "Everybody knows why," he commented in his memoirs.[33]

Between 1953 and 1957 Khrushchev and the rest of the collective leadership tried several approaches to the settlement of the German problem: rapprochement with West Germany, four-power talks, and, most important, efforts to split NATO through a diplomacy of reconciliation, peace initiative, and recognition of neutral states. None of these devices worked. By 1957 the resources of Khrushchev's new diplomacy seemed exhausted.

One Russian and Two Germans

By the spring of 1957 Khrushchev was beginning to get exasperated with the policy of West German chancellor Adenauer, seeing it as the biggest obstacle to European detente. Adenauer and his circle firmly believed that democratic Germany could survive only as a part of NATO.

A German historian concludes: "For them unification on acceptable terms, that is coupled with free self-determination, could be achieved only from a Western position of strength."[34]

The crises in Eastern Europe in 1956, like "the June events" in 1953, encouraged the chancellor to stick to his policy of nonrecognition of the GDR, covert subversion of the East German regime, and selective pressure on East European countries. Information about this policy, along with reports on the West German economic boom and the activities of "revanchist organizations" in the FRG, reached the Kremlin.[35] One memorandum suggested that if West Germany recognized the new Polish borders, then "the Polish government would no longer be interested in hosting Soviet troops on Polish territory." The Soviet Union would then have to pull her troops back, not to the Oder-Neisse line, but to her state borders. Other reports created the impression that the FRG was trying to knock Czechoslovakia out of the Soviet-led alliance system. If Poland and Czechoslovakia became neutrals, Soviet strategic positions in the GDR would be untenable. Simultaneously, the reports said, the West German government had intensified efforts to destabilize the economic situation in the GDR and to "discredit and isolate" Ulbricht.[36]

The Soviets paid close attention to cautious but persistent attempts of the Adenauer government to raise its military-political status within NATO by various means, including the sharing of nuclear technology and armaments. This drift from the 1954 pledge of the FRG to abstain from developing weapons of mass extermination was in part caused by Soviet nuclear threats during the Suez crisis and, later, by the test of Soviet ICBMs—which made U.S. security guarantees more doubtful in the eyes of the West Germans (and also the French and Italians). Eisenhower and Dulles tried to dissuade the allies from going nuclear, but their line on nonproliferation was far from firm and clear, at least to the Soviets.[37] In January 1957 Eisenhower announced plans to install medium-range nuclear weapons targeted at the Soviet Union in Turkey, Iran, Japan and West Germany. Simultaneously, Washington strategists began to discuss the idea of nuclearization of the Bundeswehr under U.S. control in order to reduce the massive presence of American troops in Europe.

On April 25, 1957, in a conversation with the Soviet ambassador to Bonn, Andrei Smirnov (who replaced Zorin in October 1956), Chancellor Adenauer did not deny that the FRG might become a nuclear power. West German foreign minister Heinrich von Brentano, present at the conversation, added: "If England and other powers have atomic weapons, why should the FRG not have them?"[38] Later the FRG sided with the United States in rejecting the Rapacki plan (presented by the Polish foreign minister Adam Rapacki but designed in Moscow) for the denuclearization of Central Europe.

Oleg Grinevsky describes in his memoirs a "restricted meeting" in Khrushchev's office. Khrushchev, Grinevsky indicates, was not fearful of West German nuclear aspirations (the Western nations "would not give him [Adenauer] nuclear weapons," Khrushchev said) but that he suspected foul play by Adenauer and was determined to exploit to the hilt lingering memories of World War II in order to discredit German militarism. In any event, this episode led to further deterioration of So-viet–West German relations. At the end of April Khrushchev retaliated by cutting off a confidential channel to Adenauer. He clearly hoped for the chancellor's defeat at the Bundestag elections in September.

After reelection in April 1958, the Adenauer government passed a Bundestag resolution opening the way to nuclear armament of the Bun-deswehr. This time Khrushchev sent his chief adviser and trouble-shooter, Anastas Mikoyan, to Bonn to warn Adenauer that the Soviet leadership would not put up with this. Mikoyan suggested returning to the Rapacki plan and stressed that the nuclearization of the FRG "would bury the idea of Germany's unity." He even added: "We are ready to grant the FRG a guarantee that if the FRG abstains from atomic weapons, we, on our side, would not use atomic weapons against the FRG even should you participate in a war against the Soviet Union."

Adenauer blandly reiterated his favorite line about the need for gen-eral and complete disarmament. Mikoyan asked him how long West Germany would continue the Hallstein Doctrine of nonrecognition of socialist countries of Eastern Europe and socialist China. Adenauer replied, tongue in cheek, that he was "considering the question of the recognition of Poland. But we are afraid that you in Moscow would think that we want to pit Poland against other East European coun-tries."[39] Those discussions strengthened Khrushchev's perception that forceful measures would be necessary to make Adenauer change his mind.

When Walter Lippmann interviewed the Soviet leader on October 24, 1958, he was surprised to find Khrushchev in a cocoon of pre-1941 fears. Khrushchev's perception of West German behavior had crystallized into a pattern. He had had a strong impression since the 1955 talks that Adenauer was afraid of war, but who could be sure that the West German military (some of them Hitler's generals) and younger politicians in the Christian Democratic Union–Christian Social Union (such as Franz-Josef Strauss) were not dreaming about an *Anschluss,* this time of the GDR and the FRG? The situation, he said, was similar to that prevailing on the eve of World War II, and U.S. policy also "was the same." Khrushchev compared Adenauer to German president Paul von Hindenburg, who had allowed Adolf Hitler into power in 1933. The Americans, he finished ominously, "may someday pay with their blood for having encouraged such people."[40] Khrushchev, for all his artistic talents, did not himself believe in what he was saying. And his exaggerated "fears" only puzzled the Americans.

Meanwhile, since the West was building up the FRG, Khrushchev felt that he had to fulfill his promises to turn the GDR into a full-fledged ally, sovereign, and equal to other East European members of the socialist bloc. Massive Soviet aid in late 1953 and early 1954 had helped stabilize the economic situation in the GDR and had slowed the flight of well-trained workers to West Germany. But by the end of 1954 and during 1955 emigration resumed with new force, induced by the growing prosperity in West Germany. However great Soviet assistance, many in the Soviet government began to recognize slowly that it could not solve the GDR's structural problems. And then there was the personality factor—the leadership of Walter Ulbricht, the Stalinist first secretary of the SED. Throughout 1955 and particularly after the 20th Party Congress, Soviet ambassador Georgii Pushkin criticized Ulbricht for failing to follow the Soviet example of destalinization. After the crises in Poland and Hungary, however, this criticism of Ulbricht's hostility to reform fizzled out.

By early 1957 Khrushchev and his supporters understood that there was no alternative to stability in the GDR and that they would have to pay for it. This understanding became explicit in June, during the fierce power struggle between Khrushchev and the "anti-party group" led by Molotov, Malenkov, and Lazar Kaganovich and including Dmitrii Shepilov, Kliment Voroshilov, Nikolai Bulganin, Maksim Saburov, and Mikhail Pervukhin. Denouncing the opposition on behalf of Khrushchev before a Central Committee plenum, Mikoyan recalled that Molotov and his group had refused to give three billion rubles of credit to the GDR and other countries of Eastern Europe. "Nikita Sergeevich

[Khrushchev]," said Mikoyan, "immediately sensed the political crux of the issue." He explained to the elite audience: "If we do not strengthen the regime inside East Germany, then our army will be surrounded by fire. And we maintain an army of half a million there. . . . And what does the loss of East Germany mean? We know what it means."[41] Soviet policy in the GDR had fallen into a trap: economic stability and self-sustained growth in East Germany were impossible without the renunciation of state controls, but if socialism were renounced there would be no raison d'être for the GDR.

Some years later, by which time Soviet subsidies had helped the Ulbricht regime meet popular demands for food and consumer products, some Soviets began to see a bitter irony in the fact that the East Germans enjoyed a much better living standard than their Soviet occupiers and supporters. But at the same time the Soviets strained their generosity, East German economic stability increasingly came to depend on the prosperity of the FRG: during the rest of the 1950s and later, the West German government deliberately encouraged "inter-German trade" on terms extremely favorable to the GDR. The further irony, therefore, was that in spite of the Soviet aid, the GDR's "independence" (from the West) had no economic basis.

The sicker the GDR became, the more passionately the Soviets stuck to its defense. Marshal Vasilii Sokolovskii voiced the widespread sentiment on this issue in his address at a party conference of GSFG in early October 1961, on the eve of the 22nd Party Congress. There was no alternative to unconditional support of the GDR. "It was Beria," he said, "who came up with a theory that asked, Why do we care about those Germans, let Adenauer have them all. Could we tolerate that? Did we fight the last war in vain? What did our brothers, sisters, fathers and mothers die for? To reduce the results of our victory to zero?"

The marshal did not doubt that after "absorbing" the GDR, "the imperialists would then want to swallow Poland, Czechoslovakia, other people's democracies, then to extend their tentacles to the Baltics and all the Soviet Union."[42] This straight "soldierly" talk had powerful reverberations among the senior military and diplomats.

By the summer of 1958 Khrushchev was ready to give the GDR a decisive boost. This was after the triumphant launch of the Sputnik satellite, the defeat of all Khrushchev's domestic rivals, and the fall 1957 Moscow conference of the Communist parties that made Khrushchev feel like the leader of the socialist camp. Even Mao Zedong came to Moscow, for the first (and last) time since his visit to Stalin. This was the pinnacle of Khrushchev's career, and in those heady times the intractable German question became more than just an irritation for him. He was no longer in the mood for concessions or any repetition of the Austrian gambit. His aide Oleg A. Troyanovsky recalls that Khrushchev could not forget how Molotov and other members of the anti-party group blamed him for a loss of dignity and accused him of naivete and appeasement of the West through unilateral concessions.[43] Mao Zedong shared Molotov's doubts and pushed Khrushchev to demonstrate his new strength to the "American imperialists."[44] In the face of American and West German intractability, Khrushchev's policy of patience on the German question began to look like indecisiveness and procrastination.

To counter any such impression, Khrushchev agreed with Ulbricht on the need to start a diplomatic offensive to promote a peace treaty between the two German states, with the great powers serving as its guarantors. The East German leader pushed for a more hard-line Soviet *Deutschlandpolitik*. He requested a meeting with two Soviet ambassadors on October 5 to ask the Soviet government to "answer the latest letter from Adenauer in such a way that West Germany could not retain any illusions about the possibility of German reunification on Western terms."[45] Ulbricht played his customary role of a Cassandra, warning the Soviet leadership about West German revanchism. This time, however, the Soviets did not need to be persuaded. Ambassador Smirnov, acting on instructions, agreed with Ulbricht that it was time "to retaliate against the enemy's offensive by a counteroffensive on the part of the GDR.[46]

In retrospect, it is clear that Ulbricht dragged the Soviet leadership deeper into a confrontation with the West, but Khrushchev's perceptions and the dynamics of the German question were even more important in producing the Berlin crisis. Its heart was Moscow's constant concern about the unresolved German question, made more acute by Adenauer's intransigence and provocative behavior, by Moscow's own commitment to the socialist GDR and its leadership, and by the enhanced sense of power and responsibility that Khrushchev felt in 1958. All those factors conspired to make Khrushchev discard his conciliatory diplomacy and replace it with a policy of *Sturm und Drang*.

The Road to the Wall

At some point during his summer vacation of 1958, Khrushchev decided that West Berlin, the headache of the GDR and a Trojan horse of the FRG, should be turned from a problem into a solution. In November 1958 he presented the Western powers with an ultimatum: either they agree on a settlement of the German question by recognizing the existence of the two German states and "the free city of West Berlin" or the Soviet Union would sign a separate peace treaty with East Germany, thereby ceding to it the control over state borders and communications.

For the next four years the United States and other NATO countries discussed in anguish what their response to a Soviet-GDR blockade of West Berlin, or an attempt to push Western troops out of the city, should be. The most perceptive analysts, and eventually President Eisenhower himself, came to believe that Khrushchev was bluffing.

Sergei Khrushchev has recently argued that his father had started his bluff without thinking through all the consequences. According to Sergei Khrushchev, the Berlin crisis "cannot even be considered a real crisis," because his father remained in control over the situation, even during the worst moments of posturing and brinkmanship.[47]

There is much in the new documentary evidence from East German and Russian archives to confirm that Khrushchev was bluffing. The Soviet leader never intended to impose a blockade on West Berlin and swallow it. Rather, he regarded its future as a neutral free city, not an integral part of the GDR. But he did want to shut it off from the West German economy and gradually draw it into the orbit of Eastern bloc's trade and cultural contacts.

Throughout the first two years of the Berlin crisis, and even as late as early 1961, the Presidium insisted on the development of "direct contacts," including economic and cultural ties, between the GDR and West Berlin.[48] That implied open sectoral borders and encouragement of the Grenzgänger, people who lived in East Berlin but found employment in the West. According to Iulii Kvitsinskii, at that time an interpreter for Pervukhin, the Soviet ambassador in East Berlin, it was out of the question to close the sectoral border between East and West Berlin, because it "would have discredited the idea of transformation of West Berlin into a free city, and would have created panic and other unwelcome developments."[49]

Moreover, for compelling reasons Khrushchev never wanted to sign a separate peace treaty with the GDR. Any such action would have contradicted his strategy of weakening NATO and dissolving the foundations of the Cold War in Europe. It would also have meant that the Soviets would have unilaterally renounced their occupation rights and the theoretical possibility, sanctioned by Yalta and Postdam, of deciding the future of Germany along with the United States. From Stalin to Brezhnev, the Soviet Union considered such a development to be unacceptable.

Soviet diplomats, including Gromyko, kept complaining that their "friends" in East Germany (the GDR leadership) did not have an adequate understanding of the goals and tactics of the Soviet Union on West Berlin and the German question. After the fiasco of the Paris summit (May 1960) a Soviet diplomat alerted Moscow to the fact that "at least 70 percent" of SED activists were in a "fighting mood," prepared to storm West Berlin tomorrow. It goes without saying—with the Soviet troops in the vanguard.[50] And, in the presence of Khrushchev (who clearly approved his rebuke), Foreign Minister Andrei Gromyko chided Ulbricht in October 1960 because the GDR's refusal to recognize West Germany and West Berlin ran contrary to Soviet policy.[51]

Taken as a whole, Soviet diplomatic correspondence on West Berlin and the GDR stands very much in contrast to Khrushchev's public rhetoric.[52] But at first they were complementary. The first secretary (and since 1958 chairman of the Council of Ministers) used verbal threats where Stalin had used force—trying to compel the Western powers to reconsider their policies on the German question. And in retrospect, his chances were not all that bad. The determination of the Western powers to resist Soviet pressure in Berlin had diminished by the end of the 1950s. The leadership of Great Britain, very hard-line during the Berlin blockade, now attempted to mediate between Moscow and Washington. Even the Eisenhower administration's real thinking did not quite match its tough rhetoric.[53]

Much of this drift in American-British attitudes toward the German question was produced by the dangerous nuclear standoff. The threat of nuclear war by miscalculation over West Berlin loomed ever larger, and the old fear of upsetting Adenauer's position through direct talks with the Kremlin on the German question was becoming less acute. In London and even in Washington, Adenauer's foreign policy seemed increasingly provocative and out-of-date.

Khrushchev was banking on these still inconclusive trends. He was playing it largely by ear, attempting to reach a rapprochement with the Eisenhower administration, to jump-start four-power talks on the German question, and to drive Adenauer into isolation.

After his ominous ultimatum on West Berlin, the Khrushchev quietly began to sound out Western leaders on possible talks. In January 1959 he sent Mikoyan to Washington with a message to Eisenhower: "It is necessary to make a start, and while the first agreement might not be important, it is possible that it will snowball and lead to a great improvement." The Soviet guest also complained that Adenauer was pursuing his own agenda, dangerous to European stability. Perhaps the West German chancellor hoped that "by delaying a peace treaty he might become stronger, exploit the differences between us and base his position upon force."[54]

Soviet approaches to the United States culminated in the discussions between Eisenhower and Khrushchev at Camp David in September 1959. On the surface the outcome was not favorable to the Soviet Union: Khrushchev suspended his ultimatum on the German peace treaty, while Eisenhower only acknowledged that the situation in West Berlin was "abnormal" and vaguely promised talks on this subject. But from the viewpoint of the Soviet leader it was a major breakthrough for his personal diplomacy, a first step toward reducing Cold War tensions and resolving the German question.

The Camp David outcome also helped to undermine the alliances cobbled together by Dulles and to sow discord between Washington and Bonn. On the eve of his first American trip Khrushchev sent Adenauer an extraordinarily blunt letter. If, he wrote, the chancellor abandoned his irredentist policy and recognized the GDR de facto (by accepting the idea of confederation of two German states with a free city of West Berlin), then Adenauer would become a man of peace for all time and contribute to the end of the Cold War. The Soviet Union, Khrushchev continued, would prefer a settlement of the German question between the FRG and the GDR to a four-power formula, in which it was outvoted by the Western powers three to one. The Soviet leader did not conceal that he would be pleased with another Rapallo.

If Adenauer persisted, however, he would end up as a lonely and despised figure, abandoned by his own allies. Khrushchev continued: "We attribute great significance to forthcoming talks with the U.S. president." And, he added crudely, we "cannot dwell in our talks only on issues of corn and cucumbers."[55]

This letter reminds us how impatient and heavy-handed Khrushchev's personal diplomacy often was. At home he could get away with "giving hell" to the local party chiefs and administrators for a while, since there were no rivals to take advantage of his indiscretions. Not so in international relations, where every one of his faux pas was magnified by the mass media and backfired on him. For Western audiences—except for a group of perceptive Soviet watchers—Khrushchev began to look like a bull in the diplomatic china shop.

Yet even after the collapse of the Paris summit in May 1960, the Soviet leader did not change his goals and priorities: he just blamed his failure on the fact that Eisenhower, in his eyes a captive of the "dark forces," could not shake off the inertia of old policies. He decided to wait for a new and younger president on whom to try the power of his personal diplomacy.

Western historians of the Berlin crisis pay great attention to changes in the balance of strategic forces, both real and perceived. For years they speculated that U.S. nuclear superiority prevented Khrushchev from signing a separate treaty with East Germany and led him to build the Berlin Wall instead. Yet as far as the German policy of the Soviet leader was concerned, the effect was minimal. On the contrary, Khrushchev himself hoped that the threat of a nuclear war would "sober up" some "hotheads" in the West and render the situation ripe for a negotiated settlement of the German question. And of course he worked hard to enhance the political effect of the Soviet nuclear arsenal with a new series of tests, including that of a hundred-megaton superbomb at Novaia Zemlia on October 30, 1961. At a meeting with managers and designers of the Soviet atomic complex, Khrushchev called this bomb "the sword of Damocles hanging over the heads of the imperialists."[56] With this sword/shield Khrushchev thought he could continue his diplomacy on the German question with a good margin of safety.

What made Khrushchev change his policy on Berlin in the summer of 1961 was the rapid deterioration of the situation in East Germany as a direct result of the Berlin crisis. In this sense the designs of the Soviet premier backfired. Although Khrushchev failed to persuade Adenauer and his Western backers to recognize the division of Germany, he convinced hundreds of thousand of East Germans that the border would soon be closed. Hence the flight of people to the increasingly prosperous West Germany turned into a flood, and Ulbricht began to ask the Soviets to provide workers to fill the serious deficit in labor.

It is less well known that the economic situation of the GDR had become desperate even before this development. In October 1960 Ulbricht dramatically revealed to the Soviet leadership the growing dependence of the East German economy on the FRG. He warned Khrushchev that West Germany might terminate a trade agreement with the GDR, dealing a blow to its economy.[57] Ulbricht asked for massive Soviet subsidies, the scope of which shocked Khrushchev and the Soviet economic planners. A month later, during a Moscow conference of the Communist and Workers parties, the Soviet leader told Ulbricht "not to thrust your hands into our pockets." At the same time he was upset that after so many years, despite all its credit and industrial orders, the Soviet Union had failed "to liberate the GDR" from its economic dependence on the FRG. As in the past, he pledged that the Soviet Union would not leave East Germany in the lurch.[58]

But the problem only intensified. At the end of 1961 Gosplan calculated that the hidden benefits from "inter-German trade" for the GDR budget during that year amounted to 540 million deutschmarks, out of a total volume of 1,878 million. In July 1961 Mikoyan and Gromyko reported to Khrushchev and the Presidium that an economic embargo against the GDR by the FRG "and also by other countries of NATO" would cause "substantial economic damage" to the GDR.[59] At the same time West Berlin had become increasingly linked to the West German economy: in 1960 West Berlin trade with the GDR amounted to less than 300 million deutschmarks, as compared to 14 billion with the FRG.[60]

In early August 1961, at a secret meeting in the Kremlin with the leaders of Warsaw Pact, Khrushchev even tried to nudge the leadership of Poland and Czechoslovakia toward sharing the burden of support of the GDR. "Narrow nationalist" priorities, he warned, could bring the Bundeswehr to their borders. Yet the leaders of those countries gave Khrushchev's appeal the cold shoulder. The growing economic commitments to the GDR were turning into an embarrassment, and the GDR itself was becoming a black hole, forever sucking in Soviet money and resources. The most obvious manifestation of this syphoning was the crowds of shoppers from West Berlin who used the speculative exchange rate of deutschmarks to Eastern marks to stock up on subsidized food and consumer goods in the GDR. Therefore the policy of assistance to the GDR continued to lose support among Soviet elites, particularly economic managers. In October 1960 Aleksei Kosygin, chairman of Gosplan, sharply objected to the "exaggerated demands" of "friends" from the GDR.[61]

Ulbricht had insisted for many months on closing the sectoral border with West Berlin and, in the meantime, started repressions against *Grenzgänger*. As documents reveal, however, the GDR government pursued its own agenda in the crisis. Its leaders were openly disgusted with what they regarded as Khrushchev's halfway, vacillating, procrastinating policy.[62] Unlike the Chinese and North Korean leadership, however, Ulbricht lacked his own power base and therefore any real leverage on Khrushchev. His best weapon, as in 1953, was his weakness.

The idea of the Wall originated with Ulbricht, and Khrushchev found it unfortunate even long after it had been erected. The ugly concrete barrier went too much against the grain of his optimistic predictions of a peaceful and voluntary expansion of socialism. But in the summer of 1961, when the headlines about the flight of people from the GDR made a mockery of the Soviet policy of two states, he suddenly "discovered" the idea of the Wall as a third option—a way out of the corner into which he had hoped to drive the Western powers and eventually drove himself.

Initially he had concluded that time was on his side; he could just issue his ultimatum and wait for NATO to splinter. In 1961, however, it was the West that enjoyed the benefit of time; it could ignore Khrushchev's brinkmanship and wait for the GDR to collapse. Until June 1961 Khrushchev placed his last hopes on a meeting with the new American president, John F. Kennedy. But when he found Kennedy unprepared to compromise during the Vienna summit, Khrushchev unleashed—for the third time—a campaign of pressure, blackmail, and brinkmanship. Yet at the same moment the situation in the GDR forced his hand, and he finally seized upon the idea of the Wall.

According to Kvitsinskii, "in late June or early July" Ulbricht invited Ambassador Pervukhin to his country house in East Germany and told him that the "growing flow of refugees increasingly disorganizes the whole life of the Republic." "Nineteen fifty-three cannot be excluded, and he [Ulbricht] feared that the Bundeswehr could be drawn in. That would mean a war." Pervukhin reported to Khrushchev that if the borders in Berlin remained open, "a collapse is inevitable."[63] Khrushchev took some time, but then (again on vacation) made a decision: on August 13 the open border between the two German states ceased to exist—as it turned out, for twenty-eight years.

The Crisis Subsides

For the West the crisis continued through 1961 and beyond. British officials, for instance, believed that Khrushchev might be "carried away" or "forced" during the 22nd Party Congress in October 1961 to announce the signing of a separate peace treaty with the GDR.[64] Yet for Khrushchev the building of the Wall served more as a partial substitute for the diplomacy of pressure that had been a primary cause of Berlin tension.

Khrushchev considered the construction of the Berlin Wall a genuine accomplishment. He stressed in his memoirs that it allowed East Germany to "restore order" and begin to heal the shattered economy. In a more contrived argument, Khrushchev wrote that "even without the signing of a [separate] peace treaty, the GDR acquired the rights of sovereignty," since the Western powers reconciled themselves to the sector border in Berlin as the East German state border.[65]

With the gap in the socialist camp's ramparts plugged by the Wall, Khrushchev continued to apply pressure on the West. In September and October bilateral U.S.-Soviet discussions began at the foreign-ministry level as well as via a back channel, bypassing the foreign ministries. Khrushchev made sure that Ulbricht and other leaders of the bloc countries (including the People's Republic of China) were informed about those talks and used them as a face-saving device to back away from his unfortunate commitment to sign a separate peace treaty with the GDR. Secret information provided by Moscow to "the friends" (East Germans) stated that Washington and London "decided for themselves to go ahead with de facto recognition of the German Democratic Republic," although of course they could not do it publicly and formally.[66]

With the last ultimatum called off during the 22nd Party Congress, Khrushchev finally restored the relative freedom of diplomatic maneuver on the German question that he had forfeited so recklessly between 1958 and 1961. Now Moscow could turn its attention to stabilizing the GDR, particularly by solving East Germany's economic problems—a daunting task.[67]

Well into 1962 the priority of Soviet policy in Germany was to let the tension in Berlin ebb, to keep the situation under control until the population in both German states accepted the new status quo. The issue of the state border, monitored by GDR troops and police, turned out to be a minor headache for the Soviet leadership when widely publicized shootings on the border led to unnecessary increases in tension in West Berlin and the FRG. Several times between November 1961 and June 1962 Khrushchev had to take this issue up with Ulbricht.

The Wall changed the situation in Soviet-West German relations. Adenauer had to accept it. Although the chancellor was reelected again in September 1961, his policy of depending on the West and ignoring the GDR had suffered a serious blow. West German public opinion, unlike that of the Western powers, could not be indifferent to the fate of a divided Berlin and divided families, but the only way to alleviate this situation was through negotiations with the Kremlin and the GDR regime.

Adenauer was not the only one who initiated such a policy. A secret and separate channel was opened between Soviet emissaries and a group of prominent Social Democrats (involving the mayor of West Berlin, Willy Brandt, and his secretary, Egon Bahr) who were shocked by the Wall and gradually embarked on a policy of tacit recognition of and piecemeal cooperation with the GDR—what later became known as *Ostpolitik*. Khrushchev was very interested in encouraging this trend and even considered, twice, a secret meeting with Brandt.[68]

For almost three decades after the Berlin crisis, most American analysts, including some historians (such as Adam Ulam) believed that Khrushchev's decision to send Soviet missiles to Cuba was more or less linked to his desire to improve his negotiating position on West Berlin and the German question as a whole.[69] But an abundance of newly released evidence shows that this was not so. During the dark week of the Cuban missile crisis, when Gromyko's deputy V. V. Kuznetsov suggested that the Soviets might apply pressure on West Berlin again, to retaliate against the American naval blockade of Cuba, Khrushchev sharply rejected his idea as "another adventure."[70] He realized that he had overplayed his hand in Cuba, and the only thing he wanted now was to move back from the brink.

This, incidentally, highlights a fundamental difference between the way the U.S. administrations and Nikita Khrushchev looked at the German issue. For the United States it was an ultimate test of their global strategy of containment. Neutralization of West Berlin, in this globalist perspective, would have meant an unacceptable loss, and the Soviet policy directed at this goal was treated as a dagger aimed at the heart of NATO. Khrushchev did indeed hope to undermine NATO and American influence in Germany. Yet this was not his main goal; it was merely one of various approaches to his ultimate end, the confirmation of the political realities in Central Europe. In addition, Khrushchev had always been motivated by his feelings as a Communist and, more important, a war veteran: he simply could not give up on the construction of a socialist Germany, and over time he developed a personal, die-hard commitment to the GDR regime.

For all its drama, the Berlin crisis was understood by Khrushchev as an episode in the struggle to settle the German problem on the basis of recognition of the status quo—including the socialist GDR as a second, sovereign German state. When he failed to persuade the U.S.– West German alliance to accept the GDR, the Soviet leader tried to force it to do so. But this heavy-handed, ill-conceived policy dragged the Soviet Union into an international crisis and, instead of stabilizing the GDR, almost brought it down. As a result, Khrushchev had to build the Wall to save socialist Germany from extinction.

From Khrushchev's own perspective, the Berlin crisis (like the Cuban missile crisis a year later) did not end in a defeat. For him it was a crucial test of wills with Adenauer and the United States, a means to shatter the U.S.–West German axis. Although Khrushchev overplayed his hand, Adenauer's policy toward the East began its decline, eventually to be replaced with *Ostpolitik*, Willy Brandt's policy of accepting the division of Germany. Had Khrushchev stayed in power longer, the Soviet–West German rapprochement that took place after 1969 might have begun even earlier.

12

Khrushchev and Gorbachev: A Russian View

GEORGII SHAKHNAZAROV

All countries change, but they do so in different ways. Some adapt quickly and relatively easily to the circumstances of the times. Others do so slowly and with difficulty, sometimes dragging out urgently needed changes for centuries. Some undertake changes willingly, even enthusiastically, while others put up desperate resistance, as if being led off to execution.

This is how things appeared at the end of the seventeenth and the beginning of the eighteenth centuries, when Peter I decided to "open a window onto Europe" and to build his state after the example of England and Holland. To this end he had to put down the Streltsy revolt, cut off the boyars' beards (both literally and figuratively), and even sentenced to death his own son, who was involved in a conspiracy against the tsar-reformer. In order to refashion Russia it was necessary, to use Pushkin's expression, to "raise her up on her hind legs."

It was precisely this frightening yet picturesque background of events that gave grounds for the durable assertion that moribund and patriarchal Rus does not yield to innovation and is incapable of entering the circle of leading nations. This judgment is extremely superficial, disproved by the many outstanding achievements of Russia in both the distant and recent past. The truth is that, as a result of our particular conditions (the gigantic proportions of the territory, the multinational composition of Russian society, the late entry onto the path of industrial development by comparison with European nations, and the necessity of frequently fighting off invasions from East and West), the modernization of the country and its transition to a higher level of technical, economic, social, and political progress demanded long-term preparation each time. There is profound meaning in the proverb, "Russians hitch up slowly but ride fast."

Perhaps most curious is that reforms in Russia always seem to have been carried out in two stages; to put it in sports terms, they have required two tries. Every Russian Messiah inevitably had his John the Baptist, who set out to undertake transformations but did so too timidly, only halfway, without threatening the foundations of the existing order. However unimportant the direct results of their attempts to breathe new life into the traditional institutions and customs may have been, they played a significant role in the success of the next, decisive stage of reform. They did so primarily by shaping popular opinion over time, facilitating the acceptance of new ideas, and, most important, preparing a cohort of comrades-in-arms for the future reformer, whose actions, without these preconditions, would almost certainly have been doomed to failure.

The mighty figure of Peter the Great is popular throughout the whole world. But only those well versed in Russian history know that his father, Tsar Aleksei Romanov, blazed a trail for Peter in many different ways. He sent young noblemen to Europe, as one often hears today, to "study foreign experience." He not only summoned specialists from abroad (even before his time, Italian architects were invited to build the Kremlin) but gave them permission to reside permanently in Moscow as well. The so-called German Quarter was in essence Russia's first step toward an open society. Also, the Russian Law Code of 1649, which was created under Tsar Aleksei and which introduced unified principles of justice, can be considered the first step toward legal statehood.

Of course these and other changes begun by Aleksei cannot compare to Peter's grandiose reforms. But they made his work less difficult. A century later, in exactly the same way, the extremely timid reformist ideas of Alexander I, which remained for the most part on paper, helped another tsar-reformer, Alexander II, accomplish his task and put an end to serfdom.

The powerful popular disturbances of 1905–1907 forced Nicholas II to grant a constitution and to agree formally to the establishment of a partially representative government. But the tsar, who did not want to share even a small amount of his autocratic power, dismissed the first and second State Dumas. The third and fourth Dumas were also largely powerless parliaments, kept in effect in the tsar's pocket. Thus a chance offered by history was passed up. The consequence of this refusal to undertake fundamental structural reform was revolution.

Historical experience, and in particular the history of Russia, bears witness to one immutable truth: reform is capable of accomplishing any task with minimal costs only if it is begun and conducted in a timely manner and to the full extent necessary. If the powers-that-be are late in making changes that are due, or if they try to limit themselves to trivial or cosmetic alterations, such tactics will sooner or later provoke general dissatisfaction and can change the opposition into to a revolutionary one. According to Victor Hugo, the right to vote cancels the need for revolution. Hugo was right, but we should add: as long as the right to vote (with all the accompanying democratic institutions) does not lead to desperate people taking up arms, and as long as the powers-that-be do not cancel that right after the very first popular declaration of will unfavorable to them.

Another political theorem that can be gleaned from our experience is that political leaders who risk attaching their fate to the accomplishment of one or another democratic task should not expect gratitude from their compatriots. Unlike "heroic" leaders, whose names are known for their victories in war, the expansion of territory, and other glorious acts, a reformer-democrat is doomed to misunderstanding, if not oblivion. At best his or her services to the homeland will receive modest acknowledgment after two or three decades.

Just such a fate befell the reformist tandem of Nikita Khrushchev and Mikhail Gorbachev. They were both in essence working on the same historical task: to liquidate the totalitarian system, to democratize the country, and to integrate it into world society, eliminating the division of the world into opposing military-political blocs. But each formulated the task in his own way and, most importantly, acted with different methods and with a different level of determination. These and other differences can be explained by several factors.

First of all is the spirit of the time. Khrushchev's ouster and Gorbachev's coming to power were separated by twenty-one years. In the interim, Brezhnev reestablished virtually all the key institutions of the Stalinist system, stopping only at mass repression. His rule was drab and undistinguished, although not harsh. Brezhnev did not execute his political opponents or allow them to rot in jail, but rather subjected them to isolation and exile, as in the case of the dissidents Andrei Sakharov and Aleksandr Solzhenitsyn. Troublemakers from within the ranks of the nomenklatura were sent packing, either to posts as ambassadors or into the provinces. Fear remained as one of the supports of the system, but it was nowhere near the same chilling horror that existed under Stalin. Moreover, in advancing the notion of relaxing tensions and becoming involved in the European process, the regime was forced, if not to throw open, then at least to begin to lift the Iron Curtain. The number of Soviet people traveling abroad rose sharply, and forbidden literature began to flow in from the outside. The jamming of radio broadcasts could no longer prevent access to information about the real state of affairs in the country, which was lagging farther and farther behind the West in living standards and quality of technology. Alarming signs of decline were not only discussed in various secret meetings but also became the subject of conversations in academic establishments, and information on this subject occasionally even appeared in the press.

The principal alteration in the public atmosphere and in the reigning attitude can be expressed succinctly. By the middle of the 1980s the whole conscious part of society longed for changes and anxiously awaited the arrival of a new leader, one who would sharply turn the helm of the ship of state—unlike the situation in 1953, when society was not really ready for a radical upheaval. Khrushchev's exposure of the repressions, which was essentially a denunciation of Stalin, had been a shocking surprise for society. In this sense it was incomparably more difficult for him to dare to take the first step. He attacked the stronghold of the totalitarian system almost as Don Quixote attacked the windmills. And if he did not crack his own skull in the process, it was only because he was acting not from the outside but from the inside, as "chief of the garrison."

The other principal difference between the two levels of Russian reform is that Khrushchev came to power when the previous system had a large reserve of strength and was still effective, whereas Gorbachev took power in a system that was already exhausted and breathing its last breath.

This is forgotten by many of Khrushchev's critics, who reproach him for indecisiveness and for the fact that he did not try to destroy the foundations of the system. They find the reason for this in the narrowness of his views and in his blind faith in the postulates of Marxism-Leninism in the Stalinist interpretation. All this undoubtedly played a role. But let us ask ourselves a question: Why should he have launched an attack on the foundations of the system if it remained completely functional from a practical standpoint? What is more, it must be pointed out in all fairness that the early postwar years are called the "Soviet miracle," which occurred earlier than the Japanese, German, and other generally accepted postwar "miracles."

Indeed, within a few years after the war the Soviet Union completely rebuilt the destroyed cities of Sevastopol, Minsk, and Stalingrad, along with dozens of other cities and thousands of villages; the same was true of palaces in Leningrad, which were reborn in much of their old brilliance and splendor. Also rebuilt in record time was the Dnepro Hydroelectric Station, as well as many other industrial enterprises. And then there appeared the world's first atomic power station, icebreaker, and satellite. All this symbolized the country's achievement of a new level of development: it seemed to us we would easily surpass the capitalist world—which was spinning its wheels and was mired in evil—and would burst at cosmic speed into the realm of general plenitude and prosperity. Khrushchev's Seven-Year Plan was built on these hopes, and the new program of the CPSU (Communist party) was imbued with this fervor; it was sealed with the promise that today's generation of Soviet people would live under communism.

It is worth pointing out that at that time the West was bewildered by the obvious achievements of the Soviet Union. Many in fact spoke enviously about the superiority of the Soviet system of public education; they held the universal medical services for the population in high regard; and they were considering copying certain institutions of social support, which eventually became an essential element of the so-called welfare state.

In a word, Khrushchev had reason to believe that by surpassing the United States in rates of growth we would eventually be able to overtake the American farmer in milk yields. Life taught him and all of us, however, a cruel lesson. What was interpreted as the first stage of a real takeoff in the Soviet economy turned out to be the final achievement of the previous stage, its highest point, after which a decline began.

It is true that this was not immediately apparent. Iurii Gagarin's space flight occurred in the early 1960s. World records were set in the production of coal, oil, and metal. Soviet hockey players and athletes prevailed at international championships, and the Bolshoi Ballet remained the unsurpassable peak of that noble art. But all these things were the last gasps of the "Soviet miracle." Ominous signs of decline, which would later be called stagnation, appeared everywhere. At first we lost our primacy in outer space; we were unable to (we pretended we did not want to) repeat the American expedition to the moon. Following this painful blow to the pride of a power that considered itself to be the standard-bearer of progress, there came the defeat of one of its main objectives: computerization. Our industry was not able to handle the delicate materials involved, and the lag in this area soon made itself felt in the general level of production and daily life. By the 1970s practically all the technical goods manufactured in Soviet Union, from fountain pens and electric razors to automobiles and airplanes, were inferior to their foreign-made counterparts. In the end it reached the point that we were basically incapable of producing certain innovations—video recorders and cameras, complex medical instruments, measuring devices, and so on.

For the time being, propaganda skillfully concealed these deficiencies from the public. The leadership did not attach particular importance to them, as they were content that in the realm of armaments we were up to the mark. They grew concerned only when it became clear that a basic backwardness was even showing up in the quality of armaments. It was then that they began to admit that the period of extensive growth had ended and to discuss the necessity of increasing the incentive to work; they returned to the idea of economic reform. But the enfeebled leaders found in themselves neither the strength nor the courage to dedicate themselves to serious reforms. This task, vital to the country, was put off for years, until fate brought Mikhail Gorbachev to the post of general secretary of the Central Committee.

Out of this brief foray into the past arises a serious question: Why was the "Soviet miracle" so quickly exhausted? After all, economic relations, in spite of Khrushchev's experiments, remained unchanged. The political system was preserved almost untouched. Ideology remained firm, if one does not count several amendments, such as the thesis that the dictatorship of the proletariat was replaced by an "all-people's state" committed to the preservation of the leading role of the working class. Nor did the makeup of the ruling elite undergo any particular changes. A good two-thirds of its ranks continued to occupy the same offices as they had under Stalin. Nor did the incentive to work decline; on the contrary, the standard of living in the country was on the rise, albeit slowly.

Did the reasons for our decline perhaps lie outside the country? Some argue that the West understood earlier than we did the need for deep reconstruction of the economy on the basis of new technologies; that they quickly attacked this task in the late 1960s and early 1970s; and that they sped forward, leaving the clumsy, closed-minded, and innovation-resistant totalitarian system behind. There is undoubtedly a great deal of truth in that explanation. Our economic noncompetitiveness was not just our own fault; it reflected our isolation from countries "on the other shore" which were traditionally the most developed, where nine-tenths of discoveries and inventions occurred, where contemporary technology was created from which we were practically cut off.

But even this does not answer the question at hand. Lagging behind the West economically and technologically was not equivalent to stagnation and decay. We moved much more slowly, but moved all the same. The rates of industrial growth continued to wane, however, and every year it became necessary to buy more and more bread from abroad; shelves in stores grew empty, and people wasted more and more time waiting in lines. The possibility of feeding the country with oil and gas revenues, which were rapidly losing value on the world market, was vanishing.

What are we left with? We are left with the supposition that the end of the postwar Soviet miracle is tied, along with certain objective factors, to the death of Stalin. I anticipate lack of understanding, irritation, and even outrage among people who are democratically inclined and, in addition, were raised believing that the role of personality in history is limited by objective circumstances. We must leave emotions aside, however, and try to comprehend the particularity of our political system. What existed in our country in the post-Lenin period was, in the full sense of the word, unique and had no analogs in the past. It stood upon two pillars: first, the submissiveness of citizens before the state, and second, the absolute faith of the majority in the justness of the regime, which was embodied by the leader. This system was created by Stalin, and his role in it was not simply that of a leader who could be replaced, but its main element, its Koshchei spirit.[1] As soon as he was gone, the effectiveness of the system declined sharply. Throwing open the gates of the gulag and discrediting Stalin's cult of personality, Khrushchev gave the people a gulp of freedom, but he did not dare to follow through to the end the reform that had been started, to attack the very foundations of the Stalinist system. But despotism does not work without a despot.

We turn now to one more vital difference between the two stages of Russian reform. Every revolution in the beginning and every major reform in the end removes from power the prevailing class (if one is to put it in Marxist terms) or the ruling elite (according to Mosca and Pareto).[2] Success or failure is determined by the balance of forces among competing political parties and the social movements that stand behind them, as well as by the ability of the protectors of the old system or its opponents to attract to their side, if not the majority of the population, then at least its active part.

From this point of view, Khrushchev had to deal with much more powerful resistance than Gorbachev did. The nomenklatura sat firmly in the saddle and did not think of defying the mandate that had been handed down for everlasting use by the Bolsheviks. It received Khrushchev's report at the 20th Party Congress without great enthusiasm; some of the people in its ranks were probably tempted to remove the new leader from power right then and there. Nevertheless, the majority decided that the game was not worth the candle. To a significant degree Georgii Malenkov, Nikolai Bulganin, and other colleagues of Khrushchev shared his feelings regarding Stalin and were not opposed to escaping the blind submissiveness and fear that the deceased generalissimo continued to inspire in them. Moreover, criticism of the personality cult separated the current leader from the former leader and served as a kind of indulgence for the sin of participation in the crimes of the regime.

For a while Khrushchev was empowered to rule by the nomenklatura that he had renewed. In return for this privilege, however, he had to agree not to exceed a certain limit in his fits of reformism. The first secretary's autocracy, unhindered by palace upheavals, actually began only after he broke up the party organization of the Academy of Sciences' Institute of Physical Problems, which was calling for deeper destalinization, announced that "we will not give Stalin up to anyone" and especially put down the Hungarian uprising of 1956. This and certain other actions of the same sort were accepted by the ruling Communist elite as a guarantee that the reforms would be realized in "reasonable proportions" and that they would not upset the status of the ruling elite.

I will allow myself in this connection to relate an episode from my own life. In 1952, upon completing graduate studies at the Academy of Sciences' Institute of State and Law and defending my dissertation for the degree of candidate of jurisprudence, I was invited to join the publishing house Politizdat, where I was soon put in charge of editing directories and dictionaries. After the 20th Party Congress we faced the question of what to do with the calendar sheet on which the birthday of the "leader of all peoples" was noted. I went for advice to the director of the publishing house, Mikhail S. Sivolobov, who in my presence called the secretary of the Central Committee, Petr N. Pospelov, and received the order to remove the mention of Stalin. As Sivolobov told me, Pospelov chided him for even asking such a question: as an experienced party worker, did he really not understand that there should be no propaganda about Stalin in a mass publication?

The trouble was that the calendar, whose run was in the millions and which was practically the sole spiritual food for a considerable part of our population, particularly the agrarian population, had to be sent out to the printer a year and a half before it was issued to readers. And by the time it came out, the ardor for unmasking had weakened a great deal. In addition, the Georgian government refused to allow the calendar to be imported into the territory of the republic without Stalin's date printed on it. In a word, things had changed dramatically, and people began to search for a low-ranking scapegoat. Following several summons to the Central Committee, Sivolobov announced that I would have to bear party responsibility for the "gross political error" that had been committed. When I reminded him that we had acted upon the order of Pospelov, the director objected, saying: "God help you if you mention this to the Secretariat. They will exclude you from the party completely. This way, you will get off with just a formal reprimand."

About a hundred people gathered in the hall on Staraia Ploshchad (Old Square) where the Secretariat session was held. Seated behind a long table were the party secretaries, with Mikhail A. Suslov at the head.[3] Members of the party were invited one after the other to approach the podium. As a rule they were scolded for blunders, after which they repented, received a reprimand, expressed thanks for the trust reposed in them, and quickly took their leave.

The scene that struck me in particular was the rebuke given to the editor of the magazine *Novyi Mir,* Konstantin Simonov. This fine poet, writer, and journalist underwent a real flogging because Vladimir Dudintsev's book *Not by Bread Alone* had been published in his magazine. Ekaterina Furtseva, the party secretary in charge of ideology, pounced on him like a fury, accusing him of loss of vigilance, political infantilism, and other mortal sins. To Simonov's credit, he bore himself with dignity. He said that he did not consider Dudintsev's book an anti-So-

viet work, although it was possible that there were "ideological mistakes" in it. He requested that he be relieved of the responsibility of the
editorship of the magazine.

Then it was my turn. Suslov knew the whole story very well. Nevertheless he asked why the date of Stalin's birth had not been noted. To
this I responded, as had been agreed with Sivolobov, that the date was
not a nice round figure, and that in the calendar only major anniver-
saries of great leaders' birthdays were noted. Laughter was heard in the
hall.

"What is so funny?" I asked. "After all, otherwise it would be necessary to note hundreds of names!"

"But don't you make some exceptions?" asked Suslov.

"Yes, of course," I said, "for Marx, Engels and Lenin." This time no
one laughed.

"Do you agree to receiving a formal reprimand?" suddenly asked
Suslov.

"No, I do not agree," I responded, "but is it really up to me?"

"Okay, fine, move along," said Suslov with uncharacteristically
good humor, waving me along. And Pospelov sat in the Presidium as
though nothing had happened, saying nothing.

Khrushchev, reacting to this sort of resistance, acted on the formula
"one step forward, a half-step back." In this sense Gorbachev was in a
more favorable position, at least in the beginning. The issue was not
simply that some in the upper crust of the party and government had
come to believe in the need for serious reforms. It is no less important
that over the almost two decades of Brezhnev's rule, this crust itself
had became quite enfeebled. Advancing the slogan of the stability of
cadres, Brezhnev let the word out to everyone—from republic and
provincial party leaders to ministers, marshals, and directors of public
organizations and creative unions—that they could remain in their positions until such time as the Lord should call them to Him.

The same was true for Brezhnev. This unspoken agreement was
unfailingly observed, and by the time Gorbachev reached the Central
Committee, pensioners predominated there, the average age of Politburo members exceeding seventy years. For the most part these people
were of a mind to live out their years peacefully. No matter how great
the desire to stop the young general secretary, who had, in their opinion, gone too far, each of them was afraid to join in a struggle with an

unpredictable outcome, with the threat of losing a comfortable salary and pension, treatment in a private clinic, and vacations at chic resorts.

The fact that the resistance that remained was relatively weak explains why the Politburo and Central Committee unanimously approved almost all the far-reaching initiatives of Gorbachev, and why the party sanctified with official authority such revolutionary ideas as civil society, legal government, freedom of the press, and ideological and political pluralism. The "mutiny on board" began under deep cover, but the 28th Party Congress approved a platform that was completely opportunistic from the perspective of the canons of Marxism-Leninism, while the July 1991 plenum of the Central Committee accepted, with virtually no resistance, a draft of the CPSU program that was, in effect, social democratic. After daring to try to take power in the August 1991 coup, the leaders of the nomenklatura almost immediately gave themselves up, once again showing that this stratum was historically ready for retirement. With their awkward escapade the leaders of the August putsch only played into the hands of right-wing radicals and helped to turn the direction of events in the country from difficult but still democratic reforms to novel revolutionary shocks, state coups, and a merciless struggle for power between elements of the new and the old elite.

As for differences in the personalities of the reformers. Khrushchev and Gorbachev have many similar traits: both came from a peasant background and were taught from a young age to work for their bread. Both had inherent good sense plus the ability to put practical needs before theoretical, abstract dogma. Popular wisdom and peasant cunning, tactical cleverness and political romanticism, simplicity and openness in interactions with people—all these things characterized both of them to almost the same degree.

Yet there is a great difference between them, stemming from different levels of culture. And the issue here is not simply that Khrushchev attended the Industrial Academy, whereas Gorbachev graduated from Moscow State University. (Although officially both schools are considered to be institutes of higher education, the qualitative difference between them is clear.) Far more important than the worth of the diploma is the ability to accumulate knowledge, which in turn can lift one to a higher level. Both reformers had richly gifted natures, but Khrushchev nevertheless represented the peasantry on the throne, whereas Gorbachev represented the intelligentsia.

The difference can mostly be observed in questions of culture. Long-range political vision was combined, in Khrushchev's case, with a primitive taste in art. I will not take it upon myself to judge how much the circumstances of his childhood and youth are to blame, but he had neither basic knowledge of nor any particular interest in serious music or painting, nor did he have too deep an understanding of philosophy, history, or jurisprudence. No offense is intended to the memory of this remarkable person, but precisely this lack of culture was the reason for his pounding his shoe on the table at a session of the United Nations General Assembly, for his ugly rebuke of artists and writers for the alleged ideological deviations in their work, and for the rude shouts and reprimands that, according to the testimony of eyewitnesses, he often permitted himself in relations with subordinates.

In the end, the artists themselves (such as Ernst Neizvestnyi and Andrei Voznesenskii) forgave him this sin, urging others to remember only the good that came about because of him.[4] But this aspect of Khrushchev must not be forgotten, precisely because a low level of general culture is inevitably expressed in the makeup and style of a leader's rule, a phenomenon that we witness in the case of Boris Yeltsin.

As for Gorbachev, his spiritual world developed under the influence of a different social milieu. He was an avid reader, curious, possessing a keen sense for art. From his school days on, he sought to eliminate the natural inequality of a peasant son as compared to young city dwellers. And he did this by intensely working to improve himself. By his own admission, Raisa Maksimovna Gorbachev played an important role here, instilling in her husband a love for opera and symphonic music and for literary classics. Entering into the ranks of the political elite at a relatively young age, Gorbachev took full advantage of his opportunity to interact with outstanding people—writers, musicians, artists, architects, scholars. Quite apart from his other traits, after Lenin he was the best educated leader of the Soviet government. Furthermore, during five years of close interaction with Gorbachev I never once saw him yell at anyone. When his temper flared, he could in the heat of the moment say harsh and offensive things, but he would never insult a person, not even some furious opponent.

Significant as a leader's general level of culture is, the idea that he nurtures as to the goal of his regime and the principles he places at the base of his policy are more important. Despite all the differences in circumstances and character, in this area Gorbachev continued Khrushchev. I will risk suggesting that if the latter, after everything he lived through and reconsidered, had somehow returned to power, he would have gone much farther than he initially did to champion political reform. But this is only a hypothesis.

In criminal law, importance is given to the motive behind an act. The sentence depends to a large extent on whether a person acted deliberately or not. The judgment of history is another story, however; here intent is not as important as the result of actions. What a political leader thought, what he wanted, why he acted in one way and not in another—all this, it goes without saying, should be taken into account. Meticulous biographers give intent no less, and sometimes more, attention than actions. But this, so to speak, is for the curious. In popular memory it is not plans that endure, but actions.

From this perspective, Khrushchev's most important deed was the emancipation of public consciousness. By unmasking the Stalin cult, he discredited the very idea of absolute power and raised from their knees those people who had knelt before that power. One of the foundations of autocracy and the unlimited power of general secretaries was the belief in their righteousness. But if it is publicly and officially announced that the Bogdykhan, or emperor, is to blame for heinous crimes, then there can be no place before the throne for blind worship.

As for intentions, it goes without saying that Khrushchev in no way meant to extend the devastating criticism of Stalinist repressions to all the activities of the generalissimo, let alone to the system itself. As soon as the first signs of such interpretations appeared, measures were taken to stop the impending avalanche of revelations. Boris N. Ponomarev, former head of the Central Committee's International Department, recalled how, on the order of the Politburo, a Central Committee resolution on the personality cult was drafted in a rushed session at Maksim Gorky's dacha along Rublevskoe Chaussee on the outskirts of Moscow. Its basic idea, as is well known, was that Stalin's mistakes should in no way reflect poorly on the system; that the system was working entirely normally, but the achievements of the country and the people could have been even more substantial if Lenin's legacy had been fully observed.[5]

The teaching and example of its founder were used to try to shield the system from criticism. But this effort failed. Thoughtful people who had been roused by the 20th Party Congress began to think for themselves. How could it be that one leader organized the repressions while his closest associates did not get their hands dirty? Why didn't the party rise up in protest against violations of Leninist principles? Asking these and other questions, people contrasted what they heard in Khrushchev's report with the surrounding reality; they drew additional information from the numerous articles that streamed into print after the dam of extreme censorship was breached, albeit for a short period. Moreover, printed materials from abroad began to seep into the country, and if some well-intentioned citizens still maintained their immunity from anti-Communist publications, quite a different impression was created by the critical stance of pillars of the Communist movement such as Palmiro Togliatti.[6]

However much the Khrushchev government tried to limit free thought, the process, as Gorbachev loves to say, had begun. And despite the obvious worsening of the political atmosphere by the end of Khrushchev's rule, the spirit of freedom and criticism that he introduced remained, since he himself had been a guarantor against the restoration of the previous ideological order. If Gorbachev had directly followed him, if the second and first stages of Russian reform had merged into one whole, then the country would probably already be at that point in its democratic development which it will now reach only in the second decade of the new century.

Alas, fate decreed that Brezhnev was to wedge his way in between Gorbachev and Khrushchev. Over the eighteen years of his rule, many of the beneficial consequences of the Thaw were reduced to nothing. Most important, ideological control over people's minds was established to a considerable extent. But even that regime, which it would be more accurate to call one of restoration rather than stagnation, was not able to eradicate completely the new spirit of freedom. That spirit was isolated among the creative intelligentsia; the regime made sure the infection did not soak through to the masses. This was more or less the situation until 1985; when Gorbachev came to power, he was basically forced to start again from the same point as Khrushchev: the emancipation of public consciousness.

But his approach was different as well, and the stakes were much higher. It was no longer a question of returning to criticism of Stalin but of trying to analyze the system through all its metamorphoses in an honest and serious manner. Only Lenin himself was not yet touched; nevertheless, the goal of reform was declared to be not a simple reestablishment of Leninist principles and a return to the intellectual purity of the revolutionary period, but the development of popular self-government. The goal of perestroika was to be the dismantling of the totalitarian system and the creation of civil society and a legal state; freedom of conscience was recognized, along with the right to profess any political views and to pledge allegiance to any ideology. The bonds had finally been removed from public consciousness; it must now gain maturity through self-development. Until that time it will cast about, searching for new gods and idols.

Consciousness is all well and good, but concrete results of political reform are determined for the most part by structural changes in the political and governmental mechanism. At this level Khrushchev's achievements were less impressive. His most important innovation was the prohibition included in the charter of the CPSU against occupying a ruling position for more than two consecutive terms. Beyond the fact that Khrushchev could not resist the temptation to indulge himself (by introducing the possibility of a third term in special circumstances), this law was not adopted in practice. Old apparatchiks and workers who had been promoted by Khrushchev himself remained comfortably in their seats, assured that even if they were threatened with transfer, they would not lose their material benefits and social status. First secretaries would become ambassadors, ambassadors would move to ministry positions, and ministers would become directors of trade unions, the Union of Friendship, the Committee for the Struggle for Peace, or some such organization.

We ought to admit that the way they chose their associates was the Achilles heel of both our reformers. Both were tied by too many threads to the nomenklatura environment to be able to tear themselves from its embrace. Khrushchev overestimated the personal devotion of the cohort of party leaders he had promoted. They took advantage of his vacation away from the capital in the fall of 1964 to replace him. On the other hand, if they had told him directly that it was time for him to leave, it is quite possible that they, not he, would have sat out their lives in retirement at their dachas. By 1964 both Khrushchev's reformist zeal and his capacity to rule the country were exhausted. In principle, he himself should have retired, yielding to a strong leader capable of continuing the line of the 20th Party Congress. But, alas—such is the irony of history—Khrushchev in fact chose his own successor, having raised Brezhnev to the highest position in the government.

Similar overestimation of his comrades-in-arms brought even greater tragedy to Gorbachev. All sorts of details worthy of a mystery film allow for parallels to be drawn between October 1964 and August 1991: the leader's vacation in the south, the role of the KGB. But despite the superficial similarity, the attempted coup of 1991 differs strikingly from what had happened to Khrushchev twenty-seven years earlier. In 1964 reforms were breathing their last, and the nomenklatura elite removed a leader who had become an inconvenience for them. In August 1991, however, the idea was to attack not only the president but above all the reforms themselves. In 1964 the conspirators acted dishonestly but without violating the law, whereas in 1991 it was a matter of treason.

To continue the comparison, one might point out that Khrushchev introduced virtually no innovations in the structure of the principal state institutions. The Supreme Soviet remained, as before, a establishment for show only; its deputies were carefully selected by a department of the Central Committee. Their speeches were either written out in that same department or strictly censored. The system of justice and of penal institutions went practically untouched. The rehabilitation of millions of people was conducted without structural reforms, by means of political decisions and organizational measures.

Gorbachev's "second stage of reform" began from square one in these areas. The political system he inherited was neither Khrushchevist nor Brezhnevist, but Stalinist. Convinced that economic reforms would not work without the political system's transformation, Gorbachev, in a very short historical period (only nine months separate the 19th Party Conference from the 1st Congress of Peoples' Deputies of the USSR), conducted the first free elections and created a functioning parliament. In contrast to Khrushchev, who hastened to crush opposition as soon as it made itself felt, Gorbachev consciously formed and legalized it. In this sense he did not really continue the reforms of Khrushchev, which remained within the limits of the previous system, but went a lot farther, breaking with the old order.

The same is true with regard to the overall organization of the state. From his first steps as a leader, Khrushchev was forced to deal with separatist tendencies. This was inevitable. In the Soviet Union every self-criticism by the central power gave the republics and regions the opportunity to wrest from it more rights. Khrushchev failed to take this into consideration, although he did understand the need to decentral-

ize the economy and so undertook to create regional economic councils called *sovnarkhozy*. He also advanced a formula for "increasing the
independence of the republics"; they were given some free rein, which
Brezhnev then quickly took back.

Gorbachev's reformation gave rise to a much larger wave of separatism. But the fatal blow to the Soviet Union was dealt not in August,
nor even in December, of 1991. Both those dates represented only the
final stage of an illness, one of the causes of which was the June 1990
Declaration of the Independence of Russia. Accepting this declaration,
the Supreme Soviet of the RSFSR in essence invited other republics to
follow suit. Gorbachev's desperate struggle for the preservation of the
union, one that would be transformed into a real federation or even a
confederation, ended in defeat.

Both the similarity and the difference between the two stages of Russian reform are clearest when it comes to freedom of the press. There is
no need to point out that this is the enabling condition for every democratic system. Where it exists, totalitarianism becomes impossible.

Khrushchev tore a hole in the solidly built censorship curtain,
which shielded the Russian people from every kind of undesirable (as
determined by the powers-that-be) ideological influence. The ban was
removed from such "disgraced" classics of the fatherland as Fedor Dos-
toevsky's *The Devils* and Mikhail Bulgakov's *Master and Margarita*. After a long absence, great historians of the Russian state were returned
to the readership—Nikolai Karamzin, Vladimir Soloviev, Vasilii Kliuchevskii. Radio and television began to broadcast more or less reliable
information about world events. The prohibition on showing certain
films that were sitting on shelves at Goskino (*Ivan the Terrible, Great Life*,
and others) was removed. A number of documents from the history of
the party that had previously been secret were published. Archives were
opened slightly.

But only slightly, by no more than a crack, through which the viewer
was allowed to see that fragment of reality that could, in the opinion of
agitprop, be shown without considerable damage to the system. Everything is relative, however. The creative intelligentsia, which grumbled
about the selective character of freedom of speech when Khrushchev
was in power, only fully appreciated this freedom after Brezhnev had
had enough of such liberties. Only twenty years later did the Russian
people gain free access to information and the opportunity to express

their opinions openly. Any unbiased observer must acknowledge that in the whole history of the country, the years 1988–1991 were the period when political freedom was least restricted.

Finally, a word about militarism. Neither economic nor political reforms in the Soviet Union would have been possible without the reduction of military spending to a necessary minimum. And this in turn demanded the establishment of a new modus vivendi in relations with the United States and other Western countries. Khrushchev and his advisers formulated this task and attempted to accomplish it. It is impossible to agree with domestic and foreign scholars who believe that Khrushchev's foreign policy was a chain of utter improvisations and adventures. From a historical perspective the reduction of tension that he began helped the world to hold out without any major cataclysms up until the mid-1980s.

Unfortunately, during the rule of Brezhnev, the preconditions for the normalization of international relations that developed under Khrushchev were to a large extent wasted. Some may object to this formulation, contrasting Khrushchev's well-known pranks and his impulsive breach in Soviet-American dialogue with the impressive, peaceful initiatives of the 1970s, which included the start of the all-European process, the signing of the Moscow Treaty with the FRG, and strategic arms limitation agreements with the United States.

Such indeed is the chain of events. But far more important is the fact that under the eccentric Khrushchev efforts were made to restrain militarism and to shift resources to peaceful needs, while under the "peacemaker" Brezhnev military spending reached stunning levels— as high as 40 percent of the national income.

Just as Khrushchev tried to combine a domestic reform with a relaxation of international tension, the formula for Gorbachev's reforms was "perestroika plus new thinking." The second stage of Russian reform also put an end to the Cold War.

Finally, a word about the most important element of the Soviet political system, the monopolistic domination of the Communist party. Since Khrushchev never encroached upon the basic structure of government, it seems unlikely that he would have considered a new role for the CPSU. As an orthodox Leninist, he completely shared the opinion of the founder that "not a single question should be decided by us without the knowledge of the party's Central Committee."

Or did he? At a meeting in Moscow dedicated to the centenary of

Khrushchev's birth, Gorbachev asserted that, in dividing local party organs into industrial and agricultural branches, one of Khrushchev's goals was to create something like a multiparty system, or at least a two-party system, as in the United States. If this was in fact his intention, it considerably strengthens Khrushchev's standing as a reformer. Even if he did seek to save the party from the musty, dead atmosphere connected with monopolistic domination, however, Khrushchev's political reforms were timid, halfway measures; they did not leave any deep consequences in political life and were therefore eaten up by the Brezhnev restoration, with practically nothing left behind.

In the same way, many reproach Gorbachev for launching perestroika without a clear program. This is not true. There was a certain failure to think things through during the first three years after Gorbachev became party leader, and the matter of choosing moments to act forcibly could have been handled more systematically. But this is because Gorbachev intended first to alter economic affairs radically, and only later to renovate political institutions. It was only after he became convinced that such a sequence would not work that Gorbachev turned quickly to political reform. His political program was eventually expressed in the theses of the 19th All-Party Conference and the decisions of the 28th Party Congress, and his long-term strategy was reflected in the draft program of the CPSU that was approved by the July plenum of the Central Committee. To what degree this program answered the needs of the country, and why its realization was thwarted, are other questions that remain to be resolved.

In conclusion let us note that the contradictory nature of Khrushchev's policies and the failure of his reforms are explained not only by his personality, and not simply by the resistance he encountered, but by an internal division within the Russian national consciousness among ideas of statism, the greatness of the state, and the welfare of the people.

This division left its mark on all Khrushchev's actions. He tried to humanize politics, to turn its face to the people, but he kept holding himself back. No sooner did this upstart from the people try to emancipate the countryside than the all-Russian autocrat in him grabbed him by the coattails and hauled him off toward new forms of collectivization that facilitated state control. As soon as the impressionable reformer gave society a gulp of freedom and legalized rudimentary democratic institutions, the vigilant guardian in him hurried to take them back.

The doctrinaire Khrushchev sometimes conquered the pragmatist, as the dogmatist in him did the revisionist, and the retrograde did the innovator. Across practically the whole spectrum of social problems—economics, culture, ideology, daily life—he was torn between ideas of statism and the welfare of the people.

This division is less characteristic of Gorbachev, but even he was not spared it. This contradiction was and remains the main problem of Russian reforms. Their success, to a decisive degree, depends on finding an optimal balance between the state and society. The state is necessary in all countries. In Russia it is needed even more than elsewhere, by virtue of the great expanses of land and many other factors. But state power must be carefully weighed, because as soon as the state begins to swell up, society begins to wither, and vice versa: under a weak government, society also has one foot in the grave.

Khrushchev and Gorbachev: An American View

PETER REDDAWAY

This comparison of the reformist strategies of Nikita Khrushchev and Mikhail Gorbachev, strategies that had a lot in common, aims to shed light on the reformability or otherwise of the Soviet system in the post-Stalin period. To the extent that their strategies were similar we may be able to identify those parts of the system that were the most obvious targets for reform. To the extent that they were different we may perhaps conclude that Gorbachev thought he was learning from Khrushchev's mistakes. And to the extent that they both found their strategies leading to a steady shrinking of their political base, we may consider either that the strategies were misconceived, unrealistic, and unduly "idealistic" or that perhaps no reform strategy could have succeeded. In that case the system may have long been unreformable, and the only real alternatives may have been (1) maintenance of the authoritarian status quo by using the necessary degree of coercion or (2) fragmentation and rebellion, either directly against this authoritarianism or through Khrushchevian/Gorbachevian reformism leading to a systemic breakdown and the end of empire—roughly what happened in 1990–1991.[1]

Serious problems arise, of course, in comparing Khrushchev and Gorbachev. First and most obviously, the objective social, economic, and political conditions of the late 1980s in the Soviet Union differed substantially from those of the 1950s and early 1960s. So each man was operating in a somewhat different context, with Soviet society less unprepared for change in the 1980s. Second, whereas Gorbachev rather quickly and clearly became the top leader upon Konstantin Chernenko's death in 1985, Khrushchev did not achieve that status firmly until 1955 or even 1957—years after Stalin's death in 1953. This complicates the question of exactly which years of Khrushchev's to compare with Gorbachev's tenure. This problem may, however, be less acute than it at first seems, if we bear in mind that the notion of collective leadership had at least some validity both in the years 1953–1957 and in 1985–1987, and that both men were then striving to consolidate their positions. I therefore propose to consider Khrushchev's strategy from the year 1953.

A third problem is that in this case we have eleven years to review for Khrushchev and only four for Gorbachev—only four because at least from early 1989 onward Gorbachev faced pressures from below with which Khrushchev did not have to contend, and which forced Gorbachev to change his strategy. Indeed, in my view these forces became so strong that after 1989 he no longer had any consistent strategy except the strategy of personal survival. This factor does indeed make the "objective circumstances" different enough to invalidate direct comparisons after early 1989. True, Khrushchev had some forces to contend with from below—restive intellectuals, especially in 1962–1963,[2] popular protests in 1962,[3] and the Polish and Hungarian peoples in 1956.[4] But in general I am inclined to limit Gorbachev's years for comparison to the four he had in office prior to early 1989.

All this is premised on my belief that the two men had the same central core to their strategy, namely to secure the future of Communist party rule in the Soviet Union. I have not been convinced by Georgii Shakhnazarov's implication, in the previous chapter, that Gorbachev's strategy as formulated between 1985 and 1987 included the intention to abolish the party's monopoly on power in the near future. I know of no statement in which Gorbachev directly and unambiguously makes this assertion. While in power he many times denied any such intention and labeled the idea dangerous. And since losing office he has confirmed that view: "I wanted to develop democratization in a one-party system," he said in 1993.[5] In 1995 he made the same point in a different way : "By 1988 I understood we would have to make changes outside the traditional confines of the system, but not outside the confines of socialism."[6] It is true that Alexander Iakovlev proposed in discussion, and then in a memorandum of December 1985, the idea of splitting the party into two parties, or two wings of one party. But Gorbachev, he says, considered the idea premature.[7]

The broad circumstances under which both Khrushchev and Gorbachev consolidated their power helped to shape their strategies. Here the picture is clearer regarding Gorbachev than Khrushchev, but I hold that in the latter's case too, at least by the time of his decisive defeat of Viacheslav Molotov, Georgii Malenkov, and Lazar Kaganovich in 1957, the moods and concerns that came to prevail in parts of the upper nomenklatura in the mid-1950s had a considerable influence both on that victory and on the path that Khrushchev decided to take. In other words, his victory was not simply the outcome of a power struggle among a dozen men, and the strategy he chose was not just his personal one but was influenced by wider forces within the elite. These forces felt more comfortable with him than with his opponents, partly because they thought they would be personally more secure under him and partly because they believed he would deal better with the regime's problems.[8]

To speak in more general terms, the first priority of the nomenklatura was always the security of its own power. When, therefore, the political and economic system lost its dynamism in important respects, this posed a long-term threat to that security, and the nomenklatura instinctively became concerned to regenerate the lost dynamism. The last years of Stalin's and Brezhnev's rule saw just such a loss of momentum. Aging, complacent, increasingly conservative rulers became fearful of change, mainly because it could so easily sweep them away[9]. Concern therefore developed in those parts of the political elite which were either more perceptive and forward-looking (the policy motivation) or more ambitious and impatient to be promoted (the power motive) or both. (These motives commingle in the mind of every politician everywhere, if in wildly varying proportions.)

When Stalin and Brezhnev eventually died, there were interregnums or *mezhtsarstva* (1953–1957 and 1983–1985) during which factions fought tooth and nail over the succession. True, the interregnums are not fully comparable, since Khrushchev became the party boss early in the first interregnum, in September 1953, and Gorbachev did not do so until the midway point of the second interregnum, in March 1985. Nonetheless, the party infighting in the two periods had some features in common, with the twists and turns representing the changing balance of forces not just among a few individuals but also among a wider group of the senior nomenklatura. In any case, when Khrushchev and Gorbachev won out, it was not only because they were formidable political infighters but also because the more forward-looking and ambitious elements in the elite were eventually able to make a significant contribution to the defeat of the conservative elements. Ultimately, for the more policy-minded supporters of Khrushchev and Gorbachev (many other supporters were doubtless more concerned about gaining power and privilege and thus with betting on the right horse), an attempt to redynamize the system became more compelling than the alluring but risky path of continued conservatism and inertia.

In eventually contributing to or going along with this choice, however, the parts of the nomenklatura in favor of change were also apprehensive and hesitant. The new leader might be able, with time, to weaken the nomenklatural controls over him, to exercise autocratic power over it, as had Stalin. And the dynamic new man might in fact end up imposing rash or badly thought-out new policies, thereby jeopardizing, not securing, the elite's power.

As a result, the nomenklatura of the mid-1950s and the mid-1980s were deeply divided on how much change was needed and was desirable. It was also apprehensive about the leader it eventually chose, even in the aftermath of each choice, and especially in the case of Gorbachev. After all, the nomenklatura of the post-1985 period recalled, Khrushchev did impose "hare-brained schemes" that made things worse, and he did start escaping from the elite's control, so that it was compelled to oust him in an undignified palace coup. Much of the elite that supported Gorbachev eventually came to believe that he too pursued reckless policies and was able to do so because, notwithstanding their apprehensions, he went much further than Khrushchev in escaping their control.

With all the caveats in mind, and the context of each man's accession briefly sketched, let us now proceed to some comparisons.

Both Khrushchev and Gorbachev became leader of the party at a time when stagnation and inertia in society had reached dangerous proportions. How did they build a political base? Both men took care at first to reassure the nomenklatura that they were ideologically orthodox on the leading role of the party and the importance of the armed forces. This made it easier to consolidate their power and gain the cooperation of the party's senior echelons. Thus, unlike Malenkov, they observed "Breslauer's law" about the political necessity of taking these conservative positions in the early stages.[10]

Both men saw that the problems of the economy were the most urgent ones, but they also realized the need for a comprehensive program of social and political as well as economic reforms. Although they had some radical tendencies before they reached the top, Khrushchev did not present himself as politically radical until he had been in office for two and a half years,[11] and Gorbachev prepared the ground for nearly two years before doing likewise.[12] Both men were considered to be "sound" on basic principles; therefore they could be trusted to tackle the country's problems with the unusual amount of energy and imagination that each possessed, qualities that many officials apparently felt were required if a deepening and therefore dangerous stagnation were to be avoided. We should also note here that Gorbachev had, in his "electioneering" speech of December 1984, given a clearer indication of his radical tendencies than Khrushchev ever gave, and we know something about the educational crash course of 1982–1984 that enabled him to make that speech.[13]

Part of the strategy of both Khrushchev and Gorbachev was, of course, to obtain strong support for their reform programs from the party. To that end both men deployed their extraordinary skills of persuasion and infighting within the party's upper levels. This was a prominent and time-consuming feature of their activity that Shakhnazarov neglects. In their tactical dexterity, their sense of timing, their subtle mix of benevolence and ruthlessness, their ability to catch opponents off guard with unexpected thrusts, and their considerable success at putting together top party bodies they could work with, at least for a time, they were a match for each other—although to my mind Gorbachev surpassed Khrushchev, thanks to the finer calibration of his actions and his care not to humiliate fallen opponents (with the eventually fatal exception of Boris Yeltsin) too much. Later on, both men gradually became overconfident and complacent about the extent of their power and failed to take account of how rapidly it ebbed away in the years 1961–1964 and 1989–1991.

As they tried to work out coherent programs of reform, both leaders spoke out increasingly about the need for militant efforts to change the system. Reform was essential because the faults of their predecessors had incurred heavy costs for the Soviet Union. But now, both men suggested, inspirational leadership at last was available, based on a group of people who had identified the problems, who had begun devising rational solutions, and who possessed the will to apply them. Contrary to Shakhnazarov's view that Khrushchev was the last true believer in communism among Soviet leaders, Gorbachev and Yegor Ligachev also provided leadership based on their deep personal commitment to socialism and communism. Gorbachev, like Khrushchev, repeated as late as early 1990, "I am a convinced communist." He made a passionate confession of faith in December 1990: "I've been told more than once that it is time to stop swearing allegiance to socialism. Why should I? Socialism is my deep conviction, and I will promote it as long as I can talk and work." Even after the coup of August 1991 he earnestly emphasized his allegiance to the "socialist choice" and the Communist party, which he would neither abandon nor kill.[14]

To nomenklatura audiences, the reformist message included an extra appeal: that younger, more dynamic and innovative officials could expect quick promotion. In attracting such officials, whose support was considered essential, the leaders sought to engage not only personal ambition and Soviet patriotism but, especially in Gorbachev's case, the fear that without serious reform the party's power would decline or even collapse. Even Gorbachev's early ally, Ligachev, quoted several times some obiter dicta of Lenin's which must have struck the apparat's most sensitive nerves: "All the revolutionary parties which have perished up to now, perished because they grew complacent, were unable to see where their strength lay, and were afraid to talk about their weaknesses."[15] The message could hardly have been clearer.

Apart from mobilizing the party, central to both Khrushchev's and Gorbachev's strategies was the goal of mobilizing the people behind reform. This meant activating what Gorbachev called "the wasted reserves of socialism," which were, above all, "the human factor." Thus both men spoke of great transformations, the "building of communism" (Khrushchev) and the vaguer *perestroika* (Gorbachev). Also, both pushed democratization and (though Khrushchev did not use the actual word) *glasnost* as key means of mobilization.[16]

Intellectual groups, for example, were not only allowed to organize meetings and publications with much less interference than before but also found themselves being urged to debate in public, to produce new ideas, to refine the ones the politicians adopted, and in general to promote an atmosphere of liberation and fresh thinking in society. Political prisoners such as Aleksandr Solzhenitsyn under Khrushchev, and Andrei Sakharov and Vyacheslav Chornovil under Gorbachev, were released from prison or exile and enabled to take part in these activities. What was called the Thaw in Khrushchev's time and glasnost in Gorbachev's had the same basic functions of creating a constituency for reform and encouraging collaboration in reformist thinking. As for ordinary people, the leaders aimed to inspire them by the promise of less regimentation and a better standard of living, in return for harder work. Young people found themselves addressed more in their own language; in particular they were allowed more access to international pop culture.[17]

All this naturally raised the question of political control and where to draw the line. Both leaders were keen to claim that there were no longer any political prisoners in the labor camps (Khrushchev in 1959, Gorbachev in 1988) but became exasperated at the criticism and demands from below, to which such liberalism gave rise. Both chose the same method for responding to critics who were operating "within the system"—calling in the complainers, persuading, cajoling, reasoning with them, and eventually threatening them. Khrushchev did this with the "creative intelligentsia," especially in 1962–1963.[18] He also used tougher methods against unknown dissidents completely outside the system.[19]

Gorbachev, too, called in established critics. At his meeting with editors on October 13, 1989, for example, he berated them for abusing glasnost by throwing lighted matches around in a country that resembled a huge vat of gasoline. And he and his colleagues indicated that glasnost meant "socialist pluralism," and that anti-socialism would not be tolerated, at least within the established polity. This recalled the Khrushchev-Ilichev line of 1962–1963 that "we have complete freedom to struggle for communism, but we do not have, and cannot have, freedom to struggle *against* communism."[20] When nationalism went too far for Gorbachev's taste in Georgia, Azerbaijan, Lithuania, and Latvia, bloody military reprisals were undertaken. These only made things worse, because by this stage nationalism enjoyed a base of mass support. In most of these cases Gorbachev tried rather unconvincingly to deny responsibility for the bloodshed.

In this connection, it seems to me odd for Shakhnazarov to claim that the "Declaration of the Independence of Russia" (in fact a declaration of sovereignty, not of independence) was a fatal cause of the separatism that undermined the Soviet Union. In reality Russia was two years behind the Baltic states, and the source of separatism was clearly the Baltic and Transcaucasian regions.

Both Khrushchev and Gorbachev subscribed to what they temperamentally liked, namely a socialist form of *sobornost*. This concept involves people constructively debating any problem and reaching a socialist solution by consensus. If some malicious dissenter is still dissatisfied, Gorbachev said in one speech, he will be left behind and can be ignored. This cast of mind helps to explain why Gorbachev so strongly opposed dropping the party's monopoly on power until, in 1990, this position became untenable.

Khrushchev too was orthodox in this regard, though he felt in retirement that perhaps he had been timid in not allowing more freedom: "We were consciously rather afraid of this thaw, for fear that it might produce a flood which would inundate everything. . . . The fear was that . . . the leadership . . . would not be able to lead and direct into Soviet channels the creative forces which would be let loose, nor to ensure that the output of these creative forces would serve to strengthen socialism. This concern was good, a good instinct, but perhaps a bit cowardly."[21]

The two leaders also solicited support from both Communist and capitalist leaders abroad as they set about reducing tensions with foreign countries. The aim was to win a breathing space in which to tackle domestic problems and to see whether defense spending could be held steady or even reduced. In the most dangerous region, Eastern Europe, Khrushchev introduced the notion of different roads to socialism, or polycentrism, and Gorbachev did the same. This highly risky approach produced for Khrushchev the Hungarian uprising of 1956 and his first major political crisis. For Gorbachev, the tolerant approach, coupled with his wise but difficult decision to withdraw from Afghanistan and the effective impossibility of using force in Eastern Europe in 1989, brought about the collapse of communism in Eastern Europe and gave more ammunition to his enemies at home.

For Khrushchev in 1956, and for Gorbachev in 1986, it became clear that dismissing old or unsuitable officials and appointing younger ones on anything like the scale they wanted was politically impossible because of opposition to such firings at the top level of the party. So they turned their thoughts to changing entire structures of the command economy and the main bureaucracies, as well as many of their longstanding procedures. Such structural changes would both help to ease the exasperating problems of firing and hiring large numbers of people and simultaneously create new or modified institutions with which to carry out the planned reforms.

A relatively easy change for both Khrushchevites and Gorbachevites was the relaxing (in Khrushchev's case) and the virtual dismantling (in Gorbachev's) of the many-tentacled apparatus of censorship known as

Glavlit. Both men turned instead, if in differing degrees, to the principle of trusting editors to obey centrally issued guidelines.[22] A more difficult task was gaining the nomenklatura's acceptance of proposed new mechanisms to democratize and thus revivify the party, the soviets, and workplaces such as factories and farms. Gorbachev became a radical on these issues in 1987, at an earlier stage than Khrushchev.

Crucial structural changes by both leaders centered on the system of economic management and planning. Both saw the urgent need for innovation, flexibility, and financial discipline in running the economy and the consequent necessity, above all, of breaking the stranglehold on the economy of the top-heavy state corporations known as ministries. Khrushchev's approach was to make a frontal assault. In 1957 he abolished more than half the economic ministries. He restricted most of the central planners to long-term tasks and set up a network of councils *(sovnarkhozy)* to plan and coordinate the economy at the regional level. He ensured that these were under the supervision of regional party bosses and enjoined party officials at the grass roots not to interfere in the day-to-day running of enterprises. He called on the local soviets and their executive organs to take a stronger hand in supervising the local economy.

In 1987–1988 the Gorbachevites gained party approval for a somewhat similar group of reforms, which would, had they been carried out, have broken the economic ministries, curbed the planners, given "all power to the soviets," and barred party officials from meddling in enterprises. But while the overall pattern resembled Khrushchev's scheme in some ways, there were important differences. Relatively few central ministries were abolished outright by Gorbachev. The general working principle from January 1988 on was to aim to cut ministerial staffs by half. Also, the largely unsuccessful sovnarkhozy were not revived. Their functions (between 1957 and 1965) were to be taken over from the ministries, in part by a steadily expanding socialist market based on freely negotiated contracts between state enterprises, in part by a much smaller but also expanding free market involving cooperatives and private family businesses, and in part by the soviets. (Not much of all this actually happened, as the economy became chaotic and corruption and barter arrangements flourished.)

The party conference in June 1988 made a controversial decision about the future of the soviets, reminiscent of Khrushchev's subjection of the sovnarkhozy to party supervision. It voted that the local party boss should assume a second office as chairman of the local soviet. This formula violated the principle of the Gorbachevites that there should be maximum disengagement by the party from the soviet and ministerial hierarchies. But it helped for a time to mitigate the party apparatus's sense of grievance that the reforms were threatening to strip it of many of its powers and reduce it to little more than a political debating club.

This last point helps to explain a notable difference between the two leaders over agriculture. Khrushchev was able to improve farm output, and thus public welfare and morale, in his early years by removing many restrictions from the peasants' private plots. But Gorbachev, while also concerned about public welfare, was unable to gain acceptance for the widespread introduction of family farming that he favored, which would have constituted a more radical reform than Khrushchev's. The reasons for this were complex and included the conservatism of popular culture, but a critical factor seems to have been the refusal of the party apparatus to give up a function that employed thousands of its officials as de facto managers of much of Soviet agriculture. For the Gorbachevites, meanwhile, the hard fact was that continuing food shortages fast undermined their credibility as reformers concerned for the public well-being.

As for the military forces, both the Khrushchev and the Gorbachev leaderships took the opportunity to remind them of their subservient status by dismissing their defense ministers in humiliating circumstances—Marshal Georgii Zhukov in 1957 and Marshal Sergei Sokolov in 1987. But the Khrushchevites waited until 1960 before launching a campaign for military reform, and the Gorbachevites until late 1988. When the campaigns came, they had many features in common, notably the goals of greatly reducing the size of the armed forces and of cutting the military budget.[23] If the public were to support reform, as both leaders felt was essential, resources needed to be switched to the civilian economy and the raising of living standards.

The leaders' treatment of the KGB reveals one of the few sharp contrasts between the two reform strategies, but it derived from special circumstances. Khrushchev managed to preempt Lavrentii Beria's grab for power in 1953; he thus gained the opportunity both to increase his personal security and to reform the secret police by severely cutting its apparatus and status down to size during the period after Beria's execution. Gorbachev, by contrast, trod very lightly at first, since the KGB was headed until the fall of 1988 by an opponent of his, Viktor Chebrikov. After replacing Chebrikov with an ally, Vladimir Kryuchkov, Gorbachev made some progress in the same direction as Khrushchev, subjecting the KGB to criticism, mainly about the past, apparently diminishing greatly its domestic role as a secret police, and reducing its size—in the case of the border guards substantially.

Finally, on the supremely difficult issue of how to handle the national minorities, Khrushchev in his early years as party leader took a relatively liberal position, increasing the powers of the republics and rehabilitating most of the small peoples deported by Stalin in the early 1940s. But he started reversing this trend in 1958–1959, when he saw the incipient danger of ethnic party bosses in the republics courting popularity through the quiet promotion of mildly nationalistic trends.[24] He also felt the need to relegitimize the regime by radically revamping Marxism-Leninism. All this led to the policies summed up in this sentence in the new Party program of 1961 : "Full-scale communist construction signifies a new stage in the development of national relations in the Soviet Union in which the nations will draw still closer together and their complete unity will be achieved."

By contrast, Gorbachev's first tendency was to tighten central controls, since many of the minority republics had degenerated into corrupt, feudalistic, and surreptitiously nationalistic fiefdoms. This line led to the closing down of many economic ministries in most of the republics, and to an apparent reduction in the republics' economic autonomy.

Yet before Gorbachev even saw the need to work out a coherent nationalities policy, militant nationalism had developed in an increasing number of republics. This movement was enormously accelerated by the elections to the new Congress of People's Deputies in March 1989, which destroyed or severely damaged the traditional loyalty of some of the republican party apparatuses to Moscow. Now they were forced to compete with the powerful forces of local nationalism, and mostly on those forces' terms. Only in 1990 did Gorbachev start trying to devise new and more flexible constitutional arrangements to regulate relations between the republics and the union, and to inhibit nationalist aspirations by making secession a long and testing process. But by then it was too late for such documents to have much force.

The radicalism of both Khrushchev and Gorbachev became stronger after a couple of years in office, at least partly in response to the resistance of much of the nomenklatura to proposed reforms and to extensive changes in personnel. In turn, the leaders' increased radicalism soon provoked their more moderate or conservative colleagues into going further in their resistance and plotting how to remove or at least curb them. In Khrushchev's case, his destalinization campaign and assault on the ministries were key factors in provoking Malenkov and other members of the anti-party group into an attempted coup against him in 1957, which almost succeeded. When Khrushchev managed to turn the tables and oust the plotters, he went on in early 1958 to increase his personal power still more by becoming prime minister in addition to his position as first secretary of the party.

However, his radical desire to reform most institutions and abolish others in a populist-anarchist promotion of the "withering away of the state" gradually turned all sectors of the nomenklatura against him. With public opinion, too, souring on him because of erratic food supplies and price rises on key consumer items, his power base shrank rapidly and no one resisted his ouster.

Opposition to Gorbachev and quiet sabotage of his reforms began in 1987. As he increasingly realized the effectiveness of passive resistance by conservatives in the party, led by Ligachev and parts of the Central Committee, he decided that his only way of avoiding Khrushchev's fate was to create an entirely new power base for himself and harness its authority to the reform or abolition of the existing institutions. So he instituted a new legislative hierarchy, allowed considerable choice of candidates in elections to it, and tried to free it from constant party control.

This, however, was the fateful decision that led to his own loss of control over the processes of change. Dissenting and oppositional forces of many kinds arose and forced him in February 1990 to abandon the party's monopoly on power. In a desperate attempt to prevent economic chaos, growing social disintegration, political polarization, and incipient fragmentation of the country from sweeping him away, he expanded the powers of the presidency and persuaded and cajoled 59 percent of the congressional deputies to vote him into the new office.

But the lesson of this comparison of two leaders' reform strategies appears to support the view that once Soviet authoritarianism had been undercut beyond a certain point by reforms, revolution—probably followed by years of instability, upheaval, anarchy, and even perhaps civil war—was the likely outcome. Eventually the party-state closed ranks against Khrushchev and threw him out. At first the extraordinarily pragmatic Gorbachev avoided the same fate by skillfully exploiting the rising popular discontent with the party that was released by glasnost and semi-free elections. For a time he appeared to have almost neutralized and sidelined the party. But the more successful he was at that, the more the one institution that had held everything together ceased to do so and the faster the rebellious and disintegrative trends around the country developed.[25]

How long the system would have survived if Gorbachev or someone like him had not been able to take power in 1985 is an intriguing question. An authoritarian like his challenger Grigorii Romanov could probably have ruled oppressively for many years if the nomenklatura had supported him. In 1985 the economic and social crisis was not dangerously acute. But would the nomenklatura have supported a conservative? How strong were its reformist forces at that time? Could a variant of the Chinese model—pursuing radical economic reform alongside minimal political reform—have been launched? Was Gorbachev irresponsibly impatient and wrong to try to do things the other way round? How much depended on the views and actions of one individual, Gorbachev—and, thirty years earlier for that matter, of Khrushchev?

Notes

APRF   Archive of the President of the Russian Federation
AVPRF   Archive of Foreign Policy of the Russian Federation
CPSU   Communist Party of the Soviet Union
d.   delo
DOA   Donetsk Provincial Archive
f.   fond
GARF   State Archive of the Russian Federation
o.   opis'
RTsKhIDNI   Russian Center for the Preservation and Study of Documents of Con-
            temporary History
TsAODM   Central Archive of Social Movements of the City of Moscow
TsGAOOU   Central State Archive for Social Organizations of Ukraine
TsKhSD   Center for the Preservation of Contemporary Documentation

Introduction

1. See Lazar Pistrak, *The Grand Tactician: Khrushchev's Rise to Power* (New York: Praeger, 1961); Edward Crankshaw, *Khrushchev: A Career* (New York: Viking Press, 1966); Mark Frankland, *Khrushchev* (New York: Stein and Day, 1967); Myron Rush, *The Rise of Khrushchev* (Washington, D.C.: Public Affairs Press, 1958); Robert Conquest, *Power and Policy in the USSR: The Study of Soviet Dynastics* (New York: St. Martin's Press, 1961); Carl Linden, *Khrushchev and the Soviet Leadership* (Baltimore: Johns Hopkins Press, 1966); Michel Tatu, *Power in the Kremlin: From Khrushchev to Kosygin,* translated by Helen Katel (New York: Viking Press, 1969); Priscilla Johnson Macmillan, *Khrushchev and the Arts: The Politics of Soviet Culture 1962–1964* (Cambridge: MIT Press, 1965), Roman Kolkowicz, *The Soviet Military and the Communist Party* (Princeton: Princeton University Press, 1967); Myron Rush and Arnold L. Horelick, *Strategic Power and Soviet Foreign Policy* (Chicago: University of Chicago Press, 1966); Sidney Ploss, *Conflict and Decision-Making in Soviet Russia: A Study of Agricultural Policy, 1953–1964* (Princeton: Princeton University Press, 1965); William Hyland and Richard Wallace Shryock, *The Fall of Khrushchev* (London: Pitman, 1970); A. Brumberg ed., *Russia Under Khrushchev: An Anthology from Problems of Communism* (New York: Praeger, 1962); Alexander Werth, *Russia Under Khrushchev* (New York: Hill and Wang, 1962).

2. Nikita S. Khrushchev, *Khrushchev Remembers,* translated and edited by Strobe

Talbott (Boston: Little, Brown, 1970); Khrushchev, *Khrushchev Remembers: The Last Testament,* translated and edited by Strobe Talbott (Boston: Little, Brown, 1974).

3. Roy A. Medvedev and Zhores A. Medvedev, *Khrushchev: The Years in Power* (New York: Columbia University Press, 1976); Roy A. Medvedev, *Khrushchev,* translated by Brian Pearce (Garden City, N.Y.: Anchor Books/Doubleday, 1983).

4. Martin McCauley, *Khrushchev and the Development of Soviet Agriculture: The Virgin Lands Programme 1953–1964* (London, Macmillan, 1976); R. F. Miller and F. Feher, *Khrushchev and the Communist World* (London and Canberra: Croom Helm, 1984); George W. Breslauer, *Khrushchev and Brezhnev as Leaders: Building Authority in Soviet Politics* (Boston: Allen and Unwin, 1982).

5. Sergei N. Khrushchev, *Pensioner soiuznogo znacheniia* (Moscow: Novosti, 1991); Sergei N. Khrushchev, *Khrushchev on Khrushchev: An Inside Account of the Man and His Era,* translated by William Taubman (Boston: Little, Brown, 1990); Aleksei Adzhubei, *Te desiat' let* (Moscow: Sovetskaia Rossiia, 1989); Adzhubei, *Krushenie illiuzii* (Moscow: Interbuk, 1991; Fedor Burlatsky, *Khrushchev: The Era of Khrushchev Through the Eyes of His Advisor,* translated by Daphne Skillen (New York: Scribner, 1991).

6. Nikita S. Khrushchev, *Khrushchev Remembers: The Glasnost Tapes,* translated and edited by Jerrold L. Schecter with Vyacheslav Luchkov (Boston: Little, Brown, 1990). The full Russian version of Khrushchev's memoirs was published as "Memuary Nikity Sergeevicha Khrushcheva" in *Voprosy istorii* beginning in no. 2, 1990, and finishing in nos. 5−6, 1995. See also Martin McCauley, ed., *Khrushchev and Khrushchevism* (Bloomington: Indiana University Press, 1987); Michael Beschloss, *May Day: Eisenhower, Khrushchev, and the U-2 Affair* (New York: Harper & Row, 1986); Beschloss, *The Crisis Years: Kennedy and Khrushchev 1960–1963* (New York: HarperCollins, 1991); James G. Richter, *Khrushchev's Double Bind* (Baltimore: Johns Hopkins University Press, 1994).

7. For continuing coverage of the state of Soviet archives, including materials contained therein and the degree of accessibility thereto, see issues of the *Cold War International History Project Bulletin,* published by the Cold War International History Project at the Woodrow Wilson International Center for Scholars, Washington, D.C.

8. See, for example, A. A. Gromyko, *Pamiatnoe* (Moscow: Izdatel'stvo politcheskoi literatury, 1988); P. E. Shelest, *Da ne sudimy budete* (Moscow: Edition Q, 1995); V. V. Grishin, *Ot Khrushcheva do Gorbacheva* (Moscow: ASPOL, 1996); A. M. Aleksandrov-Agentov, *Ot Kollontai do Gorbacheva* (Moscow: Mezhdunarodnye otnosheniia, 1994).

9. The Khrushchev Centenary Conference, sponsored by the Watson Institute of Brown University, was held at Brown in Providence, R.I., December 1–3, 1994.

10. William J. Tompson, *Khrushchev: A Political Life* (New York: St. Martin's Press, 1995).

Chapter 1: The Ukrainian Years

1. See Edward Crankshaw, *Khrushchev: A Career* (New York: Viking Press, 1966), pp. 137–38.

2. I have had the opportunity to be one of the first to analyze documents previously unavailable to scholars. See: Iu. I. Shapoval, "N. S. Khrushchev na Ukraine: stranitsy zhizni i deiatel'nosti," in *Tribuna lektora,* no. 10 (Kiev, 1988), pp. 23–26 (in Ukrainian). Shapoval, "N. S. Khrushchev: ocherk politicheskoi deiatel'nosti," in *Ukrainskii*

istoricheskii zhurnal,, no. 1 (Kiev, 1989), pp. 103–15 (in Ukrainian). I. P. Kozhukalo and Shapoval, "N. S. Khrushchev na Ukraine," in *Voprosy istorii KPSS*, no. 9 (Moscow, 1989), pp. 85–98. Shapoval, *N. S. Khrushchev na Ukraine* (Kiev, 1990), p. 48 (in Ukrainian). Shapoval, "N. S. Khrushchev na Ukraine: stranitsy zhizni i deiatel'nosti," in *Stranitsy istorii Ukrainskoi SSR: fakty, problemy, liudi* (Kiev, 1990), pp. 367–81 (in Ukrainian). Shapoval, "Nestandartnyi kommunist," in *Vesti iz Ukrainy*, no. 16 (Kiev, 1994; in Ukrainian). Shapoval, "Stoletnii Khrushchev," in Shapoval, *Chelovek i sistema: shtrikhi k portretu totalitarnogo perioda v Ukraine* (Kiev, 1994), pp. 195–225. Shapoval, "Khrushchev i Ukraina," in *N. S. Khrushchev (1894–1971): materialy nauchnoi konferentsii, posviashchennoi 100-letiiu so dnia rozhdeniia N. S. Khrushcheva, 18 aprelia 1994 goda* (Moscow: Gorbachev-Fond, 1994), pp. 153–62. Shapoval, "N. S. Khrushchev i L. M. Kaganovich: sosushchestvovanie i sotrudnichestvo," in *N. S. Khrushchev i Ukraina: materialy nauchnogo seminara 14 aprelia 1994 g., posviashchennogo 100-letiiu so dnia rozhdeniia N. S. Khrushchev* (Kiev, 1995), pp. 19–27 (in Ukrainian).

3. Khrushchev himself, on some forms filled out in his own hand, gave April 16 (4 o.s.) of the same year as his date of birth. See Application to the Comrade Artem Donetsk Tekhnikum (for admission in 1922), in DOA, f. 1087, o. 31, d. 1715, l. 2. The excerpt from the registration book of the village of Kalinovka, Dmitriev district (*uezd*), Kursk province (*guberniia*) (1894), is in TsGAOOU, f. 39, o. 4, d. 223, l. 27.

4. R. A. Mevedev, *N. S. Khrushchev: politicheskii portret* (Moscow: 1990), p. 15.

5. Report of the head of the Ekaterinoslav provincial gendarme administration to the police department, May 28, 1912, in TsGAOOU, f. 39, o. 4, d. 223, l. 6.

6. A. I. Adzhubei, *Krushenie illiuzii* (Moscow: 1991), p. 50.

7. Shapoval, *Chelovek i sistema*, p. 199.

8. Ibid.

9. Agenda from session of the Soviet of Worker Deputies, May 29, 1917, in DOA, f. R-42, o. 1, d. 1, ll. 39–40.

10. N. S. Khrushchev, "Memuary N. S. Khrushcheva," in *Voprosy istorii*, no. 2 (Moscow, 1990), p. 91.

11. Ibid.

12. *Rasskaz o pochetnom shakhtere* (Stalino, 1961), p. 51.

13. Ibid., p. 62.

14. A. P. Zaveniagin (1901–1956) served from 1953 as deputy minister and from 1956 as minister of medium machine construction of the Soviet Union; beginning in 1955 he simultaneously served as deputy chairman of the USSR Council of Ministers.

15. Application to the Donetsk Tekhnikum for admission to the first year of the Workers' Department, August 24, 1922, in DOA, f. 1087, o. 31, d. 1715, l. 1 (reverse side).

16. Agenda of the 9th Iuzovka regional party conference, December 23, 1923, in DOA, f. 9, o. 1, d. 7, l. 12.

17. Agenda of the plenum of the Iuzovka regional party committee, February 11, 1924, in DOA, f. 9, o. 1, d. 40, l. 21.

18. Adzhubei, p. 48.

19. Khrushchev, "Memuary," in *Voprosy istorii*, no. 4 (1990), p. 77.

20. Ibid., pp. 77–8.

21. "Posledniaia 'antipartiinaia' gruppa: stenograficheskii otchet iiun'skogo (1957 g.) plenuma TsK KPSS," in *Istoricheskii arkhiv*, no. 2 (Moscow, 1994), pp. 43–4.

22. Ibid., no. 1, p. 37.

23. F. Chuev, *Tak govoril Kaganovich: ispoved' stalinskogo apostola* (Moscow, 1992), p. 99.

24. T. I. Kharechko joined the party in 1914; between 1919 and 1921 he belonged to the Central Committee and the organizational bureau of the Ukrainian Communist party, and in 1921 he headed the agitation-propaganda department of the Ukrainian Central Committee. Because of his Trotskyite views, he was later expelled from leadership posts and probably arrested in the 1930s.

25. Agenda #2 from a plenum of the Petrov-Mar'insk district (*raion*) party committee, January 11, 1926, in DOA, f. 9, o. 1, d. 29, l. 1.

26. Agenda of the 8th plenum of the Stalino regional party committee, September 30–October 2, 1926, in DOA, f. 9, o 1, d. 262, l. 98.

27. "O kul'te lichnosti i ego posledstviiakh: doklad pervogo sekretaria TsK KPSS tov. Khrushcheva N. S. XX s"ezdu KPSS 25 fevralia 1956 gg," in *Reabilitatsiia: politicheskie protsessy 30–50-x godov* (Moscow, 1991), p. 23.

28. *Pervaia vseukrainskaia konferentsiia KP(b)U, 17–21 oktiabria 1926 g., stenograficheskii otchet* (Kharkov, 1926), p. 95 (in Ukrainian).

29. Agenda #9 of a session of a plenum of the Stalino regional committee, November 11, 1926, in DOA, f.9, o. 1, d. 264, l. 1.

30. Khrushchev, "Memuary," in *Voprosy istorii*, no. 2 (1990), p. 91.

31. Ibid., p. 83.

32. Agenda of a session of the Politburo, September 10, 1927, in TsGAOOU, f. 1, o. 16, d. 3, l. 326; agenda #13 of a closed session of the Stalino regional committee, September 12, 1927, in DOA, f. 9, o. 1, d. 381, l. 45.

33. "Posledniaia 'antipartiinaia' gruppa: stenograficheskii otchet iiun'skogo (1957 g.) plenuma TsK KPSS," in *Istoricheskii arkhiv*, no. 2, Moscow, 1994, p. 44.

34. Agenda #16 of a closed session of the bureau of the Stalino regional committee of the Ukrainian Communist party, September 26, 1928, in DOA, f. 9, o. 1, d. 381, l. 52.

35. Khrushchev, "Memuary," in *Voprosy istorii*, no. 2 (1990), p. 90.

36. Ibid., p. 91.

37. Excerpt from agenda #33 of a session of the secretariat of the Ukrainian Communist party, April 28, 1928, in TsGAOOU, f. 1, o. 20, d. 2661, l. 87.

38. A. N. Ponomarev, *N. S. Khrushchev: put' k liderstvu* (Moscow, 1990), p. 11.

39. For more details see ibid.

40. "Posledniaia 'antipartiinaia' gruppa,"p. 45.

41. Khrushchev, "Memuary," in *Voprosy istorii*, no. 5 (1990), p. 46.

42. Agenda #20 of a session of the Politburo of the Ukrainian Communist Party, April 10, 1938; resolution "O reorganizatsii natsional'nykh shkol na Ukraine," in TsGAOOU, f. 1, o. 6, d. 463, l. 2.

43. Stenographic record of N. S. Khrushchev on the work of the Ukrainian Central Committee at the 14th Congress of the Ukrainian Communist Party, June 13–18, 1938, in TsGAOOU, f. 1, o. 1, d. 548, l. 63.

44. Ibid., l. 61.

45. Resolution of the 14th Congress of the Ukrainian Communist Party on the report of the Ukrainian Central Committee, in TsGAOOU, f. 1, o. 1, d. 544, l. 500.

46. *N. S. Khrushchev i Ukraina*, pp. 182, 184.

47. Ibid., p. 189.

48. Affair of Stepan Ivanovich Usenko. Statement of acting head of the 2d depart-

ment of the Directorate of State Security of the Ukrainian NKVD, Senior Lieutenant of State Security Pavlychev, in *Arkhiv Ministerstva bezopasnosti Rossiiskoi Federatsii* (Archive of the Ministry of Security of the Russian Federation), delo R-4282, tom 1, list 70.

49. Shapoval, *Ukraina v 20–50-kh godakh: stranitsy nenapisannoi istorii*, pp. 241–256.

50. Stenographic record of N. S. Khrushchev on the work of the Ukrainian Central Committee at the 14th Congress of the Ukrainian Communist Party, June 13–18, 1938, in TsGAOOU, f. 1, o. 1, d. 548, ll. 2,4.

51. Ibid., l. 90.

52. "Na strazhe bezopasnosti Otchizny: interv'iu s Predsedatelem KGB USSR N. M. Galushko," in *Sovetskaia Ukraina* (Kiev), August 9, 1988 (in Ukrainian).

53. Stenographic record of N. S. Khrushchev on the work of the Ukrainian Central Committee at the 14th Congress of the Ukrainian Communist Party, June 13–18, 1938, in TsGAOOU, f. 1, o. 1, d. 548, l. 74.

54. Ibid., l. 78.

55. Khrushchev had barely put down the receiver when the phone rang again. It was Stalin calling back: "We've talked it over and decided that you shouldn't arrest Uspenskii. We'll summon him to Moscow and arrest him here. Don't get involved in these things." This plan had been successfully carried out against many other figures, but it did not succeed this time. The conversation was wiretapped, and Uspenskii, after leaving a note saying that he would commit suicide, fled. He was soon caught and executed. See Khrushchev, "Memuary," in *Voprosy istorii*, no. 5 (1990), p. 63.

56. S. N. Khrushchev, *Nikita Khrushchev: krizisy i rakety*, vol. 1 (Moscow, 1994), p. 13.

57. Khrushchev, "Memuary," in *Voprosy istorii*, no. 5 (1990), p. 60.

58. "Po-bol'shevistski vypolnim resheniia partii i pravitel'stva o razvitii obshchestvennogo zhivotnovodstva v kolkhozakh. Doklad tov. N. S. Khrushcheva na soveshchanii rabotnikov zhivotnovodstva Ukrainskoi SSR 15 iiulia 1939 g.," in *Bol'shevik Ukrainy*, no. 8 (Kiev, 1939), p. 19.

59. See David Joravsky, *The Lysenko Affair* (Cambridge: Harvard University Press, 1970).

60. Khrushchev, "Memuary," in *Voprosy istorii*, no. 6 (1990), p. 93.

61. Letter of N. S. Khrushchev to the Sverdlovsk provincial committee, March 25, 1943, in TsGAOOU, f. 1, o. 23, d. 408, l. 5.

62. Letter of N. S. Khrushchev to I. V. Stalin, January 26, 1944, in TsGAOOU, f. 1, o. 23, d. 862, l. 4.

63. Khrushchev, "Memuary," in *Voprosy istorii*, no. 7 (1990), p. 88.

64. Memorandum of I. A. Serov to L. P. Beria, September 27, 1939, in *Kollektsiia dokumentov Arkhiva Sluzhby bezopasnosti Ukrainy* (Collection of Documents of the Archive of the Security Service of Ukraine).

65. V. S. Parsadanova, "Deportatsiia naseleniia iz Zapadnoi Ukrainy i Zapadnoi Belorussii v 1939–1941 gg.," in *Novaia i noveishaia istoriia*, no. 2 (Moscow, 1989), p. 36.

66. *Letopis' nepokorennoi Ukrainy: dokumenty, materialy, vospominaniia*, book 1 (Lvov, 1993), p. 13 (in Ukrainian).

67. Khrushchev, "Memuary," *Voprosy istorii*, no. 7 (1990), p. 91.

68. Resolution of the Ukrainian Central Committee, "O faktakh nepravil'nogo otnosheniia k byvshim chlenam KP Pol'shi," November 2, 1940, in TsGAOOU, f. 1, o. 1, d. 20, ll. 173–4.

69. Shapoval, *Chelovek i sistema*, pp. 45−6.

70. V. Z. Siderskii, "Vospominaniia o N. S. Khrushchev," typewritten manuscript, May 7, 1990, pp. 10−11, in author's archive.

71. "Ukrainskii 'sinodik' Nikity Khrushcheva," in *Molodaia gvardiia* (Kiev), February 26, 1991 (in Ukrainian).

72. The exact circumstances of L. N. Khrushchev's death are unclear; different versions therefore appear in various publications. See, for example, "Pogib? Propal bez vesti? Zhiv?" in *Voenno-istoricheskii zhurnal*, no. 4 (Moscow, 1990), pp. 78−80.

73. Letter of N. S. Khrushchev to the Secretariat of the Ukrainian Communist Party, in TsGAOOU, f. 1, o. 23, d. 2534, ll. 1−14.

74. "Chernaia stranitsa istorii nashego naroda," in *Golos Ukrainy* (Kiev), September 10, 1994 (in Ukrainian).

75. Report of the deputy chairman of the Ukrainian Soviet of People's Commissars, V. Starchenko, and the secretary of the Ukrainian Central Committee, D. Korotchenko, to the State Defense Committee (V. Molotov) (1944), in TsGAOOU, f. 1, o. 23, d. 1318, l. 2.

76. Letter of the secretary of the Ukrainian Central Committee, D. S. Korotchenko, to the Central Committee (G. M. Malenkov), on the carrying out of the August 12, 1944, resolution of the State Defense Committee, "O pereselenii kolkhoznikov v raiony Kryma," October 1944, in TsGAOOU, f. 1, o. 23, d. 1318, l. 12.

77. See A. M. Nekrich, *The Punished Peoples: The Deportation and Fate of Soviet Minorities at the End of the Second World War*, translated by George Saunders (New York: Norton, 1978).

78. Letter of the deputy chairman of the Soviet of People's Commissars of the RSFSR, A. Gritsenko, to D. S. Korotchenko, the authorized agent of State Defense Committee on the resettlement of collective farmers to regions of the Crimea, D. S. Korotchenko, August 16, 1944, in TsGAOOU, f. 1, o. 23, d. 1319, l. 11.

79. One of the reports he studied, written by the Ukrainian Academy of Sciences economist I. N. Romanenko at the behest of the Ukrainian Central Committee, noted in particular, "The author of these lines believes that beginning with the 1897 census in which nationality was defined according to one's native language, a significant portion of the population of Ukrainian background has started to consider itself as belonging to the Russian nation." Report, Crimean ASSR on the eve of the Patriotic War, in TsGAOOU, f. 1, o. 23, d. 636, l. 48.

80. P. Knyshevskii, "Shtrikhi k portretu kremlevskoi galerei," in *Novoe vremia*, no. 9 (Moscow, 1994), p. 54.

81. Ibid.

82. "'Bolit u menia serdtse dnem i noch'iu . . . ' Iz zapisnykh knizhek Aleksandra Dovzhenko," in *Literaturnaia Ukraina* (Kiev), February 2, 1989 (in Ukrainian).

83. "Ob antileninskikh oshibkakh i natsionalisticheskikh izvrashcheniiakh v kinopovesti Dovzhenko 'Ukraina v ogne,' vystuplenie I. V. Stalina 31 ianvaria 1944 goda," in *Literaturnaia Ukraina* (Kiev), July 5, 1990 (in Ukrainian).

84. A. Dovzhenko, "Ia protiven vam i kem-to opasen," in *Istochnik*, no. 0 (Moscow, 1993), p. 126.

85. See Zhores Medvedev, *The Rise and Fall of T. D. Lysenko*, translated by I. Michael Lerner (New York: Columbia University Press, 1989).

86. Speech of N. S. Khrushchev at a session of the Politburo of the Central Committee, March 27, 1948, in TsGAOOU, f. 1, o. 6, d. 1227, l. 8.

87. Information on the carrying out of the decree of the Presidium of the USSR Supreme Soviet, "O vyselenii iz Ukrainskoi SSR lits, zlostno ukloniaiushchikhsia ot trudovoi deiatel'nosti v sel'skom khoziaistve i vedushchikh antiobshchestvennyi, paraziticheskii obraz zhizni," February 21, 1948, in TsGAOOU, f. 1, o. 24, d. 73, ll. 60–61.

88. Ibid., l. 72.

89. Letter to Comrade I. V. Stalin: "O meropriatiiakh, provodimykh v kolkhozakh ukrainy po ukreplenia trudovoi distsipliny i primenenii k litsom, zlostno ukloniaiushchimsia ot trudovoi deiatel'nosti i vedushchim parazicheskii obraz zhizni, mer, predusmotrennykh Ukazom Presidiuma Verkhovnogo Soveta SSSR ot 21 fevralia 1948 goda," April 17, 1948, in TsGAOOU, f. 1, o. 23, d. 5177, l. 44. 30

90. "Ispytanie stalinshchinoi. Dokumenty i kommentarii k politicheskoi biografii Khrushcheva," in Vecherniaia Moskva (Moscow: April 15, 1994).

91. I. M. Makoviichuk and Iu. G. Piliavets, "Golod na Ukraine v 1946–1947 gg.," in Ukrainskii istoricheskii zhurnal, no. 8 (Kiev, 1990), p. 29.

92. Khrushchev, "Memuary," in Voprosy istorii, no. 11. (1991), p. 38.

93. Ibid.

94. "Soobshchenie o plenume TsK KP(b)U," in Sovetskaia Ukraina (Kiev) March 4, 1947 (in Ukrainian).

95. Letter on the stationery of a member of the Military Council of the 1st Ukrainian Front to L. M. Kaganovich in Moscow, November 9, 1943, in TsGAOOU, f. 1, o. 23, d. 383, l. 63.

96. "Khvylevism" was named for the famous Ukrainian writer N. G. Khvylevoi (Fitilev), who was accused of "national-deviationism" in the 1920s and who committed suicide in May 1933.

97. A. Korneichuk, "Literatura Sovetskoi Ukrainy pered velikim iubileem," in Sovetskaia Ukraina (Kiev), September 2, 1947 (in Ukrainian).

98. Ryl'skii was hounded for his speech "Kiev in the History of Ukraine," given in 1943 at a ceremonial session of the Ukrainian Academy of Sciences; for his poetic works "Travel to Youth" and "Kiev Octaves"; and for his article "Shevchenko Anniversary" in 1942. See Shapoval, Khrushchev na Ukraine (Kiev, 1990), p. 38 (in Ukrainian).

99. R. A. Medvedev, N. S. Khrushchev. Politicheskaia biografiia, p. 55.

100. Khrushchev, "Memuary," in Voprosy istorii, no. 11 (1991), p. 42.

101. Kaganovich was removed "in connection with [his] transfer to work as deputy chairman of the USSR Council of Ministers." See "Soobshchenie o plenume TsK KP(b)U," in Sovetskaia Ukraina (Kiev), December 27, 1947 (in Ukrainian).

102. Khrushchev, "Memuary," in Voprosy istorii, no. 11 (1991), p. 43.

103. XVI s"ezd KP(b)U, 26–28 ianvaria 1949 g. Materialy s"ezda (Kiev, 1949), p. 70 (in Ukrainian).

104. Song about Khrushchev, text and music, in TsGAOOU, f. 1, o. 23, d. 1498, l. 7 (front and back).

105. Letter of N. S. Khrushchev to I. V. Stalin, November 15, 1944, in TsGAOOU, f. 1, o. 23, d. 1060, l.13.

106. Ibid., l. 14.

107. M. V. Koval', Ukraina vo vtoroi mirovoi i Velikoi Otechestvennoi voinakh, 1939–1945 gg. Popytka sovremennogo kontseptual'nogo analiza (Kiev, 1994), pp. 46–47.

108. Letopis' nepokorennoi Ukrainy, book 1, p. 212 (in Ukrainian).

109. Transcript of a conference of secretaries of province committees of the

Ukrainian Communist party, heads of the provincial directorates of the NKVD and NKGB, commanders of military districts, Lvov, February 14, 1946, in TsGAOOU, f. 1, o. 23, d. 2884, l. 121.

110. Shapoval, *Chelovek i sistema*, p. 47 (in Ukrainian).

111. Report of the Ukrainian NKVD to the secretary of the Ukrainian Central Committee, Comrade N. S. Khrushchev, August 24, 1945, in TsGAOOU, f. 1, o. 23, d. 3905, l. 1.

112. Letter of N. S. Khrushchev to the commander of the troops of the Carpathian Military District, Eremenko, and member of the Military Council, Mekhlis, August 27, 1945, in TsGAOOU, f. 1, o. 23, d. 3905, l. 10.

113. Memorandum concerning the gross violation of Soviet legality by so-called special MGB groups, February 15, 1949, in TsGAOOU, f. 1, o. 16, d. 68, l. 10.

114. *Letopis' nepokorennoi Ukrainy*, book 1, pp. 353–59.

115. O. Kerziuk, "Kak vypolnialis' 'spetsial'nye zadaniia.'" Retsenziia na knigu Pavel Sudoplatov, 'Special Tasks,' Little, Brown," in *Put' svobody*, no. 7 (London, 1994), p. 882 (in Ukrainian). This story, like many other assertions of P. A. Sudoplatov, demands verification. Unfortunately, many documents that throw light on this or that aspect of Khrushchev's biography still remain unavailable. Khrushchev himself does not mention a single word about these episodes.

116. *N. S. Khrushchev (1894–1971). Materialy nauchnoi konferentsii, posviashchennoi 100-letiiu so dnia rozhdeniia N. S. Khrushcheva, 18 aprelia 1994 g.* (Moscow: Gorbachevfond, 1994), p. 39.

117. *Letopis' nepokorennoi Ukrainy*, book 1, p. 39 (in Ukrainian).

118. *XVI s"ezd KP(b) U, 25–28 ianvaria 1949 g. Materialy s"ezda* (Kiev, 1949), p. 4 (in Ukrainian).

119. Ibid., p. 51.

120. "O Khrushcheve, Brezhneve i drugikh," in *Argumenty i fakty*, no. 2 (Moscow, 1989).

121. Khrushchev, "Memuary," in *Voprosy istorii*, no. 11 (1991), p. 44.

Chapter 2: The Rise to Power

1. Space considerations for this book have demanded a significant abridgment of the original text of this article. It appears in its entirety in Russian in the journal *Rossiia*, vol. 21, nos. 11–12 (Moscow, 1994) and nos. 1–2 (Moscow, 1995).

2. Nikita Khrushchev, "Memuary," in *Voprosy istorii*, no. 11 (1991), p. 45.

3. Ibid.

4. See "Upriamyi opponent Stalina," in the collection *Oni ne molchali* (Moscow: Politizdat, 1991), pp. 409–23.

5. *Novyi mir*, no. 9 (Moscow, 1952).

6. See E. Iu. Zubkova, *Obshchestvo i reformy. 1945–1964*, chapter II-2, "Molodezhnoe dvizhenie: popytki formirovaniia oppozitsii" (Moscow: Rossiia molodaia, 1993), pp. 69–77.

7. *Sbornik zakonodatel'nykh i normativnykh aktov o repressiiakh i reabilitatsii zhertv politicheskikh repressii* (Moscow: Respublika, 1993), p. 46.

8. Note of Deputy Minister of Internal Affairs S. N. Kruglov to L. P. Beria, May 2, 1953, in TsKhSD, Kollektsiia rassekrechennykh dokumentov (Collection of Declassified Documents), f. 89, p. 18, d. 26, l. 1–2.

NOTES TO PAGES 46−55

9. Note of Minister of Internal Affairs N. P. Dudorov to the CPSU Central Committee, April 5, 1956, in TsKhSD. f. 89, p. 16, d. 1, l. 7.

10. Khrushchev, "Memuary," in *Voprosy istorii,* no. 12 (1991), p. 69. I consider this account only one of many possible versions of what actually happened.

11. Ibid., p. 51,

12. *Izvestiia TsK KPSS,* no. 7 (Moscow, 1990), pp. 76−7.

13. "Postanovlenie sovmestnogo zasedaniia Plenuma Tsentral'nogo Komiteta Kommunisticheskoi Partii Sovetskogo Soiuza, Soveta Ministrov Soiuza SSR, Presidiuma Verkhovnogo Soveta SSSR," in *Pravda,* March 7, 1953. All three organs were represented at the session by far from complete delegations.

14. *Izvestiia TsK KPSS,* no. 7 (Moscow, 1990), p. 77.

15. Personal notes of CPSU Central Committee secretary P. N. Pospelov, in R'TsKhIDNI, f. 629, o. 1, d. 54, l. 2.

16. *Izvestiia TsK KPSS,* no. 1 (Moscow, 1991), p. 160.

17. Khrushchev, "Memuary," in *Voprosy istorii,* nos. 6−7 (1992), p. 86.

18. See chapter 3 in this book, "The Rivalry with Malenkov," by Elena Zubkova, as well as E. Iu. Zubkova, "Malenkov i Khrushchev: lichnyi faktor v politike poslestalinskogo rukovodstva," in *Otechestvennaia istoriia,* no. 4 (Moscow, 1995).

19. Note of G. M. Malenkov's former assistant D. N. Sukhanov to the Central Committee's Institute of Marxism-Leninism, February 28, 1988, in the author's collection of documents.

20. The Leningrad affair involved the arrest and liquidation in 1949−1950 of several up-and-coming party leaders, including Central Committee secretary Aleksei Kuznetsov and Gosplan chairman Nikolai Voznesenskii, who had been closely associated with Leningrad. Beria and Malenkov were apparently behind the affair.

21. *Izvestiia TsK KPSS,* no. 7 (Moscow, 1990), p. 77.

22. *Na boevom postu* (Moscow), December 27, 1989, p. 3.

23. Author's calculation, based on note of Minister of Internal Affairs N. P. Dudorov to the CPSU Central Committee, April 5, 1956, in TsKhSD. f. 89, p. 16, d. 1, p. 6. According to this note, there were 114,000 political prisoners on January 1, 1956, in contrast to 468,000 on February 1, 1954. See *Argumenty i fakty,* no. 5 (Moscow, 1990), p. 8. These releases should not be confused with rehabilitation. That could be realized only through a judicial review of the case, which naturally took time. Rehabilitation for the most part took place in 1956, 1957, and subsequent years.

24. See *Pravda,* March 5 and December 19−22, 1954.

25. See, for example, Khrushchev, "Memuary," in *Voprosy istorii,* nos. 6−7 (1992), p. 86.

26. *Istoricheskii arkhiv,* no. 4 (Moscow, 1993), p. 81.

27. Handwritten original of the report "O kul'te lichnosti i ego posledstviiakh," from the personal papers of P. N. Pospelov, in RTsKhIDNI. f. 629, o. 1, d. 54, ll. 73−112.

28. *Izvestiia TsK KPSS,* no. 3 (Moscow, 1989), p. 166.

29. Conversation of the author with D. T. Shepilov, February 23, 1989, from the author's collection of documents (the original recording of the conversation is in RTsKhIDNI). The text of this conversation was later published as "'Ia byl prichasten k dokladu o kulte lichnosti . . .': beseda s D. T. Shepilovym," *Ogonyok,* no. 7 (February 1996).

30. According to KGB data, from 1930 to 1953, 3,778,234 people were sentenced

for counterrevolutionary and state crimes, of whom 786,098 were shot. See *Pravda*, February 14, 1990.

31. From the report of the Leningrad party leader F. R. Kozlov at a meeting of Leningrad province party activists, July 2, 1957, in RTsKhIDNI. f. 556, o. 2, t. 664, l. 145.

32. Note of the Central Committee Department of Party Organs to the Central Committee, February 12, 1957, in RTsKhIDNI. f. 556, o. 14, d. 77, ll. 49, 55.

33. The full stenographic record of the June 1957 plenum, which lay hidden in a secret folder for thirty-six years, was published in *Istoricheskii arkhiv*, nos. 3–6 (1993), nos. 1–2 (1994).

34. *Istoricheskii arkhiv*, no. 4 (1993), p. 64.

35. Armenian Communist party first secretary S. A. Tovmasian quoted Khrushchev in a report on the June 1957 plenum to the republic party aktiv, July 3, 1957, in RTsKhIDNI. f. 17, o. 57, d. 44, l. 170.

36. Conversation of N. S. Khrushchev with the leader of the group preparing a draft for the third party program, B. N. Ponomarev, in RTsKhIDNI. f. 586, o. 1, d. 66, l. 12.

37. Speech of N. S. Khrushchev on the draft party program, June 19, 1961, in RTsKhIDNI. f. 586, o. 1, d. 201, ll. 47–60.

38. Stenographic recording of remarks of N. S. Khrushchev on the draft for the third CPSU program, in RTsKhIDNI. f. 5 86, o. 1, d. 201, l. 14.

39. See official publication of the USSR general prosecutor N. Trubin, "Novocherkassk-62: kak eto bylo," in *Pravda*, June 3, 1991.

40. See "Novocherkassk: The Chronicle of a Tragedy," *Russian Social Sciences Review*, September-October 1992. Other suppressed revolts are described in Vadim Belotserkovsky, "Upheavals the Country Did Not Notice," *New Times International*, no. 15 (1991), pp. 8–9.

41. *Pravda*, April 24, 1964.

42. The note has not been published. Regarding its content, see M. A. Suslov's statement at the October 1964 plenum of the CPSU Central Committee, in *Istoricheskii arkhiv*, no. 1 (1993), pp. 11–12, 18.

43. Report of the First Secretary of the Ukrainian Communist party P. E. Shelest at the plenum of the Ukrainian Communist party Central Committee, November 20, 1964, in RTsKhIDNI. f. 17, o. 94, d. 969, l. 16.

44. Information on the plenum has not been published. Regarding its work see M. A. Suslov's statement at the October 1964 plenum of the CPSU Central Committee, in *Istoricheskii arkhiv*, no. 1 (1993), pp. 8, 18.

45. *Izvestiia* (Moscow), November 17, 1988.

46. *Voprosy istorii*, no. 2 (Moscow, 1989), p. 115. See also *Vlast' i oppozitsiia. Rossiiskii politicheskii protsess XX stoletiia.* (Moscow: ROSSPEN, 1995), pp. 229–30.

47. "'Khrushchevskie vremena': besedy s politicheskimi deiateliami 'velikogo desiatiletiia', s A. N. Shelepinym i V. E. Semichastnym 27 marta, 22 maia 1989 g.; s N. G. Egorychevym 19 sentiabria 1990 g." in *Neizvestnaia Rossiia. XX vek* (Moscow: Istoricheskoe nasledie, 1992), pp. 270–304.

48. The October 13–14, 1964, Presidium session was not transcribed. Khrushchev's words are quoted from notes taken by A. N. Shelepin, a participant in the session, which he dictated into a tape recorder in a conversation with the author. It is included in its entirety in the almanac named in note 46, pp. 283–84. This recording was later published by Shelepin himself in *Trud* (Moscow), March 14–15, 1991.

49. Materials of the October 14, 1964, plenum were published almost thirty years later. See *Istoricheskii arkhiv*, no. 1 (Moscow, 1993), pp. 3–19.

50. N. S. Khrushchev, *Vospominaniia. Izbrannye otryvki*, edited by V. Chalidze (New York, 1982), pp. 274–6.

Chapter 3: The Rivalry with Malenkov

1. A. I. Kokurin, ed., "Vosstanie v Steplage (mai–iiun' 1954 g.)," in *Otechestvennye arkhivy*, no. 4 (1994), p. 33.

2. Report of the USSR Ministry of Agriculture and Reserves, "O nedostatkakh v sel'skom khoziaistve i merakh po uluchsheniiu del v kolkhozakh i sovkhozakh" (July 1953), in TsKhSD, f. 5, o. 30, d. 20, l. 9.

3. Stenographic record of session of the plenum of the USSR Central Committee, January 31, 1955, in TsKhSD. f. 2, o. 1, d. 127, l. 35.

4. See Protocols of the sessions of the Secretariat of the VKP(b) Central Committee, in RTsKhIDNI, f. 17, o. 116, d. 643.

5. Citation from "Plenum TsK KPSS. Iul' 1953 g. Stenogr. otchet," in *Izvestiia TsK KPSS*, no. 1 (1991), p. 210.

6. Note of N. S. Khrushchev, "O polozhenii del v Latviiskoi SSR" (June 1953), and draft resolution of the CPSU Central Committee, "O polozhenii del v Latviiskoi SSR" (June 1953), in TsKhSD. f. 5, o. 30, d. 6, ll. 20–29.

7. "Plenum TsK KPSS. Iul' 1953 g. Stenogr. otchet," in *Izvestiia TsK KPSS*, no. 1 (1991), p. 152.

8. *Sto sorok besed s Molotovym: iz dnevnika F. Chueva* (Moscow, 1991), p. 358.

9. Radiogram from V. Kuk to V. Okhrimovich, no later than July 1953, in TsKhSD. f. 5, o. 8, d. 3, ll. 33–34.

10. Stenographic record of the 4th Moscow city conference of the VKP(b) (May 23–28, 1937), in TsAODM, f. 4, o. 8, d. 3, ll. 33–34.

11. Ibid., l. 34.

12. V. P. Popov, *Rossiiskaia derevnia posle voiny. 1945–1953 gg: sbornik dokumentov* (Moscow, 1993), p. 149.

13. Report of the USSR Ministry of Agriculture and Reserves, in TsKhSD, f. 5, o. 30, d. 20, ll. 2–34.

14. G. M. Malenkov, *Rech' na piatoi sessii Verkhovnogo Soveta SSSR* (Moscow, 1953).

15. Until 1953 the agricultural tax was based on the principle of progressive rates, and was calculated from the overall sum of income from a peasant household in various forms of production, independent of the scale of that household. As a result, the most productive households wound up in the least advantageous position. Beginning in July 1, 1953, the principle of fixed tax levies per hectare of a private plot was introduced, the extent of its income notwithstanding. The overall sum of the tax decreased from 9.5 billion rubles in 1952 to 4.1 billion in 1954. See *Ekonomicheskaia zhizn' v SSSR*, vol. 2 (Moscow 1967), p. 462.

16. "Pis'mo M. Nikolaevoi—N. Khrushchevu. Noiabr' 1956," in *Izvestiia TsK KPSS*, no. 6 (1989), p. 149.

17. N. Khrushchev, "O stroitel'stve i blagoustroistve v kolkhozakh," in *Pravda*, March 4, 1951).

18. Secret letter from the VKP(b) Central Committee to the Central Committees of

the parties of union republics, kraikoms, obkoms, okruzhkoms, gorkoms, and rai-koms, "O zadachakh kolkhoznogo stroitel'stva v sviazi s ukrupneniem melkikh kolkho-zov," April 2, 1951, in *Otechestvennye arkhivy*, no. 1 (1994), pp. 46–47.

19. In his memoirs, Khrushchev recalled Stalin's derogatory remarks about Ma-lenkov made on the eve of the 19th Party Congress in 1952. See memoirs in *Voprosy istorii*, no. 11 (1991), p. 39. The Central Committee plenum of January 31, 1955, which recommended Malenkov's demotion from the post of chairman of the Council of Min-isters, charged that he "lacked necessary knowledge and experience in agricultural mat-ters." See plenum resolution "O tovarishche Malenkove, G. M.," in TsKhSD, f. 2, o. 1, d. 116, l. 7.

20. "O kul'te lichnosti i ego posledstviakh. Doklad N. S. Khrushcheva XX s"ezdu KPSS. 25 fevralia 1956 g.," in *Svet i teni "velikogo desiatiletiia": N. S. Khrushchev i ego vremia* (Leningrad, 1989), p. 98.

21. Stenographic record of session of the plenum of the CPSU Central Committee, January 31, 1955, in TsKhSD. f. 2, o. 1, d. 127, l. 30.

22. Ibid., l. 58.

23. Ibid., ll. 30, 38.

24. Ibid., l. 38.

25. *XX s"ezd i ego istoricheskie real'nosti* (Moscow, 1991), p. 110.

26. *Resheniia partii i pravitel'stva po khoziaistvennym voprosam*, vol. 4 (Moscow, 1968), p. 295.

27. Ibid.

28. In the mid-1950s, from two-thirds to three-quarters of the entire potato crop in the country, and around half the vegetables, came from private plots. All the way through 1958, up to 65 percent of meat production, and even more of milk, came from private plots. See O. M. Verbitskaia, *Rossiiskoe krest'ianstvo: ot Stalina k Khrushchevu. Ser. 40-kh - nach. 60-kh gg.* (Moscow, 1992), p. 74. An individual plot—literally a "personal supplemental plot" *(lichnoe podsobnoe khoziaistvo)*—was more than supplemental, even for peasant families. In 1955, for example, from 40 to 52 percent of the overall in-come of families came from private plots. See M. A. Beznin, *Krest'ianskoe khoziaistvo v Rossiiskom Nechernozem'e. 1950–1965 gg.* (Moscow, Vologda, 1990), pp. 11–12.

29. *Resheniia partii i pravitel'stva po khoziaistvennym voprosam*, vol. 4 (Moscow, 1968), pp. 349–351.

30. Stenographic record of meeting of secretaries of obkoms, kraikoms, and the central committees of the Communist parties of union republics, June 18, 1958, in TsKhSD. f. 5, o. 30, d. 248, l. 39.

31. *KPSS v resoliutsiiakh i resheniiakh s"ezdov, konferentsii i plenumov TsK*, vol. 4 (Moscow, 1986), p. 289; *Plenum TsK KPSS 22–25 dekabria 1959 g. Stenogr. otchet.* (Mos-cow, 1960), p. 167.

32. Verbitskaia, *Rossiiskoe krest'ianstvo*, p. 73.

33. Ibid.

34. For a summary and translations of new evidence from Russian, German, and Hungarian archives concerning the June 1953 East German uprising, see *Cold War In-ternational History Project Bulletin*, no. 10 (March 1998), pp. 61–110.

35. Stenographic record of session of the plenum of the CPSU Central Committee (January 31, 1955), in TsKhSD. f. 2, o. 1, d. 127, l. 28.

36. Resolution of the plenum of the CPSU Central Committee, "O tov. Malenkove G. M.," January 31, 1955, in TsKhSD. f. 2, o. 1, d. 116, l. 5.

37. G. M. Malenkov, "O vrednykh deianiiakh N. Khrushcheva," no date, Malenkov family archive.

38. Stenographic record of session of the plenum of the CPSU Central Committee, February 13, 1956, in TsKhSD. f. 2, o. 1, d. 183, l. 4.

39. Ibid.

40. Report of N. S. Khrushchev, "O kul'te lichnosti," with corrections of members of the Presidium of the CPSU Central Committee, in TsKhSD, f. 1, o. 2, d. 16.

41. G. M. Malenkov, "'Kul't lichnosti'—bolezn' zatiazhnaia i zatianuvshaiasia" (no date), in Malenkov family archives.

Chapter 4: Repression and Rehabilitation

1. Zhukov's speech is in the transcript of the June 1957 plenum published in *Istoricheskii arkhiv*, no. 3 (1993), pp. 19–20.

2. Even at the time of the 20th Party Congress, when Khrushchev gave his report on the personality cult, he declared that oppositionists should have undergone punishment, just not as harsh. He thought that it had not been necessary to shoot them all. In addition, he asserted that Stalin acted the way he did because he was sure that he was serving the interests of the party and the laboring masses, and that he was defending the achievements of the revolution. See APRF, f. 32, o. 1. d. 169, ll. 32–33.

3. TsAODM, f. 4, o. 7, d. 2, l. 227.

4. See *Podmoskov'e*, January 16, 1993, p. 5.

5. See *Trud*, June 4, 1992.

6. Information Memorandum, Politburo Commission for Supplementary Study of Materials Related to Repressions Which Took Place from the Thirties through the Early Fifties, and of Anti-Constitutional Practices of Those Years, pp. 11–12.

7. APRF, f. 3. o. 58, d, 179, l. 27.

8. See Alexander Nekrich, *The Punished Peoples* (New York: Norton, 1978).

9. Beria's April 4, 1953, decree stated" "It has been established by the USSR Ministry of Internal Affairs that in the investigatory work of Ministry of State Security organs, there have occurred gross distortions of Soviet laws, arrests of innocent Soviet citizens, unbridled falsification of investigatory materials, and the broad use of various forms of torture: cruel beatings of prisoners, round-the-clock handcuffing behind the back that in certain cases continued for several months, extended deprivation of sleep, incarceration in cold solitary confinement cells in an unclothed state, and others. According to orders from the bureau of the USSR Ministry of State Security, beatings of prisoners took place in locations specially designed for that purpose in Lefortovo and internal prisons and were assigned to a certain group of specially identified individuals, chosen from among prison workers, with the use of every possible instrument of torture. Such fiendish 'methods of interrogation' led to a situation in which many innocent prisoners have been brought by investigators to a condition of physical exhaustion and moral depression, with some even wholly losing their humanity. Taking advantage of prisoners in such a condition, investigator-falsifiers slipped them fabricated 'confessions' of anti-Soviet and spy-terrorist work." In GARF, f. R-9401, o. 1, d. 1299, l. 246.

10. TsKhSD, f. 5, o. 47, d. 89, ll. 30–4.

11. APRF f. 3, o. 58, d. 321, ll. 37–9, 42, 43, 45.

12. Ibid., l. 63.

13. TsKhSD, f. 3, o. 8, d. 388, l. 61.

14. Ibid., ll. 61, 62.

15. APRF, f. 3, o. 24, d. 489, ll. 23-101.

16. RTsKhIDNI, f. 39, o. 3, d. 120, ll. 115, 116.

17. These data are contained in a May 26, 1954, memorandum from Minister of Internal Affairs S. N. Kruglov. In APRF, f. 3, o. 58, d. 169, ll. 50-1.

18. *Rossiiskaia Gazeta*, April 14, 1994.

19. See L. K. Chukovskaia, *Zapiski ob Anne Akhmatove*, vol. 2, 1952–1962 (Paris, 1980), p. 7.

20. TsKhSD, f. 89, per. 18, d. 38, ll. 1, 4.

21. *Izvestiia TsK KPSS* 11 (1989), pp. 58-9.

22. APRF, f. 3, o. 24, d. 490, ll. 13-17. See also Iurii Aksiutin's chapter in this book.

23. APRF, *Dokumenty massovoi rassylki* (Documents for mass distribution), no. 294.

24. Ibid., no. 300.

25. APRF, f. 3, o. 23, d. 491, l. 53.

26. See Petro G. Grigorenko, *Memoirs*, trans. Thomas P. Whitney (New York: Norton, 1982).

27. APRF, f. 3, o. 2.4, d. 489, l. 89; TsKhSD, f. 5, o. 6, d. 1077, l. 4.

28. APRF, f. 3.

29. For further details on the Tbilisi massacre, see Iurii Aksiutin's chapter in this book.

30. [Editors' note:] An official investigation carried out by the chief military procurator's office in 1990–1991 concluded as follows: "The decision to use force, taken on the spot by Presidium members, did not receive Khrushchev's concurrence in advance. At the start, he had opposed the use of extreme measures." Report on Conclusions of Chief Military Procurator's Investigation, *Krasnaia Zvezda*, October 7, 1995, p. 7.

31. TsKhSD, f 6, o. 6, d. 1266, l. 8 (reverse).

32. Ibid., d. 1267, l. 5 (reverse).

33. Ibid., d. 1269, l. 2 and d. 1271, l. 4.

Chapter 5: Khrushchev and the Countryside

1. Nikita S. Khrushchev cited these figures himself in his keynote speech on behalf of the Central Committee to the 20th Party Congress, "Rezkoe uvelichenie proizvodstva sel'skokhoziaistvennoi produktsii—vsenarodnaia zadacha" (February 14, 1956), in *Stroitel'stvo kommunizma v SSSR i razvitie sel'skogo khoziaistva*, vol. 2 (Moscow: Gosudarstvennoe izdatel'stvo politicheskoi literatury, 1962), p. 196. All notes refer to the eight volumes of this source. The publication year of each volume is indicated in its first citation.

2. Ibid.

3. Khrushchev speech at a Leningrad meeting of agricultural workers from the provinces and autonomous republics of the northwest RSFSR, May 22, 1957, vol. 2, p. 447.

4. Khrushchev, "Po-novomu planirovat' proizvodstvo v kolkhozakh i sovkhozakh, konkretno rukovodit' khoziaistvom," speech at a Saratov meeting of agricultural workers from southeast provinces, March 18, 1955, vol. 2, p. 28.

5. Khrushchev, "Kadry i tekhnika—reshaiushchaia sila v pod"eme sel'skogo khoz-

iaistva," speech at all-union meeting of Machine-Tractor Station workers, January 28, 1954, vol. 1 (1962), p. 132.

6. Khrushchev, "Po-novomu planirovat'," vol. 2, p. 28.

7. Khrushchev, speech at Leningrad meeting, vol. 2, pp. 449–50.

8. Ibid., p. 449.

9. Ibid., p. 450.

10. Ibid., p. 458.

11. Khrushchev, "Chelovek ukrashaet zemliu," conversation with people from the Don at Veshensk village, August 31, 1959, vol. 4 (1963), p. 57.

12. Khrushchev, "Polnee izpol'zuem rezervy dlia dal'neishego pod"ema sel'skogo khoziaistva," speech at Central Committee plenum, December 25, 1959, vol. 4., pp. 68–9.

13. Ibid.

14. Ibid., pp. 71–72.

15. Ibid., p. 70.

16. Khrushchev, "Bor'ba KPSS za pod"em sel'skogo khoziaistva," speech at a conference of representatives of Communist and Worker parties of European Socialist countries on the exchange of experience in agricultural development, February 1960, vol. 4, p. 115.

17. Ibid., p. 116.

18. Ibid., p. 117.

19. Khrushchev, "Povyshenie blagosostoianiia naroda i zadachi dal'neishego uvelicheniia proizvodstva sel'skokhoziaistvennykh produktov," theses for presentation at the January 1961 Central Committee plenum, January 5, 1961, vol. 4, p. 224.

20. Ibid., p. 217.

21. Khrushchev, "Polnee ispol'zuem rezervy," vol. 4, p. 76.

22. Khrushchev, "Protiv blagodushiia, samouspokoennosti i zaznaistva pervymi uspekhami v razvitii sel'skogo khoziaistva," note to the Central Committee Presidium, October 29, 1960, vol. 4, p. 164.

23. Ibid., p. 167.

24. Ibid.

25. Ibid., p. 168.

26. Khrushchev, "Povyshenie blagosostoianiia naroda," vol. 4, p. 200.

27. Khrushchev, "Protiv blagodushiia," vol. 4, p. 163.

28. Ibid.

29. Ibid.

30. Khrushchev, "Povyshenie blagosostoianiia naroda i zadachi dal'neishego uvelicheniia proizvodstva sel'skokhoziaistvennykh produktov," speech at Central Committee plenum, January 17, 1961, vol. 4, p. 272.

31. Khrushchev, "Uspeshno pretvorim v zhizn' resheniia ianvarskogo plenuma TsK KPSS," speech at a plenum of the Ukrainian Central Committee, January 28, 1961, vol. 4, p. 396.

32. Ibid., pp. 398, 413.

33. Khrushchev, "Polnee ispol'zovat' vozmozhnosti severnogo Kavkaza dlia uvelicheniia proizvodstva sel'skokhoziaistvennykh produktov," speech at a conference of outstanding agricultural workers from regions of the northern Caucasus, in Rostov-na-Donu, February 1, 1961, vol. 4, p. 437.

34. Khrushchev, "Opiraias' na peredovoi opyt i dostizheniia nauki, dobivat'sia ob-

shchego pod"ema sel'skogo khoziaistva," speech at Voronezh meeting of outstanding agricultural workers from the provinces of the central Black Earth region of the Russian Federation, February 11, 1961, vol. 5 (1963), pp. 35–36.

35. Khrushchev, "Kadry i tekhnika," vol. 1, p. 139.

36. Khrushchev, "Prevratim vse sovkhozy v obraztsovye, vysokodokhodnye khoziaistva," speech at all-union meeting of sovkhoz workers, February 5, 1954, vol. 1, p. 165.

37. Ibid., p. 167.

38. Khrushchev, "Opiraias' na peredovoi opyt," vol. 5, p. 12.

39. Khrushchev, "O nekotorykh neotlozhnykh zadachakh v oblasti sel'skogo khoziaistva," note to CPSU Central Committee Presidium, July 20, 1961, vol. 5, p. 422.

40. Ibid.

41. Khrushchev, "Sovremennyi etap kommunisticheskogo stroitel'stva i zadachi partii po uluchsheniiu rukovodstva sel'skim khoziaistvom," speech at CPSU Central Committee plenum, March 5, 1962, vol. 6 (1963), p. 424.

42. Khrushchev, "Sovetskii narod uspeshno vypolnit programmu dal'neishego razvitiia sel'skogo khoziaistva," concluding remarks at CPSU Central Committee plenum, March 9, 1962, vol. 6, p. 4–7.

43. Khrushchev, "Za boevuiu rabotu, tovarishchi!" speech at meeting of agricultural worker delegates to the 22nd Party Congress, November 2, 1961, vol. 6, p. 56.

44. Khrushchev, "Pravil'noe ispol'zovanie zemli—vazhneishee uslovie bystrogo uvelicheniia proizvodstva zerna, miasa, moloka i drugikh sel'skokhoziaistvennykh produktov," speech at Moscow meeting of agricultural workers from provinces and autonomous republics of non-Black Earth region of the RSFSR, December 14, 1961, vol. 6, p. 236.

45. Khrushchev, "Sozdat' ustoichivuiu bazu dlia polucheniia vysokikh garantirovannykh urozhaev," speech at Krasnodar meeting of agricultural workers from the northern Caucasus, September 26, 1963, vol. 8 (1964), p. 179.

46. Khrushchev, "Sovetskii narod," vol. 6, p. 457.

47. Ibid, p. 455.

48. For an account of the unrest in Novocherkassk, see Dmitri Volkogonov, *Seni vozhdei*, vol. 1 (Moscow: Novosti, 1995), pp. 387–88.

49. Khrushchev, "Sovremennyi etap," vol. 6, p. 368.

50. Khrushchev, "Uskorennoe razvitie khimicheskoi promyshlennosti—vazhneishee uslovie pod"ema sel'skokhoziaistvennogo proizvodstva i rosta blagosostoianiia naroda," speech at CPSU Central Committee plenum, December 9, 1963, vol. 8, pp. 291–92.

51. E. Y. Zubkova, *Obshchestvo i reformy 1945–1964* (Moscow, 1993), p. 107.

52. Khrushchev, "Uspeshno osushchestvit' resheniia fevral'skogo plenuma TsK KPSS ob intensifikatsii sel'skokhoziaistvennogo proizvodstva," speech at meeting of leading workers of party, soviet, and agricultural organs, February 28, 1964, vol. 8, p. 526.

53. Khrushchev, "Povyshenie blagosostoianiia naroda," vol. 4, p. 328.

54. Khrushchev, "Uvelichenie proizvodstva sel'skokhoziaistvennykh produktov—vazhneishaia zadacha kommunisticheskogo stroitel'stva," speech at Kiev meeting of agricultural workers from the Ukrainian SSR, December 22, 1961, vol. 6, p. 270.

55. Khrushchev, "Vse sily partii i naroda na vypolnenie planov kommunisticheskogo stroitel'stva," concluding remarks at CPSU Central Committee plenum, December 13, 1963, vol. 8, p. 348.

56. See Michael Voslensky, *Nomenklatura: The Soviet Ruling Class,* trans. Eric Mosbacher (Garden City, N.Y.: Doubleday, 1984).

Chapter 6: Industrial Management and Economic Reform

The author wishes to thank Professor Philip Hanson of the Center for Russian and East European Studies of the University of Birmingham and the editors of this volume for their suggestions and comments on earlier drafts of this paper.

1. See, for example, Abraham Katz, *The Struggle for Economic Reform in the Soviet Union* (London: Praeger, 1972), pp. 97–100; Michel Tatu, *Power in the Kremlin* (London: Michael Collins, 1969), pp. 249–60 and 283–93; also Jan Ake Dellenbrant, *Reformists and Traditionalists: A Study of Soviet Discussions about Economic Reform, 1960–1965* (Stockholm: Rabén & Sjögren, 1972). Among recent Soviet/Russian writers, Gavriil Popov has drawn attention to Khrushchev's failure to move beyond the bounds of the "command-administrative system"; G. Popov, "Dva tsveta vremeni, ili uroki Khrushcheva," *Ogonek* 42 (October) 1989.

2. Katz, *Struggle for Economic Reform,* pp. 97–100.

3. R. F. Miller, "Khrushchev and the Soviet Economy: Management by Re-Organisation," in R. F. Miller and Ferenc Feher, eds., *Khrushchev and the Communist World* (London: Croom Helm, 1984), pp. 109, 113. Khrushchev himself knew these dangers firsthand from his experience with the ill-fated *agrogorod* scheme. W. J. Tompson, *Khrushchev: A Political Life* (London: Macmillan, 1995), pp. 99–103.

4. These debates, and the parallel discussions that unfolded in other communist countries, have been analyzed in a number of Western works, including Katz, *The Struggle for Economic Reform;* Gregory Grossman, ed., *Value and Plan: Economic Calculation and Organization in Eastern Europe* (Berkeley: University of California Press, 1960); Dellenbrant, *Reformists and Traditionalists.*

5. E. Liberman, *O planirovanii pribyli v promyshlennosti* (Moscow, 1950).

6. Katz, *Reform,* p. 30.

7. These included Bulganin (*Pravda,* 17 May 1955 and 17 July 1955), Pervukhin, *XX S"ezd Kommunisticheskoi Partii Sovetskogo Soyuza: stenograficheskii otchet,* vol. 2 [Moscow: Gospolitizdat, 1956], pp. 130–31, Kosygin (*Pravda,* 16 July 1960), and Podgornyi (*Pravda,* 21 November 1962).

8. *Pravda,* May 7, 1957; October 18, 1961; November 20, 1962. See also his comments on the subject in N. S. Khrushchev, "Nasushchnye voprosy razvitiia mirovoi sotsialisticheskoi sistemy," *Kommunist* 12 (August 1962).

9. This theme was addressed in Khrushchev's speeches at home and abroad: *Pravda,* May 11, 1962; November 20, 1962; August 25, 1963; and April 2, 1964.

10. *Pravda,* July 2, 1959; Miller, "Management by Re-Organisation," p. 124.

11. *Pravda,* December 15, 1963.

12. *Pravda,* April 26, 1963; June 29, 1963; and July 14, 1964.

13. Alfred Zauberman, "The Soviet Debate on the Law of Value and Price Formation," in Grossman, ed., *Value and Plan,* p. 17.

14. *Pravda,* May 8, 1953; December 12, 1953; January 5, 1954; September 21 and 28, 1954; October 9 and 14, 1954. The theme of *kontrol'* with respect to industry in particular is addressed in *Pravda,* October 20, November 2, 10, and 23, 1954.

15. *Izvestiia,* December 23, 1954, and September 22, 1956. *Pravda,* February 16, 17, 20, and 23, 1956 (criticism of the ministries during the 20th Party Congress).

16. *XX S"ezd*, vol. 1, pp. 106–7.

17. For the details of these reorganizations, which touched most sectors of industry, see *Vedomosti Verkhovnogo Soveta SSSR,* September 18, 1953, p. 1; September 25, 1953, p. 1; December 1, 1953, p. 1; December 6, 1954, p. 813; January 23, 1955, p. 3. Also *Zasedaniia Verkhovnogo Soveta SSSR: stenograficheskii otchet* 4 (1) 1954, pp. 547–48; 4 (2) 1955, p. 517; 4 (4) 1955, pp. 463–64; 4 (5) 1956, pp. 368–39. And *Direktivy KPSS i Sovetskogo pravitel'stva po khoziaistvennym voprosam,* vol. 4 (Moscow: Gospolitizdat, 1958), pp. 627–30.

18. See, e.g., the May 1955 decree on the budgetary powers of union republics; *Direktivy,* vol. 4, pp. 400–417.

19. Katz, *Reform,* p. 28.

20. The "theses" that formed the basis for the sovnarkhoz discussion were advanced in Khrushchev's own name rather than in the name of the Central Committee or any other body. *Pravda,* March 30, 1957.

21. See R. W. Davies, "Industrial Planning Reconsidered," *Soviet Studies* 8, no. 4 (April 1957), pp. 426–36.

22. *Izvestiia,* April 12, 20, and 27, 1957.

23. *Pravda,* April 4 and 16, 1957. *Izvestiia,* April 13, 20, and 27, 1957. *Sovetskaia Rossiya,* April 11, 1957.

24. For a detailed examination of the discussion and its impact on the sovnarkhoz reorganization, see Tompson, "Khrushchev and the Territorial Apparatus," D.Phil. thesis, University of Oxford, 1991, pp.153–72.

25. *Izvestiia,* April 12, 14, 16, 20 and 27, 1957; *Pravda,* April 14, 1957. See also A. Krylov, "O pravakh direktora zavoda v novykh usloviiakh," *Kommunist* 6 (April 1957), pp. 44–49. For a description of plant managers' hostility to the new sovnarkhozy, see V. N. Novikov, "V gody rukovodstva N. S. Khrushcheva," *Voprosy istorii* 1 (January 1989), p. 112.

26. This is evident both in the original theses and in Khrushchev's address to the Supreme Soviet in May. *Pravda,* March 30 and May 8, 1957.

27. These changes are described in detail in Tompson, *Khrushchev and the Territorial Apparatus,* pp. 178–81 and 227–56.

28. Nuritdin Mukhitdinov stated in 1989 that Khrushchev was recognized as the driving force behind the ministerial reorganizations that preceded the sovnarkhoz reform, not to mention the reform itself. See his interview with V. A. Starkov in "12 let s Khrushchevym," *Argumenty i fakty,* 44 (October 1989), p. 6.

29. *Pravda* and *Izvestiia,* May 17 and 19, 1955; see also "Ocherki nashikh dnei: tri dnia v Kremle," *Novyi Mir* 7 (July 1955). Malenkov had addressed many of the same issues in 1941 at the 18th Party Conference (G. M. Malenkov, "O zadachakh partiinykh organizatsii v oblasti promyshlennosti i transporta," *Bol'shevik,* nos. 3–4 (February 1941), pp. 13–17. Managers had voiced similar complaints even under Stalin; see, e.g., *Pravda,* September 10, 1940, and I. Likhachev, "Khozraschet na avtozavode imeni Stalina," *Planovoe khozyaistvo* 5 (May 1948), pp. 42–50; especially page 50, which sets out virtually the entire agenda for the Liberman debates.

30. *Pravda,* July 17, 1955.

31. *Pravda* and *Izvestiia,* May 19, 1955.

32. Zauberman, "The Soviet Debate," p. 40, no. 1. See also the list of Soviet articles on enterprise rights, profit, etc., which appeared during early 1956 in Davies, "Industrial Planning Reconsidered," p. 426.

33. *Direktivy*, vol. 4, pp. 425–43.

34. *Direktivy*, vol. 4, pp. 451–57.

35. A. Kosytsin and B. Laptev, "Khoziaistvennoe pravo sovetskogo gosudarstvo," *Kommunist* 10 (July 1965), p. 91.

36. *Pravda*, May 7, 1957.

37. *Pravda*, June 25, 1957; January 9, 1958; and June 25, 1959; *Izvestiia*, December 8, 1957; November 22, 1961; December 20 and 23, 1961; and May 24, 1962.

38. Michael Kaser, "The Reorganization of Soviet Industry and Its Effects on Decision Making," in Grossman, ed., *Value and Plan*, pp. 224–25; P. J. D. Wiles, "Rationality, the Market, Decentralization and the Territorial Principle," in Grossman, ed., *Value and Plan*, p. 201.

39. Kaser, "Reorganization," pp. 224–25.

40. N. S. Khrushchev, *Khrushchev Remembers: The Last Testament* (Boston: Little, Brown, 1974), pp. 127–28.

41. *The Times* (London), February 1, 1958, p. 5.

42. RTsKhIDNI, f. 17, o. 26, d. 770, l. 47; and Iu. I. Shapoval, *N. S. Khrushchov na Ukraini* (Kiev, 1990), p. 9.

43. Shapoval, *Khrushchov*, p. 9.

44. N. S. Khrushchev, *Khrushchev Remembers* (London: André Deutsch, 1971), pp. 18–20; *Desiatii z'izd Komunistichnoi Partii (Bil'shovikiv) Ukraini: stenografichnii zvit* (Kharkov, 1928), p. 236.

45. RTsKhIDNI, f. 17, o. 26, d. 411, ll. 25–33; *Visti VTsVK*, April 12, 1929.

46. *Tret'ia moskovskaia oblastnaia i vtoraia gorodskaia konferentsii VKP(b): Biulleten'*, no. 4 (Moscow, 1932), pp. 30–35; *IV Moskovskaia oblastnaia i III gorodskaia konferentsii VKP(b): stenograficheskii otchet* (Moscow, 1934), pp. 276, 278, 281; N. S. Khrushchev, *Stroit' prochno, bystro, krasivo i deshevo* (Moscow, 1935), pp. 7–8; Khrushchev, *Khrushchev Remembers*, pp. 62-63, 68–70; *Rasskazy stroitelei metro* (Moscow, 1935), pp. 44, 62–63, 86–88; 226–31, 257; *Piat' let moskovskogo metro* (Moscow, 1940), pp. 33; *Pravda*, March 16, 1935; *Kak my stroili metro* (Moscow, 1935), pp. 659–50.

47. *Tret'ia moskovskaia . . .*, pp. 30–35.

48. Khrushchev's primary economic focus during this period was agriculture rather than industry, but the attitudes he expressed were much the same: *Visti VTsVK*, August 3, 8, and 18, 1938, and September 29, 1940; RTsKhIDNI, f. 17, o. 45, d. 1966, ll. 97–109; f. 17, o. 45, d. 1967, ll. 4, 17–20, 26, 29, 47–50; N. S. Khrushchev, *Nashi zadachi v vosstanovlenii i blagoustroistve gorodov i stroitel'stve v selakh i kolkhozakh* (Moscow, 1945), p. 12.

49. A. N. Ponomarev, *N. S. Khrushchev: put' k liderstvu* (Moscow, 1990), p. 53, 55–56. Central State Archive for Social Movements of the City of Moscow (former Moscow Party Archive), f. 3, o. 129, d. 188.

50. *XXII S"ezd Kommunisticheskoi Partii Sovetskogo Soiuza: stenograficheskii otchet* (Moscow: Gospolitizdat, 1962), vol. 1, pp. 250–51.

51. Kendall E. Bailes, *Technology and Society under Lenin and Stalin: Origins of the Soviet Technical Intelligentsia, 1917–1941* (Princeton, N.J.: Princeton University Press, 1978), p. 265.

52. It might be argued that party work was no less dangerous than production work, and possibly more so. During much of 1937–1938, this was undoubtedly true, at least in the upper echelons of the party hierarchy. However, periodic pressure on engineers and other specialists was a feature of the system from the early 1920s until World War

II, so Bailes's assertion that there was a flight from production on the part of specialists would seem to make sense.

53. "Sovershenstvovat' rabotu partiinykh shkol," *Partiinaia zhizn'* 10 (May 1957), pp. 29–31.

54. *XX S"ezd*, vol. 1, pp. 103–4.

55. George Breslauer, *Khrushchev and Brezhnev as Leaders: Building Authority in Soviet Politics* (London: George Allen & Unwin, 1982), pp.82–144.

56. *Plenum Tsentral'nogo Komiteta Kommunisticheskoi Partii Sovetskogo Soiuza (19–23 noiabria 1962 g.): stenograficheskii otchet* (Moscow, 1962), pp. 444–52.

57. *Pravda*, November 20, 1962.

58. *Pravda*, March 6, 1962.

59. Grey Hodnett, "The Obkom First Secretaries," *Slavic Review* 24, no. 4 (December 1965), p. 642; John A. Armstrong, "Party Bifurcation and Elite Interests," *Soviet Studies* 17, part 4 (1966), pp. 426–27.

60. See, e.g., Hodnett, "Obkom First Secretaries"; Armstrong, "Party Bifurcation"; Tatu, *Power*, pp. 249–60 and 283–93; Barbara Chotiner, *Khrushchev's Party Reform: Coalition Building and Institutional Innovation* (London: Greenwood Press, 1984); Gavriil Popov, "Dva tsveta vremeni," p. 16; and Tompson, *Khrushchev and the Territorial Apparatus*, pp. 195–200, 259–62.

61. Katz, *Reform*, pp. 66–68.

62. N. S. Khrushchev, *Stroitel'stvo kommunizma v SSSR i razvitie sel'skogo khoziaistva*, vol. 7 (Moscow: Gospolitizdat, 1963), pp. 163–77. In fact, he appears to have first discussed the proposal with Brezhnev, Nikolai Podgornyi, and Dmitrii Polianskii during his Black Sea holiday earlier in the summer; Sergei Khrushchev, *Khrushchev on Khrushchev*, ed. and trans. William Taubman (Boston: Little, Brown, 1990), p. 20.

63. Tatu, *Power*, pp. 249–60 and 283–93.

64. *Pravda*, May 8, 1957; October 18, 1961; November 20, 1962.

65. Katz, *Reform*, p. 64.

66. A. Zverev, "Against Oversimplification in Solving Complex Problems," in Myron Sharpe, ed., *Planning Profit and Incentives in the USSR*, vol. 1, *The Liberman Discussion* (White Plains, N.Y., 1966), p. 148.

67. For a discussion of the earliest debates on the issue, see Katz, *Reform*, pp. 28–40.

68. *Pravda*, November 20, 1962.

69. Khrushchev, "Nasushchnye voprosy," pp. 6, 15–16; *Pravda*, November 20, 1962.

70. L. Gatovskii, "Rol' pribyli v sotsialisticheskoi ekonomiki," *Kommunist* 18 (December 1962), pp. 60–72.

71. For the dogmatic/Stalinist Khrushchev at his best, see *Pravda*, February 3, 1955; by 1964 his position had shifted noticeably: *Pravda*, February 15, 1964; October 2, 1964.

72. Katz, *Reform*, pp. 88–89.

73. *Pravda*, November 20, 1962.

74. G. Anisimov, F. Veselkov, and A. Sokolovskii, "Podvedenie itogov ekonomicheskoi diskussii," *Voprosy ekonomiki* 2 (February 1964), pp. 144–48.

75. Breslauer, *Khrushchev and Brezhnev*, pp. 35–38, 60, 78–79.

76. Popov, "Dva tsveta vremeni," p. 14.

77. *Pravda*, September 6, 1933; N. S. Khrushchev, *Itogi dekabr'skogo Plenuma TsK*

VKP(b) I zadachi moskovskikh bol'shevikov (Moscow, 1936), pp. 7, 13–18; Khrushchev, *Nashi zadachi v vosstanovlenii*, p. 12; Tompson, *Political Life*, p.50–52, 214–16.

78. S. Khrushchev, *Khrushchev on Khrushchev*, pp. 18–19.

79. *Pravda*, November 20, 1962.

80. *Pravda*, December 15, 1963, and July 14, 1964.

81. *Pravda*, May 17, 1964.

82. See the articles reproduced in Sharpe, ed., *The Liberman Discussion*, pp. 193–218; and *Pravda*, August 23, 1964.

83. Katz, *Reform*, p. 72.

84. N. A. Barsukov, "Kak byl 'nizlozhen' N. S. Khrushchev," *Obshchestvennye nauki* 6 (November 1989), pp. 130–31; P. A. Rodionov, "Kak nachinalsia zastoi," *Znamia* 8 (August 1989), p. 191; Anatolii Strelianyi, "Poslednii romantik," *Druzhba narodov* 11 (November 1989), p. 225; *Trud*, 26 (November 1989).

85. Barsukov, "Nizlozhen," pp. 130–31. Sergei Khrushchev disputes this claim, and Barsukov does not indicate what the basis for his assertion is. It is not implausible, however, given that vertical management had by that time been restored in everything but name anyway.

86. Alec Nove, *An Economic History of the USSR*, 2d ed. (London: Penguin, 1989), pp. 367–68.

87. Vladimir Kontorovich, "Lessons of the 1965 Soviet Economic Reform," *Soviet Studies* 40, no. 2 (April 1988), pp. 308–17, esp. pp. 312–14.

88. This is the view taken by Janos Kornai in *The Socialist System: The Political Economy of Communism* (Oxford: Clarendon Press, 1992).

Chapter 7: Cultural Codes of the Thaw

I would like to thank the following scholars for their comments during the preparation of this essay, for which they bear no responsibility: Mark Altshuller, Marina Bilenky, George Breslauer, Abraham Brumberg, Elena Dryzhakova, Dan Field, Genevra Gerhart, Leonid Gurevich, Nina Khrushcheva, Mark Lipovetskii, Vladimir Padunov, Aleksandr Prokhorov, Marshall Shulman, and the editors of this volume, William Taubman, Sergei Khrushchev, and Abbott Gleason.

1. N. S. Khrushchev, *The Great Mission of Literature and Art* (Moscow: Progress, 1964), p. 153. Here and throughout, unless otherwise noted, quotations of Khrushchev are taken from this authorized Soviet translation into English of his official published speeches. My interest lies not in the personal, intimate Khrushchev, approximated in his postadministrative reminiscences *Khrushchev Remembers*, but in the official representation of Khrushchev in the approved state texts.

2. I have in mind the so-called first part of "The Thaw" ("Ottepel'"), which appeared in *Znamia*, 1954, no. 5. The second part appeared in *Znamia*, 1956, no. 4 (1956) after considerable editorial resistance but with much tidier endings, according to Ehrenburg.

3. Relevant to this discussion is not only Ehrenburg's "The Thaw" but also his earlier piece, "On the Work of the Writer" ("O rabote pisatelia") in *Znamia* 1953, no. 10.

4. I would not argue that these are wholly new themes. A number of scholars of diverse disciplines and political orientations have argued convincingly that the coun-

try was already undergoing a muted destalinization in many arenas, including culture, even before the death of the leader himself; See Katerina Clark *The Soviet Novel: History as Ritual*, 2d ed. (Chicago: University of Chicago Press, 1985), pp. 211-13; Charles Gati, "The Stalinist Legacy in Soviet Foreign Policy," in Stephen F. Cohen, ed., *The Soviet Union since Stalin* (Bloomington: Indiana University Press, 1980), pp. 295-97; Henry Kissinger, *The Troubled Partnership: A Reappraisal of the Atlantic Alliance* (Garden City, N.Y.: Doubleday Anchor, 1966), pp. 189-90; Marshall Shulman, *Stalin's Foreign Policy Reappraised* (New York: Atheneum, 1965); and William Zimmerman, "The Soviet Union and the West," in Cohen, ed., *The Soviet Union since Stalin*, p. 306. Clark (*The Soviet Novel*) has also demonstrated that the major themes of Thaw culture were already familiar to the Soviet reading public, for the most part from the novels of the 1940s. My interest lies not in the putative novelty of individual themes, but rather in their configuration in the context of new historical circumstances.

5. *Literaturnaia Moskva. Literaturno-khudozhestvennyi sbornik moskovskikh pisatelei. Sbornik vtoroi*, ed. M. I. Aliger, A. A. Bek, V. A. Kaverin, et al. (Moscow: GIKhL, 1956).

6. Aleksandr Solzhenitsyn. "Odin den' Ivana Denisovicha," *Novyi mir*, 1962, no. 11. Yevgeny Yevtushenko, "Babii iar," *Literaturnaia gazeta*, September 19, 1961; "Nasledniki Stalina," *Pravda*, October 21, 1962.

7. In 1951, only eight feature films were produced in the Soviet Union. These included Grigorii Kozintsev's *Belinskii*, Igor Savchenko's *Taras Shevchenko*, Sergei Iutkevich's *Przheval'skii*, and Mikhail Chiaureli's *The Unforgettable Year 1919* (*Nezabyvaemyi 1919 god*), based on Vsevolod Vishnevskii's play. Although the figure rose in 1953 to eleven feature films, these were largely screen adaptations of already existing—that is, already censored—novels and plays. An additional twelve were either concert films or so-called spectacle films (filmed stage productions) (Naya Zorkaya, *The Illustrated History of Soviet Cinema* [New York/Moscow: Hippocrene/Novosti, 1989]).

8. Harriet Murav, "The Case against Andrei Siniavskii: The Letter and the Law," *Russian Review* 53, no. 4 (October 1994): 549-60; Julia Wishnevsky, "The Fall of Khrushchev and the Birth of the Human Rights Movement in the Soviet Union," *Radio Free Europe/Radio Liberty* 382/84 (October 8, 1984): 1-5; Pavel Litvinov, "O dvizhenii za prava Cheloveka v SSSR," in *Samosoznanie: Sbornik statei* (New York: Khronika, 1976).

9. This literocentrism was by no means the exclusive purview of the dissident community of the late Thaw period; quite the contrary, it was an orientation modeled by a broad political spectrum and a variety of culture industries. A far-flung but substantive example in late Thaw architecture is the Council of Mutual Economic Assistance (SEV) building (1964-69), designed by Mikhail Posokhin and Ashot Mndoiants to resemble, of all things, an open book. The CMEA building, which might be seen as a kind of unintentional architectural citation of the 1920 Sergei Ivanov poster ("The Book Is Nothing Else Than a Person Speaking Publicly"), derives its authority from that same Russian belief in the "magic of the book," for which Ivan Fedorov, having set up the first printing press in Muscovy exactly four centuries earlier (1564), was run out of town as a wizard.

10. This would include the work of such prominent film directors, educated in the early 1960s, as Elem Klimov, Andron Konchalovskii, Nikita Mikhalkov, Sergei Paradzhanov, Eldar Riazanov, Eldar and Georgii Shegelaia, Larisa Shepitko, and Andrei Smirnov.

11. A tribute to this late Thaw in cinema is the special issue dedicated to the Thaw

of the journal *Seans/Show,* a St. Petersburg cinema journal of the young (as they dub themselves) "retro-avantgarde," whose childhood and formative years were spent in the late 1960s. The journal, edited by Liudmila Arkus, wife of the filmmaker Oleg Kovalov, defines the Thaw almost entirely in terms of post-1964 culture. The contributors' only exception to this historical framework, significantly, is Aleksandr Solzhenitsyn.

12. S. Frederick Starr, *Red and Hot: The Fate of Jazz in the Soviet Union* (New York: Limelight, 1985), pp. 282–88, 322–23.

13. The notion of 1964 as an end to the Thaw is more credible with respect to print media as a whole than to literature per se. Insofar as a literary work's initial appearance was precisely in the "journal version" (*zhurnalnyi variant*), it was indeed more intimately linked with the press—specifically, the periodical—than in the West. This issue, which deserves a separate forum, is borne out by an examination, for example, of newspaper and magazine cartoons (in *Krokodil* and elsewhere) in the post-Khrushchev 1960s—i.e., the visual text in a print medium. As in works of literature and news journalism (but unlike in other culture industries), print cartoons after 1964 rapidly conform to a homogenous, "even-handed" satirical style. Thus, for example, the front and back covers of the weekly *Krokodil,* whose circulation had grown astronomically during the Thaw years (from 300,000 in 1953 to 1,700,000 a decade later) take on a deadening regularity—a Soviet shortcoming on the front cover, a capitalist shortcoming on the back cover—in contrast to the greater heterogeneity of the Khrushchev era. See Richard Stites, *Russian Popular Culture: Entertainment and Society Since 1900* (New York: Limelight, 1985). Although these remarks are highly speculative, it would seem that the print media—the fabled "Press" ("Pechat'") of revolutionary lore—was what *appeared* to pose the greatest potential for cultural destabilization in the post-Khrushchev period from 1964 to 1968. The Soviet Union was still, after all, very much a culture organized around the sacralic nature (and therefore the dangers) of the printed text, which hence could not be permitted the greater liberties afforded other cultural industries beyond 1964.

14. N. S. Khrushchev, *The Great Mission of Literature and Art* (Moscow: Progress, 1964), p. 74.

15. Artemy Troitsky, *Back in the USSR: The True Story of Rock in Russia* (Boston: Faber, 1988).

16. I have in mind Aleksandr Ginzburg's *Syntaxis* (1959), Iurii Galanskov's *Phoenix* (1961), Valerii Tarsis's *Sphinxes* (1965), *SMOG* (1966), and Galanskov's *Phoenix-66* (1966). The *Chronicle of Current Events* (1968–72, 1974–82) already belongs to an entirely different era.

17. Lev Anninskii, "Shestidesiatniki, semidesiatniki, vos'midesiatniki . . . : K dialektike pokolenii v russkoi kul'ture," *Literaturnoe obozrenie* 1991, no. 4, p. 12.

18. Mark Fel'dman, "Musei shestidesiatnikov," *Novoe russkoe slovo,* November 12–13, 1994, p. 15.

19. Khrushchev: *The Great Mission,* pp. 187–88.

20. A further dimension, which cannot fully be addressed here, concerns the fact that, from the early 1950s on, thousands of amnestied prisoners returned from the gulag. To the extent that their experience, language, songs, tattoos, and other signifying codes of behavior had an impact on post-Stalin culture but could not explicitly be so identified in official culture until the early 1960s, the poetics of war became a legal and euphemistic screen for other forms of compulsory state labor.

21. With their inimically wacky logic, Chinese literary scholars of Soviet literature

correctly suggest that liberal Thaw literature (read "modern revisionism") is merely the extension of the peaceful coexistence (read "capitulationist line") into the ideological sphere: "The Soviet modern revisionist writers use their works to play up the horrors of war, to oppose revolutionary war, peddle the philosophy of survival, propagate capitulationism, embellish class enemies and advertise the reactionary theory of human nature." See Hsiang Hung and Wei Ning, *Some Questions Concerning Modern Revisionist Literature in the Soviet Union* (Peking: Foreign Languages Press, 1966), p. 15, 28. The appeal and clarity of this argument fades, however, when buttressed not by the obvious choices (the novelist Viktor Nekrasov, the chansonier Bulat Okudzhava) but by such "modern revisionists" as the novelist Dmitrii Sholokhov and the poets Robert Rozhdestvenskii and Konstantin Simonov, an inscrutable list if there ever was one.

22. *Vtoroi Vsesoiuznyi s"ezd sovetskikh pisatelei. Stenograficheskii otchet* (Moscow: Sovetskii pisatel', 1956). See especially speeches by Fadeev, p. 506, and Simonov, pp. 98–99. "Bezkonfliktnosti 'teoriia,'" *Kratkaia literaturnaia entsiklopediia*, ed. A. A. Surkov, vol. 1 (Moscow: Sovetskaia entsiklopediia, 1962), pp. 557–80.

23. G. A. Moglevskaia, *Problema konflikta v proizvedeniiakh sovetskoi literatury o derevne (1921–1941)* (Moscow: Institut mirovoi literatury imeni A. M. Gor'kogo AN SSSR, 1954).

24. D. F. Ivanov, "Izobrazhenie konfliktov v literature o kolkhoznoi zhizni," in *Partiinost' literatury i problemy khudozhestvennogo masterstva* (Moscow: Izd. VPSh I AON pri TsK KPSS, 1961), pp. 77–130.

25. Indeed, in Thaw literature the idealized oil painting of the collective farm became a trope for the falsity of the past. Ehrenburg's novel *The Thaw* and Vladimir Tendriakov's story "Meeting with Nefertiti" ("Svidanie s Nefertiti," 1965), for example, contain descriptions of virtually identical (imaginary) oil paintings: Pukhov's "Feast on a Collective Farm" and the hotel manager's "Collective Farm Wedding." Both paintings are muted references to, among other things, paintings by Sergei Gerasimov and Arkadii Plastov, both from 1937 and both titled "Collective Farm Festival."

26. In Khrushchev's own words, "the struggle between the new and the old." See *The Great Mission*, p. 74.

27. Ibid., p. 114.

28. This sense of duty of the older generation in guiding the younger through the forest of post-1956 politics is strongly developed in Khrushchev's speeches. The filmmaker Sergei Gerasimov, Khrushchev maintains, should have guided his younger disciple, Marlen Khutsiev, in the making of the film originally titled *Lenin District* (*Zastava Il'icha*, 1964) but released under the title *I Am Twenty* (*Mne dvadtsat' let*): "It is legitimate to ask Khutsiev . . . and his superior, Gerasimov: How could the idea of such a film have occurred to you?" (*The Great Mission*, p. 153, emphasis mine). Khutsiev's cardinal error, in Khrushchev's view, is precisely the episode in which the protagonist meets his own father's ghost:

The son asks the father for guidance, and his father in turn asks: "How old are you?" "Twenty-three," the son replies, to which the father retorts: "And I am only twenty-one." . . and disappears. Do you really want us to believe such a thing could be true? No one is going to believe you! . . . Can anyone imagine a father refusing to answer his son, refusing to help him find the right road in life. . . . According to the authors of the film, the youth can very well decide how to live without the advice or assistance of older people. (*The Great Mission*, p. 152)

A similar anxiety of the mentor, abandoned by his own disciple, might be sensed in Khrushchev's remarks on Robert Rozhdestvenskii: "In Comrade Rozhdestvenskii's speech one could detect the contention that only the group of young writers and poets express the sentiments of all our youth, that they are the mentors of our youth. That is not true at all. Our Soviet youth has been reared by the Party." To Rozhdestvenskii's brazen co-opting of the mentor role, Khrushchev juxtaposes the "soldier-poet" Nikolai Gribachev, who accepts the mentoring of the party as "teacher and leader." *The Great Mission*, pp. 167–68.

Elsewhere, Khrushchev's "errant mentors" include the film director Mikhail Romm (whose disciples included an impressive list of young filmmakers: Andron Konchalovskii, Larisa Shepitko, Vasilii Shukshin, and Andrei Tarkovskii), as well as the Soviet novelist Viktor Nekrasov, whom he contrasts unfavorably with the pre-Soviet poet "Comrade [Nikolai] Nekrasov . . . the Nekrasov everyone knows. (*Laughter. Applause*)" (*The Great Mission*, p. 198). Among Viktor Nekrasov's many sins were his travel notes "On Either Side of the Ocean" as well as his praise of Khutsiev's film for (in Nekrasov's words) "not having dragged on to the screen by his greying mustache the all-understanding old worker who always knows all the answers." Thus, Khrushchev's anger here concerns Viktor Nekrasov's (and implicitly Khutsiev's) breaking rank with the league of mentors. As Khrushchev puts it, "One cannot read without indignation things like this written about an old worker in a supercilious, scornful tone. That kind of tone, I think, is wholly impermissible to a Soviet writer" (*The Great Mission*, p. 185). The 1967 letter, written to the Presidium of the 23rd Party Congress by sixty-two noted Soviet writers in protest of, among other things, the arrests of Siniavskii and Daniel, read like a membership list of renegade uncles, including Kornei Chukovskii, Ehrenburg, Veniamin Kaverin, and Viktor Shklovskii—all of them, as Edward Brown notes, over seventy. See Edward J. Brown, *Russian Literature since the Revolution* (New York: Collier, 1971), p. 299.

29. The self-contradictory nature of this system is evident in Khrushchev's discussions of "varnishing"—that is, presenting reality in an elevated or idealistic fashion. While vociferously opposed to pre-1956 varnishing, as in Pyrev's film *Kuban Cossacks*, Khrushchev bristles at the usage of the term for optimistic works of post-1956 culture: "Why should they be called 'varnishers'? They are not 'varnishers,' but champions of the new, of the cause of our Party and our people, who are advancing to communism with firm step." See Khrushchev, *The Great Mission*, p. 70; for similar views, see also pp. 68, 155, 211–14.

30. Significantly, the attacks on Ehrenburg focused on his scholarly competence to understand Stendhal, not on the issue of inner freedom, for which Ehrenburg's Stendhal was, in Aesopian terms, the "screen." See Lev Loseff, *On the Beneficence of Censorship: Aesopian Language in Modern Russian Literature* (Munich: Otto Sagner, 1984. Also see E. Knipovich, "Eshche ob urokakh Stendalia," *Znamia*, 1957, no. 19: 220–24; N. Tamantsev, "V chem zhe vse-taki 'Uroki Stendalia,'" *Literaturnaia gazeta*, August 22, 1957.

31. Andrei Voznesenskii's poetry, for example, is very much about the "struggle between the old and the new" in his contrastive poetic discourse ("handlebar lovers, looking like Rublev angels"), as well as about digressions ("Triangular Pear," "Parabolic Ballad"), and other forms of marked deviation from linear progression. See Andrei Voznesenskii, *Sobranie sochinenii v trekh tomakh*, vol. 1 (Moscow: Khudozhestvennaia literatura, 1983).

32. Priscilla Johnson, *Khrushchev and the Arts: The Politics of Soviet Culture* (Cambridge: MIT Press, 1965), pp. 101–2.

33. Archpriest Avvakum, "Life of Archpriest Avvakuum By Himself," *Medieval Russia's Epics, Chronicles, and Tales,* ed. Serge A. Zenkovsky, revised and enlarged (New York: Dutton, 1974), pp. 339–448.

34. See Khrushchev, *The Great Mission*, pp. 184, 172. On Ehrenburg's credibility, see Shklovskii: "I used to be angry with Ehrenburg, because in transforming himself from a Jewish Catholic or Slavophile into a European constructivist, he failed to forget the past. Saul failed to become Paul. He remains Pavel Savlovich." See Viktor Shklovskii, *Zoo, or Letters Not About Love*, ed. and trans. Richard Sheldon (Ithaca: Cornell University Press, 1971), p. 92, translation reedited by Victor Erlich, *Modernism and Revolution: Russian Literature in Transition* (Cambridge: Harvard University Press, 1994), p. 228.

35. See Khrushchev's March 8, 1963, speech: "Comrade Yevtushenko's position on abstract art coincides in substance with the views Comrade Ehrenburg defends. Evidently there is much that the poet, who is still a young man, does not understand about the policy of our Party; he wavers, his views on art problems are shaky. But his speech at the meeting of the Ideological Commission gives assurance that he will succeed in overcoming his vacillations. I should like to advise Comrade Yevtushenko and other young writers . . . not to cater to the moods and tastes of the philistines. Don't be ashamed of your mistakes, Comrade Yevtushenko. Khrushchev, *The Great Mission*, p. 176.

36. Ibid., pp. 190–91.

37. What is most curious about this extemporaneous dimension is the fact that Khrushchev—that is to say, the narrator of his speeches—fears and dreads extemporaneous speech: "You know, comrades, how difficult it is to speak in public. When you have your speech written and ready, you can sleep quietly. But when you have to speak without a written text, you sleep poorly. You wake up and think how to formulate this or that point best, and begin to argue with yourself. Speaking without a prepared text is hard work for a speaker." Khrushchev, *The Great Mission*, p. 96. The "argument with yourself" is one of the most pronounced aspects of Khrushchev's style, and it occurs precisely in the (apparently) extemporizing mode that the narrator purports to fear most.

38. Ibid., p. 106.

39. Boris Groys, *The Total Art of Stalinism: Avant-Garde, Aesthetic Dictatorship, and Beyond*, trans. Charles Rougle (Princeton: Princeton University Press, 1992), p. 81.

40. Khrushchev, *The Great Mission*, p. 521.

41. Khrushchev is not unaware of his limitations as a critic. He suffers at times, he admits, from imprecision. In a passage oddly reminiscent of the conceptualist writer Dmitrii Aleksandrovich Prigov, Khrushchev writes: "I had spent all of December 31, from early morning on, in the woods. . . . The woods were very beautiful that day. The delicate hoarfrost covering the trees gave them particular beauty. I remember reading a story in the magazine *Ogonyok* in my young days. I can't remember who the author was, but in his story he spoke of "lovely silver shadows." The story must have been well written, or perhaps my tastes in literature were less exacting then. . . . I was strongly impressed by the wintry forest on New Year's Eve. . . . Maybe the shadows weren't silvery: I haven't the words to convey the deep impression the woods made on me." See Khrushchev, *The Great Mission*, pp.178–79.

42. Ibid., p. 188.

43. Ibid., p. 189.

44. Ibid., pp 183–84.

45. Ibid., p. 191. For an account of the many cultural figures—including Magnitskii, Radishchev, and La Harpe—who conceived of Russia as a ship, see James Billington, *The Icon and the Axe: An Interpretive History of Russian Culture* (New York: Vintage, 1970), pp. 362, 741. Khrushchev's "good ship," steering its Leninist course, is matched in his speeches by a "bad ship," a Noah's ark "with all the scents of all the ideological trends and shades," by which he would appear to mean ideological coexistence in culture.

46. Khrushchev, *The Great Mission*, pp. 109–10.

47. Ibid., p. 69.

48. Khrushchev's shoe-banging episode at the United Nations, which so captivated Western television viewers that it entered into late twentieth-century telecommunications folklore, must be looked at anew in this context. It no longer matters whether this event did or did not occur; whether it was or was not typical; whether it was uncultured, charming, or any other qualities that might be discerned. What matters is the image of Khrushchev as a leader acting out ritual conflict in an unexpected and deviant gesture within the very institution that serves as symbol for the containment of international conflict. In this sense, the episode is, in its own fashion, as characteristic of the period as any other text of the Thaw.

49. See Shklovsky, *Zoo*.

50. Andrei Siniavskii, "Poslednee slovo," *Tsena metaphory, ili prestuplenie i nakazanie Siniavskogo i Danielia* (Moscow: Iunona, 1990). See also Murav, "The Case against Andrei Siniavskii," pp. 549–60.

Chapter 8: Popular Responses to Khrushchev

1. See M. Gefter, "Stalin umer vchera," ed. Iu. N. Afanas'ev (Moscow: Progress, 1988); V. A. Kozlov et al., *Istoricheskii opyt i perestroika: chelovecheskii faktor v sotsial'no-ekonomicheskom razvitii SSSR* (Moscow: Mysl', 1988); L. Piiasheva, "Tiazhelaia kolesnitsa istorii proekhala po nashemu pokoleniiu," *Druzhba narodov*, 1988, no. 7; G. Popov, "Sistema i 'zubry,'" in *Nauka i zhizn'*, 1988, no. 8; E. Anisimov, "Imperskoe soznanie v Rossii i ego retsidivy pri stalinizme," *Rodina*, 1989, no. 2; E. Batalov, "Kul't lichnosti i obshchestvennoe soznanie," in *Surovaia drama naroda: uchenye i publitsisty o prirode stalinizma* (Moscow: Politizdat, 1989); V. P. Buldakov, "U istokov sovetskoi istorii: Put' k Oktiabriu," *Voprosy istorii*, 1989, no. 10; A. O. Tsipko, "O zonakh, zakrytykh dlia mysli," *Voprosy istorii*, 1989, no. 10; L. Gordon and E. Klopov, *Chto eto bylo? razmyshleniia o predposylkakh i itogakh togo, chto sluchilos' s nami v 30–40-e gody* (Moscow: Politizdat, 1989); K. Simonov, *Glazami cheloveka moego pokoleniia: razmyshleniia o Staline* (Moscow: Novosti, 1989); I. M. Kliamkin, "Byla li al'ternativa administrativnoi sisteme?" in V. V. Polikarpov, ed., *Istoriki otvechaiut na voprosy*, vol. 2 (Moscow: Moskovskii rabochii, 1990); Iu. Borev, *Staliniada, istorii, svidetel'stva, apokrify, anekdoty* (Moscow: Sovetskii pisatel', 1990); Iu. S. Aksenov et al., *Na poroge krizisa: narastanie zastoinykh iavlenii v partii i obshchestve* (Moscow: Politizdat, 1990); A. Adamovich and D. Granin, *Blokadnaia kniga* (Moscow: Sovetskii pisatel', 1991); Iu. V. Aksiutin, O. V. Volobuev, and S. V. Kuleshov, "Mysliashchii trostnik," in A. V. Afanas'ev, ed., *Oni ne molchali* (Moscow: Politizdat, 1991); G. A. Bordiugov, "Velikaia Otechestvennaia: podvig i obmanutye

nadezhdy," in V. A. Kozlov, ed., *Istoriia otechestva: liudi, idei, resheniia: ocherki istorii Sovetskogo gosudarstva* (Moscow: Politizdat, 1991); E. Iu. Zubkova, "Ot 60-kh k 70-m: vlast', obshchestvo, chelovek," in V. A. Kozlov, ed., *Istoriia otechestva: liudi, idei, resheniia: ocherki istorii Sovetskogo gosudarstva* (Moscow: Politizdat, 1991); Iu. F. Lukin, *Sotsial'no-politicheskaia aktivnost' i protest v istorii sovetskogo obshchestva: uchebnoe posobie* (Arkhangelsk, 1991); o. V. Khlevniuk, *1937-i: Stalin, NKVD i sovetskoe obshchestvo* (Moscow: Respublika, 1992); I. V. Aksiutin, "Poslevoennye nadezhdy," *Rodina*, 1993, no. 12; Iu. V. Aksiutin, "Pochemu Stalin dal'neishemu sotrudnichestvu s soiuznikami posle pobedy predpochel konfrontatsiiu s nimi?" in M. M. Narinskii, ed., *Kholodnaia voina: novye podkhody, novye dokumenty* (Moscow: 1995); V. V. Zhuravlev, ed., *Vlast' i oppozitsiia: Rossiiskii politicheskii protsess XX stoletiia* (Moscow: Rosspen, 1995); N. D. Kozlov, *Obshchestvennoe soznanie v gody Velikoi Otechestvennoi voiny (1941–1945)* (Saint Petersburg: Leningradskii oblastnyi institut usovershenstvovaniia uchitelei, 1995); S. A. Shinkarchuk, *Obshchestvennoe mnenie v Sovetskoi Rossii v 30-e gody. Po materialam Severo-Zapada* (Saint Petersburg: SPb-UEF, 1995).

2. See Iu. V. Aksiutin and O. V. Volobuev, *XX s"ezd KPSS: novatsii i dogmy* (Moscow: Politizdat, 1991); N. A. Barsukov et al., *XX s"ezd KPSS i ego istoricheskie real'nosti* (Moscow: Politizdat, 1991); Iu. Borev, *Fariseia: poslestalinskaia epokha v predaniiakh i anekdotakh* (Moscow: Konets veka, 1992); E. Iu. Zubkova, *Obshchestvo i reformy (1945–1964)* (Moscow: Rossiia molodaia, 1993).

3. Anonymous letter to the CPSU Central Committee addressed to Khrushchev, March 1953, in TsKhSD, f. 5 (Central Committee), o. 30 (Central Committee General Section), d. 6, l. 1, manuscript.

4. Requests of party committees, labor collectives, and individual citizens on the perpetuation of Stalin's memory. Summary, March 1953, in TsKhSD, f. 5, o. 30, d. 41, ll. 45–50.

5. Letter from N. V. Kritskov to CPSU Central Committee, March 1953, in TsKhSD, f. 5, o. 30, d. 41, l. 35, photocopy.

6. Letter from Ia. B. Barshtein to CPSU Central Committee, March 6, 1953, in TsKhSD, f. 5, o. 30, d. 41, ll. 31–32, photocopy.

7. A. Bandenko, "Sergei Mikhalkov ne videl 'Oskara' Nikity . . . Interv'iu," in *Komsomol'skaia pravda*, August 4, 1995, p. 14.

8. Note of N. Mikhailov, secretary of the CPSU Moscow committee, to Khrushchev, April 4, 1953, in TsKhSD, f. 5, o. 30, d. 19, ll. 12–14.

9. Note of N. Mikhailov, secretary of the CPSU Moscow committee, to Khrushchev, April 6, 1953, in TsKhSD, f. 5, o. 30, d. 19, l. 21.

10. The leader of the underground anti-fascist organization "Young Guard" in Krasnodon, who was executed by the Germans in 1942.

11. Note of N. Mikhailov, secretary of the CPSU Moscow committee, to Khrushchev, April 4, 1953, in TsKhSD, f. 5, o. 30, d. 19, ll. 12 and 14.

12. Ibid., l. 12 and 16.

13. G. M. Malenkov, "Rech' na sessii Verkhovnogo soveta SSSR 8.08.53," *Pravda*, August 9, 1953, pp. 1–2.

14. G. Kuzovkin and A. Papovian, "Groza v nachale ottepeli: Tbilisi, 1956: besporiadki ili miatezh?" *Obshchaia gazeta*, 1996, no. 3, pp. 7–13.

15. Information of F. R. Kozlov, secretary of the CPSU Leningrad obkom, on meeting of regional party activists in Leningrad, March 16, 1953, in TsKhSD, f. 5, o. 32, d. 45, ll. 24–26.

16. Note of V. Churaev, deputy head of the CPSU Central Committee department for RSFSR party organs, on discussion of the results of the 20th Party Congress, March 19, 1956, with the note, "M. Suslov, A. Aristov, N. Beliaev, L. Brezhnev, P. Pospelov, D. Shepilov, E. Furtseva spoke." In TsKhSD, f. 5, o. 32, d. 43, ll. 8–9.

17. Ibid., l. 22.

18. Ibid., l. 62.

19. Ibid., l. 8.

20. Ibid., l. 9.

21. Information of Z. Muratov, secretary of the CPSU Tatar obkom, on discussion of the results of the 20th Party Congress, April 18, 1956, in TsKhSD, f. 5, o. 32, d. 46, l. 119.

22. Information of the secretary of the CPSU Vologda obkom on discussion of the results of the 20th Party Congress, April 13, 1956, in TsKhSD, f. 5. o. 32, d. 46, l. 91. 13.

23. Note of Grishin, major general of tank troops, on the reaction of military personnel in parts of the Moscow military district to Khrushchev's speech "On the personality cult and its consequences," with a note from Shuiskii on June 6, 1956, "Presented to Comrade Khrushchev. Archive," in TsKhSD, f. 5, o. 16, d. 46, l. 202.

24. Ibid., l. 203.

25. Ibid., l. 204.

26. Ibid., l. 207

27. Ibid., l. 208.

28. "The Communist Party has been and continues to be victorious by staying true to Leninism," Pravda, April 5, 1956, p. 1.

29. Communication of A. M. Pankratova to the CPSU Central Committee Presidium on the moods of the Leningrad intelligentsia in connection with the reading of the personality cult speech, no date, with the notes, "Comrade Pankratova's note sent by Comrade Khrushchev's secretariat to the department of propaganda and agitation" and "Comrade D. T. Shepilov has looked this over. To the archive," in TsKhSD. f. 5, o. 16, d. 46, ll. 214, 216–18.

30. Citation from R. Pikoia, "Bomba pod diktaturu proletariata: kak TsK KPSS sozdaval politicheskuiu oppozitsiiu samomu sebe," Rossiiskaia gazeta, March 15, 1996, p. 28.

31. Note of V. Churaev, deputy head of the CPSU Central Committee department for the RSFSR, on the direction of the discussion of the results of the 20th Party Congress, April 16, 1956. This document includes the signatures of the following Central Committee secretaries who looked it over: Suslov, Aristov, Pospelov, Furtseva, Shepilov, and Beliaev. In TsKhSD, f. 5, o. 32, d. 45, ll. 2–3.

32. Communication of V. Churaev, deputy head of the CPSU Central Committee department of party organs for the RSFSR, and G. Drozdov, deputy of the department of adminstrative organs, April 16, 1956, with the note, "Show to CPSU Central Committee secretaries" and the signatures of Suslov, Aristov, Pospelov, and Beliaev, in TsKhSD, f. 5, o. 16, d. 46, ll. 82–83, and 87.

33. T. Men'shikova and Iu. Solomonov, "Svet sud'by," Sovetskaia kul'tura, May 20, 1989, p. 3.

34. See V. Beletskaia, "Uznik sovesti," Ogonek, 1989, no. 5, p. 22.

35. V. Bukovskii, "I vozvrashchaetsia veter," Teatr, 1990, no. 4, p. 179.

36. Note of V. Churaev, deputy head of the CPSU Central Committee department of party organs for the RSFSR, on the discussion of the results of the 20th Party Congress, April 16, 1956, in TsKhSD, f. 5, o. 32, d. 45, l. 4.

37. Ibid., l. 5.

38. D. Danin, "Neravnaia duel' cheloveka s Bogom," *Nauka i zhizn'*, 1989, no. 12, p. 129.

39. L. K. Chukovskaia, *Zapiski ob Anne Akhmatove*, vol. 2, *1952–1962* (Paris: 1980), p. 7.

40. "K istorii poslednikh leninskikh dokumentov: iz arkhiva pisatelia A. Beka," *Moskovskie novosti*, 1989, no. 17, p. 9.

41. Citation from V. Konstantinov, "Neskol'ko utochnenii," *Druzhba narodov*, 1985, no. 3, p. 175.

42. "Posledniaia 'antipartiinaia' gruppa: stenograficheskii otchet iiun'skogo 1957 goda plenuma TsK KPSS," *Istoricheskii arkhiv*, 1993, no. 6, p. 74.

43. V. Kardin, "Ne zastriat' by na obochine," *Druzhba narodov*, 1989, no. 2, p. 245.

44. Citation from Borev, *Fariseia*, p. 37.

45. A. I. Tarasov, "Vsesoiuznaia demokraticheskaia partiia," *Voprosy istorii*, 1995, no. 7, p. 138.

46. A. Sakharov, "Vospominaniia," *Znamia*, 1990, no. 11, p. 147.

47. Author's personal archive.

48. Iu. Anokhin, "Dorogoi Nikita Sergeevich: posleslovie k iubileiu," *Segodnia*, April 21, 1994, p. 10.

49. Note of P. Ivashutin, deputy chairman of USSR KGB, to the CPSU Central Committee "on the most significant events and anti-Soviet displays that took place on the territory of the Soviet Union during the celebration of the 39th anniversary of the Great October Socialist Revolution," in TsKhSD, f. 5, o. 31, d. 141, ll. 67–8.

50. "Spravka KGB SSSR na L. D. Landau ot 19.12.57," *Komsomol'skaia pravda*, August 8, 1992, p. 3.

51. A. Liubishchev, " O smysle i znachenii vengerskoi tragedii," *Znamia*, 1993, no. 10, p. 176.

52. Letter of A. Pashkov to the editor of *Pravda*, November 30, 1956, in TsKhSD, f. 5, o. 30, d. 141, ll. 107, 109–10, 115–19, 141–50.

53. "Posledniaia 'antipartiinaia' gruppa: Stenograficheskii otchet iun'skogo 1957 goda plenuma TsK KPSS," *Istoricheskii arkhiv*, 1993, no. 4, p. 17.

54. N. S. Khrushchev, "Rech' na prieme v posol'stve KNR 17.01.57," *Pravda*, January 19, 1957, p. 1.

55. Note of V. Churaev, deputy head of the department for party organs, on anti-party speeches of individual Communists on the discussion of the letter of the CPSU Central Committee, "Ob usilenii politicheskoi raboty partiinykh organizatsii v massakh," February 12, 1957, in TsKhSD, Kollektsiia, f. 89, perechen' 6, dok. 5, ll. 1–2.

56. Ibid., February 21, 1957, dok. 6, ll. 1–3.

57. Letter of M. Petrygin to the CPSU Central Committee Presidium, January 27, 1957, in TsKhSD, f. 5, o. 30, d. 188, ll. 29–35, manuscript.

58. Letter of A. Peterson to Shepilov, April 10, 1957, in TsKhSD, f. 5, o. 30, d. 189, l. 3, manuscript.

59. List of questions asked at party meetings in Georgia, July 10, 1957, in TsKhSD, f. 5, o. 31, d. 71, ll. 38 and 41–44.

60. Anonymous letter to the USSR Ministry of Internal Affairs about A. S. Pavlenko sent on July 8, 1957, to CPSU Central Committee Secretariat, in TsKhSD, f. 5, o. 30, d. 188, l. 17.

61. Informational notes of CPSU Central Committee departments of party organs

of in the RSFSR and other union republics, July 26, August 7, and August 26, 1957, in TsKhSD, f. 5, o. 30, d. 71, ll. 2–7.

62. The author was one of the participants in these events. Here is one of the jokes he remembers from those days: "An old man from a village says to Khrushchev that it of course would not be bad to catch up with America, but that they should definitely not pass them. In reply to the natural question, "But why?" he answered, "So that they won't see our naked behinds!"

63. Letter of a group of workers to the Committee of Party Control of the CPSU Central Committee, addressed to its chairman Shvernik with a request that it be passed along to Bulganin and Khrushchev, July 1957, in TsKhSD, f. 5, o. 30, d. 189, l. 77, photocopy.

64. Note of I. Serov, chairman of the USSR KGB, to the CPSU Central Committee, December 12, 1957, in TsKhSD, f. 5, o. 30, d. 231, ll. 106–7.

65. Ibid., November 11, 1957, l. 86.

66. Z. Maslennikova, "Portret Borisa Pasternaka," *Neva,* 1988, no. 9, p. 139.

67. A. Voznesenskii, "Bez nego ia by ne pisal Ozy," *Nezavisimaia gazeta,* April 15, 1994, p. 7.

68. Citation from Borev, *Fariseia,* p. 66.

69. Information of the CPSU Central Committee General Department on letters-reactions to the decisions of the December 1958 plenum of the CPSU Central Committee, in TsKhSD, f. 5, o. 30, d. 288, l. 7.

70. Greeting from a group of Leningrad residents to Molotov, November 6, 1959. Manuscript sent on from the USSR Ministry of Internal Affairs to the CPSU Central Committee, in TsKhSD, f. 5, o. 30, d. 289, l. 180.

71. Communication of A. Shelepin, chairman of the USSR KGB, to the CPSU Central Committee, December 28, 1959, in TsKhSD, f. 5, o. 30, d. 289, l. 194. The original is a photocopy with notes that the following Central Committee secretaries looked at it: Furtseva, Pospelov, Kuusinen, and Suslov.

72. See communication of A. Shelepin, chairman of the USSR KGB, to CPSU Central Committee, September 22, 1961, in TsKhSD, f. 5, o. 30, d. 351, ll. 32–33.

73. Note of A. Shelepin, chairman of the USSR KGB, to CPSU Central Committee, September 21, 1961, in TsKhSD, f. 5, o. 30, d. 351, ll. 40–47. When this "terrorist" was arrested on September 20, 1961, they found no deadly weapons except a typewriter, one copy of the "materials" not yet sent, and the rough draft.

74. Special communication of V. Tikunov, Minister of Internal Affairs of the RSFSR, to the CPSU Central Committee Bureau for the RSFSR, September 6, 1961, in TsKhSD, f. 5, o. 30, d. 373, l. 40. It is hard to say which residents of Murom are meant; perhaps those participants in the uprising of July 8–10, 1918, in defense of the Constituent Assembly, who were shot.

75. Note of G. Schetchikov to CPSU Central Committee, September 11, 1961, with Suslov's resolution: "To Comrade Shelepin. I request that you look into this and present it to the Central Committee," in TsKhSD, f. 5, o. 30, d. 372, l. 188.

76. Communication of V. Semichastnyi, chairman of the USSR KGB, to the CPSU Central Committee, July 17, 1962, in TsKhSD, f. 5, o. 30, d. 378, l. 95.

77. Letter of B. A. Kolumbetov to CPSU Central Committee, addressed to Voronov, October 24, 1961, in TsKhSD, f. 5, o. 30, d. 378, l. 146, manuscript.

78. In Russian: *U moei milenki v zhope razorvalas' klizma: prizrak brodit po khalupe, prizrak kommunizma.*

79. Borev, *Fariseia*, pp. 67, 69.

80. Ibid., pp. 47–49, 68.

81. Letter of K. M. Kochiashvili to Khrushchev, August 30, 1962, in TsKhSD, f. 5, o. 30, d. 378, ll. 153–44.

82. Letter of N. D. Rudenko to Khrushchev, no date, in TsKhSD, f. 5, o. 30, d. 350, ll. 187, 190, 195. This letter is registered on December 27, 1961, in the General Department of CPSU Central Committee, but it also has a note from April 1, 1963, "Comrade N. V. Podgornyi has looked over" (as above, l. 186).

83. Ibid., ll. 198–99, 206.

84. Ibid., l. 211.

85. Ibid., l. 212.

86. Ibid., l. 213.

87. Communication of N. Tartshev, secretary of the USSR Chita obkom, to CPSU Central Committee, January 8, 1962, in TsKhSD, f. 5, o. 30, d. 378, l. 6.

88. Anonymous "Tezisy k vystupleniiu na plenume TsK KPSS 5 marta 1962 goda," in TsKhSD, f. 5, o. 30, d. 378, l. 6. P. Ivashutin, deputy chairman of the USSR KGB, sent this on to the CPSU Central Committee on February 22, 1962, and informed them, "Measures have been taken to locate the author" (as above, l. 5). S. Pavlov, in sending the same text to the same place on February 26, 1962, felt obliged to note, "In our opinion, this is a deception perpetrated abroad" (as above, l. 12).

89. Ibid., ll. 7, 11.

90. Note of V. Semichastnyi, chairman of the USSR KGB, to the CPSU Central Committee, February 23, 1962, in TsKhSD, f. 5, o. 30, d. 378, l. 4. There is a note: "Show to CPSU Central Committee secretaries" (as above, l. 3).

91. Ibid., ll. 23–44. The following secretaries of the CPSU Central Committee looked at it: Kuusinen, Il'ichev, Ponomarev, Suslov, and Shelepin.

92. Note of V. Semichastnyi, chairman of the USSR KGB, to the CPSU Central Committee, March 19, 1962, in TsKhSD, f. 5, o. 30, d. 378, ll. 35–36.

93. Information of N. Egorychev, secretary of the CPSU Moscow gorkom, March 19, 1962, in TsKhSD, f. 5, o. 30, d. 383, ll. 28–30, 57, 60, 65, 76, 89.

94. See Iu. V. Aksiutin, "Novoe o XX s"ezde KPSS," *Otechestvennaia istoria*, 1998, no.2, p.120.

Chapter 9: The Making of Soviet Foreign Policy

It would be presumptuous to claim that the story this author has to tell is the truth, the whole truth, and nothing but the truth. Events are of course susceptible to different interpretations. Some may have been depicted somewhat subjectively in this account because the author was intimately involved in them. The view from the White House in Washington must have been far different from that in the Kremlin. Nor is the picture as complete as it might have been had more exposure been given to the role played by some of the other countries besides the Soviet Union and the United States, particularly China, whose presence was constantly felt in Moscow. Nor is what follows a comprehensive history of international affairs in the 1950s and early 1960s, but rather the story of one man's impact on Soviet foreign policy during that period. Given those limitations, the author has tried to provide as truthful a picture as he could.

1. Marshal Zhukov's memoirs refer to heated arguments taking place particularly between Stalin and Molotov, but also with others, including Zhukov himself, partici-

pating. I also recall Alexei Kosygin saying that lively discussions were admissible in Stalin's time, but only to a point and only until a decision had been taken.

2. Dwight Eisenhower, *Mandate for Change* (Garden City, N.Y.: Doubleday, 1963– 65), pp. 145–48.

3. Charles E. Bohlen, *Witness to History* (New York: Norton, 1973), p. 411.

4. See Matthew Evangelista, "Cooperation: Theory and Disarmament Negotiations in the 1950's," in *World Politics* 42 (June 1990), pp. 502–28.

5. *Foreign Relations of the United States 1952–1954,* vol. 2, pt. 1 (Washington: USGPO, 1984), p. 844.

6. "Main Trends in Soviet Capabilities and Policies, 1957–1962," in *National Intelligence Estimates,* November 4 and 12, 1957.

7. What did Molotov really expect to happen? He may have sincerely believed that the "ruling class" in any given country would be certain to use force in the form of fascist or military dictatorship to prevent any leftist groups from coming to power even through democratic procedures, as was later the case in Chile, for instance. In this instance the leftists would also be compelled to resort to force. Or it may be that he was simply averse in principle to any revision of the fundamental tenets of Marxist-Leninist theory.

8. See Vladislav Zubok, "Khrushchev and the Berlin Crisis 1958–1962," *Cold War International History Project Working Paper,* no. 6, May 1993.

9. Thompson to Dulles, November 18, 1958, 762.00/11-1858/DSCF/USNA.

10. In my opinion, Llewellyn E. Thompson was one of the best ambassadors the United States had in Moscow, although I can obviously speak only of those I have seen in action.

11. Alistair Horne, *Harold Macmillan,* vol. 2, *1957–1986* (New York: Viking, 1989), pp. 127–28.

12. Michael R. Beschloss, *May Day: The U2 Affair* (New York: Harper and Row, 1986), p. 18.

13. Alistair Horne, *Harold Macmillan,* vol. 2, p. 226.

14. Khrushchev respected Western, particularly American, newspapermen for being so dedicated and hard-working. He admired Marguerite Higgins of the *New York Herald Tribune* for pushing through a crowd of reporters on one occasion, even though she was seven months pregnant. He spoke highly of Harrison Salisbury of the *New York Times* not only for his penetrating commentaries but also because Salisbury, although he had become a distinguished writer, would sleep in his car outside the Soviet mission on Park Avenue so as not to miss anything. The feeling of respect must have been mutual, for Salisbury devoted a chapter to Khrushchev in his last book, *Heroes of My Time* (New York: Walker, 1993).

15. Filipino delegate Lorenzo Sumulong said that the peoples of Eastern Europe had been "deprived of political and civil rights" and "swallowed up by the Soviet Union." *New York Times,* October 13, 1960, p. 1.

16. Michael R. Beschloss, *The Crisis Years* (New York: HarperCollins, 1991), p. 278.

Chapter 10: The Military-Industrial Complex

1. When Nikita Khrushchev used this expression in an interview in 1956, he meant that the more economically progressive socialism would leave the less progres-

sive capitalism behind; he did not mean that the Soviet Union wanted to destroy the United States.

2. As related in 1965 in Moscow by Lev Petrov, a Soviet Army intelligence officer (GRU) who served with those troops in 1952.

3. Nikolai Ostroumov, "Armada, kotoraia ne vzletela," in *Voenno-istoricheskii zhurnal*, 1992, no. 10, pp. 39–40.

4. Protokoly zasedanii sekretariata TsK VKP(b), in RTsKhIDNI, f. 17, o. 116, d. 643.

5. Nikita S. Khrushchev, *Otchetnyi doklad tsentral'nogo komiteta kommunistecheskoi partii sovetskogo soiuza XX s"ezdu partii*, (Moscow: Gospolitizdat, 1956), p. 40.

6. *Military Archives of Russia*, 1993, no. 1, pp. 272–73. This was the first and only issue of this journal.

7. Ibid, pp. 280–81, 283–88, 294, 305–7.

8. Interview with Khrushchev's foreign policy assistant, Oleg Troyanovsky, July 1991; See also V. Malyshev, I. Kurchatov, Al Alikhanov, I. Kikoin, and A. Vinogradov, "Danger of Atomic War and the Proposals of President Eisenhower," draft article, in TsKhSD, f. 5, o. 30, d. 126, ll. 39–41.

9. "Memuary Nikity Sergeevicha Khrushcheva," *Voprosy istorii*, 1995, no. 2 (henceforth "Memuary" 2), pp. 81–82, and no. 3 (henceforth "Memuary" 3), pp. 73–77. See also Sergei Khrushchev, *Nikita Khrushchev: krizisy i rakety*, vol. 1 (Moscow: Novosti, 1994), p. 66.

10. *Rossiiskoe raketnoe oruzhie 1943–1994 g.* (Saint Petersburg: Pika, 1993), p. 110.

11. N. Khrushchev, "Memuary" 2, pp. 79–80. See also S. Khrushchev, *Nikita Khrushchev: krizisy i rakety*, vol. 1, pp. 61–62.

12. N. Khrushchev, "Memuary" 3, pp. 69–70.

13. N. Khrushchev, "Memuary" 2, pp. 79–81. See also S. Khrushchev, *Nikita Khrushchev: krizisy i rakety*, vol. 1, pp. 62–63.

14. N. Khrushchev, "Memuary" 3, pp. 73–77.

15. Rear Admiral L. Belyshev, acting chief of shipbuilding and armaments of the navy, "Ostanetsia li Rossiia velikoi morskoi derzhavoi? Voenno-tekhnicheskaia politika i korablestroenie," *Morskoi sbornik*, 1992, no. 7, p. 3.

16. Ibid., p. 4.

17. N. Khrushchev, "Memuary" 3, "Chernomorskii flot i sel'skoe khoziaistvo Ukrainy," p. 77.

18. *Rossiiskoe raketnoe oruzhie*, p. 57.

19. Ibid., p. 56.

20. Here and elsewhere in this article, weapons systems are first cited as classified in the USSR and then as classified by NATO. If only one name for a weapons system is given, it is the Soviet name.

21. *Russiiskoe raketnoe oruzhie*, p. 60.

22. Ibid., p. 56.

23. Iaroslav Golovanov, *Korolev* (Moscow: Nauka, 1994), p. 447.

24. *Rossiiskoe raketnoe oruzhie*, p. 28.

25. Ibid., p. 31.

26. Ibid., p. 28.

27. Ibid.

28. Ibid., p. 56.

29. The renowned Soviet aircraft designer and brother of Soviet leader Anastas

Mikoyan, Artem Mikoyan, developed the MiG series of fighter planes. At the age of twenty-four, Lavrentii Beria's son Sergo was named colonel and chief engineer of the vast Design Bureau No. 1, which developed operating systems for anti-aircraft and cruise missiles. After his father's arrest in June 1953, Sergo Beria was himself arrested. Later he became director of a scientific research institute in Kiev.

30. *Russiiskoe raketnoe oruzhie*, p. 56.

31. Ibid.

32. Ibid., pp. 48–49.

33. Ibid. The range of this missile is mistakenly estimated to be more than 2,500 km; the actual range allowed for in the plan was 8,000 km.

34. Ibid.

35. Golovanov, *Korolev*, pp. 466, 473. Golovanov does not directly address Tikhonravov's role but rather praises Sergei Korolev. Nor does he directly address the issue of who created the R-7. For information on the R-7 itself, see *Rossiiskoe raketnoe oruzhie*, pp. 466–75.

36. *Rossiiskoe raketnoe oruzhie*, pp. 473–75. The R-7 was a bundle of five thrusters that were ignited simultaneously on the ground in order to avoid the as yet unsolved difficulties of igniting a rocket engine in a vacuum. The four smallest thrusters, grouped around the outside of the rocket, were jettisoned after their fuel was spent, while the large middle one continued the flight. This was called a one-and-a-half-stage design, in contrast to the generally accepted two- and three-stage designs, in which the second and third stages are ignited during the launch, in the vacuum of space, after the previous one is jettisoned. The "Atlas" followed the two-stage design.

37. N. Khrushchev, "Memuary" 2, p. 83.

38. S. Khrushchev, *Nikita Khrushchev: krizisy i rakety*, vol. 1, pp. 48–54.

39. As a consequence the new design bureau was named Saliut.

40. S. Khrushchev, *Nikita Khrushchev: krizisy i rakety*, vol. 2, p. 410.

41. Ibid. General Grabin was sent to teach students at Moscow's Bauman Technical Institute, and because they were located close to each other, his design bureau merged with Korolev's for intensified work on space projects.

42. Mikhail Rebrov, "Pobedy Sergeia Nepobedimogo," *Krasnaia Zvezda*, July 20, 1995, p. 2.

43. *Rossiiskoe raketnoe oruzhie*, pp. 12, 16, 17.

44. Ibid., pp. 10, 12, 18.

45. S. Khrushchev, *Nikita Khrushchev: krizisy i rakety*, pp. 385–89. See also Golovanov, *Korolev*, pp. 708–10.

46. *Rossiiskoe raketnoe oruzhie*, pp. 10, 12, 19.

47. This technique was designed to maintain oxygen at very low temperatures, even lower than those of liquid oxygen, thereby inhibiting its evaporation.

48. Golovanov, *Korolev*, pp. 709–10. See also S. Khrushchev, *Nikita Khrushchev: krizisy i rakety*, pp. 387–89.

49. S. Khrushchev, *Nikita Khrushchev: krizisy i rakety*, vol. 1, pp. 400–411, 436–42; vol. 2, pp. 46–52, 215–26, 482–91.

50. Ibid., p. 410.

51. "Memuary," *Voprosy istorii*, 1994, no. 5, pp. 85–86.

52. My father related this story to me many times before and after his retirement.

53. S. Khrushchev, *Nikita Khrushchev: krizisy i rakety*, pp. 413–21.

54. Ibid.

55. *Rossiiskoe raketnoe oruzhie*, pp. 10, 12, 20.
56. S. Khrushchev, *Nikita Khrushchev: krizisy i rakety*, pp. 421–22.
57. Ibid., pp. 422–29.
58. "Memuary," *Voprosy istorii*, 1991, no. 1, pp. 77–79.
59. TASS statement, in *Pravda*, January 7, 1958.
60. TASS statement, "O novom sokrashchenii Vooruzhennykh sil SSSR," *Pravda*, January 7, 1958.
61. Account of a session of the Supreme Soviet of the USSR, *Pravda*, January 15, 1960.
62. Ibid.
63. S. Khrushchev, *Nikita Khrushchev: krizisy i rakety*, pp. 488–90.

Chapter 11: The Case of Divided Germany

1. For a broader picture of Khrushchev's role in the Cold War, see Vladislav Zubok and Constantine Pleshakov, *Inside the Kremlin's Cold War: From Stalin to Khrushchev* (Cambridge: Harvard University Press, 1996).

2. In particular the documentary record on the second Berlin crisis still has gaps. See *Foreign Relations of the United States*, vol. 8, *Berlin Crisis, 1959–1960: Germany, Austria* (Washington: USGPO, 1993); *Foreign Relations of the United States, 1961–1963*, vol. 14, *Berlin Crisis, 1961–1962* (USGPO, Washington DC, 1993); also a microfiche collection, *The Berlin Crisis, 1958–1962*, National Security Archive (Chadwyck-Healey, 1992), with a guide in two volumes.

3. Among the most recent are Yuli Kwitzinskij, *Vor dem Sturm: Erinnerungen eines Diplomaten* (Munich: Siedler Verlag, 1993); Valentin Falin, *Politische Erinnerungen* (Munich: Doermer Knaur, 1993); Sergei Khrushchev, *Nikita Khrushchev: krizisy i rakety* (Moscow: Novosti, 1994); Georgii M. Kornienko, *Kholodnaia voina: svidetel'stvo uchastnika* (Moscow: International Relations, forthcoming).

4. Documents of the Ministry of Foreign Affairs of the USSR (the secretariat of the minister and the 3d European [German] Department) clearly indicate that the Soviet leadership and diplomats knew well in advance about the content of those agreements from intelligence (although some, including Andrei Gromyko, feared disinformation) and discussed, in internal correspondence, the existence of "secret military clauses" in the treaties of Bonn. Memo of Gromyko to Stalin, 21 January 1952 in AVPRF, f. 07, o. 25, papka 13, d. 144, p. 27; memo of the 3d Department to Stalin, February 26, 1953, on the position of the Soviet government with regard to the "European community of coal and steel," in AVP RF, f. 084, o. 11, papka 275, d. 51, p. 3.

5. Rolf Steininger, *The German Question: The Stalin Note of 1952 and the Problem of Reunification* (New York: Columbia University Press, 1990); the German original appeared in 1985.

6. "The documents show that in 1952–53 there were discussions in which Beria advanced the idea of neutralization of Germany." A. O. Chubarian, "Istoriia XX stoletiia: novye issledovaniia i problemy," in *Novaia i noveishaia istoriia*, 1994, no. 3 (Moscow), p. 10. The reference is probably to documents from the Archive of the President of the Russian Federation.

7. Despite recent research it is not clear whether Stalin had wanted to do this earlier, in 1945–1948. The historian Wilfried Loth has argued that the German Democratic Republic (GDR) was "Stalin's unwanted child" and that he had many times

NOTES TO PAGES 278 – 283

spurned attempts by Ulbricht, Pieck, Grotewohl, and company to begin "socialist construction" without further delay. But research also demonstrates that from the first days of the Soviet occupation the building of a police state was under way in their zone, and that this process was at a very advanced stage by 1949. See Norman M. Naimark, *The Russians in Germany: A History of the Soviet Zone of Occupation, 1945–1949* (Cambridge: Harvard University Press, 1995), chapters 6 and 7. It is possible that both arguments are correct, that in spite of Stalin's preferences, the requirements of occupation led to the emergence of the police state, almost by osmosis. It was only one step from that to the official "construction of socialism."

8. His name was on the distribution list of a Ministry of Foreign Affairs draft proposal in January 1952. See AVPRF, f. 07, o. 25, papka 13, d. 144, p. 59.

9. James Richter, "Re-Examining Soviet Policy towards Germany in 1953," in *Europe-Asia Studies* 45, no. 4 (1993), p.676.

10. Ibid., 677.

11. I could not obtain the text of the proposal, but I saw a reference to it in documents of TsKhSD, as document no. 9417, May 10, 1953, f. 5, o. 3, d. 89 1; see also Richter, "Re-Examining," p. 677.

12. Pavel Sudoplatov and Anatolii Sudoplatov with Jerrold L. and Leona Schecter, *Special Tasks: The Memoirs of an Unwanted Witness* (Boston: Little, Brown, 1994), pp. 363–64. Although much of Sudoplatov's book is based on hearsay, this is one of a number of cases of which Sudoplatov evidently had firsthand knowledge.

13. "Delo Beria: stenograficheskii otchet iiul'skogo plenuma (1953) TsK KPSS," *Izvestiia TsK KPSS*, 1991, no. 1, p. 159.

14. A letter from *Pravda's* correspondent in Berlin, P. Naumov, sent to Khrushchev "for information" (June 24, 1953), in TsKhSD, f. 5, o. 30, d. 5, pp. 84–85.

15. This line of thinking was already present in cables that Soviet chief controllers in the GDR (Sokolovsky, Yudin, Semenov) sent to the Kremlin on the day after the "events." AVPRF, f. 07, o. 30, p. 16, d. 20, p. 1–7.

16. See Hope Harrison, "Ulbricht and the Concrete 'Rose': New Archival Evidence on the Dynamics of Soviet-East German Relations and the Berlin Crisis, 1958–1961," *Working paper*, no. 5 (Washington, D.C.: Cold War International History Project, May 1993).

17. See estimates of the International Department of the Central Committee: V. Sergeev to M. Suslov (September 25, 1955), and transcripts of a meeting with the delegation of Soviet workers returned from the GDR (August 25, 1953), in TsKhSD, f. 5, o. 30, d. 34, pp. 27–30, 48–83.

18. "Delo Beria," p. 164.

19. Jerrold L. Schecter with Vyacheslav V. Luchkov, ed., *Khrushchev Remembers: The Glasnost Tapes* (Little, Brown, 1990), p. 70.

20. Maiskii to Molotov, January 11, 1944. Molotov approved the letter for distribution to Stalin and other members of the Politburo. AVPRF, f. 07, o. 6, papka 14, d. 145, pp. 7, 8.

21. Ibid.; this was confirmed by Sergei A. Kondrashev, a retired KGB official and German expert, in a telephone conversation with the author, October 23, 1993. Kondrashev is co-author with David E. Murphy and George Bailey of *Battleground Berlin: The CIA and the KGB in the Cold War* (New Haven: Yale University Press, 1997).

22. See Michael Gehler, "The Austrian Solution 1955 as a 'Model' for Germany?" in Günter Bischof and Anton Pelinka, eds., *Austria in the Nineteen Fifties*, vol. 3 (New

Brunswick: Transaction Publishers, 1995); also Günter Bischof, "Eisenhower, the Summit, and the Austrian Treaty, 1953–1955," in Günter Bischof and Stephen E. Ambrose, *Eisenhower: A Centenary Assessment* (Baton Rouge: Louisiana State University Press, 1995), p. 156; and Murphy, Kondrashev, and Bailey, *Battleground Berlin*.

23. Nikita Khrushchev, "Memuary Nikity Sergeevicha Khrushcheva," *Voprosy Istorii*, 1993, no. 8, pp. 75–77, 83.

24. AVPRF, f. 06, o. 14, p. 9, d. 107, papka 1–157; d. 116, pp. 1–77.

25. For shrewd Western guesses on Moscow's intentions, see Rolf Steininger, "1955: The Austrian State Treaty and the German Question," *Diplomacy and Statecraft* 3, no. 3 (1992), pp. 512–13, 514–15.

26. G. Pushkin, Soviet ambassador to the GDR, to Iu. Andropov, the CC CPSU, June 7, 1955, in TsKhSD, f. 5, o. 28, d. 327, pp. 147–48; A. Orlov, Soviet chargé d'affaires in the GDR, "Voprosy normalizatsii otnoshenii mezhdu SSSR i Zapadnoi Germaniei," August 23, 1955; a report of Dimitrii Shepilov, editor-in-chief of *Pravda*, to Suslov, ibid., file 328, pp. 16–25, 159–220.

27. Dmitrii Shepilov transmitting a report by *Pravda*'s correspondent in the GDR, P. Naumov, November 5, 1954, in AVPRF, f. 082, o. 42, papka 287, d. 39, pp. 227–35. G. Pushkin to the Secretariat of the CC CPSU, March 7, 1955, reported on a suggestion received from Ilya Ehrenburg and Georgii Zhukov, in TsKhSD, f. 4, o. 9, d. 1242, p. 186. The suggestion was approved by the Secretariat on March 9.

28. Instructions to the Soviet ambassador in the Federal Republic of Germany, December 17, 1955, in AVPRF, f. 06 (Molotov), o. 14, papka 201, d. 14, pp. 15–18.

29. Committee of Information report on possible positions of Western powers on major international issues at the summit in Geneva, in AVPRF, f. 595, o. 52, d. 780, pp. 96–104; memorandum from Pavel Naumov, a correspondent of *Pravda* in West Germany, July 3, 1955. Molotov and Bulganin read the letter, but it was Khrushchev who brought it to the attention of the leading "trio" of Soviet diplomats: Gromyko, Semenov, and Pushkin. See TsKhSD, f. 5, o. 30, d. 163, pp. 173–85.

30. Llewellyn Thompson, U.S. High Commissioner for Austria, felt "resentment" when he learned about the results of negotiations in Moscow. See telegram, April 18, 1955, in *FRUS, 1955–57*, vol. 5, "The Austrian State Treaty; Summit and Foreign Ministers Meetings, 1955" (Washington, D.C.: USGPO, 1988), p. 45. Khrushchev knew about American objections to the Moscow settlement; see Khrushchev, "Memuary," *Voprosy istorii*, 1993, no. 8, p. 79.

31. "Zapis' besedy Bulganina, Khrushcheva, Mikoiana, Molotova s prem'er-ministrom i ministrom inostrannykh del Danii Khansenom," in TsKhSD, f. 5, o. 30, d. 163, p. 33.

32. "Kak reshalis' 'voprosy Vengrii.' Rabochie zapisi zasedanii Prezidiuma TsK KPSS, iul'–noiabr' 1956 g.," *Istoricheskii arkhiv*, 1996, no. 2, pp. 82–104.

33. Khrushchev, "Memuary," *Voprosi istorii*, 1994, no. 5, pp. 85–86.

34. Wolfgang Krieger, "Germany," in David Reynolds, ed., *The Origins of the Cold War in Europe: International Perspectives* (New Haven: Yale University Press, 1994), p. 157. Khrushchev, according to the former diplomat and speech writer Oleg Grinevsky, "did not comprehend" Adenauer's logic and therefore "did not like him." *Tisiacha i odin den' Nikity Sergeevicha* (One Thousand and One Days of Nikita Sergeevich) (Moscow; Vagrius, 1998), p.25.

35. These organizations were set up by refugees from Prussia, Silesia, the Suden-

tenland, and other regions that under Stalin had been annexed to Poland and Czecho-slovakia in 1945.

36. Memorandum of the Committee of Information to the Presidium of the CC CPSU (November 29, 1956)."Rasschety i plany praviaschikh krugov FRG po german-skomu voprosu v sviazi s sobitiami v Polshe i Vengrii," in AVPRF, f. 595, o. 77, d. 789, pp. 437–42.

37. See Marc Trachtenberg, *History and Strategy* (Princeton: Princeton University Press, 1991); Daniel Kosthorst, *Brentano und die deutsche Einheit: die Deutschland- und Ostpolitik des Aussenministers im Kabinett Adenauers, 1955–1961* (Duesseldorf: Droste, 1993), pp. 137–42; Grinevsky, *Tysiacha i odin den'*, pp. 26–28.

38. Smirnov's report to Moscow on this conversation, in AVPRF, f. 082, o. 49, d. 335, vol. 3, pp. 12–15.

39. A. Gromyko to the CPSU, the draft of the directives to Mikoyan's delegation, April 11, 1958; Mikoyan's report on the results of his talks, in AVPRF, f. 0757, o. 3, d. 18, vol. 16, pp. 4, 6–8, 24–26.

40. Notes taken during Lippmann's interview with Khrushchev, October 24, 1958, in Walter Lippmann Papers, Yale University, Sterling Library, series 7, box 239, f. 27.

41. "Posledniaia 'antipartiinaia gruppa': stenographicheskii otchet iiun'skogo (1957) plenuma TsK KPSS," *Istoricheskii arkhiv*, 1993, no. 4, pp. 28, 29

42. TsKhSD, f. 89, o. 70, d. 6, p. 13.

43. Interview of the author with Oleg Troyanovsky, March 9, 1993, Washington D.C.; see also "Posledniaia 'antipartiinaia gruppa': stenograficheskii otchet iiunskogo (1957) plenuma TsK KPSS," *Istoricheskii arkhiv*, 1993, nos. 3–6.

44. The documentary evidence on how the Sino-Soviet relations led to the Berlin crisis is scanty. For more on that subject, see Vladislav M. Zubok, "Khrushchev and the Berlin Crisis (1958–1962)," working paper no. 6 (Washington, D.C.: Cold War International History Project, May 1993), pp. 6–7.

45. Hope Harrison, "Ulbricht and the Concrete 'Rose': New Archival Evidence on the Dynamics of Soviet-East German Relations and the Berlin Crisis, 1958–1961," working paper no. 5 (Washington, DC: Cold War International History Project, May 1993), p. 19.

46. Diary of M. G. Pervukhin, October 11, 1958, in TsKhSD, f. 5, o. 49, d. 82, pp. 213–14, 216.

47. Sergei Khrushchev, *Nikita Khrushchev: krizisy i rakety*, vol. 1 (Moscow: Novosti, 1994), pp. 416, 417, 421, 466–467.

48. M. Pervukhin to I. Ilyichev, a memorandum "On measures to develop direct contacts with West Berlin," January 7, 1961. Pervukhin noted that "in fulfillment of the decision by the Instantsiia about the buildup of influence of the Soviet Union in West Berlin through the Embassy, the Trade Mission and also some central ministeries, some practical measures have already been taken." In AVPRF, f. 0742 (Referentura po GDR), o. 57, papka 390, d. 620, vol. 1, p.19.

49. Yuli Kwitzinskij, *Vor dem Sturm*, p. 161; Pervukhin to Gromyko, July 4, 1961, in AVPRF, Referentura po GDR, f. 0742, o. 57, papka 388, d. 193/3, tom 1, pp. 23—38.

50. First Secretary of the Soviet Embassy in Berlin A. Avalduiev, June 9, 1960, in TsKhSD, f. 5, o. 50, d. 226, p. 122.

51. Record of conversation between N. S. Khrushchev and Walter Ulbricht, November 30, 1960, AVPRF, f. 0742. o. 6, papka 43, d. 4, part 1.

52. The author analyzed diplomatic messages in the collections of the International Department of the Central Committee of the CPSU and the Third European Department of the Ministry of Foreign Affairs of the USSR. On the data from the International Department see Vladislav Zubok and Zoia Vodopianova, "The Berlin Crisis, 1956–1962: New Evidence from Soviet Archives," in I. V. Gaiduk, M. L. Korobochkin, M. M. Narinskii, and A. O. Chubarian, eds., *Kholodnaia vaina: novye podkhody, novye dokumenty* (Moscow: IUI RAN, 1995).

53. William Burr, "In Search of 'Breathing Space': Eisenhower and Berlin Crisis Diplomacy, 1958–1960," unpublished manuscript.

54. Memorandum of Mikoyan's call on the President, January 17, 1959, in Dwight D. Eisenhower Library, Ann Whitman File, International Series, Box. 49. The Soviet version of the visit, somewhat doctored for the consumption of allies, is in a memorandum from V. V. Kuznetzov to M. A. Suslov, January 21, 1959, in TsKhSD, f. 5, o. 30, d. 300, pp. 1–11.

55. Letter of N. S. Khrushchev to Chancellor K. Adenauer, August 18, 1959, in AVPRF, f. 0757, o. 4, papka 22, d. 9, pp. 22–34.

56. Khrushchev's phrase was related by Andrei Sakharov to his colleagues at Arzamas-16. See Yuri N. Smirnov, *On mezhdu nami zhil . . . vospominaniia o Sakharove: sbornik* (Moscow, Praktika, 1996), p. 585.

57. The U.S. Embassy in Bonn urged the Federal Republic of Germany, in response to the cutting off of access to East Berlin, to retaliate "with something in the form of breaking of inter-zonal trade." But Bonn was prepared to do this only as part of a general Western embargo on trade with the GDR, for which "the West was certainly not ready." Daniel Kosthorst, *Brentano und die deutsche Einheit*, p. 342.

58. Record of meeting of Comrade N. S. Khrushchev with Comrade W. Ulbricht, November 30, 1960, in AVPRF, f.0742 (Referentura po GDR), o. 6, papka 43, d. 4, pp. 10–11; the translation of this document appears in Hope Harrison, "Ulbricht and the Concrete 'Rose,'" Appendix A.

59. M. Pervukhin to A. A. Gromyko, December 6, 1961, in AVPRF, (Referentura po GDR), f. 0742, o. 57, papka 388, d. 119, p. 32; A. Gromyko and A. Mikoyan to the Central Committee of the CPSU, July 21, 1961, in AVPRF, (Referentura po GDR), f. 0742, o. 57, apka 389, d. 210, pp. 36, 39.

60. AVPRF, f. 0742, o. 57, papka 389, d. 210, p. 37.

61. Harrison, "Ulbricht," Appendix A.

62. Ibid., pp. 54–55.

63. Kwitzinskij, *Vor dem Sturm*, p. 179.

64. Frank Roberts to the Foreign Office, October 6, 1961, PRO, F0371, 160555. Roberts agreed with the opinion of Lord Home, the British foreign secretary, that if the West would not signal a willingness to negotiate before the party congress, Khrushchev might save face by announcing an additional bold step in his German diplomacy.

65. *Voprosy istorii*, 1993, no. 10, p.70.

66. A. A. Gromyko to the Central Committee, in AVPRF (Referentura po GDR), 1961, f. 0742, o. 57, papka 388, d. 193/3, vol. 3, pp. 97, 98.

67. Pervukhin to Ilyichev, "Memorandum of the standing representative of the State Planning Commission of the USSR in the GDR on the results of industrial performance of the GDR during ten months of 1961," November 16, 1961, in AVPRF (Referentura po GDR), f. 0742, o. 57, p. 391, d. 720/2, p. 43.

68. See memorandums of conversations of meetings with Bahr and Brandt in December 1961 and March 1962, sent from the Soviet embassy in Berlin to the Central Committee, in TsKhSD, f. 5, o. 49, d. 489, pp. 6–8, 92; also Timothy Garton Ash, *In Europe's Name: Germany and the Divided Continent* (New York: Random House, 1993), pp. 51, 59–62.

69. See Adam Ulam, *Expansion and Coexistence: The History of Soviet Foreign Policy, 1917–1967* (New York: Prager, 1968), pp. 668–72.

70. Oleg Troyanovsky, "The Cuban Crisis: A View from the Kremlin," in *Mezhdunarodnaia zhizn'* (Moscow), 1992, nos. 3–4, p. 172; Oleg Troyanovsky, conversations with the author, Washington D.C., February 1993, and Moscow, May 1993.

Chapter 12: Khrushchev and Gorbachev: A Russian View

1. In Russian epic literature, "Koshchei" or "immortal Koshchei" personifies evil. He is depicted as a repulsive old man who cannot be killed and is resurrected again and again.

2. Gaetano Mosca (1858–1941) and Vilfredo Pareto (1848–1923) were Italian social scientists and proponents of the "circulation of elites," which may be understood in this context as a nonprogressive alternative to Marxist ideas of revolution. Both class and elite theories have their own shares of the truth. Direct power is always in the hands of a political elite, a party, or individual leaders. But they ultimately reflect the interests of those classes and social strata that occupy a dominant position, primarily those that control the economy.

3. Long considered the Communist party's chief ideologist, Suslov became a Central Committee secretary in 1947 and remained in that role until his death in 1982.

4. In the fair words of Roy Medvedev: "The very fact that during the years of his rule about 20 million people were rehabilitated—granted, in most cases posthumously—this fact alone outweighs all of Khrushchev's faults and mistakes." Roy Medvedev, *N. S. Khrushchev: politicheskaia biografiia* (Moscow: Kniga, 1990), p. 303.

5. This Central Committee resolution on the cult of personality was dated June 30, 1956, and published in *Pravda* on July 2, 1956.

6. The leader of the Italian Communists wrote a memorandum in 1957 that consisted of a critical analysis of the Soviet model of socialism, and he received a negative reaction from the Communist party leadership. We might call this the first manifestation of Eurocommunism.

Chapter 13: Khrushchev and Gorbachev: An American View

1. A systemic breakdown was also what Khrushchev, in his memoirs, identified in mostly metaphorical language as the likely outcome of too much reform. See N. S. Khrushchev, *Vospominaniia* (New York: Chalidze Publications, 1979), pp. 274–76. For even bolder speculation about patterns of reform, change, and breakdown in Russia over the last three centuries, during which a major component of the impulse for change—the desire to catch up with or even surpass the West—has remained more or less constant, see Theodore Taranovski, ed., *Reform in Modern Russian History* (New York: Cambridge University Press, 1994).

2. See, for example, Priscilla Johnson, *Khrushchev and the Arts: The Politics of Soviet Culture, 1962–1964* (Cambridge: MIT Press, 1965).

3. See Albert Boiter, "When the Kettle Boils Over," *Problems of Communism* 13, no. 1, January–February 1964, pp. 33–43, esp. pp. 35–39.

4. The number of Soviet citizens arrested in connection with destalinization and the events in Poland and Hungary must have been quite large, because the archives have yielded a report by Yuri Andropov from 1975 that gives the official number of people actually prosecuted for subversion in 1958 under article 58–10 (later article 70) of the Criminal Code as 1,416. Most of these individuals were probably arrested in 1956 and 1957. See Peter Reddaway, "Sovietology and Dissent: New Sources on Protest," *RFE/RL Research Report* 2, no. 5 (January 1993), p. 14.

5. *Obshchaia gazeta*, May 21, 1993, quoted in Donald Murray, *Democracy of Despots* (Boulder, Colo.: Westview, 1996), p. 33.

6. Interview for the BBC, *Summary of World Broadcasts*, February 17, 1995, quoted in Murray, *Democracy of Despots*, p. 4.

7. Ibid., pp. 12, 13, 15.

8. High-level representatives of these forces included Mikoyan, who understood the need both for more security in officials' careers and for economic reform; Nuriddin Mukhitdinov, who represented the desire of the non-Slavic republics for greater autonomy from Moscow; and Ekaterina Furtseva, who symbolized the desire of part of the nomenklatura for a measure of cultural liberalization. At the second tier, Khrushchev had quietly courted those party officials who had been imprisoned by Stalin and released—thanks, it seems, more to himself than to other party leaders after Stalin's death. Clearly, these people had an especially sharp concern for greater personal security. An interesting example is long-time political prisoner A. V. Snegov, who had several conversations with Khrushchev after his release. Khrushchev appointed him head of the Political Directorate of the MVD's Chief Directorate for Camps (GULag). See *Chronicle of Current Events*, no. 21, September 1971 (Amnesty International Publications, 1971), pp. 294–95, for Snegov's biography and for references to his published statements.

9. It can of course be argued that Stalin's conservatism and complacency were not dominant characteristics in his last years; among the evidence is his risky decision to authorize the North Korean invasion of South Korea and his apparent intention to launch another great purge. I would argue, however, that his apparent belief that he could easily pull off such ventures may be evidence of complacency. The Korean decision may somewhat resemble Brezhnev's decision to invade Afghanistan in 1979, an undertaking conditioned by a failure to think through the likely outcome and the likely costs to Soviet interests.

10. See George Breslauer, *Khrushchev and Brezhnev as Leaders: Building Authority in Soviet Politics* (Boston: Allen & Unwin, 1982).

11. A partial exception to this generalization was his speech of September 1953 and the fairly radical reforms of agriculture to which it led. It should also be noted that some political prisoners were released before 1956. But this was done very quietly, without publicity.

12. The diagnosis of the Soviet Union's ills in his speech at the Central Committee plenum of January 1987 was remarkably comprehensive, consistent, and sophisticated, and the proposed solutions sounded radical. Khrushchev's radical "breakthrough" came in his "Secret Speech" of February 1956.

13. See, for example, Abel Aganbegyan's description of the economic and sociological seminars organized by Gorbachev at that time, in *Eko*, 1989, no. 9, pp. 19–20.

14. David Remnick, *Lenin's Tomb: The Last Days of the Soviet Empire* (New York: Vintage, 1994), pp. 303, 149, 494.

15. See, for example, Ligachev's speech in *Pravda*, August 27, 1987.

16. Khrushchev did not use the word "democratization" but, rather, phrases with the same meaning. For example, his *Programme of the Communist Party of the Soviet Union* of 1961 decreed that "the main direction in which socialist statehood develops" should be "all-round extension and perfection of socialist democracy, active participation of all citizens in the administration of the state." See p. 92 of the official text published in 1961 by the Foreign Languages Publishing House.

17. Khrushchev's ideological framework for all this was his ardent espousal of the Marxian doctrine of the "withering away of the state." As communism was being built, the people would increasingly rule themselves. Particular features that he launched were the dismantling of some of the censorship apparatus, the promotion of "comrades' courts" and the downgrading of the regular court system, the encouragement of criticism from below (so that failing enterprise directors would be forced out), and the democratization of the soviets, with increased accountability of deputies and officials and a minimum rate of turnover of deputies. In the party the most radical measure of democratization was the limited terms and compulsory turnover of officials that were introduced in 1961 but hardly put into effect, because by then Khrushchev's power was ebbing. On most of these issues see Michel Tatu, *Power in the Kremlin: From Khrushchev to Kosygin* (New York: Viking, 1967); Martin Dewhirst and Robert Farrell, eds., *The Soviet Censorship* (Metuchen, N.J.: Scarecrow Press, 1973); Ronald Hill, "Local Government since Stalin," in Everett Jacobs, ed., *Soviet Local Politics and Government* (Boston: Allen & Unwin, 1983), pp. 21–22; and *Problems of Communism* 9, no. 6 (1960), an issue devoted mainly to "The Future Soviet Society" and "The Soviet Worker."

18. See Johnson, *Khrushchev and the Arts*.

19. For example, according to secret official documents obtained from the archives after communism collapsed, between 1959 and 1964 the average number of prosecutions per year under the two articles of the Criminal Code most used against dissidents, nos. 70 and 190-1, was around 250—a very small figure indeed by previous Soviet standards. See details on this and related issues in Reddaway, "Sovietology and Dissent." Nonetheless, as noted in n. 4, Khrushchev's hypocrisy in claiming on January 27, 1959, that there were no longer any political prisoners was considerable. In some ways he compounded this hypocrisy, shortly afterward, by presenting his justification for locking up critics in mental hospitals: "We can say that now, too, there are people who fight against communism . . . but clearly the mental state of such people is not normal." *Pravda*, May 24, 1959. For a discussion of how this method of suppressing dissent was regularized and extended under Khrushchev see Sidney Bloch and Peter Reddaway, *Russia's Political Hospitals: The Abuse of Psychiatry in the Soviet Union* (London: Gollancz, 1977), chapter 3.

20. From the speech of Leonid Ilichev on December 17, 1962; see text in Johnson *Khrushchev and the Arts*, p. 116.

21. N. S. Khrushchev, *Vospominaniia*, p. 276.

22. On Khrushchev and Glavlit see Dewhirst and Farrell, eds., *The Soviet Censorship*, esp. pp. v, 5, 8, 104.

23. In Khrushchev's case the reductions in overall personnel had begun earlier. But

only in 1960 did he announce that he would cut a third of all personnel employed at that time—a radical move that aroused widespread opposition in the military and elsewhere.

24. See for example, Iaroslav Bilinsky, "The Rulers and the Ruled," *Problems of Communism* 16, no. 5, September–October 1967 (special issue on nationalities and nationalism in the USSR), pp. 16–26, pp. 17–18.

25. See my article "Is the Soviet Union Drifting towards Anarchy?" in *Report on the USSR* 1, no. 34 (August 1989), pp. 1–5.

Index